Climate Displacement

Climate Displacement

JAMIE DRAPER

OXFORD
UNIVERSITY PRESS

Great Clarendon Street, Oxford, OX2 6DP,
United Kingdom

Oxford University Press is a department of the University of Oxford.
It furthers the University's objective of excellence in research, scholarship,
and education by publishing worldwide. Oxford is a registered trade mark of
Oxford University Press in the UK and in certain other countries

© Jamie Draper 2023

The moral rights of the author have been asserted

All rights reserved. No part of this publication may be reproduced, stored in
a retrieval system, or transmitted, in any form or by any means, without the
prior permission in writing of Oxford University Press, or as expressly permitted
by law, by licence or under terms agreed with the appropriate reprographics
rights organization. Enquiries concerning reproduction outside the scope of the
above should be sent to the Rights Department, Oxford University Press, at the
address above

You must not circulate this work in any other form
and you must impose this same condition on any acquirer

Published in the United States of America by Oxford University Press
198 Madison Avenue, New York, NY 10016, United States of America

British Library Cataloguing in Publication Data

Data available

Library of Congress Control Number: 2023943789

ISBN 9780192870162

DOI: 10.1093/oso/9780192870162.001.0001

Printed and bound in the UK by
Clays Ltd, Elcograf S.p.A.

Cover image: Port Scene by Paul Klee, Bridgerman Images

Links to third party websites are provided by Oxford in good faith and
for information only. Oxford disclaims any responsibility for the materials
contained in any third party website referenced in this work.

Acknowledgements

I started working on the topic of climate displacement as a doctoral student at the University of Reading, where I was supported by a Leverhulme Doctoral Trust Scholarship in Climate Justice. Catriona McKinnon generously gave me the opportunity to undertake this research in the first place and has been a supportive and encouraging mentor ever since. Catriona's wonderful dogs—Bear, Millie, and Ginny—also kept me company at crucial times during both the writing of my PhD thesis and, later, the book manuscript.

My supervisors at Reading, Rob Jubb and Patrick Tomlin, oversaw this project in its early stages and played an important role in shaping it from the very beginning. They have continued to give me invaluable guidance over the years, both in relation to the arguments developed in this book and in my intellectual and professional development more broadly. David Owen and Alice Baderin, my doctoral examiners, also gave me incredibly useful feedback which made writing this book possible. David first encouraged me to write this book and has continued to give me generous advice and support in the years that have followed.

Most of this book was written whilst I was a Postdoctoral Research Fellow at Nuffield College at the University of Oxford. Cécile Laborde gave me the opportunity to work on the book in an exceptionally vibrant political theory community over the course of the fellowship. Cécile also gave me excellent guidance and feedback as I worked on the manuscript. I also spent six months at the Normative Orders Cluster of Excellence at Goethe Universität Frankfurt am Main during my PhD, which was of critical importance in developing the ideas that later became this book. Darrel Moellendorf hosted me there, and kindly found me funding to extend my initial three-month stay. Darrel has been hugely supportive, both in giving me thoughtful feedback on the arguments in this book and in giving me access to an incredibly stimulating intellectual environment in which to develop my ideas.

In the final stages of writing this book, I had two exceedingly helpful manuscript workshops, one at Nuffield and one at the Britain and Ireland Association for Political Thought conference. I received highly detailed and exceptionally helpful comments on the manuscript from Megan Blomfield, Sarah Fine, Matthew Gibney, Alejandra Mancilla, David Miller, and Anna Stilz. Those comments have proved to be invaluable in fine-tuning the arguments in this book, though I have no doubt that I have not been able to do justice to the many helpful suggestions that I received.

There are a number of people who have given me their time, support, feedback, guidance, and friendship over the years as I have written this book. In Reading, the members of the Climate Justice group—Zainab Aliyu, Africa Bauza Garcia Arcicollar, Bennet Francis, Livia Luzzatto, Josep Ferret Mas, Alex McLaughlin, Lydia Messling, Callum Nolan, Jessica Omukuti, Adam Pearce, Josh Wells, and Danny Waite—created a friendly and constructive environment for developing the ideas that later became this book. Alex in particular deserves special mention for providing endless feedback on just about everything that I have ever written. I also benefited from advice and feedback from several colleagues who were friends of the Climate Justice programme, including Chris Armstrong, Stephen Gardiner, John Meyer, Henry Shue, and Steve Vanderheiden. In Frankfurt, the members of 'Team Moellendorf'—Daniel Callies, Maria Paola Ferretti, Daniel Hammer, Ellen Nieß, Brian Milstein, Lukas Sparenborg, Amadeus Ulrich, and Tatiana Višak—provided valuable intellectual support and friendship. Ellen in particular welcomed me with open arms and constantly made an effort to make me feel at home. Afsoun Afsahi and Ilaria Cozzaglio were also great sources of advice and support during my time in Frankfurt. At Nuffield, the political theory postdocs—Rufaida Al Hashmi, Sam Bagg, Jacob Barrett, Shuk Ying Chan, Maxime Lepoutre, Temi Ogunye, Ẹniọlá Ṣóyẹmí, and Tony Taylor—were highly supportive and gave me useful comments and feedback on parts of the book manuscript. I have also been fortunate to be able to rely on a network of other early-career political philosophers who have given me great advice and feedback over the years, including Eilidh Beaton, Felix Bender, Rebecca Buxton, Bradley Hillier-Smith, Zsolt Kapelner, Laura García-Portela, and Hallvard Sandven.

Dominic Byatt, my editor at Oxford University Press, first took an interest in this book project and has been very supportive in bringing it to fruition. Three anonymous reviewers also provided incisive and helpful comments which have greatly improved the manuscript. Some of the material in this book is adapted from work that has previously appeared in journal articles, and I am grateful to the publishers for allowing me to use the material here:

- 'Justice and Internal Displacement', *Political Studies* 71, no. 2 (2023): 314–31.
- 'Climate Change and Displacement: Towards a Pluralist Approach', *European Journal of Political Theory* (forthcoming).
- 'Labor Migration and Climate Change Adaptation', *American Political Science Review* 116, no. 3 (2022): 1012–24.
- 'Responsibility and Climate-induced Displacement', *Global Justice: Theory, Practice, Rhetoric* 11, no. 2 (2019): 59–80.

I am also very grateful to the audiences at conferences and workshops at which draft material from this manuscript was presented, at the University of Oxford, the University of Reading, the University of Manchester, Utrecht University, Leiden

University, Texas A&M University, the University of Minho, Goethe University Frankfurt, the University of Sheffield, and the University of Oslo.

Finally, I could not have completed this book without the unwavering support of Sophie Nodzenski, who has kept me on an even keel throughout the process, and my parents (Jonathan and Maggie) and sisters (Katherine and Elizabeth), who have been continually supportive of my academic ambitions.

Contents

1. The Moral Challenge of Climate Displacement — 1
2. Against a Treaty for Climate Refugees — 19
3. Climate Change and Community Relocation — 35
4. Climate Change and Territorial Sovereignty — 63
5. Climate Change and Labour Migration — 86
6. Climate Change and the Refugee Regime — 106
7. Climate Change and Internal Displacement — 131
8. Sharing the Costs of Climate Displacement — 154
9. The Future of Climate Displacement — 176

Notes — 190
Index — 243

1
The Moral Challenge of Climate Displacement

Climate change is not a new phenomenon for my community. For several years now, we all have observed and noticed the gradual changes in the environment, rainfall patterns, natural resources and biodiversity. But recently, the pace of change has quickened and now more than ever our activities are disrupted and we are no longer in control of our environment. Given our dependence on natural resources, we feel we are direct victims of climate change. We are now forced to migrate over long distances and to areas where we never used to venture. In order to survive, we will either have to abandon our lands or stay away from our usual locations . . . This is our form of adaptation. We have always mastered it, but if nothing is done to ensure the safety of our space and activities, we risk, one day, being forced to abandon our way of life and join the swelling ranks of the unemployed in the city.[1]

These are the words of Indigenous environmental activist Hindou Oumarou Ibrahim, from the Peul Mbororo community of pastoralist cattle herders in Chad. Climate change is threatening the livelihoods of many of those who live in the drylands of West African Sahel. Drought and desertification have long featured in the lives of rural communities in the Sahel, but increases in their frequency and severity related to climate change are putting significant pressure on the livelihoods of those who depend on the land.[2] Historically, those affected have used migration as a strategy for mitigating the impact of drought, by seeking work in cities and sending remittances to their families and kin or by moving to areas more conducive to the agricultural practices upon which they rely.[3] As the impacts of climate change unfold, this pattern is intensifying.

On the other side of the world, Native Alaskan communities are also facing the impacts of climate change. Esau Sinnok, an Arctic Youth Ambassador from Shishmaref, describes the situation facing his community:

It really hurts knowing that your only home is going to be gone, and you won't hunt, fish and carry on traditions the way that your people have done for centuries. It is more than a loss of place, it is a loss of identity. Once you see how vulnerable my community is to sea-level rise and erosion, you won't be able to deny that Arctic communities are already feeling the impacts of climate change. Despite this reality, I appreciate every day that I get to wake up and see the scenery that's still here and that I'm able to call this place home. For now. While it's too late to save the island of Shishmaref, we still have a little bit of hope that we'll be able to preserve our traditions and stay united as a culture.[4]

Shishmaref is an Iñupiaq community in the North-Western reaches of Alaska, which is in the process of relocating due to shoreline erosion, reductions in sea ice, and storm surges relating to climate change. The inhabitants of Shishmaref have witnessed the creeping effects of climate change for some time. These effects threaten not only the physical infrastructure of the settlement, but also the community networks and institutions that sustain their way of life. As the impacts of climate change make more land uninhabitable, more and more people around the world will need to move away from the lands that they have called home.

In other cases, the impacts of climate change manifest in more abrupt ways:

The rains came in the middle of the night, whilst most people were sleeping. When we woke up, there was water of about 2–3 feet and we did not know how to escape, because our village is far from the main road . . . I was very pregnant at the time, and our livestock are our livelihood so we didn't want to leave them to die, so we did not know what to do. We were rescued in boats by the army and NGOs. We are thankful to be alive, but we lost our livestock and now we are trying to rebuild our livelihood by starting from the beginning.[5]

This is the testimony of Fatay and Zulaikar, a husband and wife from the Badin district of Sindh, Pakistan, recounting their experience of the floods that hit their home. In July 2010, Pakistan was hit by severe flooding in the Indus River basin associated with heavy monsoon rains, which resulted in an estimated 10 million people being displaced.[6] The following year, flooding struck again, and destroyed an estimated 1.7 million homes.[7] We cannot say with much confidence that any particular extreme weather event is a result of the impacts of climate change, but we do know that events such as these will become more frequent and more intense as climate change progresses.[8]

At around the same time, a crisis of climate and conflict was unfolding in the Horn of Africa. An anonymous Somali farmer speaking in the Nakivale refugee settlement in Uganda explains:

We had droughts in the 1970s and 1980s. However, the government supported us at that time, which allowed us to survive . . . Since there was the war, we did not receive any support from the government. Therefore, there are combined factors that made us suffer: droughts and war. If war did not exist, then we might have been able to stay, but now that the land is looted, there is no way for us to claim it.[9]

In 2010, a strong La Niña event, intensified by warming in the Indian Ocean associated with climate change, precipitated a food security crisis in a region embattled by persistent political conflict.[10] According to CARE International, which provides services in the Dadaab Refugee Camp in Kenya (a destination for many fleeing violence in the Horn of Africa), the 2010 food crisis hit Somalia especially hard because of the persistent conflict in the region.[11] The interactions between political fragility, food security, conflict, and displacement are complex, but as climate change accelerates we can expect those interactions to be magnified.

Across the Pacific, sea-level rise and coral bleaching resulting from climate change present an existential threat to some small-island states:

> The threats posed to the Maldives from climate change are well-known. Every beach lost to rising seas, every house lost to storm surges, every reef lost to increasingly warm waters, every job lost as fish stocks dwindle, and every life lost to more frequent extreme weather events will make it harder and harder to govern our country, until a point reaches where we must consider abandoning our homeland.[12]

This was the statement of Mohamed Nasheed, the then President of the Maldives, at the General Debate of the United Nations General Assembly (UNGA) in New York in 2009. The Maldives, along with other small-island states across the Pacific such as Kiribati, Tuvalu, Vanuatu, the Solomon Islands, and the Marshall Islands, are networks of low-lying islands, many of which are coral atolls, and are particularly vulnerable to the impacts of climate change.[13] Left unabated, sea-level rise associated with climate change threatens to make these island states uninhabitable, and to put their citizens in a predicament for which there is no precedent.

Climate change is reshaping the dynamics of displacement. People have moved in response to environmental changes throughout history, but in the context of climate change such movement acquires a new moral and political significance. As the impacts of climate change accelerate, extreme weather events destroy homes, environmental degradation undercuts the viability of livelihoods, sea-level rise and coastal erosion force communities to relocate, and risks to food and resource security magnify the sources of political instability. Climate displacement presents itself as a pressing moral challenge that it is incumbent upon us to address.

Climate displacement comes into view as a matter of moral and political concern against the backdrop of humanity's continued failure to meaningfully mitigate the impacts of climate change. Since the early 1990s, there has been a concerted international effort to address climate change, but that effort has been stymied by political inertia and short-termism, the path dependencies of fossil-fuel economies, active campaigns of disinformation, geopolitical rivalries, and—perhaps most significantly—the simple reluctance of those with vested political and economic interests in the status quo to loosen their grip on power.[14] As a result, our collective ability to meaningfully tackle climate change is in serious question, and the extent to which we can expect the impacts of climate change upon displacement to be mitigated is unclear.

At the same time, we are continually failing in our efforts to address crises of displacement around the world. In Europe, this failure became visible most clearly in the lack of a coherent and equitable response to the arrival of refugees fleeing civil war in Syria in 2014 and 2015.[15] But this failure is more widespread: we need only turn our attention to the large numbers of displaced people who find themselves on the margins of society around the world to see it clearly. As borders become increasingly fortified, those who are stuck in refugee camps, crowded into substandard accommodation in cities, or undertaking dangerous clandestine journeys in order to find protection testify to our failure to address crises of displacement.[16]

These two issues come together in the phenomenon of climate displacement. But the moral challenge of climate displacement is more than just the sum of these parts. Two important aspects of the intersection of climate change and displacement raise critical questions for political theory.

First, climate change forces us to re-think the ways that we respond to the plight of the displaced. Clearly, the institutions, policies, and practices that we rely on to address displacement already stand in need of reform. But climate change is also fundamentally altering the ways in which displacement takes place, and it poses deep challenges to the ways that we ordinarily respond to displacement. If we are to take up the challenge of climate displacement, then we will need to re-think the tools that we employ in responding to displacement.

Second, climate change alters the moral landscape of displacement. Often, we think of our duties to the displaced as being duties of rescue, or perhaps as duties arising from our shared participation in a system of sovereign states.[17] But in the case of climate displacement, our contributions to climate change provide a new basis for our duties to the displaced. Climate change is not a natural misfortune, and we are not merely innocent bystanders who are well positioned to aid. Climate change is *anthropogenic*: that is, it is driven by human action. And crucially, those who have contributed most to the problem of climate change tend to be those who suffer least from its effects. Through our contributions to climate change, we are implicated in the plight of those who are displaced when the impacts of climate change manifest. The position of responsibility that we occupy raises important questions about the nature and extent of the moral duties that we owe to those who are displaced in the context of climate change.

This book develops a political theory of climate displacement. It articulates an account of the duties that we owe to those affected by climate displacement and critically examines the institutions on which we rely in discharging those duties. In doing so, the book has two main aims. The first aim is to map the moral terrain of climate displacement. Climate displacement poses distinctive questions of political morality, but it also intersects with more familiar forms of displacement and relates to existing problems in debates about migration, territory, and climate change in political theory. Clarifying the structure of the problem of climate displacement helps us to navigate its moral terrain. The second aim is to defend a substantive view of the political morality of climate displacement. As well as a map of the topic, we need to chart a course. So, this book aims to provide us with normative guidance as we respond to climate displacement.

As the testimonies above illustrate, climate displacement is a not a simple or homogenous phenomenon. Climate change and displacement interact in complex and heterogeneous ways, and a political theory of climate displacement should be sensitive to its real-world dynamics. Unfortunately, misunderstandings about the dynamics of climate displacement abound. Popular media have tended to paint a simplistic and exaggerated picture of 'climate refugees'.[18] In some cases, as we will see, these misunderstandings have been picked up in normative theorizing on climate displacement. In order to get a clear-eyed view of the issues at stake, it is crucial to get a better understanding of the relationship between climate change and displacement.

The next section of this introductory chapter reconstructs the development of our knowledge of the dynamics of climate displacement. Understanding the current state of our knowledge of the relationship between climate change and displacement is essential if we are to clarify the moral questions that climate displacement raises. But it is also crucial to understand how our knowledge has developed, so that we can see how misconceptions about climate displacement have come to hold the sway that they do and to diagnose some of the ways in which existing normative theorizing on the topic has gone awry.

The Dynamics of Climate Displacement

The idea that environmental changes can drive displacement is not new. It has a long history, stretching back at least to the work of geographers such as Ernst Ravenstein and Ellsworth Huntington in the late nineteenth and early twentieth centuries.[19] In the work of these early geographers, we can find early instances of something like empirical claims about 'climate-induced' movement. Huntington, for example, argued that the 'barbarian' invasions of Europe in the late era of the Western Roman Empire were a direct result of environmental changes.[20] According to Huntington, the 'untold hordes of nomads' on the Central Asian plains, driven by shortages of rainfall, migrated to Europe, where climatic conditions were becoming warm and habitable. They arrived 'horde by horde' and 'Rome fell before the wanderers'. Huntington believed that the environment was the engine of history, and that 'the strongest nations of the world live where the climatic conditions are most propitious'.[21]

This early and deterministic view of the role of the environment in migration fell out of favour as the disciplines of geography and migration studies developed.

In the mid-twentieth century, a combination of factors led to the 'disappearance' of the environment as a causal factor in explanations of migration.[22] First was the idea that progress was liberating humans from the constraints of nature. The idea was that as modernity has dawned, humans had begun to conquer nature, meaning that 'primitive' forms of environmental migration were being superseded by social forms of migration.[23] Second was the demise of natural determinism in twentieth-century social science. Purely natural explanations of human behaviour had come to be seen as naïve and had become tainted by their association with geographers such as Huntington, who had used 'natural' explanations of human behaviour to legitimate racist conceptions of natural hierarchy and to rationalize colonial oppression. Third was the rise of economic explanations of migration. In this paradigm, the environment was either sidelined or subsumed within economic explanations. Natural hazards, for example, become part of 'a vector of variables that translates into differences of wage productivity or rent between regions and countries'.[24] Finally, fourth was the rise of a distinct discipline of refugee studies that largely concerned itself with the political causes of forced migration.[25] By the 1970s, the environment was largely absent from theoretical attempts to explain the causes of migration and displacement.[26]

Amid growing concerns about global warming in the 1980s, the relationship between the environment and displacement became salient again, primarily among environmentalists. In 1985, a report for the United Nations Environment Programme (UNEP) introduced the idea of an 'environmental refugee' into policy circles.[27] This publication, as well as others around the same time, popularized the idea that climate change would have a significant impact on displacement.[28] Researchers were galvanized to shore up the evidence base behind this claim, and a new current of research that sought to quantify climate displacement emerged. This new current of research developed what has been called a 'maximalist' view, which stressed the significance of climate change in causing displacement.[29] The maximalist view is typified by the work of the environmental scientist Norman Myers, who infamously predicted that there would be 150 million 'environmental refugees' by 2050 and updated this figure to 200 million in 2002.[30] These figures were picked up both in the Stern Review of the economics of climate change and in grey literature such as the policy briefs and reports put out by non-governmental organizations.[31] Today, the maximalist view undoubtedly dominates policy circles and the popular imagination.[32]

Since the late 1990s and early 2000s, however, critics have argued that the maximalist view fails to take up the lessons learned within migration studies over the course of the twentieth century.[33] Myers's 'dubious' figures were challenged on the basis that they crudely assumed that anyone living in an area predicted to be affected by sea-level rise would become an environmental refugee.[34] More generally, critics argued that the maximalist view depends on untenable monocausal assumptions about the relationship between climate change and displacement, that it fails to distinguish between proximate and underlying causes of displacement, and that it uses broad definitions of 'environmental refugees' to produce inflated statistics—problems that 'strike to the core of the literature on environmental refugees', in the words of the geographer Richard Black.[35] At the same time, however, migration and refugee scholars initially adopted 'defensive postures' in reaction to the maximalist view and sometimes rejected environmental causes of displacement out of hand.[36] The long shadow cast by the environmental determinism of early geographers held back the analysis of climate displacement within migration studies.

The backlash against the maximalist view can be partly explained by the fact that the reactions of refugee and migration researchers were not only disciplinary and methodological, but also political.[37] The maximalist view was motivated by well-meaning concerns about climate change, but its shaky claims about mass displacement were deployed to serve ideological ends that many refugee and migration scholars sought to contest. The emergence of the maximalist view dovetailed with the increasing popularity of the idea of 'environmental conflict' in the early 1990s.[38] Robert Caplan's influential article 'The Coming Anarchy' splashed the following text across the front page of *The Atlantic* in 1994: 'THE COMING ANARCHY: NATIONS BREAK UP UNDER THE TIDAL FLOW OF REFUGEES FROM ENVIRONMENTAL AND SOCIAL DISASTER.'[39] Ideas such as this were leveraged to create an (often racialized) image of waves of 'climate refugees' arriving from the Global South, who would be a threat to national security or the welfare state.[40] For example, a widely circulated 2003 military intelligence report outlining the challenges of climate change for US national security predicted that 'borders will be strengthened around the country to hold back unwanted starving immigrants from the Caribbean Islands (an especially severe problem), Mexico and South America.'[41] Refugee and migration scholars sought to contest the idea that migration should be viewed as a threat. Their own perspectives, however, have not been immune to ideological appropriation. For example, the increasingly popular idea that migration is simply an economically rational form of adaptation to climate change has been criticized on the basis that it serves the interests of those who seek to make migration amenable to the interests of global capital.[42]

Today, in the wake of these debates, a more nuanced picture of the relationship between climate change and displacement is emerging. The consensus view among migration scholars is now that climate change *does* play a role in driving displacement, but that its role is complicated. Climate change impacts are generally only one part of 'patterns of multiple causality, in which natural and environmental factors are closely linked to economic, social and political ones.'[43] There is still significant uncertainty about the future of climate displacement—the Intergovernmental Panel on Climate Change (IPCC) notes that there is 'low confidence' in quantitative projections of displacement—but researchers today are renewing their efforts to locate the proper place of the climate change in causal explanations of displacement.[44]

A variety of strategies have been used in recent years in order to get a fuller understanding of the role that climate change plays in different contexts of displacement.[45] Traditional approaches make causal inferences by tracking the relationship between climatic variables and aggregate levels of displacement.[46] More fine-grained qualitative, ethnographic or historical methods seek to get an in-depth understanding of the dynamics of climate displacement in particular contexts.[47] And novel strategies such as agent-based modelling use computer simulations to examine the complex interactions between different agents' actions and climatic drivers of displacement.[48] Each of these strategies has its own drawbacks and advantages, and the findings of any particular study are likely to be limited in terms of their generalizability to climate displacement as a whole. But by integrating the insights of these different approaches, migration theorists have developed new conceptual frameworks for understanding the relationship between climate change and displacement.[49] These conceptual frameworks differ in their details, but they all stress some important features of climate displacement.

One important feature of climate displacement is that it is *complex*. The impacts of climate change are mediated through social institutions and interact with other pre-existing social, economic, environmental, political, and demographic drivers of displacement.[50] Climate impacts are usually only one part of a constellation of interrelated causal drivers of displacement. One important upshot of this is that it is rarely straightforward to attribute any particular instance of displacement to climate change. But this does not mean that climate change is unimportant in driving displacement, only that climate change is tangled up with causal drivers that interact in complex ways. We should begin our analysis of climate displacement with a recognition of this complexity.

An important aspect of this complexity is that climate displacement typically intersects with background injustices structured along classic fault lines such as those of race, class, indigeneity, and gender. In general, vulnerability to climate impacts is deeply shaped by social factors and, as Olúfẹ́mi O. Táíwò has recently argued, reflects the ongoing legacy of deeply rooted historical injustices such as colonialism and racial hierarchy.[51] Climate displacement is no different: it reflects broader social injustices that shape who is exposed to climate impacts, the resources to which they have access, and the constraints they face—all of which bears on whether, when, and how people move (or are prevented from doing so).[52]

A second important feature of climate displacement is that it is *heterogeneous*. That is, it takes very different forms in different contexts, ranging from seasonal or temporary labour migration in response to environmental degradation, through permanent community-level relocation in the face of sea-level rise, to the sudden flight of those escaping extreme weather events, and beyond.[53] In each of these different contexts, climate displacement raises different moral questions and warrants different practical responses. A political theory of climate displacement will need to make space for these differences.

These two features of climate displacement are central elements of its real-world dynamics. A political theory that aims to confront the moral challenge of climate displacement as it arises in the real world should not abstract away from them. And as we will see in Chapter 2, this has important implications for how we should approach climate displacement from a normative point of view. In particular, it helps us to see why one popular approach to climate displacement—the idea that we should put in place a treaty for 'climate refugees'—is mistaken. The idea of a climate refugee treaty rests on an idealized picture of climate displacement that obscures its complexity and heterogeneity. The upshot of this idealization, so I argue, is that proposals for a climate refugee treaty are either morally objectionable or practically inert.

This does not mean that all abstraction is objectionable. Some abstraction from the details of particular cases is inevitable, and the next section sets out some abstract distinctions that structure the inquiry that unfolds over the rest of this book.[54] A theory that did not abstract at all would be like the map with a scale of 'a mile to a mile' described by Lewis Carroll in *Sylvie and Bruno*—which, of course, cannot function as a map.[55] But a political theory of climate displacement should nonetheless be informed by a careful assessment of its empirical dynamics, lest it become detached from the practical problem that it is designed to address.

Contexts of Climate Displacement

In order to provide some structure to our inquiry, it is useful to draw some analytic distinctions between the main contexts of climate displacement that I examine over the course of this book. The distinctions that I draw here categorize different forms of climate displacement in ways that highlight the relevant moral differences between different contexts. Of course, these distinctions will not always be sharp in practice, but they can nonetheless serve to orient our moral reflection on the diverse ways in which climate change and displacement interact.

One distinction that I draw in this book is between what I call *anticipatory* and *reactive* displacement.[56] This distinction borrows from Anthony Richmond's sociological theory of migration, in which he distinguishes between proactive and reactive forms of migration.[57] Richmond argues that migration is never *only* a matter of the agency of migrants, nor *only* a matter of the circumstances in which migrants find themselves. Rather, migrants exercise agency within the context of background structures in which they are situated. Different political, economic, environmental, social, and bio-psychological factors act as 'structural constraints' and 'enabling circumstances' that alter the range of options available to them.[58]

Depending on the nature of these structural constraints and enabling circumstances, movement may be more proactive or reactive. For example, when a person whose employment is precarious and who faces discrimination in the labour market sees the impacts of climate change putting pressure on their industry, they may be more likely to move to another region where work is more readily available and discrimination is less widespread, in order to secure their long-term employment prospects. In this case, structural constraints lead to a proactive form of displacement. Or consider an individual who has little financial capital and little state support, who lives in an area affected by extreme weather events. Their lack of financial capital and state support may mean that they are unable to invest in protections against the impacts of extreme weather, and so they may be more likely to face displacement in the aftermath of an extreme weather event. In this case, structural constraints lead to a reactive form of displacement.

I use the term *anticipatory displacement* to refer to movement that is undertaken in a broadly proactive, rather than reactive, way. In the climate change context, anticipatory displacement takes place in advance of, and is oriented in terms of avoiding the harmfulness of, the impacts of climate change. It is planned, rather than being a reaction to the already harmful impacts of climate change. It uses migration as a way of mitigating the harmfulness of the impacts of climate change, either by avoiding those impacts or by rendering them less harmful.

I use the term *reactive displacement*, by contrast, to refer to movement that is undertaken in a broadly reactive, rather than proactive, way. In the climate change context, reactive displacement takes place when the impacts of climate change manifest and individuals or groups move in order to seek refuge from those impacts. It is not planned, but is rather a coping response that uses movement as a way of escaping from the harmful impacts of climate change.

The distinction between anticipatory and reactive displacement is helpful because it shifts our focus away from a different distinction that occupies a central place in debates about migration and displacement in political theory: the distinction between *forced* and *voluntary* movement. Political theorists often distinguish between voluntary or 'economic' migrants and forced migrants or refugees.[59] David Miller, for example, characterizes economic migrants as those who 'are not driven out by a fear of persecution or some other immediate threat to their human rights, but drawn in by the advantages that their new society has to offer'.[60] But in the context of climate change, many people are likely to fall somewhere between being 'drawn in' by the advantages available in a new society and 'driven out' by an immediate threat. Climate change impacts may exacerbate the structural constraints that shape people's choices, for example by exacerbating vulnerabilities to economic shocks or undermining the viability of livelihoods. Those moving in such conditions certainly exercise agency, but their movement may not be fully 'voluntary' in the sense that political theorists take to be relevant for, for example, decisions about whether or not would-be immigrants can be excluded from the territory of a state or whether they forfeit a claim to the protection of cultural minority rights.[61]

At the same time, it is important to draw a distinction between these more proactive forms of displacement and the more reactive forms of displacement of those fleeing immediate threats such as extreme weather events or political conflict. Those facing anticipatory displacement face the threat of changing background conditions that foreclose the options available to them until migration becomes either the only option or a particularly attractive one. Those facing reactive displacement, by contrast, find themselves suddenly uprooted from their homes. Both of these forms of movement may be involuntary, but this is not the most important fact about them, at least for our purposes. Anticipatory and reactive displacement are qualitatively different forms of displacement, which raise different moral concerns.

Beyond this broad distinction, I also distinguish more narrowly between several practical contexts in which climate change and displacement intersect. There are five different contexts of climate displacement that I examine over the course of this book: community relocation; territorial sovereignty; labour migration; internal displacement; and refugee movement.[62] The first three can be categorized as broadly anticipatory forms of displacement, in that they are generally undertaken in ways that can be planned and anticipated. The last two can be categorized as broadly reactive forms of displacement, in that they emerge suddenly and often unpredictably. These connections are not a matter of conceptual necessity. It is *possible* for community relocation to happen reactively, for example. But in practice, the first three contexts tend to involve anticipatory displacement and the latter two reactive displacement. These contexts are also unlikely to be exhaustive, given the unpredictable nature of the impacts of climate change. But distinguishing between these contexts provides us with a useful conceptual map of the moral terrain of climate displacement, even if it remains only a rough outline.

First is *community relocation*. Community relocation is a form of displacement that takes place when particular areas become unviable as sites for human habitation, for example due to increased risks of recurrent flooding or mudslides, or a loss of habitable land as shorelines recede. Climate change impacts create risks which can make it more difficult for established communities to stay in place, but they rarely straightforwardly force a community to relocate, because impacts of climate change can often be attenuated through *in situ* adaptation.

Second is *territorial sovereignty*. Small-island peoples face threats to the habitability of their lands due to rising seas and coral bleaching. This may just look like a scaled-up version of community relocation, but there is an important moral difference between these cases. In the case of small islands, entire political communities are under threat. At present, many of those political communities exist as territorially sovereign states. The land base that enables their exercise of territorial sovereignty, however, is threatened by the impacts of climate change.

Third is *labour migration*. Slow-onset climate impacts such as thawing permafrost, the salination of ground water, desertification, and recurring floods or droughts can gradually degrade the environmental background conditions upon which people rely for their livelihoods or subsistence. Labour migration often works as an adaptive response to the impacts of climate change for those whose livelihoods are under threat. Such labour migration can take a variety of forms—domestic or international, temporary or permanent—depending on the nature of the climate impacts involved and the opportunities for migration that are available.

Fourth is *internal displacement*. Sudden-onset disasters such as flooding, typhoons, hurricanes, wildfires, and mudslides, can trigger displacement. Climate change increases both the frequency and severity of extreme weather events such as these. The impacts of such disasters are also mediated by pre-existing social vulnerabilities. Most people displaced in this way are likely to remain within their country's borders, and so to count as 'internally displaced persons' (IDPs) under existing international legal and humanitarian frameworks.

Fifth is *refugee movement*. Under international law, forced migrants must have a 'well-founded fear of persecution' on the basis of certain protected characteristics such as religion or nationality to qualify as a refugee. In some cases, climate change impacts may magnify existing sources of political instability and indirectly contribute to situations in which persecution takes place. But beyond this, some theorists also believe that the basis for refugee status should be expanded. If they are right, then those fleeing their state for other reasons, such as the failure of their state to adequately respond to social deprivation or disasters related to climate change, may also have a claim to refugee status.

Each of these contexts raises different moral questions about what we owe to those who are displaced in the context of climate change that will be examined over the course of this book. But they are also united by their shared relationship to climate change. One way of seeing these different contexts is as different expressions or manifestations of a more fundamental transformation that is taking place in the background conditions against which we live our lives: the emergence of what Simona Capisani calls 'territorial instability'.[63] These different contexts are symptomatic of a world in which we can no longer presume a stable territorial background framework—if we ever could—and must directly confront the instability created by climate change. For Capisani, the upshot of this is that we must find new ways to protect a heretofore unrecognized basic right—the 'right to a liveable locality'—that is facing unprecedented threats.[64] The arguments that I make in this book about our duties in different contexts of climate displacement can be viewed as an interpretation of what such a right might require in relation to the different ways in which the problem of territorial instability manifests in the context of climate change.

A Note on Method

This overview of the contexts and dynamics of climate displacement gives us a starting point from which to begin a normative inquiry. But before we begin to develop a political theory of climate displacement in earnest, it is worth pausing to reflect on *why* we need such a theory in the first place. This question helps us to get a better picture of the method that we should adopt in constructing a political theory of climate displacement.

The reason that we need a political theory of climate displacement is that we are confronted with a problem—the moral challenge of climate displacement—that we need guidance to address. The emergence of climate displacement makes it impossible for us to carry on unreflectively, participating in the institutions and practices that we ordinarily take for granted. At first, the problem of climate displacement appears to us as amorphous, but empirical investigation and theoretical reflection can give it a more definitive shape. The task of a political theory of climate displacement is to help us to clarify and overcome the problem of climate displacement, by providing us with guidance on how to revise our ideals, principles, institutions, and practices in light of the new challenge that we face. This view of the task of a political theory of climate displacement takes what we might call a *problem-based approach* to normative theorizing.

This idea that the task of our theories is to help us to overcome the problems that jar us into critical reflection was one of the insights of the pragmatist philosopher John Dewey.[65] Dewey thought that theory should be problem-driven, that it should guide our behaviour in the contexts in which problems arise, rather than articulating general context- and time-transcending principles to be applied to particular cases:

> Morals is not a catalogue of acts nor a set of rules to be applied like drugstore prescriptions or cook-book recipes. The need in morals is for specific methods of inquiry and of contrivance: Methods of inquiry to locate difficulties and evils; methods of contrivance to form plans to be used as working hypotheses in dealing with them. And the pragmatic import of the logic of individualized situations, each having its own irreplaceable good and principle, is to transfer the attention of theory from preoccupation with general conceptions to the problem of developing effective methods of inquiry.[66]

For Dewey, the point of moral theories is to guide our behaviour in practical contexts in which problems emerge. The upshot of this is that the task of the theorist is to develop 'effective methods of inquiry' which can be employed within particular contexts in order to help us to navigate particular problems, rather than to elaborate 'general conceptions' and to apply them to particular cases. Political ideals and principles are 'working hypotheses' to be tested in practice, and the ultimate proof of their success lies in whether they help us to overcome the problems that jar us into critical reflection in the first place.

What does this mean in terms of the method that we should adopt in developing a political theory of climate displacement? In order to put some flesh on the bones of this Deweyan idea, we can tease out three methodological implications of the problem-based approach to normative theorizing for a political theory of climate displacement.

The first implication of the problem-based approach concerns the status of the theory that is developed over the course of the book. Dewey rejected what he called the 'quest for certainty'—the search for the 'absolute and unshakeable' in philosophy—and instead saw judgements about what we ought to do as involving an ineliminable element of uncertainty and contingency.[67] On this view, developing a political theory of climate displacement is a situated exercise, the task of which is to develop principles and institutions that help us meet to the challenge of climate displacement as it confronts us in practice. This implies a certain self-consciousness about the theory's provisional nature: principles of political morality are open to change in light of their being borne out by experience, and in light of the changing circumstances of our shared political lives.

The second implication of the problem-based approach concerns the background conditions that we take as our starting point. The challenge of climate displacement has arisen at a particular historical juncture, which features certain background conditions. If we want our theory to help us to address the challenge of climate displacement as it has arisen, then it will need to begin from the fact that we find ourselves in a world characterized by these background conditions. This is not the same as saying that our theory should be rigidly constrained by them: it may be that our theory dictates that we should work to alter or dismantle them. But we cannot imagine them away, and our theory should begin from the context in which we find ourselves.

Some of the background assumptions that I adopt in this book that should be made explicit. For one thing, I take for granted the existence of an international order composed largely of territorial states, with regimes of border control that regulate the movement of people between those states. For another, I take for granted the fact that climate change is accelerating and that it is driven in a large part by human activity. But crucially, I do not assume that the continued acceleration of anthropogenic climate change is inevitable. The first moral duty that we have with respect to climate displacement is to stop contributing to it—by radically transforming our energy systems and our systems of production so that we reach net zero emissions as quickly as possible—and this duty does not disappear when we focus on how to respond to climate displacement, even if it is not in the foreground.[68] I do not think that we should assume that we will discharge this duty perfectly, but neither do I think that we should accept the inevitability of our failure. So, in this book I envisage a relatively moderate scenario of climate displacement, in which some climate displacement occurs—whether because it is already locked in by our previous emissions or because of our failure to fully discharge our climate change mitigation duties—but in which mitigating climate change continues to be a major global priority. In the final chapter, I relax this assumption and consider the implications of a 'worst-case' scenario of climate displacement. In doing so, I respond to what Kyle Fruh calls the condition of 'anticipatory moral failure' that we are in with respect to climate displacement.[69] It is important to reflect on the possibility of our failure to contain climate displacement, but we should not treat that failure as a foregone conclusion.

The third implication of the problem-based approach is that we should begin our investigation into the moral terrain of climate displacement not by starting from general moral principles, but by investigating the moral terrain of the contexts in which the problem of climate displacement arises. We should not view our institutions and practices simply as instruments for realizing some pre-determined ideal state of affairs. Rather, we should investigate them on their own terms, examining the values and ends that are implicit within them, which we can uncover through a process of interpretation. We can then critically reflect on those values and ends and decide whether they can be reflectively endorsed or whether other values and ends would better serve our purposes. In the light of those reflections, we can propose reforms to our institutions and practices that would help us to better realize those values and ends, especially in light of the new challenges that we face. This idea has some affinities with 'practice-dependent' and 'contextualist' approaches to political theory, though I do not think it need be wedded to these approaches as their proponents understand them.[70] The theory that I develop here is an 'internal' one, in the sense that it starts with the contexts in which the problem of climate displacement emerges, but as we will see, this aspect of the theory does not preclude radical reforms to our institutions and practices.

Taken together, these considerations paint a picture of an approach to political theory in which we develop principles from the bottom up, by starting from where we find ourselves and critically reflecting upon the problems and challenges that arise in relation to our ideals, principles, institutions, and practices. Of course, this picture remains somewhat impressionistic, and much more could be said to fill it out. But it suffices to provide a broad orientation in constructing a theory. It also makes the problem-based approach readily distinguishable from a different—and perhaps more familiar—approach to political theory: *ideal theory*. Ideal theorists take the principal task of political theory to be articulating an account of the requirements of an ideally just political order.[71]

I have no objection to this way of doing political theory. It seems sensible to me to endorse a healthy pluralism about the methodology of political theory and to recognize that different approaches may be suited to different projects with different aims.[72] But one reason to adopt a different strategy here is that even if we successfully articulate an account of an ideally just political order, this leaves us with inadequate guidance for the here-and-now. Suppose, for example, that an ideally just world requires the free movement of people across borders. This tells us little about the problems that confront us now concerning, for example, who has special claims to immunity from the restrictions that are applied to movement across borders today.[73] Insofar ideal theorists aim at guiding action in the here-and-now, their theories need to be supplemented with non-ideal theories that tells us how to get from where we are now to that ideal—which itself requires a detailed investigation of the context that we face.[74] Once we are in that terrain, a problem-based approach that confronts the challenges that we face directly appears to me to be a more straightforward and promising route to take.

Outline

Armed with a clearer understanding of the empirical dynamics of climate displacement and a method for developing a political theory of climate displacement, we are in a position to lay out the contours of the approach that I take in this book. In broad terms, the approach that I take is to examine five different contexts of climate displacement in turn. In each case, I examine the moral terrain of the context and the challenges posed by climate displacement, and I articulate ideals, principles, and proposals for reform which seek to meet the challenge posed by climate displacement. Then, I step back from these different contexts of climate displacement in order to set out an account of how we can fairly distribute the costs of tackling climate displacement in ways which reflect our responsibility for its production. I call this approach the *pluralist* theory of climate displacement.

The main competitor to the pluralist theory is a proposal that has enjoyed some popularity in the nascent literature on climate displacement: a treaty for 'climate refugees'. The task of Chapter 2 is to reconstruct and critique this proposal. My central argument is that the idea of a treaty for climate refugees depends upon an idealized picture of climate displacement, which obscures its complexity and heterogeneity. I argue that this means that it would exhibit two kinds of moral arbitrariness: it would fail to treat like cases alike and fail to treat relevantly different cases differently. Then, I show how the pluralist theory avoids these problems.

Chapter 3 examines climate-related community relocation, taking the case of the relocation of the Iñupiaq village of Shishmaref, Alaska, as its central case study. I argue against two approaches to community relocation, which I call the *market model* and the *communitarian model* of relocation. I argue that the market model fragments communities and, in doing so, jeopardizes the interests that community members have in maintaining the shared social and cultural practices that they value. The communitarian model avoids the problems of the market model only at the cost of suppressing internal disagreement within communities. I defend the *democratic model* of relocation, which enables community members to make collective decisions about relocation. I then analyse two practical problems that arise in community relocation: the problems of *expertise* and *scale*.

Chapter 4 examines the threats to territorial sovereignty created by sea-level rise in small-island states such as Kiribati, Tuvalu, and the Maldives. The central issue in this context concerns the protection of small-island peoples' rights to self-determination. I examine the demands of self-determination and critically assess three proposals for small-island states: *territorial redistribution, deterritorialized statehood,* and *intra-state territorial autonomy*. I argue that a weak version of deterritorialized statehood cannot secure self-determination in any meaningful sense, and that both territorial redistribution and a strong version of deterritorialized statehood can do so only by creating significant moral costs. Intra-state territorial autonomy, if implemented in ways that reflect the values of small-island peoples, can secure self-determination while minimizing these moral costs.

Chapter 5 examines labour migration as an adaptive response to the impacts of climate change in places such as rural Ethiopia, where the impacts of climate change are undermining livelihoods. Social scientific evidence tells us that labour migration can function as a form of adaptation to climate change. As a result, some have argued that we should expand opportunities for international labour migration for those facing climate change impacts. I argue that expanding opportunities for labour migration is permissible—and may even be required—but that at the same time, states must also provide sufficient opportunities for adaptation in place, so that no one is forced to take up opportunities for labour migration in order to successfully adapt to climate change. I then examine the terms under which labour migrants may be admitted to receiving states, and I argue that when labour migration policy is used as a tool of climate change adaptation, states may not impose restrictive terms on would-be labour migrants.

Chapter 6 examines the place of the refugee regime in addressing climate displacement. I develop an interpretation of the refugee regime that I call the *membership* view, against the *persecution* view and the *basic needs* view. I then leverage this interpretation of the refugee regime to explore the ways that climate impacts interact with refugee movement, drawing on examples from Somalia, Syria, and Central America. I examine three problems in the refugee regime that are exacerbated in the context of climate change—the restrictive definition of the refugee under international law, the deterrence paradigm in international refugee policy, and the maldistribution of the costs of refugee protection between states—and I propose some reforms which seek to address them.

Chapter 7 examines the place of the internal displacement governance regime in addressing climate displacement. I develop a novel interpretation of the normative status of the IDP, which I then leverage to examine the relationship between climate change and internal displacement, drawing on the examples of Typhoon Haiyan in the Philippines and Hurricane Katrina in New Orleans. Then, I examine two problems in the IDP protection regime that are exacerbated in the context of climate change—the humanitarian character of IDP assistance, and the internalist bias in the protection of IDPs—and propose some reforms which seek to address them.

The last two chapters take a step back and adopt a broader perspective on climate displacement. Chapter 8 examines how the costs of tackling climate displacement should be shared between states. I argue that the costs should be shared according to a principle of responsibility, which says that states are liable to bear the costs of climate displacement they have created through their failure to discharge their antecedent climate mitigation duties. I then refine this principle in light of two problems, one which relates to the complexity of climate displacement, and another which relates to the indeterminacy of states' duties to mitigate climate change. Neither problem undermines the principle of responsibility, but both affect how it should be interpreted in practice.

Finally, Chapter 9 reflects on the uncertain future of climate displacement. I engage in an exercise of prospection, imaging a 'worst-case' scenario of climate displacement brought about by catastrophic climate change. My aim is not to determine what we should do in such a future, but instead to reflect on how the possibility of such a future should bear on our reasoning about climate displacement today. Although the future of catastrophic climate change is a fearsome one, I argue that we should not be motivated by fear in addressing climate displacement. Instead, I argue, we have rational grounds for a politics of hope for the future of climate displacement.

2
Against a Treaty for Climate Refugees

On 19 September 2016, the United Nations General Assembly adopted resolution 71/1, *The New York Declaration for Refugees and Migrants*. The New York Declaration explicitly recognized that people move 'in response to the adverse effects of climate change, natural disasters (some of which may be linked to climate change), or other environmental factors'.[1] The Refugee and Migration Compacts, developed in the wake of the New York Declaration, each also contain an explicit recognition of the effects of climate change on displacement.[2] In climate politics, the 2010 Cancún Agreements adopted at the 16th Conference of the Parties (COP16) to the United Nations Framework Convention on Climate Change (UNFCCC) encouraged states to pursue 'coordination and cooperation with regard to climate change induced displacement'.[3] And in 2015, a 'Task Force on Displacement' was set up under the auspices of the Warsaw International Mechanism on Loss and Damage.[4]

At present, these forms of international governance remain mostly aspirational, but they reflect the fact that climate displacement has begun to be taken seriously in the international order. As the impacts of climate change unfold, the political salience and the moral significance of climate displacement will only grow. Although there is significant disagreement over exactly how much displacement will take place as a result of the impacts of climate change, there is now a consensus, reflected by the Intergovernmental Panel on Climate Change (IPCC), that climate impacts are likely to lead to an increase in displacement over the course of the twenty-first century.[5] This creates both an opportunity and an imperative for political theorists to examine our duties to those displaced by climate impacts and the institutions through which those duties can be discharged.

This chapter takes a first step in undertaking such a task, by critically examining the idea of a treaty for 'climate refugees'. The idea of a climate refugee treaty has enjoyed significant popularity in the nascent literature on climate displacement, and it has considerable appeal at first glance. I argue, however, that the idea of a treaty for climate refugees is misguided. The first part of the chapter reconstructs the idea of a treaty for climate refugees and shows why the climate refugee treaty initially appears to be a promising option. Then, I examine the concept of the 'climate refugee' that figures centrally within such proposals in more detail. The concept of the climate refugee obscures two key empirical features of climate displacement: its *complexity* and its *heterogeneity*. This, I argue, is the root of the problem with a climate refugee treaty. Because the climate refugee treaty is blind

Climate Displacement. Jamie Draper, Oxford University Press. © Jamie Draper (2023).
DOI: 10.1093/oso/9780192870162.003.0002

to these features of climate displacement, it involves two kinds of moral arbitrariness: it fails to treat like cases alike, and it fails to treat relevantly different cases differently. The proposal for a climate refugee treaty can escape these charges only at the cost of being consigned to practical irrelevance. Exposing these problems clears the ground for setting out my own alternative—the pluralist theory of climate displacement—which disaggregates climate displacement and integrates it with non-climatic forms of displacement, rather than proposing principles for an idealized climate refugee.

In broader terms, the aim of this chapter is to dislodge a picture that holds great sway in the public imagination: the figure of the 'climate refugee'. The figure of the climate refugee by now occupies a significant place in our moral imagination. In François Gemenne's words, climate refugees have become 'the human face of climate change'.[6] But my suggestion is that the figure of the climate refugee is a 'picture' in the Wittgensteinian sense: it has 'held us captive' and prevented us from adopting alternative perspectives on climate displacement.[7] The problem is not exactly that this picture is *false*, but rather that it restricts our vision—it puts us in a situation of 'aspectival captivity'—and impedes our moral reflection on climate displacement.[8] By dislodging this picture, I hope to enable us to start afresh and look at climate displacement in a more contextually specific way.

A Treaty for Climate Refugees

The basic idea of a treaty for climate refugees is simple. In essence, it would involve an agreement between states to create a new legal status for those displaced by climate change impacts. That legal status would grant those designated as 'climate refugees' access to certain legal rights and forms of international protection, which would be guaranteed by the international community. It is a clear and straightforward response to climate displacement.

The climate refugee treaty is specified in various ways under different proposals that have been made by legal and political theorists. Perhaps the most influential example comes from Frank Biermann and Ingrid Boas, who have outlined a proposal for a new legal instrument that would be constituted as a protocol to the UNFCCC, called the *Protocol for the Recognition, Protection and Resettlement of Climate Refugees*.[9] Biermann and Boas argue that the protocol should identify a group of 'climate refugees' who would be entitled to collective resettlement, either within their state or internationally.[10] As part of the proposal, Biermann and Boas also outline a funding mechanism, which operates according to a grant system where developed countries contribute funding in proportion to their responsibility for the plight of climate refugees.[11]

Other structurally similar proposals have also been put forward. Bonnie Docherty and Tyler Gianni have called for a *sui generis* legal convention for 'climate change refugees'.[12] This convention would guarantee those identified as climate change refugees access to a range of rights, including both rights specifically related to movement (such as *non-refoulment* and immunity against being penalized for unlawful border-crossing) and various civil, political, social, cultural and economic rights.[13] Sujatha Byravan and Sudhir Chella Rajan argue for a special right to free movement for those they consider 'climate exiles'.[14] On their view, 'climate exile' status should be inscribed in an international treaty or protocol to the 1951 Refugee Convention, and should entitle its bearers to an individual right to migrate to and settle in a safe country. Historically high-emitting states would have primary responsibility for 'providing immigration rights' for climate exiles.[15] The idea of a treaty for climate refugees has also found support beyond academia. In 2011, Sheikh Hasina, the Prime Minister of Bangladesh, called for the establishment of 'an international regime under the UN' to tackle climate displacement.[16] More recently, the Environmental Justice Foundation has called for 'an international agreement that will clarify the rights and ensure the protection of climate refugees'.[17]

These various proposals all differ significantly in their details. They identify different groups of people as climate refugees (or 'climate exiles'), specify different rights and correlate duties associated with climate refugee status, and take different institutional forms—which may be more or less revisionary when it comes to existing legal practice. But despite these differences, they share an important structural feature: they take the task of addressing climate displacement to require that we pick out a group of 'climate refugees' as a category of concern and articulate a set of rights to which those in that group are entitled. In what follows, I argue that it is this core feature of a climate refugee treaty that means that it gets off on the wrong foot.

Before making this argument, however, it is worth noting why the idea of a climate refugee treaty appears attractive, at least at first glance. The main motivation behind the climate refugee treaty proposal is that it appears well equipped to address what is sometimes called, in the parlance of international legal and humanitarian practice, a 'protection gap' in relation to climate displacement.[18] A protection gap refers to the idea that existing legal frameworks in the international order fail to offer protection to some people who have justified claims to protection. In the case at hand, the existing legal frameworks that govern displacement in the international order fail to offer protection to those displaced by climate change impacts: they fall through the 'gaps' in international protection. For example, those displaced by climate impacts are not eligible for protection under the 1951 Refugee Convention, which restricts protection to those who suffer a 'well-founded fear of persecution' on the basis of certain protected characteristics.[19] Similarly, many of those displaced by climate impacts will not be eligible for protection under the regimes of governance for the protection of 'internally displaced persons' (IDPs).[20] And the fragmented and largely ad hoc system of 'complementary protection' for those who fall outside the scope of these regimes provides little comfort for those seeking firm guarantees of protection.[21]

Existing legal frameworks do not provide robust forms of protection for those displaced by climate change impacts. Clearly, the judgement that this amounts to a 'protection gap' depends upon an assumption that those displaced by the impacts of climate change *ought* to be protected under international legal and normative frameworks in some way, but I do not think that this judgement is particularly controversial. Proponents of the climate refugee treaty see their proposals as a way of closing this protection gap.[22] In my view, they are right to point out that, as things stand, the international legal order fails to protect those who have compelling claims to protection. It is only their proposed solution, the creation of a treaty for climate refugees, that I take to be mistaken.

A second reason that speaks in favour of a climate refugee treaty is that it appears to be particularly well equipped to deal with the questions of responsibility that arise in relation to climate displacement. Climate displacement is a result of human action, not natural misfortune. Those who are most responsible for climate change tend to suffer least from its effects, whereas those who have contributed the least tend to be the most vulnerable to climate change. All of this means that climate displacement raises distinctive questions about responsibility. A climate refugee treaty could be structured to reflect these considerations of responsibility. For example, Biermann and Boas propose a 'principle of international burden-sharing' which would distribute the costs of addressing climate displacement according to a principle of common but differentiated responsibility, with richer, more responsible states bearing higher costs.[23] And Byravan and Rajan argue that although humanity shares an obligation to those displaced by climate impacts, high-emitting states ought to bear the lion's share of costs of climate displacement due to their historic contributions to climate change.[24]

This is not a necessary feature of a climate refugee treaty, which could distribute the costs of addressing climate displacement in some other way, or simply leave the question of cost-sharing unanswered. But a climate refugee treaty may have an especially good chance of dealing with issues of responsibility. After all, it would be unencumbered by pre-existing frameworks for distributing the costs of protection. By comparison, we might think that if existing institutions were tasked with tackling climate displacement, then the distinctive questions of responsibility that it raises would be ignored. We can call the idea that the approach we take to tackling climate displacement should reflect considerations of responsibility the *responsibility rationale*. The responsibility rationale does give us an initial reason to favour the climate refugee treaty proposal. But as we will see, it is a mistake to think that only a climate refugee treaty could meet the responsibility rationale.

The climate refugee treaty appears, at first glance, to present a straightforward solution to the problem of climate displacement. My claim, however, is that it depends on an idealized picture of a climate refugee that obscures some crucial features of the empirical dynamics of climate displacement. As we will see, this means that it would exhibit two kinds of moral arbitrariness: failing to treat like cases alike and failing to treat relevantly different cases differently. In order to see how this problem emerges, it is useful to look a little more closely at the concept of the climate refugee.

The Concept of the Climate Refugee

Talk of climate refugees is now ubiquitous in academic, policy, and popular discourses. As we saw in the previous chapter, the concept of the climate refugee emerged in policy circles as concerns about climate change grew in the 1980s, against a backdrop of relative neglect of the environment as a cause of displacement within migration studies. Since then, its usage has proliferated. Sometimes, the term is used colloquially as a shorthand to refer to anyone whose displacement can be linked to climate change. But in proposals for a climate refugee treaty, the concept has a specific role: it picks out a group of people to whom a particular legal status, with a corresponding set of rights, is owed.

Climate refugees have been defined differently under different treaty proposals. Some use the term to refer to people displaced by climate impacts in general. Docherty and Gianni's proposal targets those who flee 'as the result of sudden or gradual environmental disruption that is consistent with climate change and to which humans more likely than not contributed'.[25] Others use it to refer to groups of people displaced by specific climate impacts. Biermann and Boas restrict their definition of climate refugees to those fleeing from three 'largely undisputed' climate impacts: sea-level rise; extreme weather events; and drought and water scarcity.[26] Byravan and Rajan's proposal targets those facing permanent displacement due to the loss of habitable land.[27] Though each of these definitions identifies a different group of people, each proposal puts the concept of the climate refugee at its centre. The concept of the climate refugee, however, is not uncontroversial. There are three objections that have been made against it which are worth examining here.

The first objection is that we should not use the term 'climate refugee' because it is legally inaccurate to describe those displaced by climate change as refugees. As legal scholars have pointed out, the international legal framework governing refugee status does not recognize those displaced by climate impacts as refugees.[28] There have been some attempts in legal scholarship to argue that at least some people displaced by the impacts of climate change could qualify as refugees, and in practice, the United Nations High Commissioner for Refugees (UNHCR) has taken on some responsibilities for protecting people displaced by the impacts of climate change.[29] But the consensus view among international lawyers—and the view taken by UNHCR itself—is that those displaced by climate change impacts do not fit the legal definition of a refugee, except perhaps in some limited cases.[30] As a result, some international legal scholars have argued that we should abandon the concept of the climate refugee. One of the main messages of an expert roundtable on climate change and displacement convened by UNHCR, for example, was that 'the terms of "climate refugee" and "environmental refugee" should be avoided as they are inaccurate and misleading'.[31]

This objection need not trouble proponents of the climate refugee treaty. While it is true that it is legally inaccurate to refer to those displaced by climate change as 'refugees', this does not tell us anything about whether or not we should use the concept of the climate refugee in normative theorizing. The question that occupies us here is not what the principles of international law currently imply for people displaced by climate change. It is rather how those displaced by the impacts of climate change *should* be treated by the international community. Proponents of the climate refugee treaty maintain that they should be granted a formal legal status, even if such a status is not currently recognized under international law. Whether or not we should designate those displaced by climate impacts as 'climate refugees' is an open question, which cannot be settled by interpretive legal argument.

A second objection is that the term 'climate refugee' is insulting or degrading for those who are displaced by climate impacts. Some Pacific Islanders facing the threat of sea-level rise, for example, have objected to being called 'climate refugees' on the basis that it constructs them as passive victims and invokes a 'sense of helplessness and a lack of dignity'.[32] Anote Tong, the former President of Kiribati, has argued that 'when you talk about refugees—climate refugees—you're putting the stigma on the victims, not the offenders'.[33] Tong's own proposal, a programme of gradual relocation from Kiribati to New Zealand and Australia, was officially termed the 'migration with dignity' policy.[34] But interestingly, some have also defended the term 'climate refugee' precisely because of what it evokes. Biermann and Boas argue that it is important to use the term because it has 'strong moral connotations of societal protection in most world cultures and religions' which would lend the protection of those displaced by climate impacts 'the legitimacy and urgency that it deserves'.[35]

This objection raises an important point: that the labels that we use have powerful effects on the ways in which people are viewed and treated in public life. It should lead us to be mindful of language that we employ in relation to climate displacement. The fact that some people fear being associated with the term 'refugee' because it connotes helplessness and passivity also reflects a great moral failing in the way that refugees are represented.[36] There is nothing inherent in the concept of the refugee that should evoke these sentiments, and these are representations that we should contest. But it is sadly unsurprising that in a world in which they are confined to camps and prohibited from integrating within society, refugees have come to be associated with helplessness and passivity.[37] Ultimately, however, this is not an objection to the concept of the climate refugee as it figures in the proposal for a climate refugee treaty—that is, it is not an objection to the idea of a special legal status for those displaced by climate impacts per se. Nothing in this objection rules out us using some other term which lacks these connotations—perhaps 'exile' or 'emigrant'—to identify those displaced by climate change for the purposes of a treaty.[38]

A third objection poses a deeper challenge for proposals for a climate refugee treaty. This objection is that the concept of the climate refugee is unhelpful because it obscures two important features of the empirical dynamics of climate displacement: its *complexity* and its *heterogeneity*. As we saw in the previous chapter, complexity and heterogeneity are central features of the dynamics of climate displacement.

Climate displacement is complex in the sense that climate change impacts typically interact with other social, economic, political, demographic, and environmental drivers of displacement. For example, when a hurricane hits a city, the damage that it wreaks is felt differently according to pre-existing structural vulnerabilities.[39] Those who live in buildings that have been reinforced may escape damage that befalls others. Those who live on the wrong side of town may see critical infrastructure destroyed. Those who have caring responsibilities or lack a vehicle may be unable to evacuate. And beyond this, it is difficult to attribute any particular hurricane to climate change, even if we know that climate change in general will increase the frequency and severity of extreme events.[40] All of this makes it difficult to isolate climate change—either in general or in terms of specific climate impacts—as 'the' cause of displacement, at least in many cases.

Climate displacement is heterogeneous in the sense that it takes different forms in different contexts, ranging from community relocation in the face of climatic hazards, through labour migration undertaken as a response to slow-onset environmental degradation, to displacement in the aftermath of extreme weather events, and beyond. Displacement that occurs in the aftermath of a hurricane will look very different from displacement that takes place in response to the gradual degradation of the environmental conditions that make it possible to make a living by engaging in subsistence farming or pastoralist herding, for example. And this form of displacement will itself look very different from that which takes place when, amid pre-existing sources of political instability, increased food prices spark conflict. Climate displacement manifests in different ways in these different contexts, and there will be morally relevant differences between each form that it takes.

Critics have argued that we should reject the concept of the climate refugee because it obscures these features of climate displacement. Mike Hulme, for example, has objected to Biermann and Boas's proposal on the grounds that the term climate refugee 'implies a monocausality about the reasons for migration that just does not exist in reality'.[41] Etienne Piguet, Antoine Pécoud, and Paul de Guchteniere have argued that the language of climate refugees is unhelpful and that it is necessary 'to disentangle the different kinds of mobility that may be connected to environmental factors'.[42]

At least at first glance, it is not clear why this should lead us to reject the concept of the climate refugee as a *legal status*. It is certainly true that the concept of the climate refugee blinds us to these aspects of climate displacement. It singles out one cause of displacement—the impacts of climate change—out of many that are often entangled. And it groups together all of those whose displacement can be linked to that cause, regardless of any internal differences within that group. But this only shows that the concept of the climate refugee is *descriptively* incomplete: that it does not provide a complete picture of climate displacement. And the purpose of the concept of the climate refugee—at least as it figures within the treaty proposal—is not to provide a full description of the dynamics of climate displacement. Rather, it is to establish a certain set of rights and duties to those granted recognition as climate refugees. Our legal concepts and categories often fail to capture the richness and complexity of social and political life, and this is not the standard to which we usually hold them. Consider, for example, the legal concept of corporate personhood. Whether or not we think that this legal concept is valuable does not depend on how well it represents truths about corporate agency. It depends on whether we think that the rights and duties that it establishes—such as the liability of a corporation to be sued in court—can be normatively justified in their own right.[43] Similarly, the concept of the climate refugee, at least as it figures in proposals for a climate refugee treaty, ought not to be evaluated in terms of how well it represents the empirical dynamics of climate displacement, but in terms of its effects in establishing certain rights and duties.

The term 'climate refugee' is not best understood as a way of representing the empirical dynamics of climate displacement, which is why I do not think we should say that the picture of climate displacement that it presents is *false*, exactly. It is a legal construction that establishes certain rights for those that it picks out. But my suggestion is that the concept of the climate refugee can nonetheless be rejected on the grounds that it obscures the complexity and heterogeneity of climate displacement. This is not because idealizing away these features of climate displacement is inherently objectionable, but because a treaty centred on the legal status of the climate refugee will predictably fail to treat like cases alike and relevantly different cases differently.

The Arbitrariness of a Climate Refugee Treaty

The central problem with the idea of a climate refugee treaty is that such a treaty would exhibit two forms of morally objectionable arbitrariness: it would fail to treat like cases alike and relevantly different cases differently. The idea that our institutions ought not distinguish between cases on grounds that are arbitrary from a moral point of view is a basic principle of formal equality, which I take to be widely shared and uncontroversial.[44] One characteristic expression of this principle is John Rawls's claim that 'institutions are just when no arbitrary distinctions are made between persons in the assigning of basic rights and duties'.[45] Where there are no morally relevant differences between cases, they should be treated alike; where there are morally relevant differences between cases, they should be treated differently—in ways that reflect those morally relevant differences.

My claim is that the climate refugee treaty will predictably create morally objectionable forms of arbitrariness in practice. But of course, all legal and institutional frameworks are likely to be over- and under-inclusive in practice, and this problem can hardly be avoided entirely.[46] So, my suggestion is not that *any* element of arbitrariness in practice means that we should reject a proposal. Rather, my suggestion is that the climate refugee treaty has a particular propensity to create morally objectionable forms of arbitrariness, because of the way it conceptualizes climate displacement. The problem is not that it is unable to accommodate borderline or hard cases. It is rather that it is unable to accommodate *typical* cases of climate displacement. This problem is not inevitable and can be avoided—or at least significantly attenuated—by adopting an alternative approach that does not depend on the concept of the climate refugee. We can take each form of arbitrariness in turn.

First is the claim that a climate refugee treaty would fail to treat like cases alike. We can distinguish between a strong and a weak version of this claim. The strong version of the claim says that whether or not someone's displacement is caused by climate change should have no bearing on the rights to which they are entitled—that it is arbitrary from a moral point of view. Jane McAdam, for example, has argued that 'a "climate refugee" treaty would privilege those displaced by climate change over other forced migrants (such as those escaping poverty), perhaps without an adequate (legal and/or moral) rationale'.[47] Under a climate refugee treaty, those displaced by climate impacts would be granted international protection, while those whose displacement is unrelated to climate change but who are otherwise in a similar position would not. Unless there is something special about those whose displacement is caused by climate change, this appears to be morally arbitrary. As Phillip Cole points out, this is actually a fairly radical objection, in that it calls into question the more general practice of distinguishing between displaced persons on the basis of the cause of their displacement, which is central to the way in which displacement is governed in the international order.[48] This point also echoes an argument about refugee status made by Joseph Carens, who argues that in determining who should count as a refugee, 'what is most important is the severity of the threat to basic human rights and the degree of risk rather than the source or character of the threat'.[49]

I am sympathetic to the claim that the needs of the displaced, rather than the cause of their displacement, are of primary moral relevance in determining who is entitled to international protection. But I do not pursue this strong claim here. This is because there is nothing in the climate refugee proposal itself that precludes others with similar needs from being granted similar forms of protection under *other* institutional frameworks. I suspect that a climate refugee treaty would, in practice, have the effect of excluding some with compelling claims to protection by hardening the bureaucratic categories that govern displacement and crowding out alternatives.[50] But in principle at least, there is no reason why a climate refugee treaty could not be supplemented with other, complementary institutional frameworks for protecting those whose displacement is unrelated to climate change.

There is also at least one morally relevant reason to preserve an institutional distinction between those displaced by climate impacts and others—namely that in the case of climate change, there are considerations of responsibility that do not arise (or arise only in different forms) in other contexts.[51] This may not bear directly on the first-order question of what we owe to particular displaced persons, but—as I argue in Chapter 8—it does bear on the second-order question of how the costs of protection should be shared. So, the responsibility rationale could give us a reason for preserving an institutional division of labour between climatic and non-climatic forms of displacement. This would seem to escape the strong version of the objection that a climate treaty would fail to treat like cases alike.

There is, however, a weaker version of the claim that the climate refugee treaty will fail to treat like cases alike that gives us reason to reject a climate refugee treaty. The weaker claim is a more minimal, internal criticism, which accepts—at least for the sake of argument—that it is justifiable to distinguish between those displaced by climate impacts and those displaced in other contexts. But it points out that the complexity of climate displacement means that, in practice, decisions about who counts as a climate refugee will inevitably involve a significant degree of arbitrariness.

Any climate refugee treaty requires us to be able to identify those who count as a climate refugee and those who do not. As we have seen, different proposals set out different definitions of precisely who they count as a climate refugee, with some focusing on specific climatic parameters and others focusing on climate change in general. But whichever they focus on, they require us to be able to distinguish between different people on the basis of the cause of their displacement. The problem with this is that the empirical finding that climate displacement is complex—that climate impacts interact with other drivers of displacement—means that it will often be difficult to differentiate those whose displacement is caused by climate change from others. The consensus view reflected by the IPCC is that 'the dynamics of the interaction of mobility with climate change are multifaceted and direct causation is difficult to establish'.[52]

This problem has both an epistemic and an ontological aspect. Under the epistemic aspect, the problem is that we may not be able to *know* when climate change is appropriately singled out as the cause of displacement. The causal chains that lead from climate impacts to displacement are messy, and it may well be beyond our capacities to untangle these threads of causation. Under the ontological aspect, the problem is that it simply may not be *meaningful* to identify climate change as a cause of displacement which is isolable from other causes, at least in many cases. The links between climate change and other drivers of displacement are often non-linear, and it is not clear that combined causes in these cases can simply be broken down into their constituent parts.[53]

As McAdam has pointed out, the complexity of climate displacement means that any attempt to identify climate refugees for the purposes of a treaty would face serious hurdles.[54] Decisions about who to count as a climate refugee will often not depend on whether one's displacement 'really is' caused by climate change, because there is often no good answer to that question. At best, decisions are likely to be made on the basis of how *salient* the climatic drivers of displacement appear to decision-makers in comparison to non-climatic drivers. In many cases, especially where climate impacts are slow-onset, the climatic aspects of displacement will be less visible and more proximate causes—such as civil conflict or labour market pressures—will be more obvious.[55] At worst, decisions may be made on the basis of the *political expediency* of making claims about the causal role of climate change. It may suit political actors to lay the blame for displacement on climate change, rather than other drivers (such as conflict), or vice versa. Indeed, we have already begun to see causal claims about climate displacement being made in this way.[56]

This problem is particularly pressing when it leads to under-inclusion, since this involves denying protection those with justified claims. Unfortunately, under-inclusion appears particularly likely, because the complexity of climate displacement makes it easy for powerful states to shirk responsibility by downplaying the causal role of climate change. But over-inclusion may be a problem too, either for reasons of fairness between claimants seeking scarce protection resources, or because a tendency towards over-inclusion may make states reluctant to sign on to the proposal in the first place. In any case, these reasons of salience and political expediency are clearly not morally relevant reasons for distinguishing between cases. The upshot of this is that there will inevitably be an element of arbitrariness in decisions about who counts as a climate refugee.

The second way that the problem of arbitrariness manifests in the climate refugee treaty proposal is in its failure to treat relevantly different cases differently. This problem arises because of the way that the concept of the climate refugee obscures the heterogeneity of climate displacement. A treaty centred on the concept of the climate refugee treats those whom it picks out as an internally undifferentiated group, whose members are all entitled to the same set of rights.

Consider the group of people identified as climate refugees under Biermann and Boas's version of the climate refugee treaty: 'people who have to leave their habitats, immediately or in the near future, because of sudden or gradual alterations in their natural environment related to at least one of three impacts of climate change: sea-level rise, extreme weather events, and drought and water scarcity.'[57] They propose that those in this group should have access to planned, voluntary, and permanent resettlement.[58] But it is not at all clear why all of those who fall within this category should all be entitled to the same set of rights to planned, voluntary, and permanent resettlement. There are important differences between those who face displacement due to sea-level rise, extreme weather events, and drought and water scarcity. Voluntary relocation and resettlement may be appropriate for at least some of those facing threats to their homes due to sea-level rise. But those who face the impacts of recurring droughts may well be better served by a programme of circular or seasonal labour migration that allows them to diversify their household's sources of income than by a programme of resettlement. Those facing displacement due to extreme weather events may be better served by a programme of disaster risk reduction and/or forms of post-disaster relief and recovery assistance than by relocation projects. It is arbitrary to grant each of these groups of people the same set of rights when there are morally relevant differences between them. This point does not only apply to Biermann and Boas's proposal; it generalizes. Any treaty for climate refugees will be inattentive to morally relevant differences between different cases, insofar as it focuses on the concept of the climate refugee, which obscures the heterogeneity of climate displacement.

A similar criticism of the climate refugee treaty proposal has been made by McAdam, who draws on fieldwork in the different contexts of Bangladesh, Tuvalu, and Kiribati to argue that 'a *universal* treaty may be inappropriate in addressing the concerns of particular communities' and that what is needed is a system of governance that 'take[s] into account the particular features of the affected population, in determining who should move, when, in what fashion, and with what outcome'.[59] What is often not appreciated, however, is that this is a *moral* objection to the climate refugee treaty proposal, not merely a practical one. It is a moral objection because it is a complaint about rights and duties being misallocated. Consider someone living in a low-lying coastal area threatened by sea-level rise who is seeking relocation within their state. On Byravan and Rajan's proposal—according to which those facing threats from sea-level rise, including in deltaic regions, count as 'climate exiles'—they would be granted 'immigration rights' abroad.[60] Not only is this right not warranted by or appropriate for their circumstances, but it is also a right that is denied to others who may see it as valuable—for example, those who wish to migrate to pursue economic opportunities. At the same time, they are denied a right to which they are entitled—the right to relocate to a safe environment within their state—which may be offered to others who are in a similar position, such as those living in the shadow of an active volcano. A climate refugee treaty would systematically misallocate the rights and duties that are appropriate for different cases of displacement, because it ignores the heterogeneity of climate displacement.

A treaty for climate refugees would exhibit two morally objectionable forms of arbitrariness. First, it would fail to treat like cases alike, because it ignores the complexity of climate displacement. Second, it would fail to treat relevantly different cases differently, because it ignores the heterogeneity of climate displacement. This problem arises because the climate refugee treaty proposal puts the concept of the climate refugee at its centre, and so treats those displaced by climate impacts as a homogenous group who can be readily identified by the cause of their displacement. To be clear, this objection is not an objection to the idea of a *treaty* for climate displacement per se, even though most proposals take the form of something like a multilateral treaty. The problem is rather that such proposals are constructed around the concept of the climate refugee. A modified treaty proposal could, in principle, avoid these problems. In order to do so, however, it would need to address climate displacement in a way that does not require us to identify particular people as climate refugees and that does not ride roughshod over the morally relevant differences between different contexts of climate displacement.

Proponents of a climate refugee treaty are likely to object that these problems are merely problems of practical implementation, which do not undermine the proposal in principle. Perhaps a climate refugee treaty might face some practical obstacles in determining who counts as a climate refugee, and perhaps it might require some contextual refinement and adjustment in order to account for cases with different characteristics. But these problems can be solved at the level of implementation and need not undermine proposals for a climate refugee treaty writ large.

The response comes at a significant cost: it consigns the proposal to practical irrelevance. Given that, according to the best scientific evidence that we have available to us, complexity and heterogeneity are central features of climate displacement, a proposal that is irreconcilable with those features will be practically inert. Perhaps some version of a climate refugee treaty *would* articulate a morally justifiable set of rights for climate refugees, in a world in which such people were readily identifiable and all had the same needs. But in a world in which complexity and heterogeneity are central features of climate displacement, it is unclear what use we have for such a treaty.

The Pluralist Theory of Climate Displacement

If the foregoing arguments are correct, then we have good reasons to object to the proposal for a climate refugee treaty. Such a treaty would exhibit moral arbitrariness, in that it would fail to treat like cases alike and fail to treat relevantly different cases differently. These problems stem from the way in which the climate refugee treaty centres on the concept of the climate refugee, which obscures the complexity and heterogeneity of climate displacement. In order to avoid these problems, my suggestion is that we should dislodge the picture of the climate refugee that has held us back and focus instead on the specific contexts in which climate change and displacement interact. The theory that I develop over the rest of this book—the pluralist theory of climate displacement—takes such an approach.

The pluralist theory has two core commitments. First is that climate displacement should be *integrated* with other, non-climatic forms of displacement. No one's fate should hang on climate impacts being identified as the cause of their displacement, given that climate impacts will most often be intertwined with other drivers of displacement in complex ways. Second is that climate displacement should be *disaggregated*, rather than being viewed as one, undifferentiated phenomenon. Different principles and institutional forms will be appropriate for the different contexts in which climate change and displacement interact.

In Chapter 1, I outlined five different contexts in which climate change and displacement interact: community relocation; territorial sovereignty; labour migration; refugee movement; and internal displacement. We should begin our analysis of climate displacement with an investigation of the problems that it poses in these different contexts, rather than by proposing principles for an idealized climate refugee. In each context, the task of the theory is to identify the problems that climate displacement creates for our institutions and practices, and to propose ways of reforming those institutions and practices that address those problems. Stated at this level of generality, the pluralist theory is compatible with multiple substantive views on what is owed to the displaced in each of these different contexts and on how our institutions should be arranged to enable those duties to be discharged. Those who disagree with the specific arguments that I make in the chapters that follow, then, can still adopt the broader theoretical framework that I suggest here.

This approach to climate displacement is not entirely unprecedented. Something like it was advocated under the auspices of a process called the Nansen Initiative, which sought to provide a framework for addressing cross-border displacement resulting from disasters, including those linked to climate change.[61] The Nansen Initiative was developed out of a conference organized by the Norwegian Government and the Norwegian Refugee Council in 2011 titled *Climate Change and Displacement in the 21st Century*. Delegates noted that 'a more coherent and consistent approach' was needed to address international displacement resulting from climate-related disasters and suggested that 'states, working with in conjunction with UNHCR and other relevant stakeholders, could develop a guiding framework or instrument in this regard'.[62] This began a consultation process, which ultimately concluded that 'rather than calling for a new binding international convention', we should instead adopt 'an approach that focuses on the integration of effective practices by States and (sub-)regional organizations into their normative frameworks in accordance with their specific situations and challenges'.[63] The Nansen Initiative's focus was on cross-border disaster displacement in particular, rather than on climate displacement more broadly, but its aims overlap significantly with the project that I am undertaking here. The theory that I set out over the rest of this book can be understood as an interpretation of what the 'integration of effective practices' for 'specific situations and challenges' might require, for climate displacement as a whole.

The main attraction of the treaty for climate refugees was that it could close the 'protection gap' in the international order for climate displacement. The pluralist theory also enables us to close that protection gap, but it does so in a different way. Where the climate refugee treaty would close the protection gap through a blanket approach that creates one legal status for all those displaced by climate impacts, the pluralist theory directs us towards a more bottom-up approach. By reforming our institutions and practices in a range of contexts in which climate change and displacement interact, we can make those institutions and practices suitable for addressing climate displacement, and so close the protection gap in relation to climate displacement.

The pluralist theory also avoids the two kinds of arbitrariness that are exhibited by the climate refugee treaty. It is able to treat like cases alike, because no one's fate hangs on their being identified as a climate refugee. This means that no one will be excluded on the basis of morally arbitrary reasons, such as that the climatic drivers of their displacement are not salient to decision-makers. At the same time, the pluralist theory is able to treat relevantly different cases differently, because it disaggregates climate displacement. This means that different principles can apply to different contexts of climate displacement, where there are morally relevant differences that our theory should reflect. So, the pluralist theory retains the main advantage of the climate refugee treaty but is also able to avoid the problems that it faces.

A second advantage of the climate refugee proposal was that it was particularly well placed to meet the *responsibility rationale*—that is, to reflect the considerations of responsibility that arise in relation to climate displacement. As we have seen, the proposal for a climate refugee treaty purchases this virtue at the price of becoming untethered from the empirical realities of climate displacement, but it is nonetheless a virtue. And since the pluralist theory integrates climate displacement with other forms of displacement, we might be worried that it will be insensitive to questions of responsibility.

This worry is misplaced. Even though the pluralist theory of climate displacement rules out identifying particular people as climate refugees and holding high emitters responsible to bear the costs of addressing their displacement, it is still able to accommodate considerations of responsibility. I explore how we can hold high emitters responsible in light of the complexity of climate displacement in greater detail in Chapter 8. But in broad terms, my argument is that we should focus on holding high emitters responsible for the increased burden of displacement *risk* associated with climate change, rather than for the displacement of particular individuals. The basic idea is that our first-order responses to displacement are becoming costlier as a result of the increased burden of displacement risk associated with climate change. We ought to redistribute those costs according to a principle of responsibility for climate change. This argument operates at the macro- rather than the micro-level, and so it enables us to hold high emitters responsible even though we often cannot identify particular individuals who are displaced by climate change. This basic idea is developed in more detail later on, so for the moment this argument remains only a promissory note, yet to be redeemed. But if my suggestion is right, then the pluralist theory is able to answer the questions of responsibility that climate displacement raises.

The pluralist theory of climate displacement is a promising alternative to the proposal for a climate refugee treaty. The climate refugee treaty initially appeared attractive because it could close the protection gap in relation to climate displacement and meet the responsibility rationale. But the proposal for a climate refugee treaty relies on the concept of the climate refugee, which obscures the complexity and heterogeneity of climate displacement. This means that it will exhibit two morally objectionable forms of arbitrariness. It will fail to treat like cases alike, because the complexity of climate displacement means that it will be unable to reliably identify climate refugees. And it will fail to treat relevantly different cases differently, because it presumes that all climate refugees have the same needs when there are morally relevant differences between them. The pluralist theory of climate displacement, by contrast, retains the central advantage of the climate refugee treaty while at the same time avoiding these problems. It abandons the idea of the climate refugee and enables us to adopt a more contextually sensitive approach to climate displacement.

Ultimately, of course, the superiority of the pluralist theory of climate displacement over the climate refugee treaty proposal will need to be demonstrated through the development of a more fully worked-out account of the principles and practices that we should adopt in each context of climate displacement. To that end, the next chapter turns to the task of examining the first context of climate displacement: community relocation.

3
Climate Change and Community Relocation

In the North-Western reaches of Alaska, the residents of the villages of Shishmaref, Kivalina, and Newtok are confronting the effects of climate change.[1] Rising sea levels, shoreline erosion, thinning ice, and permafrost exposure are gradually making the land upon which the villages are located uninhabitable. All three communities are federally recognized tribes—Iñupiaq in the case of Shishmaref and Kivalina, and Yup'ik in the case of Newtok—and many community members participate in traditional hunting practices which are bound up with the land they occupy. Many of their ancestors lived semi-nomadic lives, moving between coastal fishing grounds and inland hunting areas, which enabled them to navigate fluctuations in local environmental conditions. From the late nineteenth century, they were settled into permanent villages as part of the US Bureau of Education's sedentarization policies aimed at 'civilizing' Native Alaskan communities.[2] Today, many community members work hard to keep their culture and traditions alive. Shishmaref is at the centre of a complex food distribution network and is 'a cornerstone for Iñupiaq traditions, foods, livelihood, and culture'.[3] But as shoreline erosion and sea-level rise continue apace, these communities are struggling to maintain their way of life in the face of growing climatic threats.

The residents of Shishmaref, Kivalina, and Newtok are pursuing community relocation as a strategy of adaptation to climate change. After the collapse of successive sea defences, each community has voted to relocate. Community members have set up organizations such as the Shishmaref Erosion and Relocation Coalition and the Newtok Planning Group in order to manage the relocation process. So far, however, the process has mostly faltered. Only Newtok has begun to establish pioneer housing and infrastructure on the site of its new village, Mertarvik, nine miles away on Nelson Island. One obstacle has been funding: until recently, federal funding provided only for post-disaster rebuilding of homes in their original location after a presidential declaration of a disaster.[4] As a result, funding for relocation projects had to be sought from the Alaskan State Legislature and raised through community fundraising efforts. Residents of Kivalina even filed a lawsuit against ExxonMobil seeking monetary damages for climate change impacts, although the lawsuit was ultimately dismissed.[5] Another obstacle is bureaucratic: there is no institution formally charged with managing relocation in the USA, which means that communities have been 'caught in a maze of conflicting agency regulations' with relocation proceeding 'in an uncoordinated and ad hoc manner'.[6] Without a lead agency managing the relocation process, different agencies have been reluctant to make the first move. Finally, mistrust between residents and public authorities has marred the process, exacerbated by the colonial legacies of the state in Alaska. In Kivalina, for example, the requirements for land being selected for relocation were unclear, which meant that tribal land chosen by community vote was later found to be unfit according to ecological surveys carried out by private contractors.[7]

Community relocation is becoming increasingly widespread as a form of adaptation as the impacts of climate change accelerate.[8] Climate-related relocation projects like those in Alaska have begun to take place—with varying degrees of success—in Vietnam, China, Fiji, Papua New Guinea, the USA, Mozambique, and beyond.[9] As communities living on the frontline of climate change face growing threats, community relocation is likely to become increasingly significant as a form of adaptation to climate change. Climate impacts such as sea-level rise, coastal erosion, permafrost exposure, mudslides, extreme heat, and recurrent flooding can all put communities at risk. In the short term, the risks associated with climate change impacts such as these can often be attenuated through *in situ* forms of adaptation. But in the long term, some climate impacts may make it very difficult for those living in affected areas to remain where they are. There are limits—both physical and social—to the forms of *in situ* adaptation that communities can undertake. It is at the point of breaching those limits that relocation typically becomes a live option for communities facing threats from climate change.[10]

This chapter examines community relocation as a form of adaptation to climate change. My focus is largely on the *procedural* dimensions of community relocation—that is, on questions about how relocation decisions should be taken. Procedural justice is particularly salient in the context of community relocation, for two reasons. First is that community relocation is typically an anticipatory form of displacement, which takes place over a relatively long time horizon. This means that there is—at least in principle—time to plan relocation processes, so that they can be undertaken in ways that reflect the values, interests, and identities of those affected. Second is that the history of relocation in other contexts—such as in the context of development—gives us special reason to be concerned about procedural justice. The lesson of the litany of development projects such as the construction of mines and dams is that communities affected are often disinvested, marginalized, and silenced in the process of relocation.[11] It is important to pay close attention to procedural justice in climate-related community relocation if we want to avoid replicating these injustices.

First, I discuss the stakes of relocation projects for affected communities, focusing on the value of the shared social and cultural practices in which community members participate. Then, I examine two models of relocation—which I call the *market model* and the *communitarian model*—in turn. I argue that the market model fragments communities and so forecloses opportunities for the protection of social and cultural practices. The communitarian model has the opposite problem: it risks riding roughshod over the internal diversity of communities facing relocation and privileging one partial interpretation of the community's interests. Instead, I set out and defend an alternative that I call the *democratic model* of relocation. Finally, I examine two problems in the implementation of community relocation: the problems of *expertise* and *scale*. To minimize these problems, I argue that we need clear institutional frameworks for relocation which create robust opportunities for deliberation, clearly define the role of technical experts and affected publics, and put decision-making power directly into the hands of affected communities.

Practice-based Interests and Community Relocation

When climate impacts threaten the habitability of a geographical area, the inhabitants of that area face a range of threats to their interests. Most obviously, climate impacts threaten their ability to live a minimally decent life. This may involve threats to basic biological needs such as shelter, water, food, and clean air. Floods and wildfires can put homes at risk; increased heat and groundwater salinity can lead to a lack of freshwater supplies and arable land; and extreme heat and air pollution can threaten human health. Climate impacts can also impede the functioning of the social institutions that we need to guarantee basic security and welfare. For example, flooding may make an area difficult to navigate, making it difficult for public authorities to uphold the rule of law or distribute medical resources. Anna Stilz calls these interests—the interests that we have in 'living in some territory or other that affords us a life of a decent standard'—our *basic territorial interests*.[12]

Beyond basic territorial interests, climate impacts also threaten the interests that inhabitants have in being able to sustain a way of life that reflects their values, attachments, and commitments. Stilz calls these *practice-based interests*.[13] In Shishmaref, climate impacts not only put people's homes and property at risk, but also threaten the existence of the shared social practices that sustain a set of cultural values and a particular way of life. For example, the hunting of bearded seals (*ugruk*) plays an important social and cultural role for the *Kigiqtaamiut* people of Shishmaref. This practice is partly a subsistence strategy in a society with relatively little market activity. But it also expresses distinctive cultural values. The hunting of bearded seals is governed both by sharing customs within the wider community and by a set of traditional rules (*aqizugaksrat iniqtigutait*) that express a particular conception of human–animal relations.[14] As the impacts of climate change make remaining in Shishmaref increasingly difficult, what Kyle Powys Whyte calls the 'collective continuance' of the *Kigiqtaamiut* way of life is under threat.[15]

The shared social and cultural practices that we value are collectively created within, and tied to, particular areas. What geographers and environmental psychologists call *place*—geographical spaces that are imbued with meaning by those who engage in social, economic, ecological, religious, and cultural practices within them—is at stake in contexts of community relocation.[16] The significance of place is particularly clear in Shishmaref, where the relationship between people and land is especially salient. But the value of place is not an idiosyncratic or niche concern. Wherever people live, they engage in shared social and cultural practices that are supported by their shared occupancy of particular geographical spaces. In some contexts—for example, in large diverse cities such as Miami—there will be whole networks of interrelated practice-based interests that are threatened by climate change impacts. These social and cultural practices are more likely to be shared by various partially overlapping sub-groups that share the same space, rather than by the entire affected population, but this makes them no less significant for those affected. Beyond basic territorial interests, the cultural and social practices sustained by our relationships to particular places are of central importance to the lives and well-being of those facing the impacts of climate change.

The close relationship between place and practice-based interests means that where *in situ* adaptation to climate change is possible, it will typically be preferable to relocation.[17] And although my focus in this chapter is primarily on cases where relocation goes ahead, it is important to recognize that *in situ* adaptation is rarely straightforwardly impossible. Much depends on how much we are willing to spend to protect communities where they are, and decisions about which communities to protect in place and which to relocate are not merely technical ones.

In practice, decisions about which communities to prioritize for *in situ* adaptation often reflect and entrench existing injustices. In the USA, cost–benefit analysis is the main tool used for decisions about which communities to protect in place and which to relocate away from climate risks. But because property values are a central input in the cost–benefit calculus, decision-makers tend to prioritize protecting areas with high property values over more sparsely inhabited areas or areas with low property values.[18] The result of this is that disadvantaged people who live in these areas—often as a result of injustices such the forced removal of Indigenous peoples or racial segregation—are disproportionately relocated instead of benefiting from protect-in-place measures. One study has shown that when standard cost–benefit models are applied to decisions about coastal adaptation, then the most socioeconomically vulnerable communities tend not be protected, while the least vulnerable communities tend to be protected.[19] In some regions, such as the Gulf Coast, the results are stark: 'in the highest SoVI [socio-economic vulnerability index] category nearly all of the people affected by SLR [sea-level rise] could be compelled to abandon their property, if cost-benefit considerations dominate the decision.'[20] Clearly, we should aim to avoid reinforcing these background injustices in decisions about who to prioritize for *in situ* adaptation.

At the same time, not all communities can be protected in place. In some cases, climatic threats are so severe that *in situ* adaptation is unlikely to be viable in the long term, as in Shishmaref where the collapse of successive sea defences has made it clear that eventual relocation is inevitable. In these cases, funding *in situ* adaptation would mean investing huge amounts of resources in projects that would ultimately be unlikely to secure even the basic territorial interests of residents. And beyond this, *in situ* adaptation can be highly expensive. Economists tend to argue that we should only engage in adaptation that is efficient—where 'the cost of making the effort is less than the resulting benefits'.[21] On this view, protecting coastal properties, especially when they command a relatively low market value, is often a bad investment; it would be cheaper in the long term to encourage those at risk to relocate.[22] Some have thus argued that many *in situ* adaptation projects—such as Florida's state-funded hazard insurance for coastal properties—can create a perverse incentive to stay in risky areas.[23]

There is clearly something to this criticism: we should not encourage people to live in risky areas where *in situ* adaptation is not viable in the long term. But the cost–benefit analyses employed by economists often do not reflect the value that peoples' homes and communities have in securing their practice-based interests. If the criticism is that we should not fund *in situ* adaptation when it involves spending more than the market value of the properties affected, then it is too broad. We should be willing to finance adaptation projects that protect the value of place, even if they are not economically efficient in this narrow sense.

Anna Stilz has recently defended the principle that each person is entitled to a fair opportunity to engage in social and cultural practices that reflect their own interests, so long as this does not conflict with the basic territorial interests of others.[24] This principle reflects the idea that practice-based interests typically represent central commitments in peoples' lives and—as Elizabeth Brake points out—that 'place communities' can play an important role in supporting the primary good of self-respect.[25] Protecting practice-based interests is an important demand of relational equality: our duty to protect people's practice-based interests is part of our duty to provide the material and social preconditions for people to relate to each other as equals.[26]

This principle can be used as a basis for decisions about whether to fund *in situ* adaptation or relocation. Instead of the value that a property or piece of land commands on the market, decisions about whether to fund *in situ* adaptation should instead refer to the *use value* that a property or piece of land has for its residents in terms of their practice-based interests. This explains why we should be prepared to spend more to protect some more sparsely inhabited areas: protecting such areas can have important benefits in terms of securing the practice-based interests of residents. Even if those practice-based interests are 'expensive tastes' in comparison to those of majorities, residents of these areas have an entitlement to fair opportunities to live in ways that reflect their own values and commitments.[27] As Alan Patten has argued, equality for minority cultures sometimes requires public authorities to actively support and accommodate their practice-based interests, rather than to be disinterested in them.[28] At the same time, this principle explains why we need not subsidize just *any* expensive taste for those facing threats to the habitability of the place where they live. The owners of luxury beachfront properties do not have a stronger claim to have their properties protected simply because they command a high market value. Even though they may suffer some costs, they are more likely to retain their ability to live in ways that reflect that their own values and commitments even as they relocate.[29]

Still, there is likely to be a limit to the resources that can be spent on adaptation, and so cost can be a legitimate basis upon which to make decisions about whether to finance *in situ* adaptation or relocation. It would clearly not be reasonable to spend the same amount of money to protect the 600 residents of Shishmaref as the roughly 6 million residents of the metropolitan area of Miami. So, decisions about whether to fund relocation or *in situ* adaptation can appeal to the costs that would be involved in protecting a community in place. But they should be made on the basis of how well *in situ* adaptation would secure the practice-based interests of those affected, not on the basis of the property values of the areas affected. In some cases, relocation will be the best option, either because there is no realistic prospect of a community being able to adapt in place or because the resources that would be required to protect them in place go beyond what can be all-things-considered justified. In these cases, it is still important to maintain our commitment to protecting practice-based interests. How can practice-based interests be protected in circumstances in which remaining in place is not possible?

Sometimes there will be an unavoidable element of cultural loss when a community relocates. This is especially likely to be the case where particular places have religious or spiritual significance for members of a community, such that fundamental aspects of their sense of self and identity are bound up with a particular place. In such cases of what Jonathan Lear has called *cultural devastation*, there is likely to be an unavoidably tragic element to community relocation.[30] The only option facing those affected may be the radically non-ideal option of trying to transcend cultural devastation and to collectively construct a new way of life.[31] Material support may help communities to engage in this project, but it is unlikely to remedy the harm of cultural devastation. We should be under no illusion that this is an adequate response to cultural devastation—there will always be what Bernard Williams calls a 'moral remainder' that we should regret—even if it is the best that we can do.[32]

But relocation need not always lead to cultural devastation. Sometimes, the relationship between particular places and shared cultural and social practices is more indirect. Stilz points out that place often supports and enables the shared social and cultural practices that are sources of value for their participants, but it is not always *itself* the source of value.[33] Of course, many social and cultural practices can only be maintained in places with particular features or characteristics. The *Kigiqtaamiut* practice of hunting bearded seals in accordance with traditional rules governing human–animal relations can be maintained only in places where there are bearded seals. It may be possible to preserve the ability of community members to engage in the cultural and social practices that they value, and so to provide them with a measure of cultural continuity, even as they move to a new place.

Of course, communities cannot be straightforwardly transplanted from one location to another. There are important challenges to achieving cultural continuity in the process of relocation. One challenge is that the process of relocation itself is likely to disrupt the social and cultural practices in which community members engage.[34] Relocation involves a significant upheaval in a community's shared life and is likely to involve the disruption of social networks and practices. The psychologist Mindy Fullilove, examining urban renewal policies that broke up African American neighbourhoods in the USA, calls this phenomenon 'root shock'.[35] Fullilove argues that even if neighbourhoods were rebuilt like-for-like, it is unlikely that those affected would simply be able to navigate their social world in the same way as they did before, because the process of relocation itself can affect the social ties and networks on which we rely in our day-to-day life.[36] In the same way, relocation in the context of climate change is likely to make it difficult for those affected to rebuild the complex networks of social and cultural practices on which they had previously relied.

Another challenge is that the members of communities facing relocation are likely to have different views about how to best protect their practice-based interests in the process of relocation. Different members of the community are likely to have competing interpretations of their traditions, practices, and collective identity. They may have different priorities or expectations about the aspects of their shared lives that should be reconstructed or preserved in the process of relocation. Even in highly solidaristic and close-knit communities such as Shishmaref, these conflicts of ideas, identities, and interests will inevitably shape the process of relocation. In Elizabeth Marino's ethnography of Shishmaref, she points out that even though there are major points of agreement among the people of Shishmaref about relocation—such as their desire to remain on traditional tribal territory—there are 'wildly differing opinions about politics, religion, education, the role of the family, the role of the government, and everything else'.[37] Even in apparently more hospitable contexts for protecting practice-based interests, it will be crucial to navigate the internal disagreements among those facing relocation. This challenge will only become more significant in relocation contexts with larger, more diverse, and less solidaristic communities.

One central priority in community relocation is to find ways to enable communities to protect their practice-based interests, even in the face of disagreement about how relocation should proceed and despite the inevitable disruption that relocation will bring. We need an account of procedural justice in relocation that is attentive to the importance of practice-based interests for members of communities affected by climate impacts, but which also recognizes that the process of relocation will inevitably involve disagreement about how to protect those interests. In the following sections of this chapter, I examine three models of relocation that aim to solve this problem.

The Market Model of Relocation

One model of relocation seeks to sidestep internal disagreements about relocation among community members by giving individuals the power to make relocation decisions for themselves. In its most basic form, it would involve giving an equal bundle of resources for relocation directly to those affected—for example, an equal budget for relocation per person or per household—rather than distributing resources for relocation to the community as a whole. Each individual or household could then decide for themselves how to best use their bundle of resources for relocation. I call this the *market model* of relocation.

This basic version of the market model can be complicated by recognizing that not everyone is equally affected by climate change impacts. Some people will be more vulnerable to the same climate impacts, often because of background injustices that make them more exposed or less resilient. These differences in vulnerability mean that if everyone were simply given an equal bundle of resources for relocation, then some people would be disadvantaged relative to others. But the market model can be amended in order to account for these differential vulnerabilities. One way to do so is to view these differential vulnerabilities as a form of bad 'brute luck' for which those affected should be compensated, by providing them with extra resources so that they are no longer disadvantaged in pursuing their relocation projects.[38] A defensible version of the market model would seek eliminate the influence of these background injustices—perhaps by providing each person with a vulnerability-adjusted budget for relocation—so that each person would have the same effective ability to pursue their own relocation projects.

The market model is not explicitly defended in the literature on adaptation or relocation, at least in the pure, ideal form in which I have articulated it here. But there are currents in the politics of adaptation and relocation in which it is partially realized. In the USA, the dominant approach to relocation is 'managed retreat' from areas affected by flooding risk through voluntary buyouts of individual properties, administered through the Federal Emergency Management Agency's (FEMA) Hazard Mitigation Grant and Flood Mitigation Assistance Grant programmes.[39] In these programmes, individual property owners are offered the opportunity to sell their homes (at prices that reflect their 'fair market value' in the absence of flood risks) directly to the local government or other public authority that holds the grant, so that they can use the funds to relocate to less hazard-prone areas. There are also a range of market-based instruments—such as subsidies, property tax levies, and tradable development permits—that are used to incentivize relocation away from areas at risk of climate impacts such as flooding.[40] These are certainly not pure examples of the market model—notably, because they often leave individuals to bear much of the costs of relocation themselves—but they do bear affinities to it in that they encourage individual-level decision-making about relocation. More broadly, economists often see 'autonomous' adaptation as the preferable form of adaptation to climate change.[41] Nicholas Stern, for example, argues that 'the extent to which society can rely on autonomous adaptation ... essentially defines the need for further policy'.[42]

The market model's main advantage is that it enables those with different values and preferences to make decisions about relocation that reflect those values and preferences. The more risk-averse might relocate to a less disaster-prone area earlier, whereas risk-takers or those who place a high value on place might decide to remain in place longer. Or those who place a high value on particular aspects of their social and cultural identity—proximity to a particular location or a social context in which they can practise their religion, for example—can prioritize this aspect over others with which it might otherwise compete in collective decisions. In enabling these choices, the market model seeks to promote the value of individual liberty. And insofar as it does, then this does seem to count in its favour.

The central problem with the market model is that it makes it difficult for individuals to protect their practice-based interests. In order to be able to protect practice-based interests, members of communities need to make sure that at least a critical mass of community members remain together in environments that enable them to participate in the social and cultural practices that they value. And in order to remain together in this way, communities need to be able to rely on a range of *collective goods*—that is, goods which are enjoyed by members of a community indiscriminately, rather than being consumed privately by individuals—that sustain both their physical security and their ability to participate in valued social and cultural practices.[43] But because the market model fragments communities and disperses decision-making power, it hinders the provision of those collective goods.

A safe environment for human habitation presupposes a range of collective goods—both ecological and man-made—that create a relatively stable background framework. This includes essential infrastructure, such as sanitation systems and transport networks, and ecological goods, such as clean air or land that is suitable for building. When climate impacts threaten an area, we need to take steps to ensure that the individuals affected have access to these collective goods, in order to secure the basic preconditions for a safe, habitable environment.[44] Sometimes, this can be done through processes of *in situ* adaptation. Goods such as sea defences, expanded mangrove forests, or reclaimed land may make it possible for members of a community to remain where they are, at least for a time. But in the contexts in which relocation is a live option, these forms of *in situ* adaptation are usually insufficient or prohibitively costly.

The market model will usually enable individuals to access the collective goods that they need to protect their *basic* territorial interests. This is because it enables individuals to move to places in which there are already established frameworks for providing the collective goods that serve to protect basic territorial interests. If a resident of Shishmaref were to move to Nome or Anchorage, for example, then they would have access to an already established system for the provision of collective goods that protect their basic security and welfare. When it comes to *practice-based* interests, however, the picture is quite different. In order to be able to protect practice-based interests, communities need to make sure that at least a critical mass of community members remain together. Some collective goods will be elements of basic infrastructure that enable collective relocation. Goods such as schools, airstrips, roads, and barge landings have been identified as crucial prerequisites for the relocation of Native Alaskan communities threatened by shoreline erosion relating to climate change.[45] But beyond this, other collective goods will be necessary to support the *particular* practices that community members value. In Shishmaref, shared cultural practices that enjoy broad support—such as traditional forms of hunting and fishing—may require access to particular areas of land (such as traditional tribal hunting grounds) in order to be viable.[46]

The problem with the market model is that it leaves the supply of these collective goods to individuals acting independently of each other. Collective goods tend to be undersupplied if their provision is left to the market. The standard explanation for this in economic theory refers to two characteristic features of public goods: that they are non-rivalrous (their enjoyment by one person does not reduce the amount of the good available to others) and non-excludable (non-contributing individuals cannot be prevented from enjoying the good). For example, early warning systems that broadcast radio warnings about flash flooding or mudslides, such as those that have been put in place in the mountainous regions of Colombia and Peru, are effectively non-rivalrous and non-excludable.[47] Their benefits are accessible to all, and their use by one person does not reduce the amount of the good available to others. But because benefits are non-excludable and cannot be denied to non-contributors, each individual has an incentive to 'free ride' on the contributions of others in producing these goods.[48] If each individual does what can be rationally expected of them, then collective goods will not be supplied in the first place. One part of the problem—the 'isolation problem'—is that the outcome of each individual deciding alone may be worse for everyone. But another part of the problem—the 'assurance problem'—is that even when people decide together, each individual needs to be sufficiently confident that others will in fact contribute in order to rationally contribute their share.[49] This led John Rawls to conclude that the provision of public goods 'must be arranged for through the political process and not the market'.[50]

The market model forecloses the option of protecting practice-based interests by putting in place obstacles to collective action. It puts those facing relocation in a position where they are only able to pursue those options that they can achieve without relying on the cooperation of others. Most often, this will mean that people will disperse to different places at different times, such that valued social and cultural practices will be undermined—even if every person's preferred option is to remain with other community members. In Shishmaref, this concern is highly salient. Many residents report that one of their primary fears is that collective relocation projects will fail and that they will be scattered across different towns and villages. The Shishmaref Erosion and Relocation Coalition views this scenario as one that involves the 'annihilation of the community and an annihilation of the cultural integrity of residents'.[51]

It might be objected that this argument about the undersupply of collective goods depends too heavily on idealizing assumptions about the nature of the goods at stake and the behaviour of the individuals involved. Not all collective goods are fully non-excludable and non-rivalrous. A sea wall that benefits all members of a coastal village by protecting publicly accessible spaces and the infrastructure that sustains the community as a whole (a non-excludable good) will also protect private property on the coastline (an excludable good). And the people making decisions about how to best use the resources at their disposal may not be responsive to incentive structures in the way that orthodox economists, operating with an idealizing assumption of rational self-interest, predict.

One way of developing this line of argument is to point towards the work of those such as Elinor Ostrom who have shown the limits of the conventional economic analysis of collective goods.[52] Ostrom's research suggests that key variables such as the size of the community, the level of social trust, and the ease of monitoring compliance with rules can greatly affect whether or not formal institutions are necessary for successful cooperation in governing collective goods.[53] Similarly, we might think that under some conditions, for example in highly solidaristic communities such as Shishmaref, forms of collective adaptation which produce or maintain collective goods will emerge under the market model. Neil Adger has argued that high levels of social capital can enable collective forms of adaptation in the absence of formal institutions, pointing to the collective maintenance of coastal defences in the absence of state planning in 1990s Vietnam.[54] If this is right, then the market model may not always foreclose options for relocation that depend on collective action.

Ostrom's work helpfully demonstrates the limits of orthodox economic theory when it comes to the provision of collective goods, but it does not redeem the market model, for two reasons. The first is that it shows that we can only expect the market model to function effectively under highly constrained conditions, such as in small communities with high levels of social trust. This means that the scope of the market model would need to be limited to cases where the right social conditions obtain for it to function well. This limits its applicability considerably—and in practice, there is likely to be significant disagreement about when those conditions obtain. The second, and perhaps more important, is that appealing to the capacity of individuals to engage in collective action saps the motivation from the market model. The main attraction of the market model was that it enabled individuals to make meaningful choices about relocation according to their own preferences and values, without needing to acquiesce to the preferences and values of others. But if we recognize that successful adaptation to climate change often requires collective action, then this freedom appears illusory: it is the freedom to either cooperate with others (and so to make compromises about one's own preferences and values) or engage only in the highly limited forms of relocation that can be achieved without cooperation. Faced with these options, it is unclear why we should prefer the market model over an alternative that establishes more robust mechanisms for cooperation.

The Communitarian Model of Relocation

One alternative to the market model is the *communitarian model* of relocation. In contrast to the market model, the communitarian model of relocation foregrounds the collective aspects of relocation by treating the community itself as the relevant subject when it comes to justice in relocation. The central claim of the communitarian model is that justice in relocation requires that the interests of the community *itself* be protected in the process of relocation.

The communitarian model of relocation, as I articulate it here, draws on David Schlosberg's account of justice in climate change adaptation.[55] Schlosberg argues that when it comes to justice in adaptation, we should view communities—not only individuals—as subjects of justice. Schlosberg adopts a capabilities approach to justice in adaptation, but argues that capabilities 'can be extended to communities' and that one central concern of justice in adaptation is preserving 'the ability of communities to function'.[56] He criticizes Martha Nussbaum's and Edward Page's formulations of the capabilities approach on the basis that they remain 'squarely in the individualist frame'.[57] The upshot of ascribing capabilities to communities, for Schlosberg, is that justice in adaptation requires communities to take decisions about adaptation collectively.[58]

Schlosberg's focus on community capabilities is only a part of his broader theory of justice in adaptation. I am isolating it for analytic purposes here. He also argues that individual capabilities matter, and others have also drawn on the capabilities approach to defend collective decision-making in adaptation and relocation.[59] Breena Holland, for example, has argued that Nussbaum's proposed capability of having control over one's environment can be interpreted in terms of 'having the power to shape adaptation decisions'.[60] And Craig Johnson has drawn on Amartya

Sen's formulation of the capabilities approach to argue that 'local populations have a right to decide whether and how they relocate'.[61] I have no objection to the claim that *individual* capabilities such as these should be protected in relocation. But in my view, we need an explanation that tells us why protecting these capabilities requires collective decision-making, rather than something like the market model. After all, the market model *does* afford significant control over one's environment in one important sense: it gives each individual discretion over how to use their share of resources for relocation. The argument that I make in the next section supplies such an explanation. But before turning to it, it is worth examining the claim that communities themselves are the relevant subjects of justice in relocation.

In my view, it is a mistake to claim that communities themselves—above and beyond the individuals that compose them—are subjects of justice with interests that should be represented in decisions about relocation. Schlosberg is right to suggest that many of the concerns that arise in the context of adaptation and relocation relate to collective identity and the integrity of cultural and social practices (or as I have called them, following Stilz, practice-based interests). But there are three good reasons to reject an approach that takes the community itself to be the subject of justice in relocation.

First is that the communitarian model is *unnecessary* to accommodate the claims about the value of social and cultural practices that Schlosberg wants his account to vindicate. In his account of justice in adaptation, Schlosberg seeks to accommodate both positive claims about the value of collective identities sustained through shared social and cultural practices, and negative claims about the wrongfulness of the political exclusion of marginalized and Indigenous communities threatened by the impacts of climate change. I agree that it is essential that an account of justice in relocation is able to capture these kinds of claims. But these claims can be accommodated without abandoning the basic thesis of normative individualism: the claim that individuals, not groups, are the 'units of *ultimate* moral concern'.[62] Normative individualism, understood in this minimal sense, does not mean that social groups are unimportant in the lives of individuals.[63] A commitment to normative individualism is entirely compatible with both the claim that collective identities sustained through the social and cultural practices in which individuals participate as members of social groups are of great moral significance, and the claim that it is wrongful for individuals to face political exclusion on the basis of their membership of a social group.

There are a variety of ways in which theorists have attempted to explain the value that social and cultural practices can have for members of cultural groups—such as Will Kymlicka's argument that cultures constitute 'contexts of choice' for the exercise of individual autonomy—that do not require us to accord any moral standing to the community itself.[64] Likewise, we can recognize that the political exclusion of members of marginalized communities is wrongful, and even that members of marginalized communities can have claims to enhanced forms of political inclusion, without taking communities themselves to be subjects of justice.[65] In some cases, there will be particular reasons to treat the community itself as having the standing to negotiate collectively with state authorities. When it comes to Indigenous peoples such as the residents of Shishmaref, for example, considerations relating to tribal sovereignty and self-determination will mean that residents are entitled to demand that decisions about relocation should be conducted in terms of government-to-government relations.[66] But in recognizing these claims about jurisdictional authority, we need not take the community itself to be a subject of justice with interests apart from those of its members.[67]

Second is that the communitarian model is *insufficient* to establish that collective decision-making in relocation is normatively required. Schlosberg takes his account of justice in adaptation to provide a justification for why decisions about adaptation should be taken collectively by community members. But there is no principled reason why an approach to justice in adaptation that seeks to further a community's interests should require collective decision-making. A community's interests could—at least in principle—be advanced in ways other than through collective decision-making by its members. One alternative might be to appoint one authoritative individual or group of individuals, such as a community leader or local council, to make decisions on behalf of the community. Of course, in practice, we might be concerned that the person or persons occupying this role would abuse their power in order to advance their own interests instead—as is often the case when those managing relocation or development projects uncritically accept the authority of local elites.[68] But it is at least possible that one individual—perhaps someone particularly well attuned to the values of the community—could represent the community's interests better than its members. Schlosberg's view gives us no principled reason to prefer collective decision-making in such circumstances. If we take the community itself to have interests apart from those of its members, as Schlosberg does, then the function of collective decision-making is simply to bring those interests to light, rather than to settle any internal disagreements within a community.

Third is that the communitarian model is *unattractive* as a model of relocation. An approach to relocation that seeks to advance the interests of the community itself obscures the internal diversity of communities facing relocation. Even in highly solidaristic and close-knit communities such as Shishmaref, individuals will have a range of different perspectives that will be important in the process of relocation. As Whyte points out, there are often disagreements *within* tribal communities about what practices express tribal values, and such disagreements will bear on which forms of relocation are acceptable to community members.[69] And in larger and more heterogeneous communities, we can only expect these disagreements to be even more stark. Different people will have different interpretations of the value of their cultural and social practices, different priorities and expectations about the process of relocation, and different visions of what a successful relocation project would look like. This is obscured by an approach to relocation that focuses on identifying a set of interests that are attributed to the community as a whole.

This is important because it means that the communitarian model of relocation risks privileging one partial interpretation of the community's interests—usually the interpretation that reflects the will of the majority or those with the most power—at the expense of the interests of internal minorities. It can be easy to naturalize one partial interpretation of the community's interests by adopting what Iris Marion Young has called the 'logic of substance', according to which communities have a fixed essence or set of essential attributes which gives rise to a determinate set of interests.[70] But of course, there will always be some who do not fit the dominant mould. For those people, the ideal of community can be wielded as a tool to enforce homogeneity and to oppress and exclude.[71] Instead of adopting the logic of substance, we should view communities as being constituted by the relations in which their members stand with each other.[72] When we view communities in this way, we can recognize that members of a community will have different—and often conflicting—interests and interpretations of their collective identity. This is not to say that shared sentiments of collective identity and shared social and cultural practices are unimportant. But we should take care to avoid privileging one partial interpretation of a community's interests by obscuring the diversity within communities.

The Democratic Model of Relocation

Instead of either the market model or the communitarian model of relocation, I want to defend a third model of relocation, which I call the *democratic model* of relocation. As its name suggests, the basic idea of the democratic model is that communities should take collective democratic decisions about relocation. Communities would collectively decide if, when, and how to relocate through a process of democratic deliberation. The democratic model, so I argue, avoids the disadvantages of the market and communitarian models, while retaining their advantages. It avoids fragmenting communities and so enables those affected by climate impacts to secure their practice-based interests. At the same time, it does not privilege one partial interpretation of the community's interests, but instead allows community members to articulate their shared interests through compromise and deliberation.

One conciliatory way of interpreting the argument that I make here is by viewing it as a complement to the claims made by Schlosberg, Holland, and Johnson that exercising control over one's environment is a central individual capability that ought to be protected in adaptation policy. The argument that I make here explains why, in the circumstances in which relocation decisions take place, such a capability is best realized through collective democratic decision-making, rather than through something like the market model of relocation.

My defence of the democratic model begins with what I call the *circumstances of relocation*. These are the characteristic features of the situations in which relocation takes place that make collective democratic decision-making normatively required. In appealing to the circumstances of relocation, we might naturally think of Rawls's and Hume's discussions of the 'circumstances of justice'.[73] More recently, however, Rainer Bauböck has articulated what he calls the 'circumstances of democracy'—the conditions under which he takes democracy to be both empirically possible and normatively necessary—which are a more approximate model for the circumstances of relocation.[74] The conditions that Bauböck identifies as the circumstances of democracy include the existence of a diversity of interests, identities, and ideas among a population; the existence of fixed political and jurisdictional boundaries; and the 'relative sedentariness' of a population.[75] The circumstances of relocation are similar to the circumstances of democracy, but there are also some important differences, given the different aims of democracy, understood as a set of institutions for realizing popular self-government, and relocation, understood as strategy of adaptation to climate change.

Relocation decisions, unlike institutions for democratic self-government, do not presuppose either fixed political and jurisdictional boundaries or a relatively sedentary population. These are necessary background conditions for democracy, according to Bauböck, because they enable a democratic polity to function as a set of stable self-replicating institutions over time. Relocation decisions, by contrast, are a 'one-shot' problem, where a decision—or a set of decisions—must be taken in response to a specific, shared problem. So, relocation decisions do not need to be made through an institutional framework that is able to perpetuate itself stably and indefinitely into the future. Decisions about relocation do need a well-defined public, but that public can be defined by reference to the shared problem faced by a group of people.[76]

The existence of a diversity of interests, identities, and ideas among a population is, however, a background condition against which relocation decisions take place. Those facing relocation all share an interest in avoiding the harms of climate change, but different people will inevitably have different preferences and values that they seek to realize in decisions about whether, when, and how their community should relocate. They may have different interpretations about the value of their shared social and cultural practices, different views about how protecting those interests should be traded off against other competing priorities in relocation, and different visions of what a successful relocation project would look like. This is a basic background feature of decisions about relocation, even in close-knit communities where there are strong sentiments of collective identity.

To this we should also add a second background condition: decisions about relocation are characterized by the need for cooperation. Those in circumstances of relocation face a shared problem: that climate change impacts are threating their ability to continue living where they live. This problem demands a collective remedy because, as we have seen, the market model of relocation systematically frustrates the abilities of those affected by climate impacts to protect their practice-based interests by foreclosing options that require collective action.

These two features of the circumstances of relocation explain the need for collective democratic decision-making in relocation. The need for cooperation means that *collective* decisions are practically necessary: binding collective decisions authoritatively settle the questions of whether, when, and how relocation will take place. The diversity of interests, identities, and ideas means that *democratic* decision-making is normatively necessary: democratic procedures can settle disputes among those with competing visions of whether, when, and how relocation should take place. In the absence of a diversity of interests, identities, and ideas, decisions would be unanimous. As Bauböck points out, in such circumstances, democratic procedures would be 'pointless'.[77] This gives us the basic rationale for collective democratic decision-making in community relocation: collective democratic decision-making enables those facing relocation to cooperate in protecting their practice-based interests, while also enabling them to settle the disagreements that will inevitably arise as a result of their different interests, identities, and ideas. Two familiar, high-level principles should guide processes of decision-making in relocation: the principles of *political equality* and *deliberative justification*.

The principle of political equality is—very roughly—the idea that each participant in collective decisions about relocation should have an equal say. Political equality requires more than merely formal equality in the process of decision-making about relocation. Collective decision-making about relocation will not satisfy the principle of political equality if each individual is given a vote, but some are able to use their outsized power and influence to lobby for their own interests while others are not. Rather, political equality should be interpreted as the claim that each individual should have an equal substantive opportunity to shape the outcomes of collective decisions about relocation.[78] The basic justification for the principle of political equality is that it responds to the disagreements generated by the diversity of interests, ideas, and identities in a way that gives each person's interests equal weight. Each person has an interest in advancing their own claims about how relocation projects should be undertaken, and decision-making processes that satisfy the principle of political equality privilege no person's interests over those of another.

The principle of deliberative justification is—again, very roughly—the idea that collective decisions about relocation should be made through a dialogic process in which participants offer reasons for and against different proposals, with the aim being to come to a collective judgement that each participant finds acceptable.[79] One important point to note is that—contrary to the picture painted by some early theorists of deliberative democracy—productive deliberation need not always look like the formal argumentation of a seminar room. As theorists of deliberative democracy have by now broadly recognized, other modes of deliberation such as storytelling and rhetoric can play an important role in deliberation.[80] Different models of deliberation may also be appropriate in different cultural contexts. For example, the Pacific deliberative practice of *talanoa*—made famous through the 'Talanoa Dialogue' held at COP23—might be appropriate in contexts such as Fiji, where community relocation projects are already taking place.[81]

Deliberation can have an important epistemic function in the resolution of common problems. One way of viewing democratic decision-making procedures is to see them as methods for collective problem-solving.[82] On this view, deliberation plays an important role in marshalling socially relevant information—including both factual information and social perspectives—that is asymmetrically distributed among a public. Different people have different experiences, ideas, and perspectives that are relevant to the resolution of common problems—such as the problems facing communities that are considering relocation—and deliberation is an important way of making sure that this information is factored into collective decisions.

Deliberation also aims at generating outcomes that reflect a fair and reasoned compromise among people with different interests, ideas, and identities. Of course, it would be rare for communities to reach a genuine consensus on all aspects of relocation, and more formal procedural mechanisms will usually be necessary to resolve intractable disagreements. But deliberative processes treat people's preferences as open to change in light of exposure to competing ideas and perspectives. Ideally, they give those in the minority a chance to make their case—and to secure compromises with majorities who would otherwise not have considered their point of view. Deliberative practices can prevent those in the majority, or those with outsized power and influence, from simply forcing through decisions that reflect their preferences.[83] The idea is that when they enter into an exchange of reason-giving, the powerful are forced to make proposals that can withstand critical scrutiny and be accepted as a fair compromise by others who disagree. This is particularly important in the context of a 'one-shot' problem like relocation, where those who lose out in the decision-making process cannot be comforted by the fact that they will have future opportunities to secure outcomes that reflect their preferences.[84]

Still, even well-designed deliberative processes are unlikely to ensure that minorities will have their interests represented in collective decisions about relocation. Deliberation is an important part of the process of decision-making about relocation, but we should not be overly optimistic about its prospects for limiting the power of majorities to secure their own interests without compromise. Insincere participants in deliberative processes will often be able to concoct justifications that plausibly satisfy deliberative norms but do not genuinely aim at compromise. And even sincere participants will be affected by cognitive biases such as motivated reasoning which lead them to unconsciously interpret and evaluate justifications in ways that serve their own interests.[85] These problems mean that it would be unwise to rely solely on deliberation to limit the influence of powerful majorities in decisions about relocation.

My suggestion is that deliberative mechanisms should be complemented by giving individuals effective rights of exit. By *effective* rights of exit, I mean rights of exit that go beyond a merely formal entitlement to withdraw from the collective relocation process. After all, all but the most repressive regimes permit their citizens to move within their own state, and so those affected by relocation will typically already have a *formal* right of exit. Effective rights of exit would involve providing those who opt out of collective relocation processes with material support in relocating on their own. Individuals who opt out of collective relocation processes could be given a grant so that they could relocate on their own, for example to a nearby city or town—and perhaps the broader collective's funding for relocation could also be reduced accordingly.

To see why effective rights of exit can help to ensure that minority interests are represented in collective relocation decisions, it is helpful to introduce the distinction between 'exit' and 'voice'. Albert O. Hirschman argued that there are two main ways in which those who are dissatisfied with an organization can express their dissatisfaction: they can choose to voice their displeasure (voice), or they can choose to leave (exit). The possibilities for exit can also affect the effectiveness of voice, and vice versa.[86] And crucially, when the threat of exit is credible, then this can make voice more effective.

Effective rights of exit lower the cost of exit for those whose interests are not represented in collective decisions about relocation. Without the material support needed to relocate, the threat of exit will usually be ineffective. But when individuals can depend on a grant to finance their own relocation, their threat of exit becomes credible. A credible threat of exit gives those in the majority an incentive to take seriously the perspectives of minorities and to make compromises with them.[87] As we have seen, communities depend on a critical mass of their members remaining together if they are to protect their practice-based interests in the process of relocation. They have an interest in ensuring that they do not ride roughshod over the interests of minorities, since if they do, then those minorities can credibly threaten to leave (and perhaps even to take their share of the funding for relocation with them). So, effective rights of exit can help to ensure that deliberative processes in relocation decisions are more than merely formal procedures: they give minorities within decision-making processes a real ability to exert an influence over the outcomes of relocation decisions.

One concern that is sometimes raised is that if exit is too easy, then those who are dissatisfied will not exercise their voice.[88] If it is too easy to exit, we might be worried that the collective decision-making process will be undermined, and the democratic model will simply collapse back into the market model. But this concern underestimates the costs that typically accompany the decision to exit in the context of relocation. As we have already seen, relocating alone makes it difficult for those who choose to leave to protect their practice-based interests. And often, those who are facing relocation will be loyal to the community that seeks to relocate—they will identify with it and be invested in its success—which also raises the costs of exit.[89] So, we should expect that dissatisfied minorities will prefer to use their voice where possible. Of course, there may be some people for whom the costs of exit are low—those who do not give significant weight to their practice-based interests and who are not particularly loyal to the community—but those individuals are likely to be relatively few in number. For those people, an effective right of exit preserves their ability to make choices about relocation that reflect their own preferences and values. So long as they remain relatively few, their exit is unlikely to undermine the ability of other community members to protect their practice-based interests.

In sum, then, the democratic model of community relocation involves communities taking decisions about relocation collectively, through democratic procedures. This process should be guided by the principles of political equality and deliberative justification, and each person should retain an effective right of exit. This responds to the problem-structure of relocation: it facilitates the cooperation that is necessary for communities to secure their practice-based interests, while also taking seriously the diversity of ideas, interests, and identities among those facing the prospect of relocation.

Stated at this level of generality, the democratic model of relocation might seem fairly uncontroversial. Something like this model is implicit in the attempts at community relocation that have already been begun in places like Shishmaref. But it is important to have a clear account of the philosophical basis of the democratic model. A clear account of the underlying justification for the democratic model of community relocation allows us to see its advantages compared to the communitarian and market models. The democratic model avoids the market model's problem of fragmenting communities and the communitarian model's problem of privileging a partial interpretation of the community's interests. At the same time, it provides us with a secure foundation for collective democratic decision-making, which appeals only to the problem-structure of relocation.

The democratic model of relocation is demanding, and actual processes of relocation are likely to fall short of satisfying its principles perfectly. But the democratic model can be viewed as a regulative ideal, which serves as a critical standard for evaluating processes of community relocation in the real world. Of course, difficult questions arise when it comes to the implementation of the democratic model of relocation. In order to see how the democratic model of relocation might work in practice, it is useful to return to the case of the relocation of Shishmaref with which we began. The case of Shishmaref highlights some challenges that would need to be met in the practice of community relocation. Here, I consider two challenges—the problems of *expertise* and *scale*—that arise in the implementation of the democratic model of relocation.

Community Relocation in Practice

The process of relocation in Shishmaref has been long and difficult. Relocation was first discussed after large storms in 1973, but residents voted against it, believing that shoreline erosion could be stabilized and fearing that a vote to relocate could prevent infrastructure investments such as a planned new school.[90] But the storms continued, and the sea walls that had been put in place began to fail. After a serious storm in 2001, the community voted to relocate in 2002, and since then more serious attempts at relocation have been made.[91] Residents initially worked with two federal agencies—the United States Army Corps of Engineers (USACE) and the Natural Resources Conservation Service (NRCS)—to study possible relocation sites.[92] Neither USACE nor the NRCS had a formal mandate to study relocation sites, but both conducted a series of studies, after which the Shishmaref Erosion and Relocation Coalition selected a site for relocation called Tin Creek. Later, however, Tin Creek was found to be unviable as a site for relocation by the Alaska Department of Transportation and Public Facilities (DOT), due to the presence of permafrost that is vulnerable to melting due to climate change. After a further series of studies of suitable sites, the residents of Shishmaref once again voted to relocate—this time to a site at the West Tin Creek Hills—in 2016.[93] But planning for relocation is still ongoing, and progress has been slow. Residents have had to deal with a 'revolving door' of different bureaucrats and working groups, so that the relocation process is being constantly restarted without any awareness of previous relocation plans.[94]

It should be clear from this process that a well-defined institutional framework for relocation is necessary if anything like the democratic model of relocation is to be realized. Without a clear institutional framework, the attempts at relocation that have been made in Shishmaref have been ad hoc and largely uncoordinated. What should such an institutional framework look like?

Robin Bronen has recently argued for what she calls an 'adaptive governance framework' for community relocation.[95] An 'adaptive' governance framework is one that is flexible enough to accommodate the different circumstances of communities facing the prospect of relocation. The idea is that institutions should be designed to enable communities to select between a 'continuum of responses' including not only relocation, but also *in situ* forms of adaptation such as protect-in-place and hazard-mitigation policies.[96] On Bronen's proposal, there should be a 'clear organizational structure' for relocation, with lead agencies designated for both its planning and operational aspects, and clear guidelines for stakeholder identification and coordination, which clearly outline the role of the community in the relocation process.[97]

This is a good starting point for developing institutions for community relocation. But from the perspective of the democratic model, it is crucial to ensure that the institutional framework for relocation creates opportunities for deliberation and collective decision-making throughout the relocation process. Bronen does suggest that relocation should be 'community-based and community-guided', but it is essential that this is built into the institutional framework that governs relocation processes.[98] Beyond this, it may not be possible to specify a precise institutional blueprint for all contexts of relocation. There will usually be a range of more local considerations that bear on which actors should be given different roles and responsibilities in the relocation process. In cases such as Shishmaref that involve the relocation of Indigenous communities, it will be essential to ensure that the authority of tribal governments is respected in the relocation process. Tribal governments have standing to represent their peoples and stand in government-to-government relations with the federal authorities involved in relocation projects.[99] If public authorities engaging in relocation fail to respect the authority of tribal governments, then the process of relocation is likely to replicate the historic injustices of forced relocation and sedentarization that have made peoples such as the *Kigiqtaamiut* of Shishmaref vulnerable to climate impacts in the first place.[100]

Beyond this, there are two problems that will need to be confronted in the design of institutions for relocation. The first problem concerns the role of *expertise*. Relocation projects depend upon highly specialized technical knowledge—for example, about the nature and scale of predicted climatic hazards and about whether particular relocation sites will be suitable for development and habitation—and it is essential that such knowledge is incorporated into deliberative processes. But there is a risk that the need for technical expertise will be used to manipulate the process of democratic decision-making. In other adaptation contexts, researchers have documented the ways in which elites use technical expertise—or the guise of technical expertise—to steer, contain, and co-opt community participation and to secure outcomes that reflect their own institutional or personal agendas.[101] And in other contexts of relocation, such as in relocation for development projects like dams and mines, there is a long history of forced relocation being imposed by elites appealing to the 'technical' outcomes of cost–benefit analyses.[102] Even when technical experts act in good faith, their interventions can be counterproductive. In the case of Shishmaref, the technical judgement that Tin Creek was unviable as a site for relocation came *after* it had already been selected by a community vote, leading to frustration and distrust among residents. Missteps like this appear to confirm the—often reasonable—fears of community members that political or managerial elites are only paying lip service to participation.

This challenge is difficult to overcome entirely. So long as there are background inequalities of power, there will always be a danger that elites will exploit the need for technical expertise to steer processes of democratic decision-making about relocation in ways that serve their agendas. Indeed, the veneer of participation may make it easier for them to secure legitimacy for pre-ordained outcomes.[103] And even without such background inequalities, there is a risk that technical expertise will be misused or counterproductive. Still, there are ways in which this risk can at least be mitigated, if not eliminated, in relocation planning.

On the conventional picture of the role of expertise in democratic decision-making, there is a strict 'division of labour' between technical experts and affected publics.[104] Technical experts provide facts relevant to normative judgements, but affected publics are the ones who ultimately make the normative judgements. On this picture, one way to respond to the challenge of expertise would be to ensure that the institutional framework clearly defines and narrowly circumscribes the role of technical experts in decision-making processes, in order to preserve this division of labour and to limit opportunities for elite manipulation. And there is certainly an important place for this in the context of relocation: the role of technical experts in the planning process should be clear from the outset, so that it is clear to technical experts and community members alike what kinds of judgements they are being asked to make.

But the traditional division of labour between technical experts and affected publics is often difficult to maintain.[105] From one direction, the judgements made by technical experts often implicitly appeal to values. Value judgements may be unavoidable when technical experts made decisions about, for example, the methods that they use, the standards of evidence that they uphold, and the assumptions that they build into descriptive claims.[106] For example, judgements about the 'habitability' of particular places are likely to depend on implicit assumptions about the ways in which communities live, such as about what resources they need.[107] From the other direction, community members themselves will often have knowledge that is relevant to technical judgements. Local, practical knowledge—what James C. Scott calls 'mētis'—may not be immediately accessible to scientific experts, but it can be highly relevant for technical judgements in relocation decisions.[108] Such knowledge is often tacit, uncodified, and experiential. For example, the residents of Shishmaref have acquired an in-depth knowledge of the localized dynamics of climate change in their traditional territories through subsistence hunting practices—dynamics which are very difficult for scientists to model, given the complexity of arctic ecological systems.[109] Failing to incorporate local knowledge is not only likely to lead to negative outcomes, it is also likely to erode trust between residents and public authorities.[110] In Shishmaref, relocation that ignores local knowledge would risk recreating the forms of top-down social engineering that characterized colonial processes of sedentarization.[111]

These considerations suggest two further strategies for confronting the problem of expertise. First is that there should be opportunities for the contestation and scrutiny of the judgements of technical experts in the relocation process. Institutionalized opportunities for contestation can serve as a check on technical expertise, making sure that it is kept in its proper place in the process of democratic deliberation about relocation. As Alfred Moore has argued, the contestation of expert claims can 'reveal epistemic blind spots and bring to light potentially valuable but unexplored information' in expert judgements. And beyond this, contestation can also play a role in subjecting to the *scope* of expert judgements to critical scrutiny, by enabling community members to challenge the delegation of certain decisions or judgements to technical experts.[112] There are different ways in which opportunities for contestation might be institutionalized—for example, local advocacy organizations might be empowered to act as 'watchdogs' in relocation decisions, or 'oversight juries' of randomly selected community members might be charged with contesting the judgements of technical experts.[113]

Second is that community members themselves should be involved in the process of forming technical judgements that feed into processes of deliberation. Schlosberg argues that communities should be 'thoroughly involved in both the mapping of their own vulnerabilities and the design of adaptation policies'.[114] This is an important commitment that should be built into the institutional design of the relocation process. Involving community members in the mapping of their own vulnerabilities serves a dual function: to both ensure that local knowledge is incorporated into decision-making processes, and to act as a corrective against mistaken assumptions or blind spots that technical experts themselves may have. This will require that technical experts work closely with community members, in ways that genuinely co-construct knowledge that is relevant to relocation, rather than merely paying lip service to incorporating local perspectives.

The second problem concerns the *scale* of community relocation. Shishmaref is a small and close-knit community, in which face-to-face deliberation about relocation among residents is relatively straightforward. In this sense, it is atypical: often the communities that face the prospect of relocation will be larger and more loosely connected. In worst-case scenarios, climate impacts such as sea-level rise may even present risks to entire coastal cities. In contexts such as these, involving each affected person directly in deliberations about if, when, and how to relocate will not be practically possible, since deliberation takes time, money, and commitment—all of which are finite resources. Given its emphasis on deliberation, this raises the question of how the democratic model of relocation can be scaled up.

It is first important to note that community relocation is generally a last-resort option that is taken only when *in situ* forms of adaptation to climate change fail or are prohibitively expensive. Climate impacts such as sea-level rise can often be mitigated through *in situ* measures of adaptation. Given the size of the populations potentially affected by climate impacts in these cases, adaptation measures that aim to protect in place will often make a lot more sense than engaging in relocation, even when this involves significant infrastructural investment that might not be feasible in the protection of smaller communities. In large coastal cities facing sea-level rise, this may mean using coastal defence measures—such as sea walls, levees, and beach replenishment—so that, as far as is possible, relocation can be avoided. With these kinds of measures in place, we may be able to protect at least some parts of large coastal cities through *in situ* adaptation measures while communities that are difficult to protect in place selectively engage in relocation.

Of course, this does not mean that the problem of scale can be avoided entirely. There are still likely to be many cases in which the communities facing the prospect of relocation are larger in scale than communities such as Shishmaref. And in these contexts, it will typically not be possible for each affected person to be directly involved in time- and labour-intensive forms of face-to-face deliberation about relocation.

Democrats sometimes appeal to *representation* as a substitute for more direct forms of decision-making in large-scale contexts in which the ideal of direct democracy cannot be easily realized.[115] One way of confronting the problem of scale in the context of relocation would be to use representation as a substitute for direct forms of decision-making. Communities facing relocation would choose representatives, who would stand in a principal–agent relationship to those directly affected and would be authorized to take decisions on their behalf.[116] This would be a lot more manageable than attempting to involve large numbers of people in decisions about relocation directly.

But there are reasons to avoid relying on representation as a response to the problem of scale. For one thing, classic questions about whether representatives should act as 'delegates' or 'trustees' of those they represent—that is, whether they should be bound by instructions from their constituents or whether they should exercise their own judgement—are particularly acute from the point of view of the democratic model of relocation.[117] If representatives act as delegates, then they represent the perspectives of their constituents more closely, but there is less scope for deliberation—since deliberation requires that participants be genuinely open to changing their minds.[118] And if representatives act as trustees, then there may be more scope for deliberation, but representatives will be more detached from the constituents that they are supposed to represent—which threatens the political equality of community members. Given that the democratic model places a premium on both deliberation and political equality, this tension makes representation a less-than-ideal solution to the problem of scale.

A second problem with relying on representation in the context of relocation is that the 'one-shot' nature of relocation makes it difficult to hold representatives to account. In representative democracies, elections—at least ideally—function as ways of disciplining representatives. When representatives face the threat of being thrown out, they are incentivized to represent the perspectives of their constituents, or at least not to misrepresent them too egregiously.[119] But in the context of relocation, this mechanism of accountability cannot function in the same way. Because the selection of representatives is not a recurrent event in an ongoing project of representative democracy but is rather a response to a 'one-shot' problem, there is no future prospect of re-election to keep representatives in line. This creates significant risks that representatives will fail to properly represent the interests of community members.

These problems should lead us to turn instead to more participatory forms of decision-making in the context of relocation. Even if it is not feasible for each person to be directly involved in decision-making about relocation, we can still develop participatory institutions that enable strong forms of deliberation, and which empower community members to engage in more direct forms of decision-making. Here, we can look to institutional models that realize what Archon Fung and Erik Olin Wright have called 'empowered participatory governance' for inspiration.[120] Institutions for empowered participatory governance aim to solve practical problems by empowering groups of ordinary citizens to make decisions through processes of deliberation. Oft-cited examples include reforms to the Panchayat governance system in Kerala, India, which devolved significant power over development to individual villages, and the participatory budgeting model pioneered in Porto Alegre, Brazil, which handed power over municipal budgets to a system of regional assemblies and neighbourhood associations.[121] In these cases, significant power was devolved to 'local action units' which—while coordinated and supervised at higher scales—were authorized by state institutions to design and implement solutions to practical problems.[122] These experiments have enjoyed some significant successes. In Porto Alegre, democratizing municipal budgeting enabled citizens to reduce corruption while directing public funds towards redistributive and poverty-alleviating investment projects, such as sewage systems, housing assistance, and public schooling. Levels of participation were high, and although there were some inequalities in participation, they were not nearly as pronounced as in other democratic contexts in Brazil and did not appear to create significant barriers in deliberations.[123]

These models of empowered participatory governance point towards a strategy for confronting the problem of scale in community relocation. Even in cases where not every community member can participate directly in decision-making processes, significant powers can still be devolved to deliberative assemblies made up of members of affected communities. Those deliberative assemblies could be empowered to design and implement relocation projects for the community. In building the institutions for relocation, we can draw on the lessons of these models of empowered participatory governance in other contexts. These institutional strategies may not be a perfect way of realizing the democratic model of relocation, but they do have the potential to enable robust forms of deliberation and democratic control over the relocation process.

Critics have rightly pointed out that empowered participatory governance is no panacea for democracy.[124] It is unlikely to escape the problem of background inequalities infecting deliberative processes entirely, and it may well deflect attention away from broader structural reforms that can more effectively challenge those background inequalities. Where empowered participation governance has been successful, its successes have been fragile, and it is not clear that they can be replicated everywhere. As Fung and Wright recognize, empowered participatory governance requires high levels of commitment, and so may not be stable over the long term.[125]

These criticisms suggest that we should not be too optimistic about the prospects of empowered participatory governance as a model of democracy writ large. But they should not lead us to abandon the idea for the context of relocation. There are features of the problem-structure of relocation that make it particularly fertile ground for adopting the model of empowered participatory governance. Since empowered participatory governance institutions are being used to address a fairly discrete practical problem, rather than as a broader agenda-setting tool for reform, they are unlikely to draw attention away from broader structural efforts to combat background inequalities. And the nature of relocation as a 'one-shot' problem means that we should not be overly worried about the levels of commitment that it requires. Institutions for relocation do not need to self-replicate indefinitely, so we need not worry as much about participants becoming apathetic over time. And given the high stakes for those affected, we can expect that participants will be motivated to participate. It is true that in Shishmaref, the relocation process has dragged on in ways that have led to a collapse in morale among those facing relocation—but this is more a result of their having to navigate the process of relocation in the *absence* of robust institutions for relocation, rather than a result of participating within them.[126] Given real opportunities for participation in empowered decision-making processes, we can expect that community members would be motivated to participate.

The strategies for confronting the problems of expertise and scale that I have outlined here are unlikely to be enough to dissolve those problems entirely. There is no escaping the fact that relocation is likely to be a difficult process. But they point towards ways in which we might begin to implement the democratic model of relocation in practice as community relocation becomes more salient as a form of climate change adaptation.

Community relocation is an increasingly important form of adaptation to climate change. As the impacts of climate change continue to unfold, there are likely to be more and more circumstances in which *in situ* adaptation is no longer a realistic prospect. Communities face stark threats not only to their basic interests, but also to the shared social and cultural practices that they value. In these circumstances, we need to know how decisions about relocation should be made.

As we have seen, two answers to this question—given by the market and communitarian models of relocation—fail. The market model fragments communities and so makes it difficult for their members to protect their practice-based interests. The communitarian model risks riding roughshod over the internal diversity of the communities facing relocation and privileging one partial interpretation of the community's interests. In response to the failings of these models, I have defended a third model of relocation—the democratic model of relocation—which aims to enable community members to secure their practice-based interests while also enabling them to navigate the disagreements that will inevitably arise in the process of relocation. The democratic model is guided by two key principles, the principles of political equality and deliberative justification, and each individual should retain an effective right of exit. This model aims to enable communities to protect their practice-based interests within the circumstances of relocation.

As a regulative ideal, the democratic model is a standard that we can use for evaluating processes of community relocation. But of course, difficult questions arise at the level of implementation. The problems of expertise and scale are difficult to overcome entirely. But there are strategies for making those problems less acute. Clear institutional frameworks for relocation should be put in place, which create space for deliberation among community members. The role of technical experts should be clearly circumscribed, and there should be opportunities for the contestation of expert judgements and for technical expertise to be co-constructed in ways that incorporate the local knowledge of community members. Where relocation takes place in larger-scale contexts, empowered participatory governance institutions should be put in place, so that community members can retain a real measure of control over the process of relocation. These measures are unlikely to resolve the problems of scale and expertise entirely, but they will go some way to making it possible to implement the democratic model of relocation in practice.

4
Climate Change and Territorial Sovereignty

According to the Intergovernmental Panel on Climate Change (IPCC), global mean sea levels are expected to rise by between 0.26m and 0.82m by the year 2100, depending on the emissions pathway that humanity follows in the near future.[1] There is significant variation in sea-level rise around the world, which means that some areas are likely to face higher rises. And since 1990, actual changes in sea-level rise have tended to track the upper bounds of IPCC projections.[2] These projections also do not include the additional rise of several tenths of a metre that would occur in the increasingly likely event of the collapse of marine-based sectors of the Antarctic ice sheet.[3] Uncertainty among climate scientists and glaciologists about the dynamics of ice melt processes and their relation to sea-level rise also means that IPCC projections may well downplay a very real risk of a rise of up to 2m by 2100.[4]

In the abstract, these figures may not seem especially large, but they have the potential to have drastic implications on coastlines in some parts of the world. Small-island states such the Maldives, Kiribati, Tuvalu, and Vanuatu are networks of low-lying islands, many of which are coral atolls, which are highly vulnerable to sea-level rise and other climate impacts such as coral bleaching and storm surges.[5] Many of the islands that make up these states are little more than a metre or two above sea level. Sea-level rise creates a risk that these small-island states will become uninhabitable, at least on any scale that would enable them to sustain their populations. Some territory may simply be inundated by rising seas. But much territory is likely to become uninhabitable in advance of its actual submersion because of the effects of saltwater incursion, king tides, and coastal erosion relating to climate change.[6]

Sea-level rise raises the spectre of what Milla Vaha has termed 'state extinction'.[7] According to the rules that govern statehood in the international order, set out in the 1933 *Montevideo Convention on the Rights and Duties of States*, a 'permanent population' and a 'defined territory' are requirements for statehood.[8] If small-island states become uninhabitable, both of these criteria could go unmet.[9] At present, the main way in which the value of self-determination is protected in the international order is through the norm of *territorial sovereignty*, which gives sovereign states jurisdictional rights to make and enforce law over a defined geographical space.[10] If small-island states were to lose their control over territory and their status as sovereign states because of rising sea levels, then their citizens could lose this basis for the exercise of self-determination.

It is not inevitable that small-island states will cease to exist as sovereign states. First, we may still yet succeed in stopping climate impacts from making small-island states uninhabitable. Some coral atolls have proven to be more resilient than expected to the effects of sea-level rise so far, and aggressive emissions reductions that keep global temperature increases to 1.5°C could limit the impact of sea-level rise on small-island states significantly.[11] The Alliance of Small Island States (AOSIS) has been at the forefront of efforts to pursue this more ambitious temperature target in global climate negotiations.[12] But at the moment, the international community is falling significantly short. Even if all states were to meet the emissions reductions targets that they have set themselves—which, given their track record, appears unlikely—global temperature increases would still not be limited to anywhere near 2°C.[13] So, even though the inundation of small-island states is not inevitable, it is a real possibility that we should take seriously.

Second, the rules for the recognition of statehood in the international order are not fixed and immutable. There is little precedent for the situation of small-island peoples and a strong presumption against the extinction of states under international law, so it is not clear how those rules would be interpreted in the case of small-island states.[14] And more fundamentally, those rules are constructed, shaped, and reinterpreted by actors in international politics, and can, as such, be changed. The aim of this chapter is to examine how the practices of statehood and sovereignty could be reconfigured in light of the threat of state extinction facing small-island peoples.

One response to the threat of state extinction involves granting small-island peoples individual rights to relocate.[15] Some versions of this proposal would involve fairly extensive rights, such as a right to choose a new host state.[16] In my view, these responses—although certainly defensible—do not go far enough. Individual relocation rights should be uncontroversial: even a minimal duty of rescue would provide a basis for an individual right to relocate from uninhabitable small-island states. But individual relocation rights—even more extensive ones—do not get to the heart of the threat facing small-island peoples, since they do not account for the irreducibly collective nature of state extinction. Beyond any individual losses—of property, land, and livelihoods—state extinction threatens the collective exercise of self-determination by small-island peoples. So here, I set aside arguments for individual relocation rights—which I take to complement the proposals that I examine—and focus instead on three proposals that seek to preserve small-island peoples' collective rights to self-determination.

The first is *territorial redistribution*. Territorial redistribution would involve another state ceding territory to small-island peoples, who would then exercise territorial sovereignty over a new geographical space. The second is *de-territorialized statehood*. De-territorialized statehood would decouple statehood from territorial sovereignty. Small-island peoples would enjoy a form of 'statehood' without exercising jurisdictional authority over any particular territory. The third is *intra-state territorial autonomy*. Intra-state territorial autonomy would give small-island peoples powers to make and enforce laws in a territorial sub-unit, but those powers would be nested within the jurisdiction of another state. Before evaluating these proposals, I examine the concept of self-determination in more detail. I defend a view that says that self-determination involves a real capacity for self-government and freedom from the dominating interference of outsiders. Then, I examine the three proposals with this conception of self-determination in mind. Ultimately, I give a cautious defence of intra-state territorial autonomy. I argue that intra-state territorial autonomy can, if implemented in ways that reflect the values of small-island peoples, realize self-determination in meaningful ways while avoiding some of the moral costs associated with alternatives.

The Demands of Self-Determination

Self-determination is a central value in the international order. The right to self-determination is enshrined in the charter of the United Nations, the *International Covenant on Civil and Political Rights*, and the *Declaration on the Granting of Independence to Colonial Countries and Peoples*.[17] But this broad endorsement of the concept of self-determination obscures significant disagreement about how it is best understood. In Avishai Margalit and Joseph Raz's memorable phrase, the 'core consensus' on the concept of self-determination is 'but the eye in a raging storm concerning the precise definition of the right, its content, its bearers, and the proper means for its implementation'.[18]

One disagreement is about which groups are bearers of the right to self-determination.[19] For our purposes, this disagreement is not directly relevant. This is because we can agree that small-island peoples have a right to self-determination, even if deeper disagreements about the basis of this judgement persist in the background. After all, small-island peoples *already* exercise self-determination—and are widely regarded as being entitled to do so—and so I assume here that they have a right to self-determination. My aim is not to develop a comprehensive theory of self-determination that settles this background question, so I stay agnostic on it here.

The main disagreement that is relevant here is about the *demands* of self-determination—that is, the conditions under which the right to self-determination is satisfied. Self-determination is generally viewed as having both an *internal* and an *external* aspect.[20] The internal aspect refers to the ability of a self-determining group to exercise control over some domain(s) of its members' lives. The external aspect refers to the rights against interference by outsiders that the self-determining group enjoys. Groups can be more or less self-determining along each of these axes, and different conceptions of the right to self-determination will fill each of these aspects of self-determination in different ways.

Here, I examine three conceptions of self-determination, drawing largely on the work of Iris Marion Young.[21] The conception of self-determination that I ultimately defend—*self-determination as interdependence*—says that self-determination involves a real capacity for self-government and freedom from the dominating interference of outsiders. This is an 'ameliorative' conception of self-determination—that is, a conception that aims to capture self-determination's moral value while at the same time making sense of claims made in the language of self-determination.[22] The idea is that such a conception of self-determination is one that is worth endorsing, and so can be used as a critical tool to evaluate the three proposals for small-island states.

The first conception is what Young calls *self-determination as non-interference*.[23] On this conception, self-determination requires full and exclusive sovereignty. Internally, the self-determining group has the right to exercise authority over all domains of its shared political life. Externally, no outsiders have a right to interfere within the self-determining group's jurisdiction. On this conception, self-determination is much negative liberty at the inter-personal level, in that it gives the agent a claim against interference by outsiders and a right to make autonomous choices over self-regarding decisions.

Self-determination as non-interference is the conception of self-determination that has dominated the political imagination of the international order in the post-war era. It underlies the Westphalian picture of an international order composed of 'discrete, mutually exclusive, comprehensive territorial jurisdictions'.[24] But as a matter of practice, few states enjoy anything like self-determination as non-interference in any comprehensive sense. States face various *de jure* and *de facto* limits on the exercise of their authority, including principles of international law that bind them even when they do not consent and more informal norms that have proliferated alongside processes of globalization.[25] Developments such as the globalization of capital markets, the communications revolution, and environmental changes all mean that states rarely make purely self-regarding decisions, and often have no effective choice but to interact and cooperate with each other.[26] The non-interference conception of self-determination, then, is only imperfectly realized in the international order.

The non-interference conception of self-determination undoubtedly captures something about the value of self-determination: the idea that a self-determining group ought to be able to govern its own affairs without having to seek permission from others. But there are two important problems with the conception of self-determination as non-interference. One problem is that it cannot account for many claims made in the language of self-determination. Some groups that make claims to self-determination clearly do aspire to something like full and exclusive sovereignty, but many groups that make such claims do not. As Rauna Kuokkanen points out, advocates of Indigenous self-determination do not generally seek independent statehood with full sovereignty. Instead, they 'typically claim or seek explicit recognition as distinct peoples, greater political autonomy, and decision-making powers over their own affairs, as well as more extensive opportunities to participate in the affairs of the state'.[27] If self-determination requires full and exclusive sovereignty, then these modes of self-governance to which Indigenous groups aspire do not count as claims to self-determination, or at most count only as claims to impoverished or weak forms of self-determination.

A second problem with self-determination as non-interference is that it makes self-determination conflict with other morally important goals and values. This is because, as Young points out, it depends on the false assumption that self-determining agents are, or can be, 'independent of one another except insofar as they choose to exchange and contract'.[28] In the context of a globalized international order, the choices that states make have 'unintended consequences' that affect others, which means that international cooperation on a range of issues—for example, trade, global health, climate change, and migration—is a moral as well as a practical imperative.[29] On the non-interference conception, the value of self-determination conflicts with discharging moral duties in these domains through mandatory forms of international cooperation.

The second conception is what I will call *self-determination as cultural autonomy*. On this conception, self-determination is about a group being able to live in accordance with its own cultural values. Internally, it demands that a group is able to exercise collective control over the domain of its cultural practices. Externally, it demands that a group is free from interference by outsiders to the extent that this is necessary for the group to exercise control over its cultural practices. According to Allen Buchanan, self-determination is 'the freedom of a group to live its own distinctive common life, to express its constitutive values through its own social practices and cultural forms'.[30] Buchanan argues that we should distinguish self-determination, thus understood, from the various rights of political autonomy that might be put in place in order to protect a group's capacity to live its own way of life.[31] There is significant disagreement about the degree of political autonomy required for a group to exercise control over its cultural practices. For advocates of national self-determination, something like sovereign statehood is required for a group to be able to exert collective control over its cultural life.[32] For others, such as Buchanan or liberal multiculturalists such as Will Kymlicka, more limited rights of political autonomy or regimes of cultural minority rights are often sufficient to secure self-determination as cultural autonomy.[33]

Like self-determination as non-interference, self-determination as cultural autonomy is unable to account for many claims made in the language of self-determination. This is because, as Avner de Shalit points out, the demand for self-determination is typically a *political* demand, not a cultural one.[34] Many claims made in the language of self-determination are claims made by culturally heterogeneous groups. Colonized peoples asserting the right to self-determination in the process of decolonization, for example, were often united more by the fact of their shared subjection to colonial rule than by any cohesive ethnic or cultural identity.[35] Self-determination as cultural autonomy is unable to account for these kinds of claims because it sees self-determination as essentially being about protecting a group's capacity to maintain and direct its own culture. To the extent that self-government is required by the cultural autonomy conception, it is required only as an instrument for cultural self-preservation.

In its stronger forms, self-determination as cultural autonomy also raises some moral concerns. Even in groups that appear to share the same cultural identity, there will always be some who do not fit the mould, or who interpret cultural traditions and values in different ways to the majority (as we saw in Chapter 3). If a self-determining group wields a significant degree of power in the name of protecting or promoting its cultural values, and if it enjoys robust immunity against interference by outsiders, then internal minorities face threats of marginalization by the cultural majority.[36] Of course, not all public powers used to protect or promote cultural values will involve marginalization. But to the extent that the cultural autonomy conception of self-determination puts the cultural practices of a group beyond external scrutiny, then it is liable to foster the conditions for such marginalization.

The third conception is what Young calls *self-determination as interdependence*.[37] On this conception, self-determination is about groups being empowered to govern their own affairs in relations of non-domination with outsiders. Internally, a self-determining group must have a *real capacity* for self-government. They have a 'right to their own governance institutions through which they decide on their goals and interpret their way of life'.[38] This means that the ability of a group to govern its own affairs must be effective, not merely formal. Externally, a self-determining group must enjoy freedom from *domination*. This means that no outsider should be able interfere with a self-determining group on an arbitrary basis: interference should not issue from the unconstrained will of another.[39] This will usually involve a presumption against interference in domestic affairs—and non-interference may be a useful jurisdictional rule to protect against domination in some contexts—but self-determination itself does not provide for an absolute right against interference.[40] There are some forms of interference that are consistent with, and may even be required by, self-determination.

Self-determination as interdependence preserves the idea found in the non-interference conception that self-determination is about a group's capacity to exercise self-government, rather than merely its capacity to lead a culturally specific way of life. But it differs from the non-interference conception in that it does not view the self-determining group as an agent that can, or should, act in isolation from others. Young argues that in the context of a globalized international order, the choices made by a self-determining group will inevitably affect outsiders, which means that outsiders have a right to 'make claims on the group, negotiate the terms of their relationships, and mutually adjust their effects'.[41] This explains why self-determination does not require absolute non-interference by outsiders. At the same time, however, the choices made by outsiders can affect the prospects for a group's capacity to exercise effective self-government, even if they do not involve direct interference. Outsiders, including both other states and powerful private actors, can undermine that capacity without interfering directly in the choices of self-determining groups, for example by controlling access to resources or insisting on exploitative conditions for cooperation.[42]

This means that full and exclusive sovereignty is neither necessary nor sufficient for self-determination.[43] It is not necessary because it is possible for a group to exercise self-governance without being entirely independent from outsiders. It is not sufficient because formal sovereignty is little guarantee of the capacity to exercise self-government. A group must enjoy a *real capacity* to exercise self-government—rather than a mere entitlement to do so—for the right to self-determination to be satisfied. To secure a real capacity for self-government, we need 'settled institutions and procedures through which peoples negotiate, adjudicate conflicts, and enforce agreements'.[44] Such institutions and procedures are not a compromise with self-determination, but a condition for its realization.

Self-determination as interdependence makes sense of claims to self-determination. Young's focus is on the claims made by Indigenous peoples in the United States which, as we have seen, are not usually claims to sovereign statehood. But they often are claims to *self-government*, where Indigenous groups claim recognition as autonomous peoples who enjoy a standing to negotiate intergovernmentally with the state within which they are located.[45] Secessionist groups often seek independent statehood, but as Buchanan has argued, their claims can often be understood as claims to a means to protect themselves against dominating interference by majorities.[46] And in the context of decolonization, the claims of colonized peoples were not simply claims to non-interference. As Adom Getachew has shown, advocates of self-determination in the waves of decolonization often saw self-government as being consistent with, and even requiring, forms of international cooperation such as regional federation and a New International Economic Order, because otherwise they would remain subject to the domination of former colonial powers, even if formally independent of them.[47]

Self-determination as interdependence also makes self-determination consistent with other morally important goals and values, such as international cooperation over issues such as climate change, the prevention of transnational crime, global health governance, and trade and migration policy. On the interdependence conception, global institutions that set the terms for interaction between states need not be a compromise with the value of self-determination. Self-determination as interdependence is also consistent with limits on state power to protect minorities within a state. Human rights norms, which act as external standards for scrutiny and—in the limit case—intervention, can protect internal minorities from the power of majorities or elites. On the non-interference and cultural autonomy conceptions of self-determination, such limitations are a compromise with the value of self-determination. But on the interdependence conception, human rights norms that prevent the domination of internal minorities need not conflict with groups' rights to self-determination.

Altogether, we have good reasons to endorse self-determination as interdependence. Self-determination as interdependence makes sense of core cases of claims made to self-determination, and it makes self-determination consistent with other morally important goals and values. With this conception of self-determination in mind, we can evaluate the three proposals—territorial redistribution, deterritorialized statehood, and intra-state territorial autonomy—that have been set out for protecting the value of self-determination for small-island peoples.

Territorial Redistribution

The proposal for territorial redistribution is the most straightforward of the three proposals. The most familiar way in which groups exercise self-determination is through the rights of territorial sovereignty held and exercised through a state. Self-determining groups are able to govern themselves because, through their states, they enjoy the jurisdictional authority to make and enforce law over the geographical spaces in which their members live. Small-island peoples currently exercise self-determination in this way, but their ability to do so is threatened by the possible future uninhabitability of the land over which their state exercises jurisdictional authority. Territorial redistribution aims at restoring this state of affairs by providing small-island peoples with a new territory, ceded by some other state, over which to exercise the same kind of jurisdictional authority.

Cara Nine has made the most influential argument in defence of territorial redistribution.[48] Strictly, she does not definitively claim that small-island peoples should be granted new territory, but rather argues that they are a 'candidate' for being granted sovereignty over a new territory.[49] On her view, whether or not territory should be redistributed to small-island peoples is ultimately an all-things-considered judgement that must balance the competing claims of others with respect to the territory under consideration. But she does argue that new territorial rights for small-island peoples can be justified and that other states can be required to 'downsize' their territorial holdings in order to provide appropriate territory for the re-establishment of small-island states in a new location.[50]

Nine's argument for territorial redistribution is based on a modified Lockean proviso applied to territory.[51] On her view, a system of territorial rights is justified by it serving the value of 'the establishment of justice through the preservation of self-determining groups'.[52] When this value is undermined by a particular distribution of territorial holdings, then territorial holdings should be reconfigured so as to better serve the value that justifies the regime of territorial rights in the first place. In the case of small-island states, the value that justifies territorial rights is undermined because sea-level rise means that some groups will be unable to establish justice through self-determination, and so territorial holdings should be reconfigured. Other holders of territory must downsize their territorial holdings so that small-island peoples can continue to exercise their rights to self-determination. The question of *which* territory ought to be ceded to small-island peoples remains open. Frank Dietrich and Joachim Wündisch suggest that once suitable territories have been identified, a 'negative auction' could be held, in which local communities would bid to sell their territory, to determine which territory should be ceded to small-island peoples.[53]

I will not focus on the Lockean basis of Nine's argument here. For those who are unsatisfied with this Lockean justification, other arguments for territorial redistribution have also been given.[54] My interest is rather in the conception of self-determination upon which this proposal rests. Nine argues that self-determination is essentially concerned with self-rule. She writes that 'if a group is to be self-determining, it must rule itself. In order for it to rule itself, it must have the authority to establish justice for its members.'[55] On her view, self-determination understood in this way requires both *autonomy* and *independence*. That is, it requires that the self-determining group has 'the ability to govern itself by adjudicating, legislating, and enforcing laws on its own' and that it 'has a domain of political control independent of higher or foreign political units'.[56]

Nine's argument draws on the conception of self-determination as non-interference. This conception underpins the idea that territorial redistribution is *necessary* to protect small-island peoples' rights to self-determination. But Nine is actually fairly cautious in drawing a close link between self-determination and territorial redistribution. She writes that 'self-determination *often* requires territorial sovereignty', that 'without territorial rights, the self-determining group *may* cease to exist as a self-determining group', and that 'in order to be self-determining, a group *may* have to have territorial rights'.[57] She also raises the possibility of 'limited sovereignty'—a form of intra-state territorial autonomy—as an option for small-island states.[58] But these concessions sit oddly with Nine's claim that autonomy and independence are central to self-determination. If self-determination really does require independent and autonomous jurisdictional authority over a discrete parcel of territory, then territorial redistribution would be necessary to realize it. Others who defend territorial redistribution make this clear. Dietrich and Wündisch, for example, claim that territorial rights are a 'necessary condition' of self-determination and that the 'only way to restore the self-determining capacity of a group which has irrevocably lost its territory due to rising sea levels is to provide it with a surrogate territory'.[59]

Nine's caution is perhaps explained by her awareness that the conception of self-determination that she adopts is one among many. She writes that she 'takes the concept of self-determination largely for granted' and that the 'messy business of conceptualizing the right to self-determination must now be faced head-on'.[60] And indeed, in more recent work she has developed a theory of 'overlapping self-determination' through an analysis of the shared governance of resources such as rivers.[61] But her argument for territorial redistribution assumes the conception of self-determination as non-interference. As we have seen, this conception of self-determination is inadequate as a general conception of self-determination. Still, this does not give us reason to reject the proposal for territorial redistribution out of hand. All this shows is that the concept of self-determination does not make territorial redistribution *necessary*. But even if territorial redistribution is not necessary to protect self-determination as interdependence, it might still be *sufficient*. And if it is sufficient, it might also be morally preferable to alternatives that are also sufficient.

Territorial redistribution is likely to be sufficient to protect self-determination for small-island peoples. After all, territorial sovereignty is the means through which small-island peoples *currently* exercise self-determination, and we tend to think it does a good enough (even if imperfect) job. Territorial redistribution aims to preserve territorial sovereignty by altering the distribution of territorial holdings such that small-island peoples can continue to continue to exercise self-determination in the way that they currently do.

However, not just *any* territorial redistribution will be sufficient to realize self-determination as interdependence. The territory ceded to small-island peoples must make small-island states *viable* in their new territory.[62] The reason for this is that self-determination as interdependence requires that small-island peoples have a *real capacity* to exercise self-government, rather than a mere entitlement to do so. The territory that is ceded to small-island peoples must be of the right quality—it must be of the appropriate size, contain sufficient resources, and have the right physical features for small-island peoples to live in ways that reflect their values and commitments—if it is to be viable.[63] This puts a constraint on territorial redistribution: it must ensure that the viability condition is met, if it is to be sufficient to protect self-determination.

Even if the viability condition is met, there are two potential problems associated with territorial redistribution. I do not think that these problems are insurmountable, which partly explains why my overall defence of intra-state territorial autonomy is only 'cautious'. But they are real problems that have the potential to create some significant moral costs in the proposal for territorial redistribution.

The first problem is that territorial redistribution could provoke conflict. Redrawing borders is not generally a peaceful process and there are international norms against redrawing borders between states that aim to preserve peace and stability. The principle of *uti possidetis*, for example, says that states emerging out of decolonization should inherit the colonial administrative borders that existed immediately prior to independence, except where borders are changed by mutual consent.[64] Since then it has been invoked more broadly, in contexts such as the breakup of Yugoslavia, and has been interpreted more generally as prescribing that state borders should not be changed except by mutual consent.[65] This presumption against territorial redistribution in the international order plays an important role in avoiding conflict.

Of course, redrawing borders need not *always* result in conflict. There are some cases—such as the secession of Norway from Sweden or the dissolution of Czechoslovakia—where the process of territorial redistribution has been relatively peaceful. Whether or not the risk of conflict is significant will depend on how territorial redistribution occurs. If there are peaceful ways of redistributing territory—for example, through voluntary agreements made by representative states that are unlikely to provoke a significant backlash—then this problem may not be too serious. The main problem here is that the territories that are the best candidates for new states for small-island peoples—those of a decent size, with sufficient resources to make self-determination viable—are likely to be highly valued by the would-be ceding state and its people. We can expect that states would be reluctant to cede those territories. This problem may not be insurmountable: people value territory in different ways, and so it may be possible to find territories that have relatively little value for the peoples of ceding states, but which are valued highly by some small-island peoples.[66] But we should consider the potential for conflict arising from territorial redistribution carefully, and any such conflict would be a significant moral cost of territorial redistribution.

The second problem is that territorial redistribution conflicts with the rights of incumbent residents. Nine's argument aims to show that *states* can be required to cede a portion of their territory to small-island peoples. But the residents of the territory would also be deeply affected by territorial redistribution. It is highly unlikely that any presently uninhabited territory would be viable as a substitute territory for small-island states. And even if a group of residents were to decide through a referendum to sell their territory in a negative auction, as Dietrich and Wündisch suggest, there would inevitably be some dissenters.[67] Those residents would be faced with a difficult choice: either relocate to somewhere else within their state or become residents of a newly reconstituted small-island state. Both options appear to conflict within important individual rights. The first option conflicts with residents' occupancy rights to reside in the places where they have formed and pursued their life-plans.[68] The second option conflicts with residents' rights against being subject to the authority of another state. As Jonathan Quong has argued, each person has at least a presumptive claim against their political status being changed in this way without their consent.[69]

Neither of these rights are absolute. There are some circumstances in which it may be all-things-considered justifiable to relocate people against their will, such as where poverty-alleviating development projects are only possible if people are relocated.[70] But for relocation to be justified, a high bar of justification needs to be met, as Nine herself has argued.[71] Similarly, in cases of justified secession, individuals' claims against being put in a position where they must choose between relocating or having their political status changed without their consent might be all-things-considered overridden.[72] Perhaps the case of small-island states is like these cases: small-island peoples' claims to a new territory in which they can exercise their right to self-determination are strong enough to outweigh the claims of residents. This is not implausible—after all, the loss facing small-island peoples is a highly significant one. Incumbent residents of territories ceded to small-island peoples could be financially compensated in an attempt to minimize the costs that they bear, but any financial compensation is unlikely to be able to fully make up for the loss that they face.[73] Ultimately, the costs that fall on incumbent residents on the territorial redistribution proposal—which are to be regretted and minimized—may be unavoidable if self-determination for small-island peoples is to be secured.

Still, the rights of residents should figure in the balance of reasons that inform our judgement about territorial redistribution. In their discussion of development-induced displacement, Peter Penz, Jay Drydyk, and Pablo S. Bose argue that development projects should be guided by the value of non-maleficence, which involves 'choosing the course of action that minimizes harm compared to the outcomes of other courses of action'.[74] Similarly, in attempting to protect the value of self-determination for small-island peoples, we ought to choose the course of action that imposes the fewest costs on others. The conflict between territorial redistribution and the rights of residents is an important moral cost to the proposal. In order to know whether territorial redistribution could be all-things-considered justified, we need to know whether there are other ways in which small-island peoples' rights to self-determination can be satisfied that do not require residents' rights to be overridden.

Altogether, we can judge that territorial redistribution can secure self-determination for small-island peoples, so long as the territory that is redistributed meets the viability condition. But this does not suffice to show that we should endorse it. The proposal for territorial redistribution also has two important moral costs—the risk of conflict and the rights of existing residents—that, if possible, we should seek to avoid. This makes it important to investigate whether either of the alternative proposals for small-island peoples can secure self-determination while avoiding these costs.

De-Territorialized Statehood

The proposal for de-territorialized statehood is perhaps the least familiar of the three proposals. The conception of statehood that it articulates is quite far removed from the conception of statehood that figures in the contemporary international order. The de-territorialized state proposal seeks to preserve the status of small-island states as *states*, but it decouples statehood from territory. Because the standard model of statehood is closely tied to the exercise of territorial sovereignty, it involves reinterpreting the concept of statehood in fairly radical ways. Its proponents, though, argue that this modified conception of statehood can preserve meaningful forms of self-determination for small-island peoples.

Jörgen Ödalen has set out a model of the de-territorialized state for small-island peoples.[75] On Ödalen's model, small-island peoples would elect a 'government-in-exile' that could exercise a range of state-like capacities, while its citizens would be dispersed across different states or collectively relocated into one state. The de-territorialized state could 'represent [its citizens] at the international level, and protect the rights and interests of its citizens vis-à-vis their new host state (or states)'.[76] It could act as a 'trustee' for the assets of the state and use them to benefit its citizens by providing collective goods such as healthcare and social insurance.[77] Ödalen also suggests that the de-territorialized state could retain rights over the natural resource base in its former territory, including the maritime entitlements in its former territorial waters.[78] Significant resource rents could be extracted from these territorial waters through selling fishing rights and from deep-sea mining, assuming that maritime baselines could be 'frozen' under international law so that those entitlements would be protected even as the shorelines to which they are indexed recede.[79]

Some proponents of de-territorialized statehood are motivated by the idea that it is more feasible than the proposal for territorial redistribution, since they view it as unlikely that states would willingly cede their own territory. As such, they have spent considerable effort trying to demonstrate that it does not require too significant a departure from the principles of international law that govern statehood. Territorial sovereignty is not the only form of recognized sovereignty in the international order. Non-territorial oddities such as the Holy See and the Sovereign Military Order of Malta (the 'Knights Hospitaller') enjoy status as subjects of international law and exercise some state-like capacities without exercising jurisdictional authority over discrete territories.[80] Supranational institutions such as the EU are recognized as being 'functional' sovereigns. And governments-in-exile are also recognized at the international level as legitimate sovereigns of territory that they do not control in contexts of war and invasion.[81] Proponents of de-territorialized statehood have stressed these aspects of international law in order to emphasize that the de-territorialized state is not necessarily at odds with the principles of international law and may be more feasible than alternatives such as territorial redistribution.

The de-territorialized state proposal depends on a markedly different conception of self-determination to the proposal for territorialized redistribution. Ödalen is fairly explicit about this; he writes that we should adopt a 'more gradual understanding of the concept of self-determination' according to which self-determination comes in degrees.[82] He rejects Nine's claim that self-determination requires that a group has the authority to *establish justice* by exercising jurisdictional authority over a territory. Instead, he points to Buchanan's view of self-determination as cultural autonomy, according to which self-determination is about 'the freedom of a group to lead its own distinctive common life, to express its constitutive values through its own social practices and cultural forms.'[83] On this view, territorial sovereignty is 'but one, very radical, way of institutionalizing a group's right to self-determination.'[84] But Ödalen also claims that de-territorialized statehood could afford small-island peoples a measure of 'political' self-determination.[85] He argues that although small-island peoples would lose their political independence, the forms of autonomy that they could collectively exercise mean that they would still be meaningfully exercising self-determination.

As our earlier discussion of self-determination shows, Ödalen is right that Nine overemphasizes the role of independence for self-determination. But it also shows why the de-territorialized state proposal falls short of offering meaningful opportunities for self-determination. Self-determination, while not requiring total political independence, does require that the self-determining group has a *real capacity for self-government*. The de-territorialized state would enable small-island peoples to do some things that they would otherwise be unable to do—such as to provide club goods, extract rents from collectively owned resources, and advocate for themselves at the international level—but these capacities are more like the benefits that one might get from membership in a voluntary association than the core aspects of self-government. The de-territorialized state looks more like an expansion of civil society than it does a form of self-rule.[86] On the de-territorialized state proposal, the core aspects of self-government, such as the powers of jurisdictional authority, would still be held by the territorial state in which small-island peoples found themselves. As such, the de-territorialized state proposal appears to be insufficient to realize self-determination for small-island peoples.

There is, however, a stronger version of the de-territorialized state proposal that might be able to realize self-determination for small-island peoples. We can imagine a stronger version of the de-territorialized state, which does everything that Ödalen's de-territorialized state does, but also exercises *personal* jurisdictional authority over its members. Jurisdictional authority is usually exercised on a territorial basis in the contemporary international order, but it can also be exercised on a personal basis.[87] That is, authority to make and enforce laws can extend over groups of persons, as well as over geographical areas. When parents claim to exercise authority over their children, or when religious authorities claim to exercise authority over aspects of their members' lives, they do so on the basis of *who* they are, not *where* they are. Before the consolidation of the modern territorial state, authority was often exercised in this way.[88] A model of personal jurisdictional authority was also proposed by Karl Renner as a way of governing different national groups within the Austro-Hungarian Empire at the end of the nineteenth century.[89] More recently, personal forms of jurisdictional authority have been discussed as a way of resolving disputes between competing national groups that share territories, as a basis for language policy in multilingual states, and as a way of governing 'hypermobile' societies.[90]

The strong version of the de-territorialized state is loosely inspired by these models. It could perform core state functions such as taxing its citizens and regulating their conduct, providing a system of public education, operating a system of criminal justice, and so on. Of course, its jurisdiction would need to be limited to *some* degree. This is because some of the domains of authority are inevitably territorial. Think, for example, of rules regulating traffic or the movement of people during a pandemic, and functions such as town planning or land-use policy. In these domains, it is essential to coordinate the behaviour of those whose actions inevitably affect each other because they share the same space. For these territorial functions, some kind of power-sharing agreement would be necessary, which could be a matter of intergovernmental negotiation between small-island peoples and the other state(s) with which geographical space was shared.

The question of whether this strong version of the de-territorialized state would be sufficient to secure self-determination for small-island peoples depends on whether or not control over non-territorial competencies is sufficient for a 'real capacity for self-government'. In principle, self-determination as interdependence does not require exclusive control over *all* domains of public life. Ordinarily, proponents of personal models of jurisdictional authority restrict their focus to competencies such as the provision of public education or linguistic policy within a multilingual state. We can imagine more extensive forms of personal authority, but, at least in the world in which we live now, it seems doubtful that meaningful forms of self-determination could be realized on a personal basis. After all, some of the decisions that express the central commitments of a political community have territorial aspects: the regimes of property rights that it puts in place, the forms of land-use regulation that it adopts, how it secures the basic conditions of order and stability for those living side-by-side.[91] Without control over these functions, the strong de-territorialized state's prospects for realizing self-determination for small-island peoples inevitably remain limited. Still, we should not rule out the possibility that personal models of jurisdictional authority could, in principle, realize self-determination.

One problem with the stronger version of the de-territorialized state is that the more extensive its powers of personal jurisdictional authority, the more difficulties there will be in regulating the inevitable interactions between small-island peoples and those with whom they share geographical space. In a system where citizens of different states share the same territory, but are governed by different laws, pay taxes to different authorities, are protected by different police forces, and so on, there would be a serious risk of conflict. Every interpersonal dispute between those living side-by-side under different political authorities would have the character of an international dispute. Maintaining internal security would be a matter of policing the boundaries of another state's authority. Rainer Bauböck writes that a fully de-territorialized state of this kind would be a 'weird fantasy rather than a realistic utopia' and that 'it does not take much imagination to regard such a society as close to a Hobbesian state of nature'.[92] Here, proponents of the strong version of the de-territorialized state face a dilemma. Either the de-territorialized state is granted extensive powers of personal authority, in which case it is more likely to provide a real capacity for self-government, but it brings with it a significant risk of conflict; or its powers are more limited, in which case it is less likely to provide a real capacity for self-government.

Even if the strong version of the de-territorialized state could realize self-determination for small-island peoples, there are two further problems with the proposal. The first is that it may conflict with the legitimate claims of other states to exercise specifically *territorial* forms of authority. Any system of personal authority for one group implies a system of personal authority for any other group that shares the same territory.[93] The reason for this is simple: if we have a system where state A exercises control over some domain (say, education) for all and only Xs, then we cannot simultaneously have a system where state B exercises control over the same domain on a territorial basis (at least if there are Xs within B's territory). State B, instead of operating on a purely territorial basis, would necessarily have to operate on a personal basis: it would control education for only non-Xs within its territory. If a de-territorialized small-island state were to exercise control over some domains of public life, then the state in which its citizens were located would, as a result, no longer be able to exercise exclusive territorial sovereignty. This means that the strong version of the de-territorialized state proposal implies that the state in which small-island peoples would be located would also need to become a kind of de-territorialized state itself: it would have to give up exercising authority on a purely territorial basis.

If the host state was originally *entitled* to exercise jurisdictional authority on a territorial basis, then the de-territorialized state conflicts with the rights of states to exercise territorial sovereignty. To overcome this problem, we would need an account of why the state can be required to relinquish its claim to exercise territorial sovereignty and must instead govern on the basis of personality, equivalent to the argument given by Nine that states can be required to 'downsize' their territory. Perhaps such an argument can be given—it might be that the state's claim to exercise territorial sovereignty is conditional on small-island peoples being able to exercise some form of jurisdictional authority—but in the absence of such an argument, the strong version of the de-territorialized state proposal stands in conflict with legitimate claims to territorial exercises of jurisdictional authority.

The final problem with the strong version of the de-territorialized state proposal is what I call the problem of *proximate inequalities*. In his argument against personality-based language policies, Philippe Van Parijs argues that those living side-by-side but attending different schools and reading different media will end up facing sharp inequalities of opportunity.[94] We might worry that something similar would happen under the strong version of the de-territorialized state proposal, where those governed by different political authorities but living side-by-side would face unequal opportunities and significant material inequality. In the context in which Van Parijs makes this objection, part of its force derives from the fact that he is considering different national or linguistic groups within the same state. As such, the inequalities appear to violate the principle that the state should demonstrate equal concern for its citizens.[95] But in our context, the two communities under consideration would be citizens of different states. This might undercut the proximate inequalities objection: after all, we at least tolerate inequalities between territorial states—why not between de-territorialized states?

One response to this objection is a revisionary one likely to be endorsed by global egalitarians of some stripes: we should not tolerate these kinds of inequalities between states in the first place.[96] But another response has a broader appeal: it says that material inequalities between those who live side-by-side are morally relevant because proximity roughly tracks the density of social interaction, and social interaction should be conducted on terms of non-subordination.[97] Those who occupy the same territory will inevitably interact in the same economies and public spaces, and will develop thick relationships of the kind that are less likely to exist between those in territorially distinct states. Significant material inequalities between them will create stigma, mutual suspicion, and hostility, and will likely mean that the disadvantaged or minority group will be subordinated in the social interactions. This explains why the proximate inequalities that arise under the strong version of the de-territorialized state proposal are objectionable.

Altogether, we have good reason to reject both versions of the de-territorialized state proposal. The weaker, original version of the proposal is unable to meaningfully secure self-determination for small-island peoples, at least if we think that self-determination requires a real capacity for self-government. The stronger version may ultimately be able to realize self-determination for small-island peoples. But it can do so only with some significant moral costs: it brings with it the possibility of conflict; it conflicts with the host state's entitlements to exercise jurisdictional authority on a territorial basis; and it creates objectionable inequalities.

Intra-State Territorial Autonomy

Intra-state territorial autonomy would involve small-island peoples exercising more or less limited powers of territorial jurisdiction nested within another sovereign state. Intra-state autonomy arrangements can take a wide variety of forms, ranging from federal systems in states such as Belgium and Canada, through self-governing overseas territories such as French Polynesia, to the forms of tribal sovereignty exercised by Indigenous peoples in the USA.[98] And different justifications may underpin these different arrangements: some might be best justified as matter of rectificatory justice, some as a bulwark against the centralizing tendencies of states, and some as a way to promote the value of self-determination for national minorities.[99] My suggestion is that, if implemented in ways that reflect the values of small-island peoples, intra-state territorial autonomy could realize the value of self-determination for small-island peoples while minimizing the costs associated with alternatives.

Anna Stilz has recently argued that intra-state territorial autonomy can protect small-island peoples' rights to self-determination.[100] On her view, territorial rights are justified because they protect two kinds of interests that we encountered in Chapter 3: basic territorial interests (interests in using territory to secure basic needs and the essentials of a political framework that secures basic justice) and practice-based territorial interests (interests in using territory to secure particular valued economic social, cultural, and political practices, including through political self-determination).[101] We can appeal to these interests in order to determine a fair division of territory. On Stilz's view, basic territorial interests have lexical priority, and practice-based territorial interests must be balanced such that 'everyone [has] a chance to pursue practice-based projects that matter to them, so long as they do not deny anyone else the chance to do the same'.[102]

Stilz uses this framework to analyse the possible relocation of the I-Kiribati to Australia. She argues that the I-Kiribati have 'practice-based interests in using Australian territory . . . as a site in which to exercise political self-determination'.[103] She suggests that small-island peoples may have a claim to full and exclusive territorial sovereignty 'where they can be compactly settled on *unoccupied territory* and can form a *viable* state without *risk of conflict*'.[104] But in practice, as we have seen, these conditions are unlikely to be met. On Stilz's view, intra-state territorial autonomy arrangements represent a fair balance of the practice-based interests of both the I-Kiribati and Australians. Stilz's suggestion is that this could involve the I-Kiribati exercising territorial autonomy on the model of the limited form of sovereignty exercised by tribal governments in the USA.[105]

How does the proposal for intra-state territorial autonomy fare when it comes to protecting small-island peoples' rights to self-determination? This will depend to a significant degree on the specifics of the intra-state territorial autonomy arrangement. The proposal for intra-state territorial autonomy is essentially a compromise solution that aims to preserve the ability of small-island peoples to exercise self-determination while imposing some limits on their jurisdictional authority in order to minimize the costs associated with alternatives such as territorial redistribution. But properly designed, intra-state autonomy arrangements could protect both the external and internal aspects of self-determination.

Any intra-state territorial autonomy arrangement will rule out small-island peoples having exclusive powers of jurisdictional authority in every domain: this is built into the very concept of intra-state territorial autonomy. When it comes to the external aspect of self-determination, this means that small-island peoples would not enjoy total immunity from interference by outsiders. But in principle, any powers held by the partner state could be clearly specified and justified by reference to the need for such powers to protect important rights—such as the occupancy, cultural, and linguistic rights of incumbent residents—or to preserve the stability of the broader state. According to the interdependence conception of self-determination, the external aspect of self-determination involves freedom from domination, which means that small-island peoples have a right to be free from *arbitrary* interference by others. So long as the powers of the host state are clearly codified and justified in this way, and so long as small-island peoples can effectively check those powers, then the forms of interference involved in intra-state territorial autonomy need not be arbitrary. If the intra-state territorial autonomy arrangement is designed in the right way, then it can avoid domination and be consistent with self-determination.

When it comes to the internal aspect of self-determination, an intra-state territorial autonomy arrangement could give small-island peoples a broad range of positive capacities. A territorial sub-unit controlled by small-island peoples could have all of the powers of the weaker version of the de-territorialized state, such as the power to provide club goods such as healthcare and social insurance. It could also enjoy all of the powers of the stronger version of the de-territorialized state, such as the power to tax, provide public goods and services, and make and enforce law, but on a territorial rather than a personal basis. And beyond this, it could also exercise control over necessarily territorial functions, such as planning, land-use regulation, and resource management. These capacities are likely to be important for some small-island peoples, since much land in small-island states is held under customary forms of land tenure that do not treat land as a commodity.[106] As Stilz points out, intra-state territorial autonomy arrangements could enable small-island peoples to preserve these forms of tenure, and more broadly to shape public spaces in line with their own values and commitments.[107] Small-island peoples would not enjoy total control over all domains of their political life because, as we have seen, some limits on their jurisdiction would be necessary to protect the rights of incumbent residents. But the broad range of powers that they could enjoy would concern core aspects of self-governance. Under a suitably well-designed intra-state autonomy arrangement, the powers that small-island peoples would have could certainly amount to a real capacity for self-government.

At the same time, intra-state territorial autonomy could minimize the moral costs associated with alternative proposals such as territorial redistribution. It is unlikely that these costs could be eliminated entirely, at least while preserving the ability of small-island peoples to exercise self-determination. The incumbent residents of the territories marked out for small-island peoples would certainly experience significant changes. They would still have to choose between being subject to a new political authority—though not a new sovereign state—and relocating within their state. And it is unlikely that the risk of conflict over the territory handed over to small-island peoples would be eliminated entirely. But an important aim of intra-state territorial autonomy is, so far as is consistent with the self-determination of small-island peoples, to accommodate the rights of incumbent residents and to minimize the potential for conflict. Incumbent residents could have a range of constitutionally codified rights, such as rights to exemptions from new forms of land and property tenure and rights to the provision of public services in now-minority languages. If these rights were properly codified and enforced, then this might go some way to reducing the potential for conflict by minimizing the grievances between incumbent residents and relocated small-island peoples.

Still, the extent to which intra-state territorial autonomy can both secure self-determination for small-island peoples and minimize the costs imposed upon incumbent residents will depend on the specifics of any intra-state territorial autonomy arrangement. This is another reason why my defence of intra-state territorial autonomy is 'cautious'. Partly, this will be a matter of identifying a suitable territory that provides a basis for the exercise of some form of territorial autonomy by small-island peoples. There are several criteria that will be important in identifying suitable territories.

One is the functional compatibility between the territory and the goals, livelihoods, and ways of life of small-island peoples. Suitable territories might include other islands where fishing can continue to be an important part of the lives and livelihoods of small-island peoples, or where there are similar cultural and spiritual meanings associated with land—though, of course, there is a great deal of heterogeneity among small-island peoples in terms of their relationship to land.[108] Another is the political relationship between the small-island peoples and the partner state in which they are relocated. If small-island peoples were to be incorporated within a state with a lot of *de facto* power in the region, or with whom there has been a long history of domination, then this is likely to generate conditions under which there is a standing threat that the partner state will encroach upon the self-governance of small-island peoples. Given the long history of colonial domination of small-island peoples by European settlers in the Pacific—including an attempt to resettle of the people of Nauru in the 1960s due to extensive phosphate mining on the island—small-islanders may well view the prospect of being incorporated within a former colonial power such as Australia with suspicion.[109] So, it will be important to identify territory within a partner state that small-island peoples can trust and/or where small-island peoples would not be subject to a significant imbalance of *de facto* power.

Once a territory has been identified, an agreement would need to be made with the partner state about the form of self-government that small-island peoples could exercise. There are three models of intra-state territorial autonomy that could be promising options for small-island peoples. Each of these has its own drawbacks and advantages—there is no ideal solution that solves all potential problems simultaneously—and which model is most appropriate is likely to depend on the priorities of small-island peoples facing relocation.

One model is already relatively familiar in the Pacific: self-governance in 'free association' with another state.[110] Both Niue and the Cook Islands are self-governing territories in free association with New Zealand and have extensive powers of self-government. Free association on this model would involve small-island peoples having extensive rights to govern their own territory but would give the partner state powers to act on their behalf in some domains—such as defence and foreign policy—under some conditions.[111] The distinguishing feature of free association is that it would give each partner the power to unilaterally dissolve the partnership.[112] For small-island peoples, this would provide a check against the partner state overstepping its power, since they would be able to unilaterally exit the relationship of free association and gain independence. But there are also disadvantages to this model. From the perspective of the partner state, the ability of small-island peoples to unilaterally secede from the partnership may raise a concern about the security of the rights of incumbent residents. This means that it may be difficult to find a state that is willing to turn over some of its territory on these terms. From the perspective of small-island peoples, the unilateral ability of the partner state to end the relationship makes free association potentially less stable than some alternatives.

Another model is what is sometimes called 'federacy' or 'asymmetric federalism'.[113] This is the form of autonomy enjoyed by the Åland Islands (in relation to Finland) and Greenland and the Faroe Islands (in relation to Denmark). Under this form of intra-state autonomy, small-island peoples would have fairly extensive powers of self-government with relatively little influence on the partner state, and vice versa, though the precise division of competencies would be a matter for negotiation. Unlike free association, however, federacy could only be dissolved through mutual agreement. This would make the arrangement more stable and could provide both partners with greater assurances. But without the ability to unilaterally declare independence, small-island peoples would inevitably have less independent power to check overreaches by the partner state. The powers of the partner state could be clearly limited and codified in treaties and constitutions, however, and perhaps held in check by the international community.

A third model would involve small-island peoples becoming constituent units of federations.[114] This alternative would involve small-island peoples enjoying some rights of self-government, but their powers would be more limited as they would form part of a larger federal state. This model of governance would look more like the case of Hawai'i in the USA or Tasmania in Australia. The clear disadvantage of this model is that it gives small-island peoples much less extensive powers of self-government than alternatives. But there are also some advantages. Small-island peoples might be able to exercise some influence in the broader state and their closer relationship with the overall state could create more opportunities for them to benefit from redistributive policies.

There are trade-offs between these different models and possible hybrid models that could be negotiated. Ultimately, small-island peoples will need to decide for themselves which intra-state autonomy arrangement best reflects their own values and commitments. After all, the decision about what their future looks like—even if it must be negotiated with a partner state—is a decision that small-island peoples should be able to make for themselves as a matter of their own self-determination. Sometimes a distinction is drawn between 'constitutive' self-determination, which is when a group makes a choice about its own political status (as in cases of secession), and 'ongoing' self-determination, which is when a group exercises control over its common life.[115] In the case of small-island peoples, these two forms of self-determination come together: small-island peoples are already constituted as a self-governing collective, and the decision about what kind of political status they should have is one that they should collectively take as a matter of their own self-government.

The main objection that I anticipate being levied against the proposal for intra-state territorial autonomy is that it does not provide *statehood* for small-island peoples. Both territorial redistribution and the de-territorialized state seek to preserve some form of statehood for small-island peoples, though proponents of each employ a markedly different conception of statehood. An opponent of intra-state territorial autonomy might argue that so long as small-island peoples do not enjoy statehood, their right to self-determination is not satisfied. After all, they currently enjoy statehood, and are entitled to do so, and the possibility of their losing it has arisen through no fault of their own. So, we might think that any adequate response to the predicament of small-island peoples must ensure that they retain statehood.

In my view, this objection misunderstands the value of statehood. States are valuable insofar as they enable us to realize or protect morally important values, such as the value of self-determination. Particular 'political forms'—be they modern territorial states, ancient city-states, or communes—are constellations of power and authority that arise in particular conditions and purport to solve particular problems of social organization.[116] It is a mistake to treat any particular political form, such as the modern territorial state, as being intrinsically valuable or essential to the human good.[117] The value of the state depends on its capacity, under certain socio-historic conditions, to secure goods such as self-determination. Though self-determination has in recent history been closely tied to sovereign statehood, the connection between the two is not one of conceptual necessity. Our priority should not be statehood itself, but the value of self-determination. And in the context of the threat facing small-island peoples, my suggestion is that statehood is not the best way to realize the value of self-determination.

This chapter has examined the threat of 'state extinction' faced by the peoples of small-island states. Sea-level rise in small-island states presents a distinctive challenge: the self-determining status of an entire political community is under threat. In our response to the predicament of small-island peoples, we should aim to protect their rights to self-determination.

The first section of the chapter examined the concept of self-determination in greater detail and defended a view according to which self-determination involves freedom from domination from outsiders and a real capacity to exercise self-government. Then, I used this conception of self-determination as a critical tool to evaluate three proposals for the future of small-island states threatened by sea-level rise: territorial redistribution, the de-territorialized state, and intra-state territorial autonomy.

The weak version of de-territorialized statehood cannot secure self-determination for small-island peoples, and territorial redistribution and the strong version of de-territorialized statehood can do so only in ways that create some significant moral costs. Intra-state territorial autonomy could realize self-determination while minimizing these moral costs. But the defence of intra-state territorial autonomy that I have given is cautious. In order to secure self-determination and to minimize the moral costs of alternatives, intra-state territorial autonomy must be implemented in the right way. It must both minimize the costs associated with alternative proposals—by protecting the rights of incumbent residents—and it must reflect the values and commitments of small-island peoples.

Finally, it is critical to recognize that this future for small-island peoples is not inevitable. It may still be possible to prevent the inundation of small-island states with a combination of rapid and aggressive emissions reductions and *in situ* adaptation to sea-level rise. To the extent that this is possible, it is clearly preferable to any of the proposals examined here, which all involve a range of significant moral costs. Our first commitment should be to prevent the threats to the self-determination of small-island people from materializing. But there is a realistic prospect that we will fail in this collective endeavour, and in the event that we do, our collective duty to secure the value of self-determination for small-island peoples does not disappear. In such a situation, intra-state territorial autonomy—although certainly a non-ideal option—may be one promising way of securing the value of self-determination.

5
Climate Change and Labour Migration

In rural Ethiopia, smallholding farmers are battling with droughts of increasing frequency and intensity. Drought has long featured in the lives of Ethiopian smallholders, who have developed a range of methods for resisting its adverse impacts. Many engage in 'agrodiversity' (maintaining a variety of staple crops) in order to reduce the risks of drought, in contrast to the received wisdom of maximizing yields by intensively cultivating a single crop.[1] Smallholders also replace income lost due to drought by engaging in off-farm labour, such as selling firewood or charcoal.[2] And informal insurance arrangements such as the practice of *iddir*, where payments are made into a collective fund which pays out when certain shocks (such as food shortages, the death of livestock, or unexpected medical or funeral expenses) occur, are also widespread.[3]

The impacts of climate change are stretching the capacity of these risk-management strategies. Ethiopia is among the countries most vulnerable to climate change, ranking 161st out of 182 countries on the Notre Dame Global Adaptation Initiative (ND-GAIN) Index in 2022.[4] Changes in temperature and precipitation associated with climate change have damaging impacts on crop yields in Ethiopia, and those impacts are likely to become even more damaging as climate change unfolds.[5] And an overwhelming majority of Ethiopians—around 85 per cent—live in rural areas and depend on rain-fed agriculture, which means that they are especially vulnerable to climate impacts such as drought.[6] Although smallholders in Ethiopia are often able to absorb the impacts of more familiar shocks, the evidence suggests that existing strategies of risk management are insufficient in the face of 'extreme' rainfall shortages, which instead lead to a significant decrease in consumption among those already at or below the poverty line.[7]

One alternative to these traditional risk-management strategies is labour migration. When members of a household migrate and take up waged labour abroad, they can generate an additional stream of stable income through remittances.[8] In Ethiopia, the more a community is at risk of food insecurity, the more likely it is that members of that community will migrate abroad in order to assist relatives, and the greatest levels of out-migration occurred in famine years.[9] At the household level, labour migration can function as a strategy of adaptation. The case of Amina, a smallholder in South Wollo, is illustrative:

> Amina is 60 years of age and owns two oxen, nine other cattle, and 15 shoats . . . During the 1983–84 drought she sent two children (sons) to neighbouring

Djibouti to work and one of them still sends cash remittances. Amina depends heavily on this source of cash, to buy food and livestock... In the post-drought period of 2000 to 2003 she was able to increase herds from 13 to 15 cattle and three to 23 sheep, and actually was better off in 2003 than in 1997.[10]

Labour migration enabled Amina's household to diversify its sources of income, decrease household consumption, and invest in productive assets such as livestock.

This pattern of climate change risks and responses is not unique to Ethiopia. Around the world, those who rely on their local environment for their livelihoods or subsistence face growing threats from the impacts of climate change. Across a broad range of contexts, climate impacts are detrimental to livelihoods, lead to food insecurity and increased food prices, exacerbate existing structural inequalities, worsen existing poverty, and trigger new poverty traps.[11] Recently, some academics, policy-makers, and international institutions have suggested that international labour migration should be promoted as a strategy of adaptation to climate change.[12] As the case of Amina—and a growing body of social scientific evidence—shows, labour migration can make it possible for some people living in precarious environments threatened by climate change to survive, and perhaps even to thrive. Advocates of using labour migration policy as a tool of climate change adaptation have pointed out that if high-income states were to open their borders to more labour migrants from regions affected by climate change, then those facing risks associated with climate change would be better placed to protect themselves against its worst outcomes.

This chapter examines the prospects and pitfalls of using labour migration policy as a tool of climate change adaptation. I examine the question of whether, and under what conditions, states may permissibly use labour migration policy as an instrument of climate change adaptation. I argue that states may permissibly use labour migration policy as a tool of climate change adaptation—and that they may even have a duty to do so—but that they are subject to two moral constraints. First is that states must also provide acceptable alternative options for *in situ* adaptation. This is so that those who are vulnerable to climate impacts are not effectively forced to migrate. Second is that receiving states may not impose restrictive terms on would-be migrants in order to make admitting labour migrants less costly from their point of view. In the context of climate change, such terms unfairly shift the costs of adaptation onto the most vulnerable.

My focus in this chapter is on *international* labour migration, even though the evidence suggests that much labour migration relating to climate change will take place within state borders.[13] This reason for this is twofold. First, the amount of labour migration that is internal or international itself depends at least in part on the opportunities for international migration that are made available, and so it is important to know what opportunities for international migration *should* be made available in the first place. Second, the proposals for expanding opportunities for international labour migration that I examine in this chapter raise important questions about states' duties to facilitate forms of mobility that they presently restrict. Of course, there are important normative questions about intra-state movement relating to climate change as well, some of which are discussed more fully in Chapter 7.[14] But restrictions on internal freedom of movement—such as those applied under the Hukou system in China, for example—are highly controversial both in theory and in practice.[15] Unlike international movement, internal mobility is typically unrestricted, and so it should be fairly uncontroversial to suggest that states are permitted to facilitate voluntary intra-state migration in response to climate change.

Labour Migration as Climate Change Adaptation

Climate change adaptation, in the broadest sense of the term, is simply 'the process of adjustment to actual or expected climate and its effects'.[16] This includes a broad range of actions, such as the construction of levees and sea walls, the subsidization of flood insurance, the development of early warning systems for typhoons, and so on. One common strategy of climate change adaptation is to make those who face those impacts more *resilient*—that is, better able to protect themselves against the harms associated with climate impacts.[17] We are not always able to prevent people from being exposed to climate impacts, as was the aim of the adaptation interventions discussed in Chapter 3, but we can often make those who are exposed better able to cope with the threats that they face.

We know that differences in vulnerability to climate impacts are often attributable to socioeconomic status, and that those in poverty are especially at risk of harmful outcomes.[18] As such, one way to make people more resilient is to make them better off. Those who are better off are often able to use the resources they have available to them to make climate impacts less harmful—for example, by using capital to invest in irrigation systems that make them less dependent on particular patterns of rainfall. Indeed, one of the reasons why poverty and disadvantage are so troubling is that they severely inhibit our ability to enjoy secure 'functionings' under conditions of risk and insecurity.[19] This link between poverty and vulnerability helps to explain why climate adaptation goals often overlap with broader development and poverty eradication goals.[20]

We also have clear evidence that labour migration from low- to high-income states is effective in reducing poverty.[21] At the household level, labour migration can work as a strategy for increasing incomes and spreading risk. Those who move from a low- to a high-income state can increase their own income, and the remittances they send to family members can make them better off, free up resources for investment in productive assets, and provide a stable income stream that is unaffected by income shocks in the country of origin.[22] Remittances may also indirectly benefit non-migrant households, for example by stimulating local economic activity.[23] Temporary and 'circular' forms of labour migration are often particularly effective in promoting poverty reduction and development, partly because migrants who plan on returning tend to remit a higher proportion of their income.[24] Of course, labour migration is not a silver bullet for poverty reduction and development, and I discuss some of its potential downsides below. But some of its purported problems—such as that only the relatively better-off migrate or that remittances are largely spent on conspicuous consumption and foster dependency rather than aiding development—are often overstated.[25] Overall, we can be confident in the judgement that labour migration from low- to high-income states is an effective way of reducing poverty.

This evidence on the relationship between labour migration and poverty gives us good reason to believe that labour migration can function as a mechanism of climate change adaptation.[26] Those who are vulnerable to climate impacts are often vulnerable because of their poverty and disadvantage, and so we can expect that if labour migration helps to alleviate poverty and disadvantage, then it will also help to make people more resilient to climate impacts. The direct relationship between labour migration and resilience to climate impacts has been studied less extensively than the relationship between labour migration and development, but a number of studies show that labour migration can promote resilience to climate impacts. As well as the evidence from Ethiopia cited above, studies in Vietnam, Nepal, Mexico, and the Philippines; across South Asia; and in large-scale cross-national contexts have all demonstrated that labour migration can have this adaptive function.[27] These results are not unambiguous, but overall they lend support to the idea that labour migration policy can work as a tool of adaptation to climate change. Researchers working on the climate–migration nexus increasingly argue that migration is a form of adaptation to climate change, precisely because it can make those vulnerable to climate change impacts more resilient.[28]

As a result of this body of social scientific evidence, some have argued that high-income states should expand opportunities for labour migration in order to promote adaptation to climate change. In a report for the World Bank, Michael Webber and Jon Barnett have argued that developed states should enable the adaptive function of labour migration by reducing barriers to entry, encouraging firms to recruit from among those vulnerable to climate impacts, reducing the transaction costs of remittances, and providing housing and employment assistance to labour migrants.[29] The Asia Development Bank suggests that 'international migration can play a key role in fostering the resilience of households and communities'.[30] It recommends that governments negotiate regional or bilateral freedom of movement agreements and expand opportunities for both permanent and temporary labour migration. In a report for the UK government, Richard Black and his colleagues have recommended that circular migration schemes between low- and high-income countries be expanded, and that labour migration policies support those most at risk of being trapped in place due to environmental changes.[31]

Under all of these proposals, high-income states would open their borders to greater numbers of those most vulnerable to climate change impacts, in order to promote the resilience of their households and communities. We can expect that individuals who take up opportunities for labour migration would remit a portion of their increased income to their families and communities, enabling them to better protect themselves against the impacts of climate change—though no labour migrant would be obliged to do so. The most defensible versions of the proposal will also involve high-income states adopting more active policies— such as encouraging recruitment from climate-vulnerable areas, financing skills training programmes, providing housing and employment assistance to labour migrants, paying for travel costs, and capping fees on remittance transfers—to promote the adaptive function of labour migration. Different configurations of policies will likely be appropriate in different contexts, depending on (among other things) the dynamics of labour markets in receiving states and communities affected by climate impacts and the pre-existing policy frameworks that regulate labour migration. And different configurations will also be more or less demanding for the receiving state. But in general, these more demanding policy packages promise to better achieve the goal of promoting adaptation to climate change.

In order to serve their aim of promoting adaptation to climate change, labour migration policies would need to be targeted towards communities that are vulnerable to climate change impacts and that stand to benefit from labour migration. As we saw in Chapter 1, the empirical evidence suggests that climate change impacts are often intertwined with pre-existing social, economic, demographic, environmental, and political drivers of migration in complex ways, which means that it is difficult to identify particular individuals whose migration can be attributed to climate change.[32] This means that it would be unwise to make eligibility for labour migration programmes conditional on individuals proving that they need to move because of climate change: such a requirement would be effectively impossible to meet. A more promising approach would be to identify and target particular geographical and sectoral 'hotspots' for climate pressures that could be alleviated through labour migration.[33] This may prove to be over-inclusive in some cases, but labour migration has three important advantages that should negate any concerns about over-inclusivity.

First is that labour migration is likely to be a particularly effective tool of adaptation. The resources that labour migration can generate for development and poverty alleviation are significant in scale. The World Bank estimates that remittance flows are three times higher than official development assistance, and those remittances translate into significant reductions in poverty.[34] If those benefits travel to the context of adaptation—as we have good reason to expect—then they are likely to be similarly significant.[35] Labour migration may also be less likely to be maladaptive than other interventions. As we saw in Chapter 3, top-down adaptation interventions are often maladaptive because of problems such as elite capture and inequitable participation in planning.[36] Labour migration decisions taken at the household level are a form of bottom-up 'autonomous adaptation', which means that they may be less liable to become maladaptive in this way.[37]

Second is that labour migration is likely to be a 'no-regrets' form of climate adaptation.[38] As we have seen, labour migration from low- to high-income states can help to achieve other morally important goals, such as development and poverty alleviation. Of course, a labour migration policy that is tailored towards climate change adaptation may look somewhat different from a labour migration policy that is tailored towards poverty alleviation or development. But this feature of labour migration means that even if it is over-inclusive or proves to be ineffective in reducing vulnerability to climate change in some contexts, it is nonetheless likely to yield benefits in these other domains.

Third is that labour migration is likely to be particularly cheap as an adaptation strategy. It costs little to open borders to those vulnerable to climate impacts. In fact, the costs may even prove to be negative at the aggregate level, because states often derive benefits from opening their borders to labour migrants, who may fill skill shortages in the host state's labour market or sustain an aging population.[39] As such, proponents of labour migration often describe it as a 'win–win' or 'triple-win' strategy and argue that it will be a pareto-improvement for migrants, sending states, and receiving states.[40]

Still, there are some potential downsides to labour migration, and the proposal for using labour migration as a tool of adaptation should be refined in light of them. The fact that labour migration is overall beneficial for migrants, sending states, and receiving states is consistent with labour migration involving some more local costs. Some economists have argued that labour migration depresses the wages of the least advantaged workers within the receiving state.[41] This is a real concern in some sectors and contexts, but we should be careful not to overstate the effects of labour migration on domestic workers. There is also a significant degree of 'complementarity' in the skills profiles of labour migrants and domestic workers—which means that they do not usually compete for the same jobs—and decreases in the wages of domestic workers are mostly driven by the declining power of unions and structural reforms in the economy that favour capital over labour, not labour migration.[42] Still, there may be some local costs as a result of increased labour migration, particularly on previous cohorts of immigrants who compete in the same markets as incoming labour migrants.[43] Where there are such costs, increased labour migration should be paired with broader redistributive policies—such as investments in education and skills training, increases in public sector employment, and labour reforms that increase the power of workers—to ensure that they do not fall upon the shoulders of the least advantaged.[44]

Even economists who stress the impacts of labour migration on the wages of domestic workers typically agree that the aggregate benefits of labour migration offset the costs to domestic workers, and so such programmes can be financed through taxes on the gains made by firms that benefit from labour migration.[45]

Another cost that we might be worried about falls on those who stay behind. The emigration of those with highly valued skills or who provide important care services may create a 'brain drain' or 'care drain' in stayee communities.[46] As with the effects of labour migration on the wages of domestic workers, this is a real concern in certain sectors and contexts, but as a general phenomenon it is less widespread than is often assumed.[47] Skilled emigration is also often accompanied by a 'brain gain', where remittances enable investments in education or where returning migrants share knowledge.[48] And here too, there are policies that states can adopt—such as retaining skilled workers by increasing salaries, encouraging diasporic networks through dual nationality, encouraging men to take on care-giving responsibilities at home, enabling migrant workers to bring dependent family members with them, and investing in the provision of institutional care services—that limit the costs of brain and care drain without sacrificing the benefits of labour migration.[49] The most defensible proposal for using labour migration as a tool of climate adaptation would involve receiving states financing policies such as these that limit the effect of brain or care drain, so that significant costs are not imposed on already disadvantaged stayee communities.[50] In contexts where the costs of brain or care drain cannot be effectively limited, then this cost should count against the proposal. There is a further question about whether this cost provides a good justification for states to continue to restrict immigration from would-be sending states.[51] But even if it does, then this only limits the scope of the proposal to promote labour migration as a form of climate adaptation, rather than undermining it altogether.

A final concern involves the gendered dynamics of labour migration. Gender affects who migrates, under what conditions, and for what purposes.[52] One way in which gender affects the dynamics of labour migration is through gender norms that affect household migration decisions, which often confine women to domestic roles while men engage in waged labour. In Ethiopia, women's mobility decreased while men's mobility increased under conditions of drought, because migration among men was primarily associated with waged labour whereas migration among women was primarily associated with marriage, which is difficult to finance during a drought.[53] Another way in which gender affects the dynamics of labour migration is through occupational segregation in labour markets, where gender norms affect which jobs are effectively open to women and men. These norms are especially important in the context of labour migration, since labour migration tends to involve a self-reinforcing cycle in which labour migrants follow in the footsteps of previous successful migrants.[54] So, we see starkly gendered divisions in labour markets: among Hispanic migrants in the USA, for example, a significant majority of those working in the construction and agricultural sectors are men, while a significant majority of those working in the domestic services sector are women.[55]

Given these dynamics, we might be concerned that the proposal for using labour migration as a tool of climate change adaptation will replicate traditional gendered divisions of labour—both within households and within labour markets more broadly. This is also a real concern, but it should not lead us to abandon the proposal altogether. Even if migration decisions taken within the household are influenced by gender norms that confine women to particular roles—either domestic roles or roles that involve waged labour—this does not give us a good reason to restrict labour migration opportunities that would otherwise be granted. Limiting opportunities for migration on this basis would not be an effective way to combat harmful gender norms—those norms would still pervade household decision-making and limiting labour migration would only serve to foreclose one potentially valuable option for those who are seeking to protect themselves against climate impacts. Nor does this give us good reason to attempt to intervene in migration decisions taken within the household in an attempt to disrupt the role of gender norms. Even if well-intentioned, any such intervention would involve an objectionable and imperialist form of interference—which Serene J. Khader calls 'missionary feminism'—that suppresses, rather than enhances, the voices of the women with most at stake.[56]

What receiving states *can* do, however, is take active steps to ensure that the labour market opportunities that they create undermine, rather than reinforce, the gendered dynamics of labour markets. Negatively, this would involve the aggressive enforcement of anti-discrimination policies designed to ensure that labour market opportunities are both formally and effectively open to all. Positively, this would involve policies that subvert the gender dynamics of labour markets, such as incentives for firms that recruit more women and subsidies for care services that enable women to enter the labour market.[57] In these ways, the gendered dynamics of labour migration would not be uncritically replicated through the proposal for using labour migration policy as a tool of climate adaptation. Rather, the proposal could be used as an opportunity to address—even if only in a limited way—the gendered inequalities of the international labour market.

Labour Migration and the Right to Stay

The evidence suggests that labour migration can increase resilience to climate change. And properly calibrated, labour migration policies can promote adaptation to climate change and their downsides can be limited. Should we then endorse the adoption of labour migration policies that encourage labour migration from climate-vulnerable areas to high-income states? In answering this question, it is instructive to turn to an analogous debate about the role of labour migration policy in the project of tackling global poverty. This debate provides a useful entry point for our analysis, but as we will see, the context of climate change alters its moral terrain.

Political philosophers tend to agree that there is a duty to alleviate global poverty, though many disagree about the grounds, character, and extent of that duty. In debates about the relevance of this duty for migration policy, Kieran Oberman has argued that states may not permissibly use migration policy as a means to address global poverty, because doing so would involve violating a 'right to stay' held by those who would need to migrate in order to alleviate their (or their household's) poverty.[58] Oberman argues that we have a powerful interest in being able to remain where we live, which is underpinned by at least three values: freedom of movement (including the freedom *not* to move), cultural membership, and territorial attachment.[59] If we use migration policy to address poverty, rather than more direct forms of aid, then we force people to migrate in order to alleviate their poverty, and thereby to sacrifice these morally important interests, which amounts to a violation of their right to stay.

If Oberman is right, then something similar could be said of using labour migration policy as a tool of climate change adaptation: using labour migration policy as a tool of climate change adaptation is impermissible, because it violates the rights to stay held by those vulnerable to climate impacts. I argue, however, that this conclusion does not follow from a closer examination of Oberman's argument. Oberman's argument can be upheld in the context of climate adaptation. But properly understood, it does not rule out using labour migration policy as a tool of climate adaptation.

In its original context, Oberman's argument relies on a claim that is likely to be controversial: that high-income states are constrained in how they alleviate poverty abroad by the 'right to stay'. To say that this claim is likely to be controversial is not to say that it is incorrect—I remain agnostic on that point here—but this claim bears on the prospects for the success of the argument when applied to the context of climate change adaptation. Although Oberman's argument faces an important challenge in its original context, that challenge does not arise when it is applied to the context of climate change adaptation, which means that it can be upheld.

The basic interests that Oberman argues underlie the right to stay—freedom of movement, cultural membership, and territorial attachment—clearly have significant moral weight. In my view, Oberman is right to suggest—as theorists of territorial rights have recently pointed out—that we have powerful and non-substitutable interests in being able to remain in the places where we form and pursue our life-plans.[60] The important question for our purposes, however, is what duties the right to stay imposes on would-be admitting states. For Oberman, the right to stay is a *human right*, which is violated when people have no reasonable alternative apart from migrating.[61] He takes this to mean that all states, including those contemplating how to discharge their duties to the global poor, have positive duties to ensure that the right to stay is fulfilled.[62]

For some, however, Oberman's claim that these interests ground a human right will appear too strong, at least if a 'human right to stay' means that outsiders are under a positive duty to enable those in poverty to stay where they are, rather than a mere negative duty not to expel or remove them. On some views, there is a 'division of labour' between states when it comes to human rights protection.[63] In the first instance, states are responsible for protecting and fulfilling the human rights of their own members. The failure of a state to protect and fulfil the rights of its members is a matter of international concern that may give rise to *pro tanto* duties on the part of the international community to act, for example by assisting states that lack capacity or interfering with states that lack will.[64] But other states are not themselves required to protect and fulfil the rights of non-members abroad—only to *respect* those rights by not violating negative duties that stem from them.[65] If we adopt this view, then states that expand opportunities for those in poverty to migrate do not violate the right to stay. Those in poverty are *already* in a situation where they do not have any reasonable options, after all. States that expand opportunities to migrate do not, in so doing, create or exacerbate the conditions of poverty facing the would-be migrant. So, they do not violate a negative duty that stems from the right to stay by expanding opportunities to migrate.

Still, we might think that if states have a duty of *justice* to alleviate poverty, they must discharge that duty in ways that pay due regard to the interests of the global poor. If states are to discharge their duties of justice to the global poor, they should do so in ways that do not require the global poor to sacrifice some morally important interests, such as their interests in being able to stay where they live. After all, duties of justice give their beneficiaries something that they are owed by right, not something that can be made conditional on them sacrificing other morally important interests. Even if the right to stay is not a human right, or even if a 'human right to stay' does not mean that states have positive duties to enable the global poor to stay where they live, the fact that poverty alleviation is a duty of justice means that states that are required to perform it must do so in a way that does not require the poor to sacrifice morally important interests.

This response explains why rich states may not require the poor to sacrifice their interests in staying where they live, but it leaves Oberman's argument open to an important challenge. This challenge comes from those who claim that our duties to the poor are only duties of justice, rather than duties of charity, when we are *responsible* for their plight.[66] The distinction between duties of justice and duties of charity is itself a matter of disagreement, but one popular gloss is that duties of charity are imperfect duties, meaning that we have some discretion about when and how they are to be performed, and they do not provide grounds for complaint when they are not discharged.[67] If we take this view then, at least where they are not responsible for it, rich states should enjoy some discretion about how to discharge their duties to alleviate global poverty. The poor do not have grounds for complaint if rich states only offer them opportunities to alleviate their poverty through migration, since the alleviation of their poverty is not something that they are owed by rich states as a matter of justice.

If these two claims—first, that states do not violate the human right to stay by expanding opportunities for migration, and second, that states are entitled to exercise discretion about how and when to discharge their duties to the poor—are correct, then it appears that states are morally permitted to choose to address global poverty through immigration policy (and only through immigration policy). That being said, it remains an open question whether Oberman's argument ultimately succeeds or fails, because there are important counter-arguments available to him. For instance, he might argue that using immigration policy to tackle global poverty goes beyond the limits of the discretion that imperfect duties afford us. Or he might contest the claim that we only have duties of justice to the global poor when we are responsible for their plight. Or he might argue that rich states *are* responsible for global poverty, at least in many cases—perhaps because of the history of colonial exploitation that has structured development processes or because of the role of rich states as 'rule-makers' in a global economic order that keeps some states chronically underdeveloped.[68] The important point here is not the ultimate success of Oberman's argument, but rather that it is open to contestation on the grounds that the would-be admitting states are not responsible for the conditions of poverty that face the global poor.

This is important because in the otherwise analogous case of climate change adaptation, would-be admitting states are clearly responsible for the plight of those who need to adapt. It is a basic feature of adaptation that it only arises as a need in response to the threats and risks associated with climate change, which are largely the effect of the energy-intensive economies of high-income states in the Global North.[69] Unlike in the case of poverty, there is no real debate to be had about whether the causes of the need for adaptation are endogenous or exogenous. Those most vulnerable to climate change are, by and large, those least responsible for it, and so those who need to adapt to climate change are responding to conditions imposed upon them by others. The upshot of this is that the moral duty to promote adaptation to climate change is a duty of justice—not a duty of charity—*even* on those views which maintain that we only have duties of justice when we are responsible for the plight of those who need our assistance. Whatever its prospects for success in the case of poverty, when it is applied to the case of climate change adaptation, Oberman's argument can be upheld.

This would appear to imply that the proposal for using labour migration as a tool of adaptation is impermissible. Since states discharging their duty to promote climate adaptation are constrained by the right to stay, and since using labour migration as a tool of climate adaptation violates the right to stay, states may not use labour migration policy as a tool of climate adaptation. But to get a full sense of what the right to stay implies for the proposal to promote labour migration as a strategy of climate adaptation, we need to distinguish between a strong and a weak interpretation of Oberman's argument. At some points, Oberman makes the strong claim that it is impermissible for states to use immigration policy as a tool for poverty alleviation at all, at least where there are possible alternatives. He writes that 'immigration should not be used to address poverty when there are alternatives available'.[70] At other points, he makes the weaker claim that it is impermissible for states to structure the options available to the global poor such that they have no reasonable poverty-alleviating alternatives to migration. He claims that 'a migration-based approach to global poverty *that does not seek to assist desperately poor people in their home state* . . . violates the human right to stay' and that 'when rich states rely on migration to address poverty, *instead of searching for alternatives*' they violate the right to stay.[71]

These claims are importantly different, and only the weaker claim follows from Oberman's argument. The right to stay imposes constraints on the behaviour of would-be receiving states, but it does not always rule out using immigration policy to tackle global poverty. This is because of the sense in which the poor are 'forced' to migrate. They are forced to migrate not in the sense that they are subject to direct threats of coercion, but rather in the sense that they *lack acceptable alternatives* to migration.[72] Those who are put in a position where they must migrate in order to alleviate their poverty have no effective choice but to do so.[73]

The upshot of this is that Oberman's argument does not rule out using labour migration policy as a tool of climate adaptation. It only means that states must *also* provide acceptable alternative options, so that the vulnerable are not forced to migrate in order to successfully adapt. So long as states provide acceptable alternative options that enable the vulnerable to stay where they live if they choose, they can permissibly also offer opportunities to migrate. The right to stay is only violated when states structure the options available to the vulnerable so that they have no acceptable alternatives to migration that enable them to adapt where they are. But this does not rule out using labour migration policy as one tool among many in the project of climate change adaptation. This is important, because some people may prefer to take up opportunities for labour migration rather than to remain where they live. For many would-be migrants, what Valeria Ottonelli and Tiziana Torresi call a 'migration project' is a central part of a broader life-plan.[74] Adopting immigration policies that seek to address vulnerability to climate change, among other alternatives, could be one way of enabling such projects.

Of course, exactly when alternatives are 'acceptable' is difficult to establish. For one thing, there are a variety of different adaptation interventions that may be relevant to contexts in which labour migration is a viable option—such as encouraging crop diversification, expanding local employment opportunities, putting in place social safety nets, expanding access to credit, and even direct cash transfers—and the heterogeneity of climate impacts and the circumstances of vulnerable communities makes it difficult to determine in the abstract which options are appropriate. For another, different theories of justice in adaptation will set different normative standards for adaptation policy: for example, they will tell us whether adaptation must protect certain capabilities, meet certain standards of procedural justice, make those vulnerable to climate impacts as well-off as they would have been in the absence of climate change, and so on.[75]

But even in the absence of such a theory, we can establish a rough critical standard for judgements about when alternatives are acceptable. Alternative adaptation options need not be *fully* just—only *sufficiently* just—for us to treat labour migration decisions as voluntary decisions. A standard of full background justice is far too demanding as a general standard for assessing the voluntariness of decisions. Such a standard would render all decisions made against a background of injustice involuntary, which—if we believe that contemporary societies involve widespread injustices—would effectively render all decisions involuntary.[76] Instead, we should adopt a more minimal standard for making judgements of voluntariness. Ottonelli and Torresi and Serena Olsaretti both suggest a standard of basic needs.[77] In my view, we should understand 'basic needs' fairly capaciously here, so as to count as involuntary cases where decisions are made to avoid having to sacrifice important interests—interests such as preserving family and community ties, cultural membership, and so on—rather than merely survival needs. This standard captures the sense in which those who are put in a position where they must choose between sacrificing these important interests and foregoing successful adaptation to climate change are forced to migrate. On this standard, states must ensure that there is some alternative option available to would-be migrants which does not require them to sacrifice any basic needs, understood in these broad terms.

Where does this leave us with respect to the place of labour migration policy in climate change adaptation? Labour migration policy, we know, can be an effective tool of adaptation. But Oberman's argument shows that states cannot permissibly use *only* labour migration policy to promote adaptation to climate change. Doing so would fail to pay due regard to the morally important interests that those vulnerable to climate change have in being able to remain where they live. States should also provide adaptation interventions in climate-vulnerable areas that give those who want to stay an effective ability to do so. This does not rule out using labour migration as a tool of climate change adaptation—it only rules out making successful adaptation *conditional* on taking up opportunities for labour migration. In other words, if labour migration is to be used as a tool of climate change adaptation, it must be one tool among many, and those who are vulnerable to climate change must be offered real opportunities for adaptation where they are.

A Duty to Promote Labour Migration?

So far, we have seen that high-income states are permitted to use labour migration policy as a tool of climate change adaptation, so long as they also provide *in situ* alternatives for adaptation. But beyond this, I also want to suggest that they may have a *duty* to use labour migration policy to promote climate adaptation, at least in some circumstances. The justification for this claim stems from the fact that labour migration may be a particularly cheap and effective form of adaptation to climate change.

Since the overall budget for adaptation is limited, adaptation interventions should be designed to be cost-effective. We should aim for our overall package of adaptation interventions to fulfil our duties of justice to promote adaptation as fully as we can. Given that labour migration appears to be a particularly cheap and effective form of adaptation to climate change, we can expect that it will take up relatively little of any overall budget for adaptation while providing significant adaptive benefits. The more opportunities for labour migration are taken up, the less need there will be for other, more expensive and less effective, forms of climate adaptation. As such, high-income states have at least a *pro tanto* duty to offer opportunities for labour migration as a form of adaptation to climate change. They have this duty because expanding opportunities for labour migration will take up relatively little of the overall budget, and so will enable states to discharge more fully their more general duties to promote adaptation to climate change.

But the claim that states have a duty to use labour migration policy as a tool of climate adaptation depends on three conditions. First, it depends on the claim that labour migration is cost-effective holding true. Given what we know about the way in which labour migration reduces poverty, the links between poverty alleviation and resilience to climate change, and the costs associated with other forms of adaptation, we do have good reason to believe that labour migration will be cost-effective. But ultimately, research on the relationship between labour migration and climate adaptation is still in its infancy, and further research will be needed to determine how confidently we can make this claim.

Second, it depends on the claim that other moral values do not override considerations of cost-effectiveness. Cost-effectiveness is an important consideration when it comes to selecting policies, but other moral values will also bear on which policies are acceptable. For example, we ought to ensure that policies targeted at ameliorating the condition of those affected by climate impacts do not express disrespect or compromise their standing as equals.[78] It is for this reason that the duty to promote labour migration is only a *pro tanto* duty.

Finally, the third condition is that there is a scarcity of adaptation finance. The overall costs of adaptation are difficult to measure, but one review suggests that they are likely to be somewhere between $25 billion and $100 billion per year, with some estimates being even less optimistic.[79] Although significant pledges for adaptation finance have been made—the international community has pledged $100 billion annually through the Green Climate Fund—actual contributions have fallen significantly short. In total, only around $10 billion has been contributed since the fund's inception in 2010, meaning there is a significant scarcity of adaptation finance.[80]

Of course, the scarcity of the overall budget for adaptation is not a fixed constraint. It is an artefact of the unwillingness of high-income states to contribute enough to adaptation finance. Regardless of their attitude towards using labour migration as a tool of climate change adaptation, states clearly have a duty to increase their contributions to adaptation finance. It is only by doing so that they will come close to being able to discharge their duties of justice to those vulnerable to climate change impacts. But if states were willing to *radically* increase their contributions, such that there was no longer a scarcity of adaptation finance at all, then it would be permissible for them to ignore considerations of cost-effectiveness and exercise discretion about whether or not to offer opportunities for labour migration as a form of adaptation. In circumstances of an abundance of climate adaptation finance, there would no longer be a principled reason to suggest that states have a duty to offer opportunities for labour migration as a form of climate adaptation, at least on the assumption that states have a more general discretionary right to exclude would-be immigrants.

If this is correct, then the duty that high-income states have is a disjunctive duty: they have a duty *either* to offer opportunities for labour migration as a form of adaptation (alongside *in situ* alternatives), borne of considerations of cost-effectiveness that bind them within a context of scarcity, *or* to increase the overall budget for adaptation to such a degree that they no longer need be constrained by considerations of cost-effectiveness. But until and unless states do radically increase their contributions, they have at least a *pro tanto* duty to offer opportunities for labour migration as a form of climate change adaptation (alongside *in situ* alternatives).

Fair Terms for Labour Migration as Climate Adaptation

If the foregoing arguments are correct, then labour migration policy may play an important role in adaptation to climate change. And labour migration is also likely to be attractive from the point of view of states that seek to fill labour shortages in key sectors or sustain an aging population. The economies of many industrialized democracies increasingly rely on the 'non-standard' forms of labour performed mainly by migrant workers.[81] But some have recently criticized proposals for promoting labour migration for precisely this reason. Romain Felli argues that the proposal to promote labour migration places the onus to adapt on individuals and configures labour power in ways that serve the interests of capital.[82] As he puts it, promoting labour migration as a strategy of climate adaptation involves 'dragging even more individuals into capitalist relations of production' and configuring labour power 'in ways that are as little threatening to the accumulation of capital as possible'.[83]

In response to this criticism, it is first important to note that if states abide by the constraint that I have articulated above—that is, if they put in place sufficient alternative options for adaptation *in situ*—then the onus to adapt is no longer placed on individuals. If states fund effective local adaptation interventions alongside promoting labour migration, then no one needs to be 'dragged' into the labour market against their will. Some people may choose to take up opportunities to migrate—particularly those for whom a 'migration project' is an important part of their life-plan—but their choice to do so would be a genuinely voluntary one. It would be made against a background of acceptable alternative options that would enable them to stay where they are, if they so choose.

This criticism does, however, raise an important point about the *terms* under which labour migrants are admitted to high-income states. Part of the reason why labour migration is attractive to receiving states is that they can impose restrictive terms on labour migrants, which ensure that they maximize the benefits of labour migration and minimize its costs. Receiving states often restrict migrant workers' labour rights such that they are unable to join trade unions or change employer; restrict access to social rights such as social security, pensions, and public healthcare; and restrict access to family reunification.[84] These restrictions help to explain Felli's concern about the configuration of labour power under the proposal to promote labour migration as a form of climate change adaptation.

In my view, receiving states may not permissibly restrict the rights of labour migrants in order to make labour migration less costly from their point of view. This is not because would-be migrants cannot voluntarily accept such terms, but because in the context of climate change adaptation, such restrictions unfairly shift the costs of adaptation onto the most vulnerable. In defending this claim, my focus is on temporary labour migration in particular. Temporary labour migration is particularly relevant for the context of climate change adaptation, since the climate impacts that generate the need for adaptation are often seasonal or intermittent in nature.[85] And restrictive terms are often seen as most justifiable in the case of temporary labour migration, since permanent migrants are usually thought to acquire a claim to equal citizenship over time.[86] If my argument can demonstrate that restrictive terms cannot be justified even in the case of temporary labour migration, then this gives us good reason to think that restrictions will be unjustifiable in other cases as well.

Empirical research on migration policy suggests that there is a trade-off between the rights that temporary migrant workers enjoy and the overall number of temporary workers that are accepted: the more expansive the set of rights, the lower the number of temporary workers.[87] Given the contribution to poverty alleviation and development made by labour migration, some economists have argued that trade-offs between rights and numbers can be justified, though they vary in the trade-offs that they find acceptable. Eric Posner and Glen Weyl's rather extreme proposal is that we should 'make the U.S. more like Qatar' by significantly restricting the basic rights of migrant workers and accepting the existence of a 'caste system' between migrant workers and citizens.[88] Branko Milanovic makes the more moderate claim that some rights restrictions, including the introduction of lower 'tiers' of citizenship, are justifiable.[89] Perhaps the most modest version of the proposal comes from Martin Ruhs, who argues that some limited restrictions on means-tested benefits can be justified, that employment may be restricted to a particular sector (but not to a particular employer), and that rights to family reunion can be restricted only if temporary migrants do not meet a minimum earnings threshold.[90]

Some rights restrictions are unjustifiable in any context, because they expose temporary workers to significant risks of abuse. Abuse is widespread within many temporary migration schemes. For example, live-in caregivers in Canada face wage theft and violence, and construction workers in Gulf states under the Kafala system have their passports removed and are extorted for 'debts' owed to recruitment agencies.[91] The position of vulnerability that temporary migrant workers occupy means that they are exposed to the dominating power of unscrupulous employers, who can credibly wield the threat of deportation against them.[92] Some rights, such as core labour rights, will need to be safeguarded to protect against abuses such as these.[93]

But we need not determine precisely which rights must be guaranteed here, because the claim that I defend here would preclude even more minimal restrictions. That claim is that in the context of climate adaptation, it is impermissible for states to restrict the rights of temporary workers in order to make accepting greater numbers less costly for themselves. I remain agnostic here on whether some trade-offs may be justified in other contexts, but in the context of climate adaptation, even more minimal trade-offs of the kind that Ruhs suggests cannot be justified.

Ordinarily, the debate about restrictions on the rights of temporary migrant workers focuses on whether temporary migrants can voluntarily accept the terms offered to them. Economists often appeal to the 'revealed preferences' of temporary migrants—who do in fact accept such terms—as evidence of their voluntary acceptance.[94] The problem with this is that the willingness of temporary migrants to accept such terms is often a result of the fact that the alternatives available to them—such as a life of desperate poverty—are so dire.[95] Against a background of unacceptable alternatives, it is unreasonable to interpret the willingness of labour migrants to accept such terms as an expression of genuinely voluntary choice. But in situations in which migration really is voluntary, perhaps would-be migrants can waive at least some rights. On Robert Mayer's view, for example, so long as would-be temporary migrant workers 'negotiate from a position of sufficiency', then 'yielding certain rights in exchange for better pay and adventure' is unobjectionable.[96]

How does this bear on the situation of those adapting to climate change? At first glance, it appears that those vulnerable to climate impacts are akin to those in poverty, in that they need to migrate in order to ameliorate the dire conditions they face. Their 'choice' is made against a background of unacceptable alternatives, and so we cannot treat it as voluntary. But if—as I have argued that they must—states provide real opportunities for adaptation *in situ*, then would-be migrants would have acceptable alternatives. Under such conditions, perhaps those vulnerable to climate impacts really can voluntarily waive some rights. Temporary labour migration, even under restrictive conditions, may well be chosen voluntarily, given that for at least some would-be migrants, the 'migration project' that figures in their life-plan is explicitly temporary in character and oriented towards the home state rather than the receiving state.[97] Perhaps in some cases, some of those adapting to climate change really could voluntarily accept restricted regimes of rights.

But whether or not restrictive terms are voluntarily accepted is not the only basis upon which to judge whether they are unjust. Another standard is that of *fairness*. Fairness better explains why it is impermissible for states to offer restrictive terms to temporary labour migrants, at least where temporary migration schemes are a tool of climate adaptation, rather than merely an agreement for mutual advantage or an instrument of charity.

As we have seen, the duty to promote climate change adaptation is a duty of justice that arises as a result of the actions of high-emitting agents who have brought about the problem of climate change. The costs of the duty to promote climate change adaptation, including through labour migration, should be shared on fair terms. Of course, what terms are 'fair' is a matter of significant disagreement. Some argue that the costs of adaptation should be distributed according to historic responsibility for climate change, some argue that they should be distributed according to ability to bear those costs, some argue that they should be distributed according to a beneficiary pays principle, and some argue that a hybrid approach is appropriate.[98] In Chapter 8, I examine these disagreements more closely.

For the moment, however, we need not settle these debates. This is because as a matter of mid-level principle, these competing views generate what Henry Shue has called a 'core practical convergence' on who should bear the costs of adaptation.[99] Of course, there will be some 'peripheral theoretical divergence' about exactly which states are required to bear which costs for adaptation, depending on which principle, or combination of principles, we adopt.[100] But on any plausible conception of fairness in sharing the costs of adaptation, the high-income states that are candidates for accepting labour migrants will be required to bear the lion's share of the costs, whether because they bear the greatest responsibility for climate change, because they have derived the most benefits from it, or simply because they are most able to bear those costs. Those most vulnerable to the impacts of climate change, by contrast, will be required to bear at most minimal burdens, whether because of their lack of responsibility for climate change, because of the relatively few benefits that they have derived from it, or because of their relative inability to bear those costs. This convergence is not accidental—it arises because contribution, benefit, and capacity often travel together. As Shue points out, 'those who contributed to the problem of excessive emissions thereby both benefitted more than others and became better able to pay than most others'.[101] According to one attempt to quantify how the burdens of adaptation should be shared on the basis of a combination of these principles, the Least Developed Countries (LDCs) should only be required to bear 1.8 per cent of the costs of adaptation collectively, even on the conservative assumption that states should not be held responsible for emissions before 1990.[102]

With this standard of fairness in mind, it is easy to see why states that offer restrictive terms to would-be migrant workers in order to reduce the costs that they bear act wrongly. By restricting the rights available to migrant workers, receiving states shift the costs of adaptation onto the most vulnerable, who must themselves bear significant costs—for example, the costs of the risk of facing unemployment without social insurance, or the costs of using their own financial resources to support family members who would otherwise be eligible for public benefits. Given that states have duties to share the costs of adaptation on fair terms, and given that competing conceptions of fairness converge on the principle that high-income states should bear the overwhelming share of the costs of adaptation, shifting the costs of adaptation onto the most vulnerable is patently unfair. Note that this does not mean that those vulnerable to climate change impacts cannot be required to bear *any* costs—here I leave open the question of precisely what costs they can be required to bear. But imposing costs upon the least advantaged *in order that* the most advantaged can reduce their own burden violates the demands of any reasonable view of fairness. It would, to borrow a phrase from Shue, be akin to asking the poor to pawn their blankets so that the rich can keep their jewellery.[103] Restrictive terms for labour migration as a form of adaptation can thus be ruled out on grounds of fairness.

This chapter has examined the role that labour migration should play in the broader project of adaptation to climate change. Given that we have good evidence to suggest that labour migration can help to build resilience to climate change, it has begun to be promoted as a tool of adaptation to climate change. I examined the role that labour migration can play in adaptation to climate change and set out the most defensible version of this proposal. I then argued that states may permissibly use labour migration as a tool of climate change adaptation, but only if they also offer adaptation alternatives *in situ*. If they fail to do so then they make successful adaptation conditional on taking up opportunities for labour migration, which fails to pay due regard to the interests that those vulnerable to climate impacts have in being able to stay where they live. I also argued that states may have a duty to provide opportunities for labour migration, given that it may be a cheap and effective way to promote adaptation in the context of a scarce adaptation budget. Finally, I argued that states may not restrict the rights of migrant workers in order to make accepting would-be migrant workers less costly from their point of view. This is not because would-be migrants can never voluntarily accept such terms, but because such terms unfairly shift the costs of adaptation onto the most vulnerable.

If the arguments that I have presented in this chapter are correct, then the labour migration policies that are morally justified will look quite different from those that have been proposed by international institutions, policy-makers, and academics so far. But fair opportunities for adaptation to climate change are something that high-income states owe to the most vulnerable, not something that they can make conditional on their deriving benefits from it.

6
Climate Change and the Refugee Regime

Delmira de Jesús Cortez Barrera was born in El Paste in El Salvador, about a mile from the Guatemalan border.[1] Until 2012, she lived there with her family, who were day labourers working on bean and maize plantations. But after a coffee blight, repeated storms, and a drought led to massive reductions in crop yields, their work dried up. Cortez moved to the city of Ahuachapán to take up work in a brick factory. There, she encountered the *maras*—violent transnational criminal gangs involved in drug trafficking, extortion, and protection rackets. One day, after she had lived in the city for two years, Cortez's husband was taken from her home and executed in broad daylight by a hitman. With nothing to return to in El Paste, she moved with her infant son to the outskirts of San Salvador. Now, she sells *pupusas* on the street for $7 a day. At the end of the road where she works, teenagers stand guard for the gang, and in her apartment building in San Marcos, gang members collect protection payments.

Cortez has resolved to move to the USA. Like many others fleeing Central America, she is unlikely to be received as a refugee. Gang violence has flourished in the region in the aftermath of civil wars—in which the USA played an important role through Cold War-era coups and proxy wars—but those who flee are not usually granted refugee status.[2] The deprivation brought by climate change, through impacts such as drought and crop blight, makes many Central Americans easy targets for the *maras*. Many of those who flee engage in undocumented migration, either by using clandestine smuggling routes to avoid detection by border forces or more openly through the so-called migrant caravans travelling via Mexico that have sparked a fierce backlash of repressive detention and family separation policies in the USA.[3] As a result, climate change has been described as the 'unseen driver' behind the caravans.[4] As we will see, the relationship between climate change and refugee movement is complex and indirect. But as the impacts of climate change accelerate, we can expect the connections between climate change and refugee movement to be magnified.

This chapter examines the place of the refugee regime in responding to climate displacement. The first part of the chapter reconstructs the normative logic of the refugee regime and examines the ways in which climate change interacts with refugee movement. I defend an interpretation of the refugee regime that I call the *membership view* against the *persecution view* and the *basic needs view*. Then, I examine several ways in which climate change interacts with refugee movement, including through its relationship to conflict, deprivation, and disasters. The second part of the chapter analyses some of the dysfunctions in the refugee regime that are exacerbated in the context of climate change. I examine the definition of the refugee in international law, the deterrence paradigm in international refugee policy, and the maldistribution of the costs of refugee protection between states. Taken together, this analysis gives us an account of the role that the refugee regime should play as part of our broader response to climate displacement and the ways in which the refugee regime needs to be reformed in order to play its part.

It is also important to clarify what this chapter is not, since my usage of the concept of the 'refugee' may invite some confusion. My aim here is not to set out a theory of the normative status of 'climate refugees'. From a legal point of view, that term is somewhat misleading, since climate impacts themselves do not provide grounds for the ascription of refugee status under international law.[5] Often, however, the term is used to suggest that a group of people identified as 'climate refugees' *should* be granted international protection under the auspices of a new international climate refugee treaty. In Chapter 2 I argued against this proposal, on the basis that it depends on an unhelpfully idealized picture of climate displacement. So, my aim here is not to propose or defend a special normative status for climate refugees. Rather, it is to investigate what role the refugee regime—the body of rules and norms governing refugee status in the international order—might play in responding to climate displacement.

The Refugee Regime

According to the norms of the contemporary international order, states are entitled to decide whether to admit or exclude those who seek to enter their territory, largely at their discretion. The idea that states are entitled to exercise this power is a central part of what Joseph Carens calls the 'conventional view' of the morality of immigration.[6] As Sarah Fine puts it, control over admission and exclusion is generally viewed as 'a central, legitimate, undeniable aspect of sovereignty'.[7]

The refugee regime is an important exception to this sovereign privilege. Under international law, refugees are entitled to avoid the restrictions that states might have otherwise imposed upon their entering their territory or remaining within it. The central way in which the rights of refugees are protected is through the principle of *non-refoulement*, according to which no state is permitted to 'expel or return ("refouler") a refugee in any manner whatsoever to the frontiers of territories where his life or freedom would be threatened on account of his race, religion, nationality, membership of a particular social group or political opinion'.[8] In practice, this means that once someone has made a claim for asylum in a state, they cannot be deported to their home state unless it is determined that they do not have a genuine claim to refugee status.[9] This provision also extends to preventing states from punishing asylum-seekers for entering their territory illegally.[10]

Beyond *non-refoulement*, refugees are also entitled to various rights under international law that can be grouped under the heading of 'refugee protection'.[11] Basic rights such as rights to freedom from detention, physical security, family unity, and judicial assistance are supposed to be guaranteed to all refugees.[12] More expansive rights are also granted to some refugees—with significant variation between states—including rights to work, to public relief, to housing, to travel, and so on.[13] In recent years, refugee protection has focused on providing 'durable solutions' for refugees.[14] The three durable solutions for refugees that are central to the practices of refugee protection are *repatriation* to the home country, *resettlement* in a third country, or local *integration* in the state of asylum.[15]

Who qualifies for the protections associated with refugee status? According to the 1951 *Convention Relating to the Status of Refugees*, refugees are those who are outside of their country of origin and who are unable or unwilling to return because they have a 'well-founded fear of being persecuted for reasons of race, religion, nationality, membership of a particular social group or political opinion'.[16] Originally, refugee status was restricted to those originating in Europe before 1951, but these geographical and temporal restrictions were removed through the 1967 *Protocol Relating to the Status of Refugees*.[17] According to a strict reading of the definition of a refugee under international law, to qualify as a 'convention refugee' one must be outside of the country of one's origin (the 'alienage condition') and unwilling or unable to return on the basis of a reasonable fear of persecution based on certain protected characteristics (the 'persecution condition').[18] This account of refugee status forms the historic core of the refugee regime as it developed in the aftermath of the Second World War.

But, as James Hathaway has argued, refugee status is an 'extremely malleable legal concept'.[19] Since its inception, the refugee regime has grown and developed significantly. The practices of states, international organizations, and courts have all 'stretched' the refugee regime beyond the 1951 Convention.[20] Refugee status is now often assigned on the basis of group membership, rather than on the basis of individual status determination.[21] Those who have fled situations of generalized violence—rather than targeted persecution—are also now often recognized as refugees.[22] Importantly, the United Nations High Commissioner for Refugees (UNHCR) has noted in technical advice that it is the 'vital need for international protection'—and not their persecution—that 'most clearly distinguishes refugees from other aliens'.[23] Multilateral instruments such as the European Union's 2004 and 2011 Qualification Directives have been used to develop common criteria for the determination of refugee status, and courts have developed an influential and more expansive interpretation of persecution as 'the sustained or systemic denial of basic human rights demonstrative of a lack of state protection'.[24] Developments such as these in the practices of refugee protection mean that it is crucial to go beyond a strict reading of the 1951 Convention and 1967 Protocol to understand the status of the refugee in the contemporary international order.

The 1951 Convention and 1967 Protocol are also not the only documents which define the status of the refugee. Other regional human rights instruments reflect a broader view. The Organisation of African Unity (OAU)'s 1969 *Convention Governing the Specific Aspects of Refugee Problems in Africa* takes the refugee to include

> every person who, owing to external aggression, occupation, foreign domination or events seriously disturbing public order in either part or the whole of his country of origin or nationality, is compelled to leave his place of habitual residence in order to seek refuge in another place outside his country of origin or nationality.[25]

Similarly, the 1984 *Cartagena Declaration on Refugees* signed by a number of Latin American states takes the refugee to include 'persons who have fled their country because their lives, security or freedom have been threatened by generalized violence, foreign aggression, internal conflicts, massive violation of human rights or other circumstances which have seriously disturbed public order'.[26]

These are the basic legal contours of the contemporary refugee regime. Much more could be said about the ways in which the refugee regime has grown and developed. And as we will see, there are some important ways in which the norms of the refugee regime have been eroded and undermined. But this brief characterization of basic principles of the refugee regime gives us a starting point from which we can develop a normative theory of refugee status.

Who Is a Refugee?

A normative theory of refugee status should provide a morally defensible account of who has a justified claim to refugee status and the rights that it implies, while also providing a compelling interpretation of the role that the refugee regime plays within the international order. But there are different currents in the practices of refugee protection that suggest different interpretations of the refugee regime.

A first interpretation of the refugee regime can be called the *persecution view*. According to the persecution view, only those with a well-founded fear of persecution who flee their country of origin qualify as refugees, and so have a claim to asylum and the rights associated with refugee protection. This interpretation hews closely to the 1951 Convention and its 1967 Protocol and reflects the idea that the refugee regime's role is to address the situation of those who face political persecution in their country of origin. But it is important to note that the persecution view does not seek to preserve the status quo. For proponents of the persecution view, the expansion of UNHCR's mandate and the broader judicial interpretations of refugee status are mistakes in the development of the refugee regime. Instead, asylum should be reserved for those who flee threats of persecution in their home state.

The persecution view has been defended by Max Cherem and Matthew Lister and, on different grounds, by Matthew Price.[27] Cherem and Lister both defend the persecution condition on the basis that persecution is a distinctive harm that the provision of asylum is uniquely suited to address. Unlike others in need of assistance, those who face persecution are distinctive in the sense that their country of origin has '*repudiated* their membership' or 'actively turned against them'.[28] Following Michael Walzer, they note that political membership is a 'non-exportable good'.[29] Asylum—as a surrogate form of political membership—is an appropriate remedy for those who have been driven to seek protection abroad because their status as political members has been denied through persecution at home. By contrast, other remedies, such as food or development aid, can be exported to other 'necessitous strangers' who do not face persecution and who do not need to cross borders to secure a remedy.[30]

Price's defence of the persecution view focuses on the expressive dimension of asylum. Drawing on John Rawls's stylized distinction between 'outlaw' and 'burdened' societies, he argues that one function of asylum is to express condemnation of regimes that persecute their citizens (or permit them to be persecuted by private actors).[31] Granting asylum to those who flee 'outlaw' states because they face persecution is a way of condemning those states, and may even induce them to change their behaviour.[32] But granting asylum to those from 'burdened' societies would be unjustified, since doing so would express condemnation where it is not warranted. On this view, asylum is an 'arrow in the quiver of a human rights-oriented foreign policy'.[33]

Neither of these arguments give us good grounds to restrict refugee status to only those who meet the persecution condition. Although Cherem and Lister's arguments do point towards an important distinction between refugees—whose plight can be best addressed through the provision of asylum as a form of surrogate political membership—and others in need of assistance, their focus on persecution is overly narrow. Others who do not face persecution may also need a form of surrogate political membership—not because their status as members of a state has been *denied*, but because that status is *ineffective*.[34] When civil wars break out, regimes collapse, or states fail to effectively establish control over their territory, many people flee because their state can no longer protect them against violence and insecurity. These people do not face persecution—at least, not in the orthodox sense of the term—but they do need to have their status as political members reaffirmed in order for their plight to be remedied.[35] On the rationale that Cherem and Lister give for refugee status, those whose political membership is ineffective appear to have an equally valid claim as those whose political membership has been repudiated.

Price's expressive argument about the role of asylum recovers an important current in the historical practices of refugee protection.[36] But it does not justify restricting refugee status to only those facing persecution. One problem is that as the expressive significance of asylum waxes and wanes, so too does the international community's commitment to protecting refugees. As T. Alexander Aleinikoff has pointed out, the grant of asylum served a particular ideological function in the Cold War, when Western states offered permanent resettlement to political dissidents from the Eastern Bloc in order to 'score ideological points' against communist regimes. But as the ideological usefulness of welcoming refugees declined, states instead sought to contain refugees in their regions of origin.[37] Treating the refugee regime as an instrument of foreign policy makes refugee protection depend on the strategic utility of welcoming refugees. This points towards a more basic problem with Price's expressive argument: it ignores the role of the refugee regime *for refugees*. It does not provide a moral justification for the persecution condition that can be accepted from the perspective of those making a claim to refugee status. The absence of persecution is not a good reason to deny the claims of many of those who seek asylum for other reasons—such as state breakdown or indiscriminate violence—given that asylum is an appropriate remedy for their plight as well. This does not mean that there are no morally relevant differences between those facing persecution and those who need asylum for other reasons, but it does mean that restricting refugee status to those facing persecution cannot be justified.

Given these problems with the persecution view, we might be inclined to adopt a broader alternative, which we can call the *basic needs view*. In its simplest form, the basic needs view says that anyone whose basic needs (or basic rights) are unmet in their home state has a claim to refugee status. Kieran Oberman argues that 'a rational asylum system would give priority to those in the most need'.[38] Persecution may be a sufficient condition for refugee status on this view, but it is not a necessary one, since it is only one way in which basic needs can go unmet. On the basic needs view, the more recent developments in the refugee regime that have expanded the grounds for refugee status are to be welcomed as progressive developments. Broader definitions of refugee status such as those found in the OAU's 1969 Convention and the 1984 Cartagena Declaration bring the refugee regime closer in line with its proper purpose, which is to secure unmet basic needs.

The simple version of the basic needs view confronts the problem that it flattens any distinction between refugees and other persons in need of assistance. There are a great number of people whose basic needs are unmet around the world—indeed, chronic poverty means that many of them are worse off than those who are traditionally understood as refugees. The implication of this view is that there is there is no morally relevant difference between refugees and others in need of assistance—an implication that some, such as Oberman, happily accept.[39] But treating all of these people as refugees ignores the distinctive nature of asylum as a response to those in need. There is an important difference between those who need to avail themselves of asylum in another state and those whose basic needs could—at least in principle—be met in other ways, such as through the provision of aid.[40] If we want to preserve a distinction between refugees and others in need of assistance, then this simple version of the basic needs view must be revised.

Most defenders of the basic needs view avoid this problem by arguing that refugees must also meet the alienage condition.[41] David Miller argues that refugees are 'people whose human rights cannot be protected except by moving across a border, whether the reason is state persecution, state incapacity, or prolonged natural disasters'.[42] This view avoids being over-inclusive by making refugee status conceptually related to cross-border migration. Miller argues that one thing that is distinctive about those who satisfy the alienage condition is that they are in a position of vulnerability vis-à-vis the state in which they claim asylum.[43] In claiming asylum, they put themselves at the mercy of the receiving state and thereby impose upon that state a special duty to consider their claim and to comply with the obligation of *non-refoulement*. But although Miller's argument may explain why states have special duties to refugees who claim protection at their border, it cannot supply a defence of the alienage condition. The position of vulnerability that asylum-seekers occupy vis-à-vis the state in which they claim asylum is not itself the ground of the would-be refugee's claim to admission. At most, this position of vulnerability specifies and conditions a pre-existing duty that the international community has to those with a valid claim to international protection.

More generally, it is a mistake to turn to the alienage condition to revise the basic needs view. For one thing, as Eilidh Beaton argues, the alienage condition has the effect of making would-be refugees bear the burdens of dangerous journeys to exit their state.[44] But for another thing, this amendment also conflicts with our considered judgements about who is entitled to the rights associated with refugee status. Consider those protected by international agencies such as UNHCR *within* their country of origin. Since the early 1990s, UNHCR's Comprehensive Refugee Policy has seen it become increasingly operationally involved in states that are producing refugees, often by setting up 'safe havens' within conflict countries that pre-empt the need for cross-border movement.[45] If we adopt the alienage condition, then those protected by UNHCR in these circumstances should not count as refugees. But those protected in these circumstances would have fled across borders, were it not for UNHCR's provision of protection in their home country. Many within 'safe havens' seek international resettlement under the auspices of the refugee regime, and they appear to have a compelling claim. The fact that they have not yet crossed an international border does not appear to make a morally significant difference to their plight. If we think that such people should qualify as refugees—perhaps as 'internal refugees'—then the alienage condition cannot be necessary for refugee status.

Instead of either the persecution view or the basic needs view, my suggestion is that we should adopt what I call the *membership view*.[46] According to the membership view, refugees are those who are unable to appeal to their state for the protection of their human rights, because their state has lost the standing to act as the ongoing guarantor of their human rights. Such persons have lost the protections associated with political membership and have a justified claim to international protection from the international community, which is usually best provided through asylum as a form of surrogate political membership in another state.[47]

The membership view, as I articulate it here, draws on David Owen's theory of refugeehood. On Owen's view, the 'basic form' of the refugee is 'a figure for whom the international order (via a representative state) stands *in loco civitatis*'—that is, in the place of the state—by 'taking on responsibilities for which the refugee's state is otherwise accountable'.[48] The international order is a regime of governance structured by two central norms: those of state sovereignty and human rights. These norms are made compatible through a 'division of labour' in which each state is responsible for securing the human rights of its members.[49] But when states fail to secure the human rights of their members, this creates a 'legitimacy problem' for the international order.[50] In this situation, the international order acts as a substitute for the state, usually through providing asylum to those whose states have failed to protect their rights. The refugee regime functions as a 'legitimacy repair mechanism'.[51] Refugees are those who lack the protection associated with political membership—they are, in Emma Haddad's words, 'between sovereigns'—and so have a claim to protection from the international community.[52] On this view, the duties that we owe to refugees are not a matter of rescue or charity, but are rather duties to remedy the 'foreseeable failures' of the international state system.[53]

On the membership view—or at least my version of it—not just *any* human rights deficit would justify the ascription of refugee status. For the ascription of refugee status to be justified, the state must have lost its *standing* to act as the ongoing guarantor of its members' human rights: the 'membership relationship' between a person and their state must have broken down.[54] Some members of a state may not have all of their human rights protected all of the time, but their state may still be basically competent and acting in good faith. In these cases, those affected still have a claim to assistance, but their claim is that the international community should 'supplement'—not 'substitute'—their state as the guarantor of their rights.[55] But in other cases, the state will fail more comprehensively to secure the human rights of some of its members. This can happen through either the state's *unwillingness* or *inability* to secure the basic rights of its members. The state may display unwillingness to secure the rights of some members, for example by engaging in particularly egregious rights violations (such as persecution), such that even one-off violations are sufficient for them to lose their standing. Or the state may display an inability to secure the rights of some of its members, by chronically or systematically failing to secure their human rights. In both of these cases, those affected have a claim that the international community should act *in loco civitatis*. As we will see in Chapter 7, this clarification is important for distinguishing the refugee from the 'internally displaced person' (IDP) and those eligible for 'complementary protection'.

On the membership view, neither the persecution condition nor the alienage condition is strictly necessary for refugee status. Persecution is one way in which states can lose their standing as the ongoing guarantor of their members' human rights, but it is not the only way. States may lose their standing if they are unable to protect their members against civil conflict, generalized violence, famine, and/or extreme poverty. Similarly, alienage is often indicative of the fact that the state has lost its standing, but it is not conceptually required. As Haddad puts it, the 'swapping of responsibility between the national and the international does not necessarily take place at the border'.[56] Rather than alienage or persecution, what is of fundamental moral significance for refugee status is that a person finds themselves in a situation in which their state has lost its standing to act as the ongoing guarantor of their human rights.

The membership view provides both a plausible interpretation of the role of the refugee regime and a morally defensible account of who has a claim to refugee status. As an interpretation, it provides an account of the function of the refugee regime that coheres with the idea that the international order is structured by the twin norms of human rights and state sovereignty. As a moral argument, it provides a principled basis for restricting refugee status that those making claims to it can accept. It says that all persons have a basic right to the protection of their human rights, and that guaranteeing this right is the collective responsibility of the international community. When states fail to provide such protection, those whose states have failed them have a claim to protection from the international community.

Climate Change and Refugee Movement

Climate change contributes to situations in which persons have a valid claim to refugee status in a number of ways. Here, I examine the role of climate change in magnifying the sources of political conflict, exacerbating conditions of social deprivation, and increasing the risk of disasters. These are examples of the complex relationship between climate impacts and refugee movement, but they do not provide an exhaustive account of the ways in which climate change can interact with refugee movement.

The first way that climate change interacts with refugee movement is through its relationship to conflict. The idea that climate change drives conflict enjoys significant popularity in international politics, especially in UN discourses about climate change.[57] Ban Ki Moon, the then-Secretary General of the UN, wrote in the *Washington Post* in 2007 that the conflict in Darfur 'began as an ecological crisis, arising at least in part from climate change'.[58] But the causal relationship between climate change and conflict is complex, and remains highly contested in the empirical literature.[59] Two broad arguments about the causal relationship between climate change and conflict can be distinguished.

The first is the argument implicit in Moon's diagnosis of the conflict in Darfur: that climate change has a *direct* role in driving conflict by creating resource scarcity that, combined with population growth, drives inter-group conflict.[60] On this view, climate change creates conflicts that are fundamentally driven by competition over scarce resources. This argument enjoys significant popularity among lay publics and is frequently invoked in global politics, but the empirical evidence supporting it is weak.[61] Economic and sociopolitical drivers of conflict are typically dominant in apparently 'climate-driven' conflicts, and whether or not resource scarcities lead to conflict depends on how they are managed by political institutions, and so this argument has been widely criticized on the basis that it depends on a simplified and deterministic picture of conflict.[62] It is certainly possible that climate change could create resource scarcities that drive conflict in the future—and so this argument should not be ruled out—but for the moment, this argument is best viewed as a popular myth that is unsupported by the evidence currently available to us.

The second argument is that climate change has an *indirect* role in driving conflict by exacerbating the underlying tensions that lead to conflict. At its best, this argument is more cautious about the claims that it makes for climate change.[63] There are different hypothesized mechanisms through which climate impacts have an indirect role in driving conflict. One pathway involves climate impacts that affect agricultural production—such as droughts and changes in temperature—driving up the price of food. In contexts of existing political fragility, economic shocks such as short-term increases in food prices can make conflict more likely by heightening perceptions of inequality, reducing a government's ability to retain control through patronage networks, and lowering the 'opportunity costs' of participating in violent conflict for those with existing grievances.[64] Another pathway involves climate impacts such as floods and disasters driving internal migration, usually from rural areas to urban centres, which can magnify existing sources of instability such as ethnic tensions or high unemployment rates.[65] Crucially, in both of these pathways the role of climate change is heavily mediated by contextual sociopolitical factors such as state capacity, levels of socioeconomic development, recent histories of conflict, and existing inter-group inequalities. And even with this caveat, the empirical results for these mechanisms are mixed, with different studies finding competing effects even for the same cases.[66]

The classic example of disputed claims about the relationship between climate change and conflict is the civil war in Syria that began in 2011. Those who argue that climate change was a contributing factor in the Syrian civil war tell roughly the following story.[67] In the years preceding the conflict, there was a prolonged drought in the Fertile Crescent region which—according to climate modelling—was made significantly more likely by anthropogenic climate change. Crop failures and livestock mortality resulting from this drought drove rural–urban migration, especially from North-East Syria, where the drought was most severe. Rural–urban migration exacerbated existing grievances about chronic unemployment, inequality, corruption, and housing and food prices, contributing to the conflict by magnifying existing sources of political instability. This argument does not posit a direct link between climate change and conflict, and no one is suggesting that climate change was the only (or even the principal) driver of the conflict. But those who make this argument do see climate change as an important contributing factor.

This research was widely reported—sometimes with a degree of sensationalism—but each step in the argument has also been contested.[68] Researchers have argued that climate models do not give us grounds to make confident judgements about the role of climate change in drought, that claims about both the scale of rural–urban migration in the years preceding the conflict and the role of drought in driving it are not well established, and that we do not have sufficiently clear evidence that rural–urban migration fed the underlying tensions that led to the breakout of conflict.[69] This research does not purport to conclusively demonstrate that climate change had *no* role in the Syrian conflict, but it does suggest that we should be cautious about making firm judgements about its role.

Beyond this, some have also cautioned against highlighting the connections between climate change and conflict in cases such as Syria. They argue that the 'securitization' of climate change—that is, the framing of climate change as an issue of national or international security—serves a dangerous ideological function.[70] Even well-meaning attempts to motivate action on climate change by highlighting its links to conflict may backfire, and function instead to provide rationalizations for increased military expenditure, the fortification of borders, and exceptional forms of governance that quickly become the norm. So, these critics suggest that we should not focus our attention on the relationship between climate change and conflict.

In light of this disagreement and complexity, what should we make of the relationship between climate change and conflict? Clearly, climate change is not the most important factor in driving conflicts such as those in Syria. We should avoid a crude environmental determinism that overreaches the evidence available to us and ignores the political and historical contexts in which conflict occurs. We should also be careful not to overstate the relationship between climate and conflict, especially given the political uses to which claims about the relationship between them are sometimes put. But this does not mean that we should avoid investigating that relationship altogether. In my view, the best way of responding to concerns about the securitization of climate change is to contest the political uses to which claims about the relationship between climate and conflict are put, not to rule out the idea that there is a relationship by fiat. It is reasonable to judge that climate change has a relationship—albeit a complex and indirect one—to conflict. But the claim that there is an indirect relationship between climate change and conflict is best viewed as a plausible hypothesis. It is important that we investigate that hypothesis further, including by tackling some of the methodological problems that currently hinder research on climate and conflict.[71]

We will probably never know exactly what role climate change played in the conflict in Syria, or in others like it. To the extent that climate change exacerbates the drivers of conflict, we should expect that the refugee regime will have an increasingly important role to play in tackling climate displacement. And although it is clearly important that we try to develop a better understanding of the relationship between climate change and conflict, there is one sense in which the precise nature of that relationship is unimportant. Conflicts such as the civil war in Syria create an environment in which those affected cannot depend upon the protection that is supposed to be afforded to them as members of their state. Those displaced in conflict situations clearly have a claim to refugee status on the membership view. Crucially, they have that claim regardless of whether or not climate change played a causal role in driving the conflict that led to their displacement.

The second way in which climate change can interact with refugee movement is through its role in exacerbating conditions of social deprivation. Climate change impacts are detrimental to livelihoods, lead to food insecurity, worsen existing poverty, and trigger new poverty traps.[72] As we saw in Chapter 5, the primary response to such social deprivation is adaptation, which may include both *in situ* forms of adaptation (such as crop diversification) and forms of adaptation that involve migration (such as international labour migration or community relocation). But in some cases, adaptation to climate change will fail, or will prove insufficient to tackle social deprivation.

Social deprivation itself will not usually provide grounds for the ascription of refugee status. In the first instance, the international community's role will be to assist states whose members face social deprivation, rather than to replace the state in its protective functions through providing asylum. But those who flee social deprivation may have a claim to refugee status, on the membership view, in cases where the state's failure to secure the socioeconomic rights of its members is sufficiently severe that it is indicative of the state having lost the standing to act as the guarantor of its members' human rights.[73] In such cases of 'failed governance', those who flee have a claim to international protection.[74]

More commonly, social deprivation driven by climate change will exacerbate other drivers of refugee movement. One example of this is the Central American case with which this chapter began. The Northern Triangle countries—Honduras, Guatemala, and El Salvador—have high levels of corruption, crime, and violence. Gang violence is a significant driver of displacement from the Northern Triangle, with children being especially at risk.[75] In some areas, transnational criminal gangs such as Mara Salvatrucha (MS-13) and the 18th Street Gang (Barrio 18) operate with such impunity that they have effectively usurped the state's control over parts of its territory.[76] Those who flee the violence associated with gang activity in the Northern Triangle—typically (though not exclusively) to the USA—are often denied refugee status because they are not targeted or persecuted by their state, even though they are treated as *de facto* refugees by international organizations.[77] But on the membership view, they have a clear claim to refugee status. Those fleeing gang violence find themselves unable to appeal to the protection that is supposed to be guaranteed to them by their states.

As the story of Delmira de Jesús Cortez Barrera illustrated, climate change impacts such as drought can make people more vulnerable to gang violence. Although direct research on the relationship between climate change and gang violence is limited, we do know that climate change drives social deprivation, and that social deprivation increases vulnerability to gang violence. Climate change impacts such as rising temperatures and increased incidences of crop disease and pestilence are leading to significant reductions in yields of crops such as coffee and maize in Central America, creating food insecurity and poverty.[78] Research from the World Food Programme (WFP) suggests that poverty and food insecurity drive emigration from the Northern Triangle at least in part through their role in increasing vulnerability to violence.[79] Those facing poverty and food insecurity are especially vulnerable to gang violence—for example, because they are unable to pay extortion fees or because they are more easily coerced into participating in gangs. María José Méndez calls this dynamic the 'silent violence' of climate change.[80]

As in other contexts, the link between climate change and refugee movement here is complex and indirect. It is difficult to quantify, partly because of the complexity of the relationship between climate change and other drivers of displacement and partly because it is difficult to gather data about gang violence. But to the extent that climate change increases vulnerability to gang violence through its role in producing social deprivation, it plays an indirect role in driving refugee movement.

The third way in which climate change can interact with refugee movement is through its role in increasing the risk of disasters such as hurricanes, droughts, and floods. One consequence of climate change is an increase in the frequency and intensity of extreme weather events such as these.[81] And we know that extreme weather events can drive displacement, especially among those who are already vulnerable along other axes.[82] Disaster displacement is usually internal, and (as we will see in Chapter 7) many of those displaced in the course of disasters are best treated as IDPs rather than as refugees. But in some contexts of disaster displacement, it may be more appropriate to treat the displaced person as a refugee. Strictly speaking, the morally relevant distinction here is not whether displacement is internal or cross-border—as we saw above, the membership view admits of the possibility of 'internal refugees'—but rather whether or not the membership relationship between the displaced person and her state has broken down. The distinction between cross-border and internal displacement will often roughly track the status of the membership relationship, since those who cannot rely on the protection of their state will often flee across borders to find protection elsewhere. But it is only an imperfect proxy. In some cases of disaster displacement—both internal and cross-border—some of those who are displaced may well have a claim to refugee status.

One example of the role of climate change in driving refugee movement through disasters comes from the Horn of Africa. In 2011-12, there was a severe drought in East Africa, which precipitated a food security crisis in the region. It is difficult to know with much confidence whether any particular extreme weather event such as this can be attributed to climate change. But according to one study that used the techniques of 'probabilistic event attribution' to examine the East African drought, the failure of the rains in early 2011 was likely due to anthropogenic climate change.[83] In Somalia, the drought precipitated a famine that affected millions of people. Famines are not just a matter of absolute food shortages—although the proximate cause may be shortages created by events such as droughts, the way in which political institutions manage shortages is a major determinant of whether food shortages become famines.[84] The famine in Somalia—a country already wracked by insecurity and conflict—was no different. The lack of a centralized government and the insurgency being waged by Al-Shabaab, especially in the south of the country, made Somalia especially vulnerable.[85] During the famine, an estimated 1.3 million people were displaced within Somalia, while around 290,000 people fled across the borders to Kenya and Ethiopia.[86] Many sought refuge, and were received, in major refugee camps such as the Dadaab camps near the Kenya-Somalia border.

As in the other examples that we have examined, the relationship between climate change and refugee movement here is complex and indirect. We should not expect to be able to straightforwardly identify particular people whose displacement can be attributed to climate change in contexts such as these. But on the membership view, those facing famine in Somalia—both those who fled across borders and those displaced internally—have a strong claim to refugee status, regardless of whether their displacement can be clearly attributed to climate change. The inability of the state to secure their basic rights gives them a claim to protection on the part of the international community.

The idea that climate displacement is complex has been a theme in our inquiry. The three ways in which climate change contributes to refugee movement that we have examined here—through conflict, deprivation, and disasters—exemplify this complexity. On the membership view, what is important in each of these cases is not the precise role that climate change has played in driving refugee movement. Rather, the vulnerable position in which displaced people who are unable to appeal to their own state for protection find themselves is of central moral importance for refugee status. Climate change can exacerbate the social forces that put people in this precarious situation, but the presence or absence of the fingerprints of climate change does not determine who has a claim to refugee status.

Climate Change and the Dysfunctions of the Refugee Regime

The refugee regime is deeply dysfunctional. The international community consistently fails to abide by the rules and norms that govern refugee protection in international law, let alone to live up to the moral values and principles that underlie those rules and norms. Those who find themselves on the margins of society—undertaking dangerous clandestine journeys, crowded into urban slums, and languishing in refugee camps—testify to our collective failure to meaningfully address the plight of refugees. According to Serena Parekh, this failing is a structural one, which 'emerges from the social and political structures, systems, policies, and norms that make up the refugee protection system'.[87] The system of refugee protection today leaves large numbers of refugees in precarious and vulnerable positions, unable to access what Parekh calls the 'minimum conditions of human dignity'.[88] This injustice is not just a matter of isolated incidences of wrongdoing, it is a result of the structural failings in the global system of refugee protection.

Climate change exacerbates the dysfunctions of the refugee regime. Here, I focus on three key dysfunctions in the refugee regime that are exacerbated in the context of climate change: the restrictive definition of the refugee in international law; the deterrence paradigm in international refugee policy; and the maldistribution of the costs of refugee protection. These dysfunctions certainly do not exhaust the problems of refugee protection—notably, I do not discuss the warehousing of refugees in camps here—but they are areas in which climate change plays an important role in aggravating the structural failings in the refugee regime.

The Definition of the Refugee

The first dysfunction in the refugee regime concerns the definition of a refugee set out in the 1951 Convention. The 1951 Convention restricts refugee status to those fleeing persecution on the basis of their race, religion, nationality, membership of a particular social group, or political opinion. But as we have already seen, the aim of a morally justifiable refugee regime would be to provide international protection to all of those who cannot rely on their own states to protect their basic rights. And although persecution undoubtedly remains important, it is by no means the only way in which the bond between the member and their state is broken. Climate change—through its role in magnifying the sources of political instability, exacerbating conditions of social deprivation, and increasing the likelihood of disasters—can contribute to situations in which the membership relation breaks down. The definition of the refugee in international law should be broadened, so as to capture those with normatively valid claims to refugee status.

At first glance, an attractive way of addressing the deficits of the 1951 Convention would be to include explicit recognition of climatic drivers of displacement as grounds for refugee status. In a report for the New Economics Foundation, Molly Consibee and Andrew Simms have argued that the 1951 Convention should be revised to include environmental drivers of displacement.[89] They make this argument on the basis of the idea of 'environmental persecution', arguing that the environment can be used 'as an instrument of harm'.[90] But while it is certainly true that the environment can be used as an instrument of harm, international lawyers typically reject the idea that climate impacts can be a form of persecution.[91] There may be some cases involving climate change in which the persecution condition is met—such as when governments withhold disaster relief from a particular social group—but in general, extending the persecution condition in this way is not a plausible interpretation of the concept of persecution as it figures in the refugee regime. In any case, even if climate change impacts could be understood as cases of 'persecution', it is unclear what work the 'environmental' clause would be doing, aside from making an implicit part of the 1951 Convention explicit. And perhaps most importantly, this argument implicitly accepts the moral justifiability of the persecution view. As we have seen, this view unduly limits the grounds for the ascription of refugee status.

Another defence of expanding the list of causes in the 1951 Convention is given by Lister. Lister has argued that some people displaced by climate change impacts—specifically, 'those displaced by climate change or other environmental disruptions of expected indefinite duration, where international movement is necessitated, and where the threat is not just to a favored or traditional way of life, but to the possibility of a decent life at all'—should be granted refugee status.[92] Lister argues that granting refugee status to this group of people would require 'modifying or adding to the current terms of the UN refugee convention', but that it would not require a radical departure from the refugee regime, and that therefore this approach has the virtue of 'progressive conservatism'.[93]

One problem with Lister's view is that it suffers from the same problem facing a climate refugee treaty identified in Chapter 2: given the complexity of climate displacement, it will rarely be possible to judge with any degree of confidence that a particular person's displacement is attributable to climate change. The examples just considered of the ways in which climate change and refugee movement interact illustrate this complexity. If the 1951 Convention were reformed to include 'climate change' as a basis for refugee status, then we would usually be unable to identify those with a legally valid claim. But another issue is that this approach leaves the more basic problem with the current definition untouched. Adding climate change to the list of grounds of refugee status would not enable others with a normatively valid claim to refugee status—such as those fleeing breakdowns of public order—to make a legally valid claim to refugee status.

These problems suggest that a more promising avenue is to move away from a refugee definition based on the causes of displacement. What is of primary importance—and what our legal definition of a refugee should aim to approximate—is identifying those whose relationship with their state has broken down, such that they have a claim that the international community should act *in loco civitatis*. Although some causes of displacement (such as persecution) may be indicative of the membership relation breaking down, they are not constitutive of a claim to refugee status. Insofar as causes of displacement figure in the legal definition of a refugee, they should do so only indicatively.

It is difficult to specify in the abstract what the precise wording of the definition of a refugee under international law should be. The membership view does not easily translate into the language of legal statutes. Designing legal codes is a complex process that requires us to think carefully about the ways in which legal language may be (mis)interpreted in both good and bad faith.[94] It would be unwise to make the principle that 'refugees are those whose states have lost standing as the ongoing guarantor of their human rights, for whom the international community should act *in loco civitatis*' the legal definition of a refugee. This would lend itself to a wide latitude for interpretation and—although some latitude for interpretation may be valuable to accommodate the changing threats to refugees—there is a danger that too much scope for interpretation would enable states to shirk their responsibilities to refugees.

This problem does not only affect the membership view. Alex Aleinikoff and Leah Zamore have recently proposed the concept of 'necessary flight' as a standard for determining who has a claim to international protection.[95] The test for whether an individual is eligible for international protection is whether she can offer a 'persuasive and reasonable justification' for her decision to flee or if 'the situation itself readily attests to her decision'.[96] This standard also lends itself to wide latitude in interpretation. What counts as a 'persuasive and reasonable justification' and when a situation 'readily attests' to a decision to flee are likely to be subject of significant disagreement.

Ultimately, whether or not someone meets the normative conditions for refugee status is a matter of judgement, which is not easily codified. But we can critically evaluate legal definitions in terms of how well they ensure that those with a normatively valid claim to refugee status can gain recognition as refugees. The aim of a legal definition of a refugee should be to capture those picked out as refugees by the membership view of refugee status.

Another problem facing our efforts to reform the 1951 Convention is what Luara Ferracioli calls the 'feasibility dilemma'.[97] The consensus view among scholars of international law is that any attempt to renegotiate the 1951 Convention would likely lead to a weakening of protections for refugees, rather than a more inclusive definition of refugee status.[98] States routinely attempt to evade their responsibilities to refugees, and most commentators expect that a renegotiation of the terms of the 1951 Convention would merely provide them with an opportunity to rid themselves of their legal obligations. Alexander Betts has argued that we should not aim to reopen the 1951 Convention for negotiation but should instead push for a series of more incremental reforms, such as more thoroughly institutionalizing the OAU definition of a refugee, encouraging UNHCR to supply wider guidance about how the 1951 Convention definition should be interpreted, and establishing greater legal precedent for the international protection of those who fall outside of the scope of the 1951 Convention.[99]

These are sensible ways to broaden the practical application of the refugee regime in the short to medium term, in which the political context for refugee protection is hostile. But in the long term we should aim for more robust and durable change by building the political will necessary to reform the 1951 Convention in a more inclusive way. As Ferracioli argues, we have *dynamic* duties with respect to reforming the 1951 Convention—that is, duties to create the conditions in which we can achieve more ambitious reform.[100] In the context of climate change, this aim is all the more important: it is critical that we lay the groundwork for a more expansive conception of refugee status to develop over time as the impacts of climate change accelerate.

The Deterrence Paradigm

The second dysfunction in the refugee regime is the dominance of what Thomas Gammeltoft-Hansen and Nikolas F. Tan call the 'deterrence paradigm'.[101] The deterrence of refugees and asylum-seekers is now the primary objective of refugee policy in the Global North. The policies that states in the Global North adopt force refugees to undertake dangerous clandestine journeys, often by engaging the services of human smugglers, that present serious risks to their safety. In the context of climate change, these dangers are magnified, and the moral imperative to provide safe and legal routes to asylum acquires a renewed significance.

The norm of *non-refoulement* means that refugees must be territorially present to claim asylum. States in the Global North exploit this requirement by ensuring that there is no safe and legal route for refugees to reach their territory and claim asylum in the first place. There is no 'queue' to be joined by those seeking asylum in the Global North. States in the Global North typically do not provide visas to those from states that are producing refugees and they impose punitive 'carrier sanctions' on airlines that transport those without visas.[102] They adopt a bewildering array of techniques—usually termed 'non-entrée' or 'non-arrival' measures—designed to prevent or deter refugees from reaching their territory.[103] Such techniques include the interdiction of refugees travelling by land and sea, the extra-territorialization of immigration enforcement through 'remote control' policies, the criminalization and detention of refugees and asylum-seekers, the fortification and militarization of border walls, and the use of creative legal fictions that 'shift' the border and create legal spaces of exception.[104] Infamous examples include Australia's use of offshore processing in Nauru, Frontex's Integrated Border Management strategy, the USA's policy of family separation and detention at the southern border, and most recently the UK's Asylum Partnership Arrangement with Rwanda. As Parekh puts it, the message of these policies is clear: 'you are not welcome; do not seek asylum here.'[105]

Deterrence policies do not have a strong effect in deterring refugees and asylum-seekers, but they do make the journeys that they undertake much more dangerous.[106] The techniques used by states in the Global North push refugees to take dangerous clandestine journeys to find protection. For many refugees, the alternatives to seeking asylum are so intolerable that they feel they have no choice but to try and evade the restrictions that states impose. So, when states block off safe and legal routes to seeking asylum, refugees turn to more dangerous routes, such as crossing the Mediterranean Sea in small boats or trekking for days in the Sonoran Desert. And as the techniques that states use to prevent the arrival of refugees become more sophisticated, refugees increasingly engage the services of people smugglers. Parekh argues that the deterrence paradigm makes using the services of people smugglers a 'de facto requirement for claiming asylum in the West'.[107] People smugglers provide an essential service for many refugees seeking to claim asylum, but theirs is a brutal business.[108] The position of vulnerability that refugees occupy makes them easy targets for unscrupulous smugglers, who extort them for huge sums of money and engage in vicious forms of abuse, including routine sexual violence.

Climate change exacerbates the dangers of the deterrence paradigm—not only by exacerbating existing drivers of refugee movement, but also by making the routes that refugees take more dangerous. Take the Sonoran Desert route from Mexico to the USA, through which refugees and asylum-seekers are pushed as part of the US government's Prevention Through Deterrence policy.[109] This route is incredibly dangerous, with many of those who make the crossing dying in the desert, mostly due to heat-related stress. According to US Border Patrol, around 8,000 people have died crossing the Sonoran Desert since 1998—though the true number is likely to be much higher, both because US Border Forces do not actively search for bodies in the Sonoran Desert and because scavenging vultures destroy and disperse human remains.[110] 'Desert border crossings', the anthropologist Jason De León writes, 'are cruel, brutal affairs in which people often die painfully and slowly from hyperthermia, dehydration, heatstroke, and a variety of other related ailments'.[111] And as the impacts of climate change accelerate, the risks of heat-related deaths in the Sonoran Desert will only increase. One recent study estimated that increased temperatures associated with climate change will increase the 'costs of migration' in terms of heat stress by between 29.6 per cent and 34.1 per cent over the next thirty years. As the authors put it, this means that 'undocumented migration across the southwest border of the United States will become increasingly dangerous over the next 30 years, which will likely result in increased mortality of migrants'.[112]

The predictable result of the intricate web of policies and practices designed to prevent refugees from making asylum claims—which David Scott Fitzgerald calls an 'architecture of repulsion'—is that refugees take great risks in making dangerous journeys, placing their lives in the hands of people smugglers.[113] And as the impacts of climate change accelerate, those routes will only become more dangerous. In the context of climate change, the moral imperative to dismantle the deterrence paradigm and to provide safe and legal routes for refugees to claim asylum acquires a renewed significance. This moral imperative has both a positive and a negative element.

Positively, states should work to create and expand safe and legal avenues for those seeking asylum. This might involve expanding resettlement programmes that enable asylum-seekers to make claims without having to leave their country of origin or—where possible—actively providing carriers from refugee-producing regions.[114] Canada's Refugee Resettlement Program, through which some asylum-seekers can make claims directly to the Canadian government without having to leave their country, is—though by no means perfect—one example of what this might look like.[115] But crucially, such programmes should not replace more traditional routes to claiming asylum. One criticism of 'in-country processing' is that it is often used as a way of restricting access to asylum: a token few refugees are resettled, while many more are summarily returned to their country of origin. This was the operative dynamic of the in-country processing of Haitian refugees by the USA in the 1990s.[116] But in many cases, states that are producing refugees will not cooperate with in-country processing, or it will simply be too dangerous for refugees to wait for their claim to be processed within their country of origin. So, although access to asylum from within refugee-producing states should be expanded, it should not be used as a substitute for other routes to asylum or as an excuse to deny the claims of those who do not or cannot avail themselves of this option.

Negatively, states should dismantle the deterrence paradigm that makes seeking asylum so dangerous. This is an ambitious goal: it requires a paradigm shift in refugee policy, including the demilitarization of borders, the decriminalization of asylum-seeking, the end of offshore processing and legal spaces of exception, the removal of carrier sanctions, and more. But ultimately, it is only by dismantling the deterrence paradigm that the right to seek asylum can be adequately protected. It is the architecture of repulsion itself that pushes refugees into making dangerous clandestine journeys and makes them vulnerable to abuse and exploitation at the hands of people smugglers, and it is only by dismantling that architecture that the root of the problem can be addressed.

States in the Global North are likely to argue that the restrictive policies that they adopt serve a legitimate purpose: not in repelling refugees, but in repelling those who do not have a valid claim to refugee status. At least on the assumption that states have a broad discretionary right to control admission to their territory—with refugees being an exception to the rule—restrictive migration controls might be defended on the grounds that they are a legitimate means through which states can exercise this right. The flows of people using clandestine migration routes are often 'mixed', with refugees travelling alongside other undocumented migrants seeking entry.[117] On this view, the fact that refugees are casualties of border control policies may be something to be regretted and minimized, but it is ultimately just an unfortunate side effect of the right of states to control migration to their borders, which requires them to be able to effectively deter those without a valid claim to refugee status.

The problem with this response is that even if states do have a broad discretionary right to control admission to their territory, this does not mean that any enforcement mechanism they use can be justified.[118] In the moral evaluation of border enforcement, the state's interest in preventing the arrival of unauthorized migrants needs to be weighed against the predictable effects of enforcement policies on the rights of undocumented migrants and refugees. The right to seek asylum is a basic right that should be guaranteed as a matter of the legitimacy of the international order. We should therefore see it as a constraint on the range of border control policies that states can legitimately adopt. This need not rule out *all* border control, as some policies may not threaten the right to seek asylum.[119] But it does mean that the policies that make up the deterrence paradigm cannot be vindicated by an appeal to the state's right to exercise discretionary control over admission.

The Costs of Refugee Protection

The third dysfunction in the refugee regime is the maldistribution of the costs of refugee protection. The least advantaged states host the lion's share of the world's refugee population and so bear an unfair share of the costs of refugee protection. In the context of climate change, that unfairness is likely to be exacerbated.

This makes it all the more pressing that we develop robust forms of international cooperation that share the costs of refugee protection fairly.

At present, the distribution of refugees between states is largely governed by what Matthew Gibney has called the 'tyranny of geography'.[120] Since it is generally easier for refugees to reach the territory of states that are nearby, states that are geographically proximate to refugee-producing regions tend to host the greatest share of refugees. And for their part, states in the Global North exacerbate this inequality through the use of deterrence measures that contain refugees in their region of origin. As a result, states that are already among the least advantaged bear the largest share of the costs of refugee protection. At the end of 2020, 73 per cent of refugees globally were hosted in countries neighbouring the country that they had fled.[121] The states hosting the largest numbers of refugees were Turkey, Colombia, Pakistan, and Uganda, reflecting the fact that their neighbours Syria, Venezuela, Afghanistan, and South Sudan were producing the highest numbers of refugees. Generally, the burdens of refugee protection fall disproportionately on the least advantaged states. In total, 86 per cent of the global refugee population was hosted in developing states and only one developed state (Germany) was in the top ten hosting states. The Least Developed Countries (LDCs)—including Bangladesh, the Democratic Republic of the Congo (DRC), Ethiopia, Rwanda, Sudan, Tanzania, and Uganda—hosted 27 per cent of the world's refugee population, despite accounting for only 14 per cent of the global population and 1.3 per cent of global gross domestic product (GDP).

This maldistribution is likely to be exacerbated in the context of climate change. We know that the least advantaged states are most vulnerable to the effects of climate change.[122] Partly, this is a matter of geography: climate impacts are worse in the warmer latitudes in which the least advantaged states tend to be located. But it also reflects the background inequalities of wealth and power in the international order: part of the reason why the least advantaged states are vulnerable to climate impacts is *because* they are worse off. All but two of the states that are on 'high' or 'very high' alert in the Fragile States Index—Yemen, Somalia, DRC, Central African Republic, Chad, Sudan, and Afghanistan—are also in the top ten states most vulnerable to climate change, as measured by the Notre Dame Global Adaptation Initiative (ND-GAIN) Index.[123] Obviously, this is a somewhat crude indicator of the likely impacts of climate change on refugee movement, but it illustrates that we can generally expect that the least advantaged states will be most affected by the impacts of climate change on refugee movement. In turn, states that are geographically proximate, typically also among the least advantaged, will bear the brunt of the costs of refugee protection. By contrast, states in the Global North and their neighbours, which already insulate themselves from refugee flows through deterrence policies, are generally least vulnerable to climate impacts and best able to protect themselves through adaptation measures.

The context of climate change makes it all the more important for states to develop robust forms of international cooperation that address this maldistribution by sharing the costs of refugee protection more fairly. Although the international community has formally acknowledged the unfairness in the distribution of the costs of refugee protection, robust attempts to develop fairer burden-sharing arrangements are lacking. The most recent attempt to develop a common framework for refugee burden-sharing, the 2018 *Global Compact on Refugees*, notes that there is 'an urgent need for more equitable sharing of the burden and responsibility for hosting and supporting the world's refugees'.[124] But aside from a vast array of stakeholder meetings, networks, conferences, steering groups, and consultative mechanisms, its only concrete outcome is the establishment of a Global Forum in which states can make non-binding pledges to contribute to refugee protection. It is, as Hathaway puts it, 'a bureaucrat's dream' but a decidedly 'tepid' response to the problem of refugee burden-sharing.[125]

What would a fair distribution of responsibility for refugees look like? In answering this question, we can distinguish the question of *where* refugees should be hosted from the question of *who should pay* for the protection of refugees. In practice, these two issues are run together, as the costs of refugee protection are largely left to lie where they fall when refugees claim protection in a state. And much work on refugee burden-sharing in political theory treats these two questions as synonymous: theorists treat the question of what counts as a 'fair share' of refugee protection as a matter of how many refugees each state should host.[126] But refugees can be hosted in one state while another state finances their protection. This means that we can separate the question of how the costs of refugee protection should be distributed from the question of where refugees should be hosted.[127]

Alex Betts and Paul Collier have recently leveraged the idea that the costs and the locus of refugee protection can be separated to argue that refugees should continue to be primarily hosted in states in the Global South while rich states in the Global North finance their protection.[128] They argue that this would respond to both Northern states' desires to keep refugees out of their territory and Southern states' concerns about the fairness of hosting the lion's share of the global refugee population. But while this would be an improvement on the status quo, it is not a proposal that we should endorse from the standpoint of justice. For one thing, it enables states in the Global North to leverage their existing advantages to confine states in the Global South to the role of hosting refugees. For another, it gives no real voice to refugees in decisions about where they should be hosted.[129]

Decisions about *where* refugees should be hosted should balance the claims of both refugees and hosting states. Competing claims might be settled in a number of ways, but one promising proposal is the system of preference-matching developed by Will Jones and Alexander Teytelboym.[130] On this proposal, both states and refugees would submit their preferences, which would be used to determine a distribution of refugees that best satisfies both sets of preferences. Refugees might prefer to live in states where they already speak the language, or where there are more opportunities for them to practise their religion or to participate in particular cultural practices. For their part, states might make claims about their 'integrative capacity' on the basis of factors such as their population density or the existence of diasporic networks for particular groups of refugees.[131] The preference-matching proposal is promising, but needs to be subject to a moral constraint: the preferences that both states and refugees submit should be *morally legitimate*. Some preferences—such as Poland's expressed preference for admitting only Christian refugees from Syria—should be ruled out on the basis that they are discriminatory or xenophobic.[132]

The question of how the *costs* of refugee protection should be distributed can be understood as a question about how states should cooperate in the provision of a global public good.[133] The refugee regime, viewed as a mechanism for preserving the legitimacy of the international state system, is a good that benefits all states collectively. At the moment, states in the Global North are free riding on the efforts of states in the Global South. A fair distribution of the costs of refugee protection would start from the idea that refugee protection should be *equally burdensome* for each state. This would mean adopting an 'ability to pay' principle for the distribution of the costs of refugee protection, with states bearing the costs of refugee protection in proportion to their wealth. This principle treats each state as an equal partner in the cooperative project of maintaining the legitimacy of the international state system through refugee protection, and privileges no particular state's interests over those of others.

The principle of equal burdens is, however, only a benchmark—that is, a default distribution from which departures can be justified. One way in which departures from this distribution can be justified is by appeal to *responsibility*. When states culpably impose additional costs on the refugee regime as a whole, they should be held liable to bear the costs that they create.[134] For example, where states wrongfully engage in military intervention abroad and create refugees, they should be held responsible to bear the costs associated with the protection of the refugees that their intervention creates.[135] This principle reflects the idea that it would be unfair for states that unilaterally impose a greater cost on the refugee regime as a whole to expect others to pick up the tab. Another way in which states can incur liabilities of this kind is through their contributions to climate change. As we will see in Chapter 8, there are some additional complications that arise in assigning responsibility for climate change, but states ought to be held responsible for the additional costs that they impose on the refugee regime—as well as other institutions for governing displacement—through their failures to discharge their climate mitigation duties.

The refugee regime has an important role to play in the project of tackling climate displacement. As we have seen, the refugee regime has an important function in the international state system: to reconcile the norms of state sovereignty and human rights, and so to make good on the idea that each person is entitled to live in a world where their basic rights are guaranteed. As the impacts of climate change accelerate, it will only become more important that the refugee regime is able to play this role. Though there will not be particular people whom we can identify as 'climate refugees', climate change has the potential to magnify the drivers of refugee movement through its relationship to conflict, social deprivation, and disasters. It is critical to make the refugee regime fit for this purpose.

As it stands, the refugee regime is failing. The deep dysfunctions in the refugee regime—including the restrictive definition of the refugee in international law, the deterrence paradigm in international refugee policy, and the maldistribution of the costs of refugee protection between states—are only likely to be aggravated in the context of climate change. These structural failings in the refugee regime need to be addressed in order for the refugee regime to play its part in the project of tackling climate displacement. Root-and-branch reforms are needed for the refugee regime to fulfil its purpose. This includes reforming the 1951 Refugee Convention to broaden eligibility for refugee status, dismantling the deterrence paradigm and providing safe and legal routes for those seeking asylum, and developing robust forms of international cooperation for sharing the costs of protection between states. These are ambitious goals, but it is only through ambitious reform that the refugee regime will be able to rise to the challenge of climate displacement.

7
Climate Change and Internal Displacement

In the early morning of 8 November 2013, Typhoon Haiyan made landfall in the Eastern Samar region of the Philippines. Typhoon Haiyan, known locally as Typhoon Yolanda, was one of the most destructive tropical storms in the history of the Philippines, causing widespread destruction and the deaths of at least 6,300 people. In the aftermath of the destruction, around 4 million people were displaced across the Philippines. Evacuation centres were overcrowded and makeshift shelters were set up in schools, but even then, the vast majority of those displaced were dispersed and staying outside of formal spaces of protection.[1]

Only days after the disaster struck, Yeb Saño, the lead climate negotiator for the Philippines, spoke at the 19th Conference of the Parties (COP19) of the United Nations Framework Convention on Climate Change (UNFCCC) in Warsaw. Saño spoke movingly of the devastation that had struck his home city, Tacloban, and in an impassioned plea to the delegates, he called for action:

> We refuse, as a nation, to accept a future where super typhoons like Haiyan become a fact of life. We refuse to accept that running away from storms, evacuating our families, suffering the devastation and misery, having to count our dead, become a way of life ... Super Typhoon Haiyan made landfall in my family's hometown and the devastation is staggering. I struggle to find words even for the images that we see from the news coverage. I struggle to find words to describe how I feel about the losses and damages we have suffered from this cataclysm ... We can fix this. We can stop this madness ... Can humanity rise to the occasion? I still believe we can.[2]

Typhoon Haiyan stands as a stark illustration of the kinds of events that we can expect to see unfold as the impacts of climate change manifest.

One of the main consequences of extreme weather events such as Typhoon Haiyan is internal displacement. According to the Internal Displacement Monitoring Centre (IDMC), around 38 million people were newly displaced within the territory of their state in 2021.[3] The majority of those people—around 22.3 million—were displaced by weather-related events such as cyclones, floods, and wildfires. As with other forms of climate displacement, the relationship between climate change and disaster displacement is complex. Extreme weather events cannot always be straightforwardly attributed to climate change, and their impact on displacement is mediated by social facts about vulnerability and resilience, which are often structured along classic fault lines such as race, class, and gender. But as the impacts of climate change accelerate, extreme weather events such as Typhoon Haiyan will become more frequent and intense. As such, we can expect that internal displacement will become even more significant as the impacts of climate change unfold.

Internal displacement has only come into view as a matter of political concern in the international order relatively recently.[4] In the late 1980s and early 1990s, international institutions and NGOs turned their attention to the phenomenon of internal displacement, and an international protection framework concerning the conceptualization and treatment of 'internally displaced persons' (IDPs) emerged.[5] International legal principles concerning the treatment of IDPs have been articulated and codified in international legal frameworks such as the 1998 *Guiding Principles on Internal Displacement*, the 2006 *Great Lakes Protocol*, the 2009 *Kampala Convention*, and the 2010 Inter-Agency Standing Committee (IASC) *Framework on Durable Solutions for Internally Displaced Persons*.[6] These forms of international governance for internal displacement are likely to be of increasing importance, and to face significant stress tests, as the impacts of climate change accelerate.

Political theorists have paid relatively little attention to internal displacement so far.[7] Most work on displacement in political theory has focused on movement *between* states rather than movement *within* states. This narrow focus on international movement has obscured the normative significance of internal displacement. In order to critically evaluate the ways in which IDPs are treated in practice, we need a normative theory that tells us who is eligible for IDP status, what rights those people have in virtue of that status, and what correlate duties other agents owe. And in the context of climate change, we need to diagnose the problems that arise for the governance of internal displacement, in order to be able to reform the internal displacement governance regime such that it is equipped to deal with the moral challenge of climate displacement.

This chapter examines the role of the internal displacement governance regime in the project of tackling climate displacement. The first section of the chapter develops a normative theory of IDP status through an interpretation of some of the central components of the concept of the IDP in international legal practice. The second section of the chapter examines the challenges that climate change poses to the governance of internal displacement. I examine several ways that climate change and internal displacement interact. Then, I analyse two key dysfunctions in the internal displacement governance regime that are exacerbated in the context of climate change—the humanitarian character of IDP protection and the lack of international cooperation in tackling displacement—and propose some reforms designed to address them. Taken together, this provides us with an account of the role that the internal displacement governance regime can play in tackling climate displacement, and the ways that it needs to be reformed in order to fulfil this role.

Who Is an IDP?

The main international legal framework that governs the protection of IDPs is the 1998 *Guiding Principles on Internal Displacement*. According to the Guiding Principles:

> Internally displaced persons are persons or groups of persons who have been forced or obliged to flee or to leave their homes or places of habitual residence, in particular as a result of or in order to avoid the effects of armed conflict, situations of generalized violence, violations of human rights or natural or human-made disasters, and who have not crossed an internationally recognized State border.[8]

The Guiding Principles set a number of standards concerning the treatment of IDPs, which define and prohibit the 'arbitrary' displacement of persons (Principles 5–9), govern the treatment of IDPs while they are displaced (Principles 10–23), set out the roles of national governments and humanitarian actors in protecting IDPs (Principles 24–27), and set standards for ending IDP status (Principles 28–30). Unlike the 1951 Refugee Convention and its 1967 Protocol, the Guiding Principles are a piece of 'soft law' and are not themselves legally binding. The definition of the IDP in the Guiding Principles is a *descriptive* definition, which does not confer a legal status on those that it identifies.[9] There is no comprehensive multilateral treaty equivalent to the 1951 Convention and its 1967 Protocol that governs IDP status or enshrines the rights of IDPs international law.

As a matter of practice, however, the Guiding Principles do enjoy a certain *de facto* authority.[10] The rights that they set out are systematized from existing bodies of human rights law, which means that states are formally committed to many of their provisions even though the Guiding Principles are not themselves legally binding. The Guiding Principles have also been incorporated into national legislation in a number of states and into regional conventions such as the 2006 *Great Lakes Protocol* and the 2009 *Kampala Convention*. The United Nations treats the protection of IDPs as an issue of international concern and has developed an inter-agency 'cluster approach' to coordinate action between international institutions to protect IDPs.[11] Today, we can speak of the existence of a nascent regime of governance for the protection of IDPs based around the Guiding Principles. That regime has had some uptake among states, but there is a way to go before it is firmly established in the international order.

The definition set out in the Guiding Principles identifies two key conditions that displaced persons must meet in order to count as an IDP: the *involuntariness condition* ('persons who have been forced or obliged to flee') and the *non-alienage condition* ('and who have not crossed an internationally recognised State border'). As Roberta Cohen and Francis Deng put it, the two 'distinctive features' of the IDP are that 'movement is involuntary or coerced and that the populations affected remain within their national borders'.[12] In order to develop a normative theory of IDP status, we can examine each of these conditions—involuntariness and non-alienage—in more detail.

Non-Alienage

We can begin with the concept of *non-alienage*: the fact of not having crossed an international border. At first blush, non-alienage seems to be an obvious and central aspect of internal displacement. After all, 'internal' is in the name. But it is worth interrogating the moral significance of non-alienage, for two reasons. First is simply that it is important to understand the moral relevance of (not) crossing an international border for the rights to which one is entitled. Second is that our view on the relevance of non-alienage for IDP status will bear on a conceptually related question about the relevance of alienage for refugee status. As we saw in the previous chapter, alienage is a necessary condition for refugee status under international law. But I argued—and others have also argued—that alienage is not necessary for the justified ascription of refugee status from a normative point of view.[13] If this is correct, then some people who are displaced within their state may well have a claim to refugee status, and we will need to know how to distinguish such 'internal refugees' from IDPs.

My suggestion—a somewhat revisionary one from the perspective of international law—is that non-alienage *itself* is not the morally relevant feature that distinguishes the IDP from the refugee. But this does not mean that there is no morally significant distinction between IDPs and refugees, nor that non-alienage can have no practical role in the identification and protection of IDPs. On the view that I defend, the morally relevant feature that distinguishes the IDP from the refugee is the status of the relationship in which they stand with their state. Refugees, as we saw in the last chapter, are those who cannot claim protection from their state because their relationship with their state has broken down, such that their state has lost the standing to act as the guarantor of their human rights. IDPs, by contrast, *can* claim protection from their own state, and their state retains its standing as the guarantor of their human rights. Their relationship with their state remains fundamentally intact—though it may well be compromised or degraded due to their displacement. The IDP represents the other side of the coin from the refugee when viewed from the perspective of membership. Non-alienage, on this view, is best interpreted as an imperfect proxy for tracking the status of the membership relationship. This view allows for the existence of 'internal refugees' but maintains a distinction between the normative status of the IDP and the normative status of the refugee.

To defend this view, we can begin by noting that when location matters morally, it matters because it marks out some other morally relevant feature, such as the relationship of jurisdictional authority in which a person stands. An important feature of the contemporary international order is—as we saw in Chapter 4—that jurisdictional authority is largely organized on a territorial basis. Another important feature is that states are charged with the primary duty of respecting, promoting, and fulfilling the human rights of their own members and have standing to act in that capacity—this is part of a 'division of labour' that makes human rights compatible with a system of territorially sovereign states.[14] Ordinarily, these two features work together, in that states discharge their duties to respect, promote, and fulfil the human rights of their members by exercising jurisdictional authority over the territory in which their members are located.

But these two features can also come apart. States' duties to their members persist even when they are no longer under their territorial jurisdiction: for example, when a tourist is on holiday abroad, their state still has a duty to provide them with diplomatic protection. And equally, states can lose their standing to act as the guarantor of their members' human rights even within their own territory. When a state loses its standing vis-à-vis some of its members who remain within its territory, those members can be viewed as 'internal refugees'. But, as we saw in Chapter 6, not just *any* human rights deficit will mean that the state loses its standing in this way. Sometimes, the state will be basically competent and acting in good faith, but it will be unable to secure the human rights of all of its members all of the time. In such cases, the international community's primary responsibility is to 'supplement', rather than 'substitute', the state in protecting its members' human rights.[15]

We can distinguish, then, between cases where the membership relationship has broken down and cases where it remains fundamentally intact—even if compromised to some degree. A useful way of illustrating this difference is by analogy with a distinction used in a different context by Tamar Schapiro, who distinguishes between an 'offence' and a 'betrayal' against a moral relationship:

> An offense issues from the standpoint of one whose basic commitment to the relationship is not in question. As such it has a bearing on the degree of perfection of the relationship, but it does not undermine the relationship's basic integrity. A betrayal, by contrast, issues from the perspective of one who is legitimately subject to the demands of the relationship, but whose fundamental commitment to the relationship is in question. As such, betrayals throw the basic character of the relationship into question.[16]

This analogy is helpful in mapping the conceptual terrain of the membership relationship. The analogy is not perfect, since the language of 'betrayal' suggests that the state must intentionally disregard its members' human rights (rather than merely chronically fail to secure them) in order to lose its standing. But it nonetheless illustrates that it is possible for particular human rights to go unfulfilled without the membership relationship having fundamentally broken down. The status of this relationship does not perfectly map onto the territorial jurisdiction of the state; it can remain intact when a person is outside of the territory of the state, and it can break down when they are within the territory of the state.

My suggestion is that when a person is involuntarily displaced but their relationship with their state remains fundamentally intact, they are best viewed as an IDP rather than a refugee. To see why, we can consider cases where the two come apart. One such case was mentioned in the previous chapter: we saw that the international community sometimes creates 'safe zones' within conflict countries in an attempt to pre-empt the need for international flight. If we took non-alienage to be of fundamental moral significance, then those protected in safe zones would count as IDPs rather than refugees. But on my view, we can explain why they are entitled to the more robust protections associated with refugee status that only the international community can provide.

We can also consider a case where a person is displaced across a border, but where their state retains its standing as the guarantor of their human rights. In April 2014, when the banks of the Mamoré River burst after heavy flooding in Bolivia, some 120 families in the border region of Guayaramerín fled across the border and were sheltered in Brazil, as floods prevented them from being easily moved to Bolivian shelters.[17] Suppose that if Brazil failed to provide adequate protection, Bolivia would have fulfilled its obligations of diplomatic protection and would have provided protection within Bolivia if necessary. These families, despite being displaced and being outside of their own state, would still stand in the right kind of relationship for us to describe their state as the guarantor of their human rights. It would be strange to treat such people as refugees, even if they were displaced outside of the territory of their state. After all, it was merely for reasons of efficiency that their protection took place in Brazil. The agent with the primary duty to ensure the protection of their human rights remained Bolivia, even if the responsibilities associated with this relationship had been informally transferred to Brazil. If we take the status of the membership relationship to be morally basic in drawing the distinction between IDPs and refugees, we can explain this judgement by appealing to the fact that the membership relationship remained intact.

This latter case opens up conceptual space for the possibility of an IDP who is outside of the territory of their state, which may appear counter-intuitive. It is worth recognizing, however, that my focus here is on the underlying philosophical basis upon which the rights associated with IDP and refugee status should be granted. Non-alienage may still play a practical role in IDP protection. As we can see from this case, it is rare for a person to be displaced outside of the territory of their state and for their state to be in a position to protect their human rights. Generally, a state needs to have jurisdictional authority over the territory in which a person is displaced in order to discharge its duties to protect and fulfil their rights. This means that, as a rule, we have good reason to treat those outside of the territory of their state as being eligible for international protection—perhaps by ascribing them some kind of 'complementary protection' status.[18]

Non-alienage has some practical significance as a proxy for identifying IDPs. It is not, however, itself a morally relevant basis for IDP status. This interpretation of non-alienage has critical potential because non-alienage is not always a *good* proxy. In some cases which have traditionally been viewed as cases of internal displacement, particularly in conflict situations, states have in fact lost their standing as the guarantor of their members' human rights. James Hathaway suggests that a significant source of the relative popularity of the IDP label among states is that it has proven to be a convenient way for states to shirk their responsibilities to would-be refugees in conflict situations. As he points out, 'these persons would in most cases have qualified for refugee status had they not been encouraged, and at times compelled, to remain inside their own country'.[19] In cases like these, my view has the advantage of being able to explain why these displaced people, even if they have remained inside their state, are entitled to the more robust forms of international protection associated with refugee status.

This interpretation of non-alienage implies a revision of the practices of IDP protection. It means that when we ascribe IDP or refugee status, we make a judgement about whether or not the individual concerned is entitled to international protection or whether they should appeal to their state to protect their human rights. Civil conflict will often (but not always) be indicative that a state has lost its standing to act as the ongoing guarantor of its members' human rights, at least vis-à-vis some segment of its membership. Other forms of displacement (such as disaster displacement) will often be a matter of a state trying to uphold its responsibilities in good faith but facing exigent circumstances which mean that its capacities are under pressure. Historically, many of the cases that have motivated the development of the IDP protection regime have been cases of civil conflict.[20] On my view, it may be more appropriate to treat those who are displaced in such cases as refugees, rather than IDPs.

Involuntariness

The second distinctive feature of the IDP is that IDPs have been 'forced or obliged' to move: their movement is *involuntary*. A fuller interpretation of the concept of involuntariness is necessary to clarify who counts as an IDP. As we will see, it also helps us to clarify the rights associated with IDP status.

We can distinguish between at least two conceptions of involuntariness. One conception of involuntariness draws inspiration from Joseph Raz's conception of autonomy. Raz argues that in order to undertake genuinely autonomous action, individuals must have an 'adequate range of valuable options' available to them.[21] If an individual's choice is made from among a set of options which is overly constrained, then her choice is not a genuinely autonomous one, and so it is in this sense involuntary. This is the conception of involuntariness that we encountered in Chapter 5, when considering the position of those deciding whether to take up opportunities for labour migration in the context of climate change. Applied to the context of IDP protection, we might say that movement is involuntary—and that those on the move count as IDPs—when it is *not* chosen from among an adequate range of valuable options. Call this the *broad view* of involuntariness.

A second conception of involuntariness can be called the *narrow view*. The narrow view says that involuntariness is best understood in a more specific sense for the purposes of IDP protection: in the sense of it being *reactive*. The idea of reactive movement comes from Anthony Richmond's sociological theory of migration, in which he distinguishes between proactive and reactive movement.[22] Ideal-typically, reactive movement is precipitated by sudden events and changes, which 'disrupt the normal functioning of the system' and 'destroy . . . the capacity of a population to survive under the prevailing conditions'.[23] Proactive movement, by contrast, is typically planned and anticipated, even though the options available to those on the move may be structured by a range of political, economic, environmental, social, and bio-psychological 'structural constraints'.[24] Reactive displacement, as we saw in Chapter 1, is a coping response that uses movement as a way of escaping harmful events.

My claim is that for the purposes of an account of the normative status of the IDP, we should adopt the narrow view. But before defending this claim, it is worth noting that the narrow view does not claim that all proactive or anticipatory forms of movement are always fully voluntary. It seems entirely sensible to suggest, for Razian reasons, that movement in response to slow-onset economic decline or environmental degradation is properly thought of as involuntary (though clearly, those moving in these circumstances do exercise a degree of agency). The narrow view just says that one specific kind of involuntary movement—reactive displacement—is the proper concern of the IDP protection regime. Those affected by other forms of involuntary movement may well have important normative claims with respect to that movement. My claim is only that we should be concerned with reactive movement for the purposes of an account of the normative status of the IDP.

There are two reasons to prefer the narrow view over the broad view. The first reason is that the broad view's capacious understanding of involuntariness fits poorly with the practices of IDP protection. The causes of internal displacement identified in the Guiding Principles—armed conflict, generalized violence, human rights violations, and disasters—provide central examples of the kind of movement that the IDP regime is suited to address: the movement of those who find themselves suddenly uprooted from their homes. Displacement that involves the rapid disruption of background conditions of stability is importantly different from anticipatory forms of involuntary movement and demands a different kind of response. Anticipatory forms of involuntary movement are better governed through programmes such as labour migration regulation or planned relocation projects, as we saw in Chapters 3 and 5. If we take seriously the particular function of the IDP protection regime, then we should restrict our understanding of the involuntariness of internal displacement to the more specific sense of reactive movement to stop us from inflating the concept of the IDP.

A second reason concerns the distinctive nature of the harm of reactive displacement. The IDP protection regime's specific focus on reactive displacement can be vindicated by recognizing that the narrow view captures a distinctive harm that is not captured by the broad view. We can see the role of the IDP protection regime as being to respond to this distinctive harm.

The harm of reactive displacement can be understood in terms of the interest that we have in being able to form and pursue our own life-plans against relatively stable background conditions. In order to make and pursue life-plans, we depend on a relatively stable background framework. Our life-plans are *located* in the sense that they are organized around our 'expectations of continued use of, and secure access to, a place of residence'—including secure access both to our homes and to shared spaces in which we participate in social practices.[25] Reactive displacement involves sudden disruptions that destroy the stable background conditions against which we form and pursue our life-plans. These disruptions upset the expectations that we have to continue to be able to securely use and access particular spaces, including our homes, which enable us to form and carry out our plans.

Anticipatory displacement may also affect our life-plans and expectations, but it does not do so in the same way. Rather than needing to re-establish a stable background against which we can develop any plans at all, we can respond to slow-onset changes either by revising our plans and adjusting our expectations, or by working to prevent or alter the changes in circumstances that threaten our existing plans. This does not mean that those affected by anticipatory displacement do not suffer a harm: the foreclosing of the options available to them is certainly harmful, and it may be no less significant than the harm of reactive displacement.[26] The crucial point is rather that this harm is of a qualitatively different kind, and that it warrants a different response. This provides us with a principled basis for adopting the narrow view for determining who counts as an IDP: the narrow view captures a distinctive harm, the destruction of the located background of relative stability upon which our life-plans rest. The IDP protection regime's function is best interpreted as being to address this specific harm.

This conception of involuntariness can also help us to clarify the content of the duties that we owe to IDPs. Since IDP status picks out those who face the harm of reactive displacement, the rights and duties associated with IDP status can be unpacked by reference to justified claims that IDPs have to be protected against that harm. Anna Stilz and Margaret Moore have both recently argued that the interest in forming and pursing life-plans gives rise to what they respectively term 'occupancy' and 'residency' rights.[27] We can employ the concept of occupancy rights to clarify the duties that states have with respect to internal displacement.

Stilz and Moore both argue that occupancy rights have two components: first, a liberty to reside in a particular space; second, a claim against removal from that space.[28] Reactive displacement, however, can be precipitated by purely natural disasters and need not involve any agent infringing upon the claim-right against being removed. My suggestion is that occupancy rights imply a *positive* duty on the part of the state to protect and maintain the background conditions of relative stability upon which we depend, and to restore them when they are disrupted, rather than merely a negative duty not to disrupt background conditions of relative stability. This means that even if events which precipitate displacement arise naturally, without any infringement of a claim-right against removal, states may commit a wrong if such events lead to reactive displacement.

The precise extent of this duty should be made clear. It would not be reasonable to expect states to prevent all cases of displacement which arise under any circumstances. Displacement is hard to predict, occurs suddenly, and may be of such scale that it is not feasible to stop everyone from being displaced. Despite our best efforts, displacement may still, tragically, occur. In such cases, I do not think we can say that those affected have been *wronged*, even if they have been harmed. But we can still specify the rights that individuals have against their state with respect to displacement. On my view, such rights include, first, a right to the reduction of the risks of displacement to tolerable levels, and second, a right to have background conditions of relative stability restored quickly and effectively when displacement does occur.

The first right is not strictly something that is owed to IDPs but is rather a right that each person has that their state should make reasonable efforts to prevent them from becoming an IDP. Perhaps ideally states would reduce the risk of reactive displacement to zero, but this will not be possible or reasonable in most circumstances. A threshold of 'tolerability' is more sensitive to the fact that it is not practically possible to entirely eliminate all risk of reactive displacement and reflects the idea that low levels of risk need not disrupt our ability to form and pursue life-plans. What counts as a 'tolerable' level of displacement risk is hard to specify in the abstract and may well vary across circumstances. It should, however, be low enough to enable to reasonable people to depend upon a background of relative stability.[29] In practice, protecting this right will require states to invest in projects such as disaster risk reduction and climate change adaptation. Most of the time this will involve *in situ* forms of adaptation to climate change, but it may also, in some cases, involve the forms of anticipatory movement examined in Chapters 3 and 5.

The second right can only be fulfilled through the provision of assistance once displacement has occurred. We must recognize that our best efforts to protect against displacement may fail, and that when they do, those who are displaced have a right to a background of relative stability that enables them to form and pursue their own life-plans. The duty to restore the background conditions of relative stability quickly and effectively is the correlate of that right.

There are broadly three ways that this duty can be discharged: return, local integration, and resettlement. In international legal practice, these are taken to be the 'durable solutions' to internal displacement and have been codified most clearly in the IASC Framework.[30] Each of these options can restore the background of stability in its own way. Often, return will be the preferable solution. It may enable IDPs to reconstitute their original plans by reclaiming property and lands. It may also have additional significance in terms of preserving IDPs' ability to participate in valued cultural or religious practices with connections to particular places or enabling them to assert their status as equal members of the community from which they have been displaced.[31] In some cases, however, return may not be possible or desirable. A disaster may mean that there is a lack of habitable land, or in more protracted situations of displacement, those affected may begin to develop new life-plans and expectations in the environments in which they find themselves. In such cases, local integration may be a preferable way of nurturing those plans and expectations, by ensuring that they rest on stable background conditions. Where local integration is not desirable, resettlement may be preferable. Resettlement projects for IDPs, if undertaken well, will allow IDPs to exercise some measure of choice over the new environment in which they will live. They may enable IDPs to move to a new environment which provides particular goods (for example, resources or access to culturally valued practices) that enable them to pursue their own life-plans.

The best way to restore background conditions of stability is likely to depend on particular circumstances of different IDPs, and in international legal practice IDPs are supposed to enjoy the 'right to choose freely between return, local integration, or resettlement'.[32] One rationale for this is that IDPs know their own circumstances best, and so will often be best placed to know which durable solution best fits their circumstances. But this is not the only or best rationale. Even if IDPs are mistaken about which option best suits their circumstances, they should still have the power to decide between these options. This reflects the idea that we value not only the life-plans that we happen to have, but also our ability to autonomously form and pursue our own life-plans.[33]

Taken together, these two rights specify the content of the state's positive duty to protect its members against the standard threat of displacement. The narrow view of involuntariness clarifies who has a normative claim to IDP status, and the rights that are associated with that status.

Climate Change and Internal Displacement

As the impacts of climate change accelerate, one of their central consequences will be an increase in internal displacement. The main way in which climate change interacts with internal displacement is through disasters such as typhoons, floods, and wildfires, although there are also some other mechanisms through which climate change interacts with internal displacement. Its precise scale is hard to quantify, but social scientific research suggests that most climate displacement will take the form of internal displacement of one form or another.[34] Not all of those who are displaced within their state by climate impacts will count as IDPs in the sense that I have construed them here, but a great many of them will.

The example of Typhoon Haiyan with which we began illustrates the central way in which climate change interacts with internal displacement: disasters. Anthropogenic climate change makes extreme weather events such as Haiyan more frequent and intense. And extreme weather events such as Haiyan drive displacement. The damage that they wreak can be immense: homes and critical infrastructure are destroyed, crops and livelihoods are ruined, and families are separated. Displacement due to weather-related disasters already outnumbers displacement due to conflict and development, making up nearly 60 per cent of all internal displacement in 2021.[35] And as the impacts of climate change unfold and extreme weather events become more frequent and intense, that number is only likely to increase.[36]

As with other forms of climate displacement, displacement driven by disasters is complex. One aspect of complexity lies in the relationship between climate change and disasters. For one thing, it's not always clear which events should count as 'disasters' in the first place. Anthropologists point out that whether or not particular climate impacts are experienced as a disaster depends upon the way in which they are mediated by the social and physical infrastructure of the societies that they affect.[37] Climate scientists tend to treat 'extreme' weather events as aberrations from otherwise stable climatic conditions, but their judgements depend on baseline assumptions about 'normal' climatic conditions that can be controversial.[38] Beyond these conceptual questions, we also lack good information about the extent to which particular events are related to climate change. Although we can say in general terms that anthropogenic climate change leads to an increase in the frequency and severity of extreme weather events, it remains difficult to judge that any particular event was a consequence of climate change. The developing science of 'probabilistic event attribution' hopes to give us statistical grounds for relatively confident judgements about the probability that particular events would have happened in the absence of anthropogenic climate change, but it remains in its infancy.[39]

Another aspect of this complexity is that disasters are deeply social phenomena. In order to understand disasters, it is crucial to understand not only the physical hazards associated with climate change, but also the social mechanisms through which they affect people. The concept of vulnerability—the aspects of a person's circumstances that affect their ability to cope with hazards—is central to the study of disasters.[40] And as Richard Black and his co-authors have shown, vulnerability and its converse, resilience, bear significantly on how extreme weather events affect displacement.[41] The structural constraints associated with a person's social position in society affect their capacity to mobilize resources to cope with hazards, the opportunities to which they have access, and the extent to which they can rely on formal or informal assistance from others.

The social nature of vulnerability means that the differential impacts of disasters often reflect background injustices structured along classic fault lines such as race, class, gender, indigeneity, and disability. In 2005, Hurricane Katrina provided a vivid illustration of this.[42] The enduring legacy of racial segregation in New Orleans meant that Black residents were concentrated in the areas worst affected by the hurricane.[43] As the disaster unfolded, evacuation messages were less likely to reach, or to be trusted by, low-income and Black residents of New Orleans, many of whom stayed where they were because they were concerned that public authorities would not protect their property or communities, or because they provided care for someone who was unable to leave.[44] The evacuation plan for the city depended on residents being able to escape by car, but rates of car ownership were much lower among Black and low-income communities.[45] The city's racialized and socioeconomically disadvantaged groups also returned to the city at a much lower rate.[46] As a result, the impacts of the disaster fell most heavily on low-income and Black residents.

Public policy has an important role in structuring vulnerability and resilience to disasters. The racialized failures of the government response to Katrina are notorious.[47] But there are also positive examples of interventions through disaster risk reduction and climate change adaptation that make individuals and groups more resilient in the face of disasters. Cuba—which faces a wide variety of natural hazards—has been widely praised by international actors for its sophisticated disaster management system.[48] Cuba integrates policy in construction, urban planning, early warning systems, and evacuation plans into one comprehensive framework for disaster management.[49] It also has widespread education surrounding disaster planning, and its approach appears to enjoy broad support among its population.[50] Of course, there are aspects of Cuba's 'specific political and economic context'—its top-down, command-and-control structure, for one—which may limit its generalizability.[51] But there are lessons that can be learned from it, too. Developing an integrated and competent system of disaster management—and crucially, one that pays close attention to the background injustices that affect vulnerability—is an important part of the duty to reduce the risk of internal displacement.

As in other contexts of climate displacement, the complexity of disaster displacement gives us reason to think that those displaced by the impacts of climate change will not usually be readily identifiable. But we do not need to know whether or not any particular individual was displaced by climate impacts to know that a functioning regime of governance for internal displacement is an important part of tackling climate displacement. We can expect significant increases in the numbers of people facing disaster displacement in the context of climate change. Though we may not know exactly which people are displaced by climate impacts, we do know that many of them will need to call on the protection of the IDP protection regime.

Disasters are the main way in which climate change interacts with internal displacement. But there are other connections as well. Another way in which displacement may be exacerbated in the context of climate change is through the failure of adaptation to avert foreseeable threats to background conditions of stability. Threats to food security, health, and economic stability are predictable impacts of climate change, which are often best addressed through climate change adaptation (including, sometimes, community relocation and labour migration, as examined in Chapters 3 and 5). But there also limits to adaptation.[52] Some climate impacts may be of such scale that successful adaptation is difficult to achieve. And even where successful adaptation is possible, maladaptation that results from failures in the governance and planning can *increase* vulnerability to climate change impacts.[53] Our primary duty here is to ensure that adaptation planning is as successful as it can be. But to the extent that adaptation planning fails, we can expect to see an increase in the number of people with a claim to protection as an IDP.

Another way in which climate change may precipitate displacement is not through its impacts, but through measures taken to mitigate it. The phenomenon of 'green-grabbing'—the 'appropriation of land and resources for environmental ends'—often involves removing people from the lands that they occupy in the name of conservation.[54] Some areas of land—particularly rainforests, but also grasslands, savannahs, and peatlands—act as 'carbon sinks' that sequester carbon from the atmosphere and so contribute to the project of climate change mitigation.[55] Conservation projects that seek to preserve and enhance terrestrial carbon sinks have often conflicted with the occupancy rights of local communities, and particularly of Indigenous peoples, whose informal or customary forms of land tenure make them especially vulnerable to dispossession and displacement.[56] The most infamous example is a UNFCCC initiative called Reducing Emissions from Deforestation and Degradation (REDD+), under which developing countries are compensated for protecting and enhancing their rainforests instead of exploiting them for their own economic benefit. In practice, major consequences of REDD+ projects have included the exclusion of Indigenous peoples from their lands, the capture of conservation funding by local elites, and the centralization of natural resource management.[57] Indigenous activists have been vocal critics of REDD+. At COP13 in Bali in 2007, the International Forum of Indigenous Peoples on Climate Change argued against the REDD+ programme on the basis that it would 'increase the violation of our human rights, our rights to our lands, territories and resources, steal our land, cause forced evictions, prevent access and threaten indigenous agriculture practices, destroy biodiversity and culture diversity and cause social conflicts'.[58]

Chris Armstrong has argued that conservation projects such as REDD+ need not, in principle, conflict with the occupancy rights of Indigenous communities.[59] As he points out, the rights that Indigenous peoples claim over these lands are typically not rights of 'full liberal ownership' that would entitle them to exploit natural resources for their own economic benefit. Usually, they are *use rights* to occupy particular areas and to pursue ways of life that reflect their own values—ways of life that are generally compatible with conservation efforts. Indeed, Indigenous peoples are important actors in the *defence* of sustainable land and resource use against extractive industries, and they often face violent reprisals as a result.[60] If conservation projects were properly implemented, then they would not need to lead to displacement.

But even if there is no *deep* conflict between local claims to occupancy and global claims to conservation, it is still important to take seriously the claims of Indigenous peoples over the land that they occupy. As Megan Blomfield has argued, treating land as simply part of the 'global commons' because of its role in carbon sequestration implies that conservation goals are the only normative consideration at stake in their governance and risks incentivizing land-grabs by elites in the name of conservation.[61] Safeguarding the occupancy rights of Indigenous peoples means enabling them to manage the sustainable use of their lands, and empowering them to resist domination by powerful elites and centralized state bureaucracies. This implies, at the very least, a deep transformation of the governance of conservation projects such as REDD+.

This judgement draws on a convergence in the implications of local claims to occupancy and global claims to conservation. But if local claims to occupancy and global claims to conservation were to genuinely conflict—say, if a local community started heavily exploiting its natural resources for its own economic benefit— could the goal of conservation justify their displacement? Principle 6.2(c) of the Guiding Principles says that states should not permit development projects that cause displacement unless they are 'justified by compelling and overriding public interests'.[62] The benefits associated with the conservation of terrestrial sinks—like the benefits associated with development—could be highly significant, given their important role in climate mitigation.

But conservation projects would need to meet a very high bar of justification for them to justify displacement, and it is unlikely that they will meet this bar in practice.[63] The right to occupancy is a basic right, and so should weigh heavily in our judgements about the permissibility of conservation projects that involve displacement. Proponents of a displacement-inducing project would need to show not only that it has weighty conservation benefits, but further that its *marginal* benefits, compared to other possible courses of action, are sufficient to outweigh occupancy rights. Conservation goals can typically be achieved without displacing people from their lands—for example, through land-use regulations that prevent certain uses of land which are incompatible with conservation. And even if this high bar of justification could be met, then conservation projects would also need to be implemented in a way that met standards of procedural and substantive justice, including the empowered participation of affected communities in planning and implementation, the protection of the cultural integrity, and fair compensation and benefit-sharing.[64] This would rule out *reactive* displacement of the kind that we have examined in this chapter. If any displacement were to be all-things-considered justified, then it would look much more like the forms of planned relocation examined in Chapter 3. So, although the recent history of REDD+ suggests that reactive displacement is likely to occur because of conservation projects aimed at mitigating climate change, we should view such displacement as a consequence of our failure to discharge our duties to reduce the risk of internal displacement, rather than as an acceptable side-effect of climate mitigation.

Climate Change and the International Protection of IDPs

The protection of IDPs is generally viewed as a domestic issue. This idea is reflected in Principle 3.1 of the Guiding Principles, which says that 'national authorities have the primary duty and responsibility to provide protection and humanitarian assistance to internally displaced persons within their jurisdiction.'[65] But at the same time, internal displacement is treated as a matter of international concern. The international community plays an important role in IDP protection through a range of international agencies, including the United Nations High Commissioner for Refugees (UNHCR), the World Food Programme (WFP), the International Organisation for Migration (IOM), the World Health Organisation (WHO), the United Nations Children's Fund (UNICEF), and the Office of the High Commissioner on Human Rights (OHCHR).[66]

The dual character of IDP protection raises the question of what duties the international community has in the protection of IDPs. And in the context of climate change, having a fuller understanding of those duties is all the more important. My claim is that although the IDP's state is the primary duty-bearer of their rights, the international community has a collective duty to supplement the state in its protection of IDPs. In the context of climate change, that duty has two important implications: first, that the international protection of IDPs should be treated as a matter of justice, not charity; second, that robust forms of international cooperation in sharing the costs of IDP protection between states should be established.

Why does the international community have duties to supplement the protection of IDPs by their own states? At first glance, there seems to be no principled reason why the international community should be involved in IDP protection. After all, I argued before that IDPs are partly defined by the fact that—unlike in the case of refugees—their state retains its standing as the guarantor of their human rights. According to the norms of the international order, each state is responsible for the protection of the human rights of its members, and IDPs remain members of their state. So, at first glance, it appears that the state is the only agent with a duty of justice to protect IDPs under its jurisdiction. Other agents might decide to contribute to IDP protection, but doing so would be a matter of charity, not a matter of justice.

One reason why the international community might have a duty of justice to protect IDPs is if its members bear *responsibility* for their plight. Laura Valentini argues that 'we have duties of justice towards the needy when our agency has contributed to their plight ... and duties of charity when our "hands are clean" but we can still help them at reasonable costs'.[67] According to Valentini, this helps to explain our moral intuition that we have duties of justice to those affected by the Haitian earthquake of 2010, but that assistance to those affected by the earthquakes of 2011 in New Zealand and Japan is a matter of charity. Our duties of justice in the Haitian case arise from the fact that the historic injustices inflicted upon Haiti—including its colonial past and the reparations it was forced to pay to France, its occupation by the United States, and the economic liberalization that was thrust upon it by the World Bank and the International Monetary Fund (IMF) as a condition for the receipt of loans—have enduring effects that have made it particularly vulnerable to disasters.[68]

Valentini is right to suggest that responsibility can ground duties of justice with respect to IDPs. When particular agents are responsible for internal displacement, they incur remedial duties of justice which mean that they can be required to bear the costs of addressing displacement (at least, absent any powerful countervailing reasons to redistribute those costs).[69] This explains why firms involved in extractive industries such as oil and mining, and public authorities involved in large-scale development projects such as the construction of dams, can be required to bear the costs of addressing displacement for which they are responsible. And as we will see, this also explains why high emitters incur remedial duties to bear the costs of addressing climate displacement—though there are some additional complications in the case of climate change. But in my view, the international community has a duty of justice to assist in IDP protection even when its members bear no responsibility for internal displacement.

The reason why the international community has duties of justice to assist in the protection of IDPs even when its members bear no responsibility for displacement is that they have a collective responsibility to uphold and maintain a robust regime of human rights protection. Simply leaving each state free from interference to discharge its human rights duties is insufficient to ensure that human rights are robustly protected and expresses only a weak commitment to human rights norms. States that are genuinely committed to universal human rights protection should recognize that states need the 'positive' capacity to mobilize the resources necessary to address human rights threats such as the threat of displacement.[70] Where states do not enjoy that positive capacity, there is a predictable risk that they will fail to protect their members' human rights. Establishing provisions for assistance in protecting human rights can be a matter of preserving the 'background justice' of an international order structured by a commitment to human rights protection.[71]

Displacement is a 'standard threat' against which states have a duty to protect their members.[72] Addressing this standard threat requires the state to be able to mobilize the resources necessary to protect its members' rights. But disadvantaged states may need to call on international assistance to protect their members—whether because of their own lack of capacity, because of the enduring effects of historic injustices, or simply because accidents of geography leave them more vulnerable to disasters. They will foreseeably be unable to mobilize resources at a large scale in the way that addressing displacement requires. When acting alone, their immediate capacities to respond to displacement can be overstretched. As Roberta Cohen points out, situations of displacement are often particularly acute:

> Many governments do not have the resources, capacity or will to address the needs of the displaced, so that attention understandably shifts to the international community. The Guiding Principles on Internal Displacement... make clear that the international community has an important role to play in addressing the protection and assistance needs of IDPs, even though primary responsibility rests with their governments.[73]

Principle 25 of the Guiding Principles says that 'international humanitarian organizations and other appropriate actors have the right to offer their services in support of the internally displaced' and that 'consent thereto shall not be arbitrarily withheld'.[74] On my view, this principle is too weak. In an international order committed to universal human rights protection, the international community has a collective duty to ensure not only that each person has a state that is charged with the protection of their human rights, but also that each state has the support it needs to make that protection effective.

At the moment, the protection of IDPs is largely treated as a matter of charity. This is true of both the duties that states owe to IDPs in their own jurisdiction and the duties that the international community owes to assist states in protecting

IDPs. As a result, there are serious failures in the implementation of IDP protection, and those failures are only likely to become more severe as the impacts of climate change accelerate.

One aspect of the problem is that being labelled as an IDP does not give the individual any specific rights under international law. Although the sources from which the Guiding Principles are drawn are in human rights law, and while there is evidence of widespread formal recognition of the relevance of the principles, the lack of legal standing given to IDPs makes it difficult for them to claim their rights.[75] This is partly a result of the political context in which the Guiding Principles were drafted. According to Cohen and Deng:

> There was no support for a legally binding treaty given the sensitivity surrounding the sovereignty issue. Second, treaty making could take decades, whereas a document was needed urgently. Third, sufficient international law already existed to protect IDPs. What was needed was a restatement of the law tailored to the explicit concerns of IDPs.[76]

The result of this, however, is that states are under no formal obligation to recognize the Guiding Principles as authoritative in their treatment of IDPs. And the implementation of IDP protection is patchy at best, even in states which do formally recognize their obligations to IDPs. Phil Orchard notes that 'given the soft law nature of the principles, governments which make a commitment at the international level to protect their own IDPs have only done so rhetorically'.[77] One study of the implementation of IDP protection found serious failings in a number of countries where IDP protection has been incorporated into national legislation, including in Colombia, Sudan, Pakistan, Nepal, the Democratic Republic of the Congo, Georgia, Kenya, the Central African Republic, and Turkey.[78] In some cases this is due to a lack of political will, but in others it is due to a lack of state capacity.

Where the problem is a lack of state capacity, it is compounded by the lack of binding international obligations in IDP protection. Any international assistance that is given for IDP protection is treated as discretionary. Where assistance is given, it is rarely allocated in ways which fulfil the international community's duty of justice to assist in IDP protection. Studies of the flows of international assistance in the wake of disasters suggest that assistance is largely allocated not on the basis of need but rather along the lines of former colonial ties, shared languages, geographical distance, and—in many cases—the economic interests of donor countries.[79] The humanitarian character of international assistance in the practices of IDP protection means that those states which depend on international assistance are at the mercy of donor countries. There is no guarantee that international assistance will be provided, let alone that it will be provided in ways which fulfil the international community's duty of justice to assist in IDP protection.

This problem is only likely to be exacerbated in the context of climate change. Developing states—those that are already most vulnerable to climate impacts—are likely to feel the brunt of economic losses associated with climate change.[80] We can expect that this will make it more difficult for them to mobilize the resources they need in order to address displacement. For their part, richer states are likely to take advantage of the discretionary nature of international assistance by directing their resources inward towards their own competing priorities, or outward, but in line with their own strategic interests. The status of the Guiding Principles as soft law means that states are likely to find it easier to renege on their commitments in providing assistance to disadvantaged states as the impacts of climate change increase the pressure on the resources needed in order to discharge duties to IDPs.

One way to address the problem of humanitarianism would be to push for the transformation of IDP governance from 'soft' to 'hard' international law.[81] In the context of IDP governance, hardening soft law could mean several different things. It could mean negotiating a multilateral treaty on internal displacement, delegating authority to an international institution to adjudicate disputes over who has a claim to protection as an IDP, formal recognition of obligations to provide assistance to disadvantaged states, or states transposing the Guiding Principles into effective domestic legislation. Harder forms of international law increase the costs that states take on if they renege on their commitments, allow less space for self-serving interpretations of legal commitments, and can create more capacity for enforcement, especially when international commitments are incorporated into domestic law.[82]

My aim here is not to prescribe a precise blueprint for hardening soft law in IDP governance. Walter Kälin has argued against pursuing a multilateral treaty for internal displacement on the basis that states are not ready to recognize a legal status for IDPs. Instead, he argues that we should seek to 'build consensus from the "bottom up"'.[83] Kälin may be right to suggest that the political context is not ripe for a binding treaty, but this need not preclude attempts to harden the international law of IDP protection. Other options—including pursuing the implementation of IDP protection in national legislation, which Kälin himself prefers—may be more politically palatable while moving in the right direction.[84] One good example is the 2006 *Great Lakes Protocol*, which seeks to formalize responses to internal displacement in the Great Lakes region and explicitly requires member states to recognize the Guiding Principles and implement them into national legislation.[85]

It is important to note, however, that one reason why states are reticent to commit to hard law in IDP protection is because they fear that they will bear disproportionate costs as a result of doing so. If the Guiding Principles in their current formulation were to form the basis of a treaty, then disadvantaged states would justifiably be concerned that they would be required to bear significant costs compared to advantaged states, because the Guiding Principles do not contain strong provisions for international assistance. Similarly, if only provisions for international assistance were strengthened without formalizing the claims that IDPs have against their states, then advantaged states would be concerned that they would have no guarantee that disadvantaged states would use the resources to address internal displacement.

One useful way of moving forward in hardening the law of IDP protection would be to ensure that *both* the obligations that states owe to their IDPs *and* the obligations of assistance that advantaged states owe to disadvantaged states are hardened at the same time. If moves were made to harden both domestic and international obligations to IDPs at the same time, then this would avoid either increasing the costs borne by disadvantaged states or incentivizing them to extract benefits from advantaged states while reneging on their commitments to IDPs.

This would provide an opportunity to address a second problem in the practices of IDP protection that is exacerbated in the context of climate change: the 'internalist bias' in IDP governance.[86] As it stands, the IDP governance regime operates on the presumption that the causes of internal displacement are the actions (or omissions) of the state in which displacement occurs. This fails to account for *external* causes of internal displacement. There are a number of ways in which external processes and events can drive internal displacement, including through military intervention abroad and the activities of multinational corporations involved in mining, oil extraction, and deforestation. But one major way in which internal displacement can be driven by external factors is through the impacts of climate change. As we have seen, extreme weather events are predicted to become more frequent and intense as a result of anthropogenic climate change, and so high emitters increase the risk of internal displacement through their contributions to climate change. Disadvantaged states bear the bulk of this burden of displacement risk—partly because they tend to be located in more vulnerable climatic zones, and partly because their pre-existing disadvantages mean that they have fewer resources to protect themselves against climate impacts—while they themselves contribute relatively little to the problem of climate change. Advantaged states, by contrast, are less vulnerable to climate impacts such as extreme weather events, are better able to protect themselves against those impacts, and contribute most to the problem of climate change.

Climate change creates a problem of unfairness in the distribution of the costs of IDP protection. High-emitting states are currently reaping the benefits of their energy-intensive economies but are unilaterally imposing the burden of displacement risk that they are creating on disadvantaged states. This is not only a moral problem in its own right, but is also likely to strain the commitments required to sustain the fragile project of IDP protection. States that are most affected by internal displacement in the context of climate change have a reasonable complaint that they are being required to bear a disproportionate share of the costs of the IDP protection regime, and their commitment to that regime may weaken as a result.

This bears on how the costs of IDP protection should be shared between states. As we have seen, states are in the first instance responsible for addressing the internal displacement of their own members, but the international community also has a collective duty to assist disadvantaged states in protecting IDPs. The costs of discharging this collective duty should be shared on fair terms. As we saw in the discussion of the refugee regime in Chapter 6, one fair way to share the costs of this collective duty would be on the basis of a principle of equal burdens. The principle of equal burdens treats each state as an equal partner in the cooperative project of international IDP assistance, and privileges no particular state's interests over those of others.

But as we also saw in Chapter 6, the principle of equal burdens is only a benchmark, from which departures can be justified. One justification for departing from the principle of equal burdens refers to responsibility: when states are responsible for causing internal displacement, they can be held liable to bear the costs associated with addressing it. In the case of climate change, high emitters can be held liable for the costs associated with the burden of displacement risk that they impose upon the IDP protection regime. This should be reflected in the way in which the costs of IDP protection are shared between states, as a matter of fairness. Climate change involves some complications that affect how this idea should be interpreted in practice, which I discuss further in Chapter 8. But in broad terms, we can say that states should be held responsible for the costs of addressing the displacement associated with their contributions to climate change.

The protection of IDPs is a central part of the project of tackling climate displacement. As we have seen, the normative status of the IDP implies a set of rights that its bearer can claim and correlate duties that others—in the first instance, their own states—owe. This chapter has set out an interpretation of the normative status of the IDP, according to which IDPs are those who are reactively displaced but who still remain in the right kind of relationship to their state for it to have standing to act as the guarantor of their human rights. This interpretation allows us to maintain a conceptual distinction between IDPs and 'internal refugees' while also diagnosing the specific harm that the IDP protection regime is best suited to address: the harm of having the background conditions of relative stability, upon which we depend to form and pursue life-plans, undermined. The rights of IDPs—to the reduction of displacement risks to tolerable levels, and to the restoration of background conditions of stability through return, local integration, or resettlement—are the justified claims that they have to be protected against this harm. The international community, I have argued, also has a collective duty to provide disadvantaged states with the support that they need to protect their own IDPs.

Climate change plays an important role in driving internal displacement. The main way in which it does this is by making extreme weather events such as typhoons, floods, and wildfires more frequent and intense. But measures taken to mitigate climate change—such as rainforest conservation projects—can also be implicated in internal displacement when they are carried out in ways that do not pay sufficient attention to the occupancy rights of local communities. In the context of climate change, it is all the more important that both the domestic and the international duties associated with IDP protection are strengthened, and I have suggested that hardening the presently soft forms of international law that govern internal displacement is an important goal for reform. An important part of that process will be ensuring that high-emitting states are held responsible for the costs associated with addressing the displacement that they have created through their contributions to climate change. In Chapter 8, I examine the question of how the costs of addressing climate displacement should be shared in more detail.

8
Sharing the Costs of Climate Displacement

Over the past five chapters, we have examined a range of contexts of climate displacement: community relocation, territorial sovereignty, labour migration, refugee movement, and internal displacement. Addressing climate displacement across these contexts involves a variety of actors discharging a range of first-order duties. These include the duties of governments to plan and manage relocation for local communities, the international community's duties to negotiate and implement new forms of territorial autonomy in partnership with small-island peoples, high-income states' duties to put in place labour migration schemes that target those vulnerable to climate impacts, the international community's duties to host refugees and provide safe and legal routes for their protection, states' duties to reduce the risks of internal displacement and to protect internally displaced persons (IDPs), and the international community's duty to assist disadvantaged states in protecting IDPs in their jurisdiction.

Discharging these duties to the displaced involves bearing costs.[1] This chapter shifts the focus of our inquiry from the first-order question of what duties we owe to those who are displaced in the context of climate change to the second-order question of how the costs of discharging those duties should be shared. Although there are different actors who are best placed to discharge the first-order duties that we owe to the displaced, the costs of discharging those duties should be shared fairly among the duty-bearers. The aim of this chapter is to determine what distribution of costs is fair.

My central claim is that the concept of responsibility has an important role to play in a fair distribution of the costs of addressing climate displacement. The idea that those who are responsible for climate displacement should be held responsible for bearing the costs of addressing it has a powerful intuitive appeal. As Henry Shue puts it: 'all over the world parents teach their children to clean up their own mess'.[2] It also reflects an important feature of climate displacement: that it is *anthropogenic*. Through our contributions to climate change—and our negligent failures to avert its impacts—we have brought about the problem of climate displacement. And crucially, not everyone has had an equal hand in its production. If it is to reflect this feature of climate displacement, a political theory of climate displacement will need to make space for the concept of responsibility.

Stated in these broad terms, the idea of responsibility for climate displacement is only an inchoate idea. One task of this chapter is to clarify and defend the responsibility view. I argue that we should understand the responsibility view as a principle that says that states should bear the costs of addressing climate displacement in proportion to their failures to discharge their antecedent climate duties. I then defend the place of responsibility in light of two important obstacles to assigning responsibility for climate displacement. The first obstacle is the *complexity* of climate displacement. The complexity of climate displacement makes it difficult to know when we can hold contributors to climate change liable for displacement. The second obstacle is *disagreement* about the content of states' antecedent climate duties. Disagreement about the extent of states' antecedent climate duties makes it difficult to know who should be held responsible to bear the costs of addressing climate displacement.

In Chapter 2, we examined the main competitor to the pluralist theory of climate displacement: the proposal of a treaty for climate refugees. We saw that one of the main advantages of the climate refugee treaty proposal—the *responsibility rationale*—was that its costs could be distributed in line with responsibility for climate change. When rejecting the climate refugee treaty proposal, I claimed that the responsibility rationale could also be met by the pluralist theory of climate displacement. In clarifying and defending the place of responsibility in tackling climate displacement, another task of this chapter is to make good on that claim.

The first part of the chapter examines the idea of responsibility in general and shows how it can be applied to climate displacement. Then, I show how the responsibility view can surmount the two main obstacles that it faces, which stem from the complexity of climate displacement and disagreement about antecedent climate mitigation duties.

Responsibility

Responsibility, as David Miller puts it, 'has proved to be one of the most slippery and confusing terms in the lexicon of moral and political philosophy'.[3] In order to clarify the role of responsibility in the distribution of the costs of tackling climate displacement, it is first important to understand the contours of the concept and its role in our moral reasoning more generally.

Judgements of responsibility play an important role in our moral reasoning: they serve to justify the ascription of moral blame and praise or the imposition of liabilities. Importantly, judgements of responsibility are not purely descriptive, but have an inevitably moralized component. When we make judgements of responsibility, we are not only making factual claims about who did what; we are also making claims about the conditions under which we think it is fair or justified to *hold* an agent responsible—where holding an agent responsible has implications in terms of the ascription of blame and praise or the imposition of liabilities.[4]

Miller distinguishes between two kinds of responsibility: *outcome* and *remedial* responsibility.[5] Outcome responsibility 'has to do with agents producing outcomes'.[6] But rather than capturing a purely causal relation, outcome responsibility refers to the idea that an outcome can be 'credited or debited' to a particular agent. Outcome responsibility is a backwards-looking judgement about whether the relationship between an agent's action and a particular outcome is of the right kind to morally implicate them in the outcome. For an ascription of outcome responsibility to be apt, there must be not only some causal relation between the agent's action and the outcome, but, crucially, there must also be *agency* involved.[7] This need not require intention: one can be outcome responsible for producing outcomes negligently. But nor is just *any* connection between an agent and an outcome sufficient, since otherwise agents could be outcome responsible for the remotest consequences of their actions. Rather, in assessing outcome responsibility we must apply a standard of reasonable foresight.[8]

Remedial responsibility, by contrast, is 'a special responsibility, either individually or along with others, to remedy the position of the deprived or suffering people'.[9] Remedial responsibility is a forward-looking judgement that picks out the agent(s) who are rightfully given the task of putting a wrongful situation right. The ascription of remedial responsibility can be justified on the basis of one or more relevant connections that an agent has to a wrongful situation. According to Miller's 'connection theory' of responsibility, outcome responsibility, moral responsibility, causal responsibility, benefit, capacity, and community can all justify the ascription of remedial responsibilities.[10]

My argument in this chapter makes use of both of these concepts. The basic claim that I advance is that outcome responsibility for bringing about climate displacement can justify the ascription of remedial responsibility for bearing the costs of addressing climate displacement. So, it is important to understand why outcome responsibility can justify the ascription of remedial responsibility.

Outcome responsibility identifies a relation between an agent and an outcome that is morally relevant in the context of assigning remedial responsibility: it identifies cases where an agent is the *author* of the outcome in question. Authorship is morally relevant because it captures the idea that we value being able to control our liabilities and exercise choice. In cases that do not meet the conditions for outcome responsibility, we are not in control of our actions and are not exercising genuine choice (either because we are not exercising genuine agency or because we could not reasonably have foreseen their outcomes).[11] When an agent does exercise choice and control over their actions, they are the author of the outcome. In such cases, our presumption is that the agent is responsible—remedially—to bear the costs associated with the outcome, just as they are permitted to reap the benefits associated with it.[12] T.M. Scanlon explains this in terms of the 'symbolic value' of treating others as agents with the standing to make choices and bear their consequences.[13] Treating one another as agents who are capable of making choices and who can legitimately expect to bear the costs and reap the benefits of those choices expresses a form of respect for moral agency. This idea, I take it, captures the intuitive core of the slogan that people should 'clean up their own mess'.

It is important to note that outcome responsibility only justifies a *presumption* that the outcome responsible party should bear remedial responsibility. There may be countervailing reasons which mean that, all things considered, we should ascribe remedial responsibility elsewhere. An absolute principle of responsibility-sensitivity might have chilling effects or put some people in positions of disadvantage that compromise their standing as moral equals.[14] Or, if ascribing remedial responsibility on the basis of outcome responsibility would mean making the very poor bear significant costs, we might refer to another ground of remedial responsibility, such as capacity or community. But in general, the idea that those who are outcome responsible for a state of affairs should be held remedially responsible for bearing the costs involved in addressing the unacceptable outcomes of that state of affairs makes sense of our everyday moral reasoning and can be vindicated in terms of the respect for moral agency that it expresses.

This account of responsibility can be brought to bear on climate displacement. Discharging our duties to those displaced in the context of climate change generates a set of costs, and the question of who should bear those costs is a question about how remedial responsibility should be assigned. Outcome responsibility for the situation of those displaced in the context of climate change is a criterion that can be used to determine who should be held remedially responsible to bear those costs.

Responsibility for Climate Displacement

The international community has a collective duty to tackle climate change. Although there are important open questions about how exactly we should understand and discharge that duty, some of which I examine below, I take this basic idea as a starting point in my account of responsibility for climate displacement. In practice, tackling climate change is the aim of a 'regime complex' in the international order, with the United Nations Framework Convention on Climate Change (UNFCCC) at its centre.[15] One of the central questions that arises within that regime concerns how the costs of discharging that duty should be shared between states. Some of the most persistent disagreements about climate change—both in political theory and in climate negotiations—can be viewed as disagreements about what terms of cooperation in the project of tackling climate change are fair.[16]

Addressing climate displacement is an important part of the broader global project of tackling climate change. Alongside mitigation, climate change adaptation—of which the response to climate displacement is one part—is one of the central 'pillars' of global climate policy.[17] In practice, it is often difficult to get states to cooperate in financing adaptation to climate change. Unlike mitigation, the benefits of adaptation are primarily local rather than global. Mitigation benefits everyone by contributing to the production of a global public good—a stable climate system—but adaptation primarily benefits those who are most vulnerable to the impacts of climate change.[18] But this does not provide a good moral reason to let the costs of adaptation lie where they fall. The costs of adaptation and the costs of mitigation are intimately connected: the more mitigation we undertake, the less adaptation is required. If adaptation were left out of global efforts to tackle climate change, then states could simply shift the costs of their failure to mitigate climate change onto the shoulders of those most vulnerable to the impacts of climate change. This explains why it is appropriate to treat the costs of adaptation—including the costs of tackling climate displacement—as a remedial responsibility to be allocated between states.

We have good reasons to treat states as the primary bearers of responsibility when it comes to sharing the costs of tackling climate displacement. One reason is simply that states are the primary participants in the cooperative global project of tackling climate change. They are the actors that have signed up to global climate treaties, and so have incurred promissory obligations to abide by the norms embedded in those treaties, which include duties to share the costs of adaptation on fair terms.[19] Another reason is more fundamental: states are the agents with the capacity to tackle climate change. Although emissions reductions undertaken by individuals and firms are certainly important, there is an important division of labour between states on the one hand, and individuals and firms on the other. States have powers of coordination through which they can create and maintain conditions of 'background justice' so that the uncoordinated private decisions of individuals and firms do not interact in ways that create injustices.[20] Through the policies that they adopt—their macro-economic policies, energy market regulations, incentives for green investment, and so on—states make important choices that bear significantly on the prospects for tackling climate change. And when they fail to use their powers of coordination to put in place appropriate policies—or, worse, actively pursue policies that exacerbate climate change—they can be held responsible for the outcomes they produce.[21]

The principle of responsibility for climate displacement that I defend says that states should be held remedially responsible to bear the costs of tackling climate displacement that they have brought about through their failure to discharge their antecedent climate duties. Through their failures to discharge their climate change duties, states bring about the problem of climate displacement. It is on this basis that they should be held responsible for bearing the costs of remedying climate displacement. States' failures to discharge their antecedent climate duties make them outcome responsible for climate displacement, and their outcome responsibility justifies the ascription of remedial responsibility to bear the costs of addressing climate displacement.

This formulation might seem somewhat opaque at first glance. Why hold states responsible for their *failure* to discharge their antecedent climate duties, rather than directly for their contributions to climate change? The reason why we should hold states responsible for their failures to discharge their antecedent climate change duties, instead of their contributions to climate change directly, is that not all contributions to climate change provide a good basis for judgements of responsibility. There are two reasons that speak against holding states responsible for their contributions to climate change directly.

First is that some contributions to climate change may be morally permissible. A sufficiently high atmospheric concentration of greenhouse gases leads to dangerous climate change impacts, but some low level of gases can be emitted safely. Policy-makers often use the concept of a global 'carbon budget' to quantify the amount of greenhouse gases that can be safely emitted before global temperature rises exceed a particular limit, such as 1.5°C or 2°C above pre-industrial levels.[22] There are important disagreements—both scientific and normative—about how the global carbon budget should be determined. And once the budget has been set, there are also normative questions, some of which I examine below, about how rights to emit the available emissions should be distributed between states. But assuming that *some* greenhouse gas emissions are morally permissible, then we need to know not just how much any particular state has emitted, but whether or not they have exceeded their 'fair share' of the global carbon budget.[23]

Second is that states may be able to offer justifications and excuses for their contributions to climate change. Poorer states might claim that they are entitled to a greater share of the global carbon budget than others because they need to emit some greenhouse gases in order to pursue morally important goals such as poverty-alleviating development.[24] Historically high-emitting states might argue that they were excusably ignorant of the effects of their early emissions, and so should be excused for exceeding their share.[25] Of course, there are also counter-arguments that aim to show that these justifications and excuses are not valid. But the immediate point is not the success of any of these justifications and excuses; it is rather that we cannot know when a particular state has exceeded its fair share of the global carbon budget without settling these questions.

The idea that states should be held responsible for their failure to discharge their antecedent climate duties makes space for both of these kinds of reasons. States should be held responsible for failing to discharge their climate duties as they would be specified under the terms of a fair international climate agreement, rather than for their contributions to climate change directly. The idea of states' duties under a fair international climate agreement provides a 'baseline' from which we can judge states' failures. Clearly, this means that we need an account of states' antecedent climate duties in order to judge the extent of their failures, and I explore this question below. But even in the absence of such an account, we can say in broad terms that states can be held responsible for their failures to discharge their climate duties.

At least since the adoption of the Rio Declaration and the UNFCCC in 1992, states have attempted to coordinate their behaviour to enable them to tackle climate change. Through their participation in global climate negotiations, states collectively set the aims of global climate policy and specify each state's climate duties. But the international community is manifestly failing in this collective endeavour. To differing degrees, states are failing to discharge their climate duties, and as a result we are witnessing—and will continue to witness—climate impacts that lead to outcomes such as displacement. States' failures to do their part in tackling climate change have brought about the problem of climate displacement, and it is on the basis of these failures that we should hold states responsible to bear the costs of addressing the plight of those displaced in the context of climate change.

For the ascription of outcome responsibility to be apt, the consequences of an action or omission must be reasonably foreseeable.[26] The harmful consequences of states' failures to discharge their climate duties clearly meet this standard of reasonable foresight. Even if states were unaware of the harmful effects of their *early* emissions before scientific knowledge about climate change became widespread, they were clearly aware—or, at least, should have been aware—that their failure to do their part in the project of tackling climate change would have harmful consequences. And even if states did not specifically foresee that *displacement* would be a consequence of climate change, this does not undermine the ascription of outcome responsibility. We can still be held outcome responsible when we foreseeably cause indeterminate harms. Miller uses the example of a man who recklessly shoots an air rifle in the woods and hits a passer-by: even if the man believed in good faith that the woods were empty, he should have known better.[27] Similarly, even if states did not anticipate that displacement would be a consequence of their failures to tackle climate change, they should have known better. And in fact, states have no excuse for not anticipating the consequences of their failure: the possibility of displacement resulting from climate change was foreseen by the scientific community as early as the first Intergovernmental Panel on Climate Change (IPCC) report in 1990.[28] Indeed, the point of the cooperative project of tackling climate change is to avoid significantly harmful outcomes, and displacement—alongside other major harmful outcomes such as food insecurity and the spread of infectious diseases—is a paradigmatic example of the kind of harmful outcome that efforts to tackle climate change seek to avoid.[29]

This account of responsibility for climate displacement treats state *inaction*, rather than action, as the basis for assigning outcome responsibility. A critic might object that we should hold states responsible for what they have done, not what they have failed to do. But this objection is misplaced. For one thing, states' failures to discharge their climate duties do often involve actions that contribute to climate change—for example, the subsidies and tax breaks that they provide for fossil-fuel energy.[30] But more importantly, even inaction can express agency in the way that is relevant for judgements of responsibility. States have it within their power to decide whether or not to act on climate change, and their decisions to enact—or not to enact—robust climate policies have major consequences for the prospects of tackling climate change. Their negligent failure to do so is a reason to 'debit' them with the outcome of climate displacement.[31]

In broad terms, we have good reason to hold states outcome responsible for climate displacement, on the grounds that it is their negligent failure to discharge their antecedent climate duties that has brought about the problem of climate displacement. Their outcome responsibility justifies the ascription of remedial responsibility to bear the costs of addressing climate displacement.

This broad account of responsibility for climate displacement, however, faces two important obstacles. The first obstacle is a result of the complexity of climate displacement. As we have seen over the course of this book, the complexity of climate displacement makes it hard to tell when particular people are displaced by the impacts of climate change, as opposed to other drivers of displacement with which climate change is typically entangled. This makes it difficult to judge when particular instances of displacement fall within the scope of states' remedial responsibilities. The second obstacle is a result of holding states responsible for their failure to discharge their antecedent climate duties. There is significant disagreement about the content of states' climate duties, expressed in both philosophical analyses of those duties and in disagreements in global climate negotiations. This makes it difficult to judge when states bear outcome responsibility for climate displacement, since we need an account of states' antecedent climate duties to know the extent to which they have failed to discharge those duties.

Responsibility and the Complexity of Climate Displacement

The complexity of climate displacement has been an important theme in our inquiry. Climate impacts interact in complex ways with political, economic, social, demographic, and environmental drivers of displacement.[32] And vulnerability to climate displacement is structured by pervasive background injustices, with those who are most disadvantaged along other axes bearing the brunt of the displacement-related harms of climate change. Over the past few chapters, we have seen some of the complex ways in which climate change impacts interact with other drivers of displacement. Climate change is sometimes described as a *structural injustice*—that is, an injustice that arises from the complex interaction of many different individual actions, mediated by rules and norms that shape the options available to individual agents and systematically put some people in positions of disadvantage.[33] In the case of climate displacement, this is an especially fitting diagnosis.

One important upshot of this diagnosis, however, is that it makes it difficult to identify particular people whose displacement can be attributed to climate change. For one thing, it is often difficult to determine whether specific weather events or processes can be linked to climate change. But even if we know that a particular event or process is a result of climate change, the complexity of climate displacement means that it is difficult to know whether a person's displacement was caused by climate change, as opposed to the other drivers of displacement with which climate change impacts are often entangled. As we saw in Chapter 2, attempts to isolate climate change as the cause of particular cases of displacement are fraught, and any real-world assessment of the causal role of climate change is likely to involve a significant degree of arbitrariness.

When it comes to assigning responsibility for climate displacement, this appears to present a problem. If we cannot tell when someone's displacement can be attributed to climate change, how can we hold states responsible for their displacement? My suggestion is that instead of holding states responsible for the displacement of particular individuals at the micro level, we should instead hold them responsible for the increased burden of displacement risk associated with their failure to discharge their climate duties at the macro level.

Ordinarily, when we make judgements of responsibility, we identify discrete harmful outcomes caused by discrete individual actions or series of actions and assign responsibility on the basis of a clearly identifiable connection between the two. This is the basic model of responsibility attribution that underlies the practices of tort law.[34] The tort model of responsibility generally works well enough as the basis for making judgements of responsibility in our day-to-day lives. But in the context of climate change, the causal complexities involved in the chains that lead from emissions to impacts undermine our ability to make these straightforward judgements of responsibility. When it comes to climate displacement, not only are the causal chains from emissions to impacts complex, but causal complexities also bedevil the causal chains between impacts and displacement. This feature of climate displacement creates problems for the tort model of responsibility. As Dale Jamieson puts it, our ordinary model for thinking about responsibility 'collapses when we try to apply it to global environmental problems'.[35] Eric Posner and David Weisbach have argued that causal complexities involved in climate change give us reason to reject responsibility-sensitive approaches to climate change justice.[36] And theorists of structural injustice often suggest that we should focus on making forward-looking rather than backward-looking judgements of responsibility.[37] But it is a mistake to think that causal complexity makes us completely unable to make judgements of responsibility.

Instead of adopting a tort of responsibility, we should adopt an 'insurance' model of responsibility for climate displacement.[38] On this approach, we do not seek to establish responsibility for particular incidences of displacement that are attributable to climate change. Instead, we see the relevant 'outcome' for which states are held responsible as the increased level of displacement risk created by climate change. States can be held outcome responsible for the share of the displacement risk that they have imposed through their failures to discharge their antecedent climate change duties, and they can be held remedially responsible to bear the costs associated with the increased burden of displacement risk that they have created.

The basic idea of the insurance model is helpfully illustrated by an analogy with workers' compensation insurance.[39] In late nineteenth-century Germany, demands grew for a procedure for compensating workers involved in industrial accidents without the need to establish fault on the part of employers. Doctrines such as the 'fellow-servant' rule (an employer is not liable if a co-worker contributed to the injury) and the 'contributory negligence' rule (an employer's liability is diminished to the extent that the employee contributed to their own injury) heavily favoured employers and made successful litigation for tort claims a long, costly, and difficult process.[40] As Robert Goodin puts it, 'insofar as the injury occurred through some complicated set of causal interactions, blame would be somehow apportioned among all those whose negligence contributed to the outcome'.[41] Difficulties in establishing responsibility in the face of casual complexities meant that workers were systematically disadvantaged and employers rarely had to pay out compensation. In 1884, under the Chancellorship of Otto von Bismarck, the Workers' Accident Insurance Act established a system of mandatory workplace insurance for employees. The statute prevented employees from bringing tort claims against employers for workplace accidents, but it ensured that employees received compensation for injuries without having to establish fault. The system became the model for modern systems of workplace insurance that exist in many legal systems today.

In the same way that the causal complexities in workplace accidents motivated a turn to insurance-based systems of compensation, the causal complexities in establishing responsibility for climate displacement motivate a turn to an insurance model for addressing climate displacement. On the insurance model, all of those who face displacement are owed certain duties, which vary according to the different forms that displacement can take (as we have seen in Chapters 3–7). The regimes of governance that we have for addressing displacement are akin to the systems of social insurance that 'pay out' when people are displaced. Just as workers do not have to prove that their employers are responsible for industrial accidents under workers' compensation insurance schemes, neither do displaced persons have to prove that their displacement can be attributed to climate change in order to make valid claims to protection.

On the insurance model, climate change operates as a *risk multiplier* that makes displacement more likely.[42] In the same way that employers who make their employees engage in particularly risky forms of work pay higher insurance premiums to offset the predictable costs of those risks, states should bear the costs associated with the increased burden of displacement risk associated with their failure to discharge their antecedent climate duties. When it comes to apportioning responsibility between states, the insurance model draws on the idea of 'market share liability'.[43] Instead of holding agents responsible on the basis of an identifiable connection between their actions and an outcome (as on the tort model), market share liability involves holding agents responsible for a harm in proportion to the share of the risk of that harm that they, in combination with a number of agents, have created. It provides a way of approximating responsibility in conditions where we cannot individuate responsibility for particular harms.[44]

I am not the first person to suggest that an insurance model of responsibility is appropriate for climate displacement. Fanny Thornton and Peter Penz have both argued that the complexity of climate displacement means that we should turn to insurance as a means of corrective justice.[45] As Thornton suggests, an insurance-based approach provides a measure of 'rough justice' that escapes the problems of causal complexity affecting more fine-grained approaches that depend on identifying particular victims and particular perpetrators.[46] But where Thornton and Penz are focused on specific insurance-based legal and policy instruments that could be implemented in the context of climate displacement, the point that I am making here is more basic. At the level of principle, it is more appropriate to think of responsibility in terms of the insurance model than the tort model in the context of climate displacement. The insurance model allows us to preserve the intuition that responsibility matters in sharing the costs of addressing climate displacement, but it takes an appropriately realistic view of the complexity of climate displacement. There are a number of ways that the insurance model could be implemented, but the basic idea would involve redistribution from responsible states—in proportion to their failure to discharge their climate duties and thus the magnitude of the increased burden of displacement risk that they have created—to those who are actually discharging our first-order duties to the displaced. The aim is to ensure that those discharging first-order duties to the displaced are not left to shoulder the costs associated with the increased burden of displacement risk created by states that have failed to discharge their climate duties.

However we implement the insurance model, we need to have an approximate idea of both the extent of states' failures to tackle climate change and the impact of those failures on aggregate levels of displacement. In the next section, I examine how we can hold states responsible in the face of disagreement about the extent of their failures to tackle climate change. But first, it is important to examine our knowledge of the impact of climate change on aggregate levels of displacement. As we saw in Chapter 1, attempts to quantify the overall number of people displaced by the impacts of climate change present formidable challenges. The early empirical literature that attempted to predict overall numbers of people displaced by climate change was stunted by unreasonable assumptions built into models which projected migration patterns into the future.[47] As such, we might be worried that the epistemic demands of the insurance model go beyond our epistemic capacities.

There are some reasons to be optimistic about our ability to quantify the impact of climate change on displacement. The science of modelling climate displacement is developing, and new forms of spatial-vulnerability modelling such as 'agent-based modelling' are improving our ability to make better predictions and estimates of the impact of climate change on displacement.[48] Better data and more sophisticated methodological tools will be necessary to make presently crude estimates more precise. But as Robert McLeman points out, the 'prospects for linking migration data and climate information at regional, national, and sub-national scales are promising in the near term'.[49] As the science of modelling climate displacement advances, we can expect to see more fine-grained estimates of the impact of climate change on displacement. Another way in which we can make approximate judgements about the impacts of climate change on displacement is by learning from the actuarial practices of insurers who seek to calculate the cost of risks under conditions of imperfect information. By looking to the costs that insurers would expect to bet against when providing insurance against displacement risks, we can make judgements about the expected costs of the impacts of climate change on displacement.[50] We could then make judgements about the costs of climate change—perhaps through a scientific facility such as the IPCC—that draw on both our best models of climate displacement and actuarial calculations about the cost of insuring against it. As our knowledge improves, we could compare our judgements about the expected costs against the actual costs of addressing climate displacement, and update and revise our judgements accordingly.

Still, our judgements will only approximate the costs of addressing climate displacement. As such, some residual unfairness in the distribution of the costs between states might persist. If the impacts of climate change on displacement were overestimated, then states held responsible on the basis of their failure to discharge their climate duties would bear more than their fair share of the costs of tackling displacement. And if the impacts of climate change on displacement were underestimated, then non-responsible parties charged with addressing displacement would bear more than their fair share.

But tolerating this residual unfairness is still preferable to the alternatives. Ignoring responsibility entirely would simply exacerbate this unfairness, since it would mean that responsible states could unilaterally impose costs on non-responsible parties by failing to discharge their climate duties. This not only incentivizes states to fail to discharge their climate duties, as Shue has argued, but is also patently unfair.[51] Falling back on the tort model of responsibility would be little better. If non-responsible parties had to prove that a case of displacement were attributable to climate change in order to recover costs from responsible states, then the problems afflicting the climate refugee treaty proposal that we examined in Chapter 2 would simply arise in a new context. Given the complexity of climate displacement, it would be effectively impossible to meet this standard of proof. The tort model of responsibility would largely replicate the unfairness involved in ignoring responsibility in the first place. Although it may not be perfect, the insurance model at least approximates responsibility for climate displacement.

Another concern that we might have with the insurance model of responsibility is that it creates a 'moral hazard' that increases the risk of displacement. In economic theory, a moral hazard refers to the idea that being insured against a harm can incentivize risky behaviour, since the risk-takers no longer bear the full costs of the risks that they take.[52] When someone has comprehensive personal liability insurance, they might be more prone to carelessness around others' property, safe in the knowledge that their insurance will cover any costs for which they would have otherwise been held liable. Similarly, we might think that the insurance model of responsibility will make those at risk of displacement engage in behaviours that increase their vulnerability, such as buying property in areas at risk of flooding instead of investing in forms of adaptation that minimize their risk of displacement, safe in the knowledge that if they are displaced that they will not need to bear the costs of remedying their displacement.

Whatever its merits in other contexts, the concern about moral hazard has little force in the context of climate displacement. The main reason for this is that the 'pay-out' in the case of climate displacement is not an attractive one. Even when we respond to it in the best way we can, displacement involves serious non-monetary costs for those it affects. Although displacement is a heterogeneous phenomenon, it is typically a highly traumatic experience.[53] And when people engage in behaviour that increases their vulnerability to displacement, it is far more often because they face structural constraints that limit the options available to them, not because they do not fear the experience of displacement. So, although the insurance model would—ideally, at least—ensure that the financial costs of addressing displacement do not fall on the displaced, it is highly unlikely that the availability of insurance against those financial costs would incentivize people to heighten their vulnerability to displacement.

In fact, the insurance model may even incentivize forms of adaptation that lower the risk of displacement. One important part of states' climate duties is their contributions to financing *in situ* forms of adaptation to climate change. But at the moment, many states are shirking those duties, and climate adaptation is chronically underfunded as a result.[54] As things stand, their failures have few consequences, because the costs of climate change are mostly left to fall on the shoulders of those at risk of displacement. But if the insurance model were implemented, it would no longer be cost-free for states to withhold adaptation finance. If states were held liable for the risk of displacement that they create through their failure to discharge their climate duties, then we can expect that they would seek to reduce that risk by investing in adaptation.

Finally, we might think that the insurance model has broader implications than I have suggested here. The insurance model begins with a recognition that climate displacement is complex and multi-causal, such that climate change is only one of a constellation of casual drivers that are intertwined. If we hold states responsible for their share of the risk of displacement that climate change creates, then should we not also hold states (and other agents such as firms) responsible for their contributions to *other* risks of displacement that they create? If states are responsible for globally uneven development processes, or for non-climate forms of environmental degradation, or conflict—all of which increase the risk of displacement—then should we not hold them responsible for their share of this risk as well?

This is a perfectly plausible extension of the argument that I have made here. Although my focus here has been on states' responsibilities for the risk of displacement that they create through their failures to discharge their climate duties, there are a range of other ways in which states (and other actors) increase the risk of displacement. In principle, there is no reason why they should not be held responsible for those contributions as well. In some cases, the connection between an agent's actions and a person or group's displacement will be sufficiently clear and direct that the agent can be held responsible under the tort model of responsibility. Firms that engage in extractive industries such as mining for minerals can often be held responsible on the basis of a fairly clear connection between their activities and the displacement of local communities.[55] In other cases, the connection will be more diffuse. It may be hard to determine with much precision when states are responsible for increasing or heightening vulnerability to displacement through their role in chronic underdevelopment abroad, for example.[56] But in principle, there is no reason why they should not be held responsible in much the same way, so long as judgements of outcome responsibility can be made for the connection between their activities and the increased burden of displacement risk. Holding states and other actors responsible in this way would be complementary to holding states responsible for the increased risk of displacement that they create through their failure to discharge their climate duties.

Responsibility and Disagreement in Global Climate Policy

On the account of responsibility for climate displacement that I have set out, states should be held responsible for their failure to discharge their antecedent climate duties. This clearly presupposes an account of the content of those duties. But discussions about states' climate duties—both in political theory and in climate negotiations—are marred by persistent disagreement. In the face of this disagreement, how can we hold states responsible for their failures?

In order to understand how states can be held responsible for their failure to discharge their climate duties in the face of disagreement, it is first important to understand the nature and scope of that disagreement. We can do so by examining three concepts that have been sticking points in UNFCCC negotiations about climate change and the competing interpretations of those concepts that political theorists have defended. A closer look at those concepts reveals that the scope for reasonable disagreement about states' climate duties, while significant, is not so large as to make the problem of measuring states' failures to discharge those duties intractable.

The first concept is 'dangerous climate change'. The aim of tackling climate change is to achieve the 'stabilization of greenhouse gas concentrations in the atmosphere at a level that would prevent dangerous anthropogenic interference with the climate system'.[57] In practice, temperature targets have often been used to make the idea of dangerous climate change more determinate.[58] A target of 2°C above pre-industrial temperatures was agreed upon at the 15th Conference of the Parties (COP15) in Copenhagen in 2009, and states agreed on 'pursuing efforts' to limit the temperature target to 1.5°C at COP21 in Paris.[59] But ultimately, these temperature targets are proxies for amounts of expected climate-related harm. In UNFCCC agreements, dangerous climate change is climate change that should be avoided. A judgement about what counts as 'dangerous climate change' is a judgement about the amount of expected climate-related harm that we should, all things considered, permit.[60]

Simon Caney calls this question the question of the 'just target' of climate policy.[61] It is not as straightforward as it initially appears. We might think that the common-sense answer to the question of how much climate-related harm we should permit is simply 'none'. Unfortunately, this answer will not do. For one thing, we are already experiencing climate-related harms at current levels of warming and will continue to do so in the future due to the inertia of the climate system, regardless of how much we emit.[62] But perhaps more importantly, we also need to consider the costs of *avoiding* warming.

The lower the target, the fewer emissions will be available in the global carbon budget. But emissions can be instrumental for the pursuit of poverty-alleviating development, at least in circumstances in which fossil fuels remain cheap sources of energy for the global poor. This means that a lower target, with a correspondingly smaller carbon budget, may limit the prospects of tackling global poverty. At the same time, a higher target creates a greater risk of climate-related harm. And since vulnerability to climate change has a close relationship to development, those harms disproportionately affect the poor and hinder their prospects for development. So, there is an internal tension between achieving human development and tackling climate change. To some extent, this tension can be attenuated by technological developments (such as the falling price of renewables) and particular climate policies (such as technology transfers to developing states) that 'decouple' emissions from economic growth.[63] But when we make a judgement about dangerous climate change, we make a judgement about the relative importance of both poverty reduction and climate mitigation, on the basis of a set of assumptions about technological progress and climate policy levers that we can use to reduce the depth of that tension.

Competing interpretations of dangerous climate change express different judgements on both the normative and empirical aspects of these questions.[64] But, given the magnitude of the harms that we can expect from climate change, there is a good deal of consensus that an ambitious target of 1.5°C is justified, and widespread acceptance that no more than 2°C should be tolerated. There are some who think that the 2°C target should be abandoned, but they remain outliers.[65] Darrel Moellendorf—whose work puts the tension between poverty alleviation and climate change mitigation at its centre—defends the 1.5°C target on the basis that the impacts of climate change at 2°C would do much more to prolong global poverty than the sacrifices involved in achieving the more ambitious target.[66]

The second concept is the 'right to sustainable development'. Article 3.4 of the UNFCCC says that parties 'have a right to, and should, promote sustainable development'.[67] The right to sustainable development reflects the idea that the project of human development is a morally valuable one that we have reason to endorse. But the 'sustainable' qualifier is supposed to constrain the pursuit of development, so that it does not create morally unacceptable costs—including costs that threaten human development itself.[68] Respecting the right to sustainable development involves 'ensuring that developing and underdeveloped states are allowed emissions allotments sufficient to achieve development within a plan of global emissions reductions'.[69] Like the concept of dangerous climate change, the right to sustainable development attempts to navigate the tension between tackling climate change and pursuing poverty-alleviating development.

Different interpretations of the right to sustainable development involve different views about the needs that the right protects and the assumptions that we should adopt about the level of emissions required to meet those needs. Moellendorf argues against a narrow focus on basic needs and in favour of understanding human development in terms of the Human Development Index (HDI).[70] In his earlier work, he also suggests that we should use the emissions levels of countries with 'high' rankings on the HDI as an indicator of the per capita emissions levels that we can expect of states that achieve human development goals, though this assumption has to some degree been superseded by developments in clean energy technology.[71] A more restricted view is expressed in Shue's claim that emissions from less developed countries ought to rise 'insofar as this rise is necessary to provide a minimally decent standard of living' and his claim that 'the economic development of the poor nations must be as "clean" as possible—maximally efficient in the specific sense of creating no unnecessary CO2 emissions'.[72] One attempt to quantify the right to sustainable development is the 'Greenhouse Development Rights' framework, which sets a 'development threshold' at 1.25 times the poverty threshold, at 'the level at which a "middle class" (or "consuming class") begins to emerge in the developing world'.[73] As with the concept of dangerous climate change, these competing interpretations of the right to sustainable development express different judgements about the relative priority of tackling climate change and pursuing poverty-alleviating development.

The third concept is 'common but differentiated responsibilities and respective capabilities' (CBDR-RC). The basic idea of CBDR-RC is that while all states have duties to tackle climate change, the content of their duties should be differentiated on the basis of their responsibility for the problem and their ability to address it.[74] In climate negotiations, CBDR-RC has been expressed in different ways. In the Kyoto Agreement, states were divided into Annex I and non-Annex I states depending on their level of economic development and legally binding emissions reduction targets were imposed on Annex I states.[75] This distinction was abandoned in the Paris Agreement. Instead, it was agreed that developed states should 'take the lead' in economy-wide emissions reductions (though which states are 'developed' is not specified) and that each state's 'Nationally Determined Contribution' (NDC) should be based on 'its highest possible ambition, reflecting its common but differentiated responsibilities and respective capabilities'.[76]

The main sticking point in interpreting CBDR-RC has been the role of responsibility. 'Differentiated responsibilities' is often interpreted as referring to the differential *historic* responsibility that states have for their contributions to climate change, as was the argument made under the Brazilian Proposal for the Kyoto Protocol.[77] In climate ethics, the 'Polluter Pays Principle' (PPP) aims to capture the normative significance of responsibility in CBDR-RC. The idea of the PPP is that those who have caused the problem of climate change—either directly through the impacts of their emissions or indirectly through their overuse of the scarce resource of the earth's capacity to absorb greenhouse gases—should be held responsible to bear the costs of tackling climate change.[78] Debates about whether 'excusable ignorance' about the effects of early emissions means that historically high-emitting states should not be held liable arise at this juncture. Some have also defended the 'Beneficiary Pays Principle' (BPP)—which says that states that have benefited from emissions should bear the costs of tackling climate change—as a way of capturing the normative significance of history that avoids the counter-arguments that have been made against the PPP.[79]

The other central component of CBDR-RC is states' relative ability to bear the costs of tackling climate change. This is the 'respective capabilities' component of CBDR-RC. The most common way of interpreting this part of CBDR-RC is in terms of the 'Ability to Pay Principle' (APP), which says that states engaged in the cooperative project of tackling climate change ought to bear costs in proportion to their ability to bear those costs.[80] The idea is that a progressive rate of contribution according to national wealth will ensure that no state faces a disproportionate burden in tackling climate change, as with progressive rates of taxation for funding public goods and services.

There is some disagreement about the fairness of the APP—some have argued that it would be unfair to make the 'responsible rich' bear significant costs—but most of the disagreement about it concerns the relative weight that we should give to ability and responsibility.[81] But even if we give significant weight to responsibility, ability will play an important role in determining states' climate duties. The right to sustainable development suggests that some less developed states should be exempted from responsibility for their historic emissions, and so an account of states' climate duties will be incomplete if it relies only on the concept of responsibility and not ability.[82] Most have defended accounts that involve some balance between responsibility and ability.[83]

This brief analysis gives us a better sense of the nature and scope of some of the main disagreements about global climate policy. But perhaps surprisingly, it also reveals that there is a good deal that reasonable deliberators can agree upon. The implications of the competing interpretations of these concepts overlap, and we can view the overlap between them as a what Cass Sunstein calls an 'incompletely theorized agreement' about global climate policy.[84]

Take first CBDR-RC. As Shue has argued, the competing moral principles that have been used to interpret CBDR-RC (the APP, PPP, and BPP) each 'yield initial duties that are unconditional and overdetermined even if later peripheral theoretical divergence may leave the ultimate limit on the extent of the duties contested'.[85] These principles all suggest that developed states should bear the lion's share of the costs of tackling climate change while the least developed states should bear the fewest costs. By and large, developed states have the greatest ability to bear the costs of tackling climate change, have contributed most to climate change, and have benefited most from emissions. The least developed states, by contrast, are least able to bear the costs of tackling climate change, have contributed least to the problem, and have benefited the least from emissions. As we saw in Chapter 5, this is not accidental: it is a result of the fact that historic processes of industrialization that created fossil-fuel economies have generated much of the wealth of the Global North.

Competing interpretations of the concepts of dangerous climate change and the right to sustainable development also converge in their implications. The right to sustainable development, however capaciously or restrictively it is understood, suggests that the least developed states should bear the fewest costs. If the 'development' aspect of the right to sustainable development is emphasized, it suggests that the least developed states should bear the fewest costs because imposing mitigation costs upon them hinders their pursuit of human development. If the 'sustainable' aspect is emphasized, it suggests that the costs of climate change should be minimized overall, because they will tend to fall disproportionately on the most vulnerable and hinder the project of human development. The concept of dangerous climate change also suggests that the costs that fall on the least developed states should be minimized. Depending on how we interpret the concept, it suggests either that we should avoid imposing excessive mitigation costs on the least developed states, because doing so would hinder poverty alleviation, or that we should ensure that those most vulnerable to climate change do not face significant climate-related harms.

These imperatives overlap because the least developed states *are* most vulnerable to the impacts of climate change. The 'skewed vulnerabilities' of climate change are partly a matter of geography—less developed states tend to be in more vulnerable climatic zones—but they are also partly a consequence of the relationship between development and vulnerability.[86] As the IPCC points out, differences in vulnerability to climate change arise in part from 'multidimensional inequalities often produced by uneven development processes'.[87] The reverse of this relationship is also true: developed states are able to insulate themselves against the impacts of climate change at least in part *because* they are developed. Since development can make states less vulnerable to climate change, we have good climate-based reasons to promote it in the least developed states. And since climate change can hinder development among the most vulnerable, we have good development-based reasons to prevent harmful climate impacts from befalling the least developed states. This means that ultimately, as Moellendorf puts it, 'climate mitigation is a pro-poor project'.[88]

This does not mean that there are no trade-offs in global climate policy or that disagreement about global climate policy is only apparent. Important disagreements about the precise extent of states' climate duties will persist. But we should not lose sight of the fact that there is significant space for agreement on climate policy among those with competing priorities. Reasonable deliberators about climate change should agree on three basic principles. First, aggressive action on climate change is a moral imperative. Second, developed states should bear the greatest share of the costs of tackling climate change. Third, the least developed states should not bear significant costs in the effort to tackle climate change. These principles form the core of any reasonable interpretation of the central concepts embedded in the global climate policy regime.

The incompletely theorized agreement on these core principles is enough to get discussions about holding states responsible for their failures off the ground. States should be held responsible for their failures to discharge their climate duties when they fall foul of any of these three principles. This is a minimal standard for holding states to account. Given that competing conceptions of fairness in global climate policy converge on these principles, states cannot reasonably object to being held responsible for these failures on grounds of fairness. The costs associated with the increased burden of displacement risk created by climate change can be apportioned to states in proportion to the extent to which they have failed to meet this minimal threshold for fairness in climate action.

In practice, this will mean that developed states that have not made significant efforts to tackle climate change will be liable for significant costs associated with climate displacement, while the least developed states will be exempted from bearing costs. Of course, this does not resolve the problem of disagreement entirely. The precise details of how to measure these failures will inevitably still need to be thrashed out in negotiations. But this does provide us with a principled constraint and a basis upon which to critically evaluate those negotiations. Although states might reasonably disagree about some elements of global climate policy, they cannot reasonably reject these core principles.

There are two main objections to relying on the incompletely theorized agreement on fairness in global climate policy to hold states responsible for climate displacement. First is that there may be a more straightforward and determinate way of measuring states' failures. One alternative way to determine the content of states' climate duties would simply be to refer to the commitments that they have already agreed upon in climate negotiations under the UNFCCC. After all, the central purpose of the UNFCCC is to enable states to adjudicate between competing conceptions of fairness in global climate policy.[89] When states persistently and reasonably disagree about their climate duties, they should settle their disagreements through fair procedures that generate authoritative prescriptions for global climate policy. Since states have agreed upon terms for cooperation through the UNFCCC, can we not simply hold them responsible for their failures to meet the targets that they have already set, for example through their NDCs?

The problem with this approach does not lie in the procedural failings of the UNFCCC. There are certainly significant procedural injustices in climate negotiations, and background inequalities in power inevitably affect the prospects for fair and effective cooperation.[90] But overall, we do have good reason to treat its outcomes as legitimate. For one thing, the consensus-based decision-making procedure of the UNFCCC does give each party a fairly significant say over decisions.[91] In fact, some commentators argue that it would be better to move from multilateral to 'minilateral' approaches that sacrifice a broad base of participation in the name of efficiency.[92] But for another, the standards of legitimacy that we adopt should be sensitive to the aims of an institution and the alternative options that are available.[93] Given the high stakes of tackling climate change and the lack of credible alternative methods for securing cooperation on climate change, we have good reason to treat the UNFCCC as legitimate.[94]

The reason that we cannot appeal to targets that have already been agreed upon in UNFCCC negotiations is because existing targets do not represent a reasonable conception of fairness in global climate policy. Estimates from Climate Action Tracker suggest that even if all states met their most ambitious emissions reductions targets, warming would only be limited to around 2.4°C.[95] This lack of ambition effectively amounts to a decision to put significant burdens on those who are most vulnerable to climate change—the least developed states—in the future. So, current targets cannot function as a credible baseline for the assessment of states' failures to discharge their duties. Even if they met all of the targets that they have set themselves, they would still not have remained within the terms of a fair international climate agreement. It may be possible to assess states' failures in this way in the future. The Paris Agreement works on the basis of a 'pledge and review' system that aims to ramp up ambition over time.[96] Existing targets are too weak, but it is possible for them to become stronger over time. If states succeed in setting targets that collectively ensure that the three basic principles of fairness in tackling climate change are met, then there is a good case for holding them to account on the basis of those targets. But in the meantime, we still need a basis upon which to make judgements about states' failures. Even if it remains only an approximation, the core agreement on fairness in climate policy provides a basis for such judgements that states cannot reasonably reject.

The second objection is that it is unreasonable to hold states responsible for their failures in the absence of clearly specified duties to tackle climate change. Paul Bou-Habib has recently argued that without legitimate institutions of climate governance that specify the content of their climate duties, states cannot be held responsible for breaches of those duties.[97] On his view, the 'social complexity' of climate change means that states could not have been reasonably expected to know that they were in breach of their duties, and so claims of 'preinstitutional liability' cannot be justified. The basis for this judgement is epistemic: social complexity 'makes it difficult for actors to obtain the facts that they need in order to tell what their rights demand of others from one situation to the next and whether those rights are actually being fulfilled'.[98] Legitimate climate-governance institutions solve this epistemic problem by providing authoritative interpretations of states' climate duties. In our context, this objection suggests that in the absence of determinate and fair terms of cooperation on climate change, states could not have been reasonably expected to know that they were breaching their climate duties, and so should not be held responsible for their failures. If successful, this objection is forceful. According to the theory of responsibility that I have drawn on here, states should be held to a standard of reasonable foresight, and this objection suggests that this condition was not met.

This objection overestimates the knowledge that states need to reasonably judge that they were in breach of their duties.[99] Even if Bou-Habib is right to suggest that states cannot reasonably be expected to know the full extent of their duties without institutions that render their duties determinate, they do not need to know the full extent of their duties to be held responsible on the grounds that I am proposing. Since I am proposing that states should be held responsible for breaches of those duties when they go beyond the limits of reasonable disagreement, they only need to know the rough parameters of what fairness in global climate policy requires. At least since the adoption of the UNFCCC in 1992, states have known—or can be reasonably expected to have known—that any reasonable conception of fairness in global climate policy would condemn some of their failures. Since it is on the basis of those failures that they are being held liable, they have no recourse to the complaint that they could not have known better.

The anthropogenic nature of climate displacement evokes a powerful moral intuition: that those who are responsible for bringing about climate displacement should be held responsible for bearing the costs of addressing it. In this chapter, I have sought to clarify and defend that intuition. As we have seen, responsibility plays an important role in our everyday moral reasoning as a basis for judgements about the imposition of liabilities. In the context of climate displacement, it has an important role in determining how the costs of addressing climate displacement should be shared between states. States should be held responsible for their failures to discharge their antecedent climate duties, because through those failures, they have brought about the problem of climate displacement.

But the attribution of responsibility for climate displacement is not straightforward. For one thing, the complexity of climate displacement makes it difficult to know what costs states should be held responsible to bear. In light of this complexity, I argued that we should hold states responsible not for the displacement of particular individuals, as on the tort model of responsibility, but on the basis of the aggregate burden of displacement risk that they have imposed, as on the insurance model of responsibility. For another thing, disagreement about the content of states' climate duties makes it difficult to know when they should be held responsible for their failure. I argued that despite this disagreement, there is a core consensus on fairness in global climate policy that no state can reasonably reject. States should be held responsible for their failures when they are incompatible with this core consensus. These two modifications to the responsibility view allow us to approximate responsibility for climate displacement, while at the same time taking an appropriately realistic view of the empirical and normative complexities involved in holding states responsible for climate displacement.

9
The Future of Climate Displacement

The perspective on climate displacement that I have articulated in this book puts its empirical dynamics at its centre. The pluralist theory starts from the complexity and heterogeneity of climate displacement and aims to push back against simplistic and idealized pictures of 'climate refugees'. It aims instead to disaggregate climate displacement and to integrate it with other, non-climatic forms of displacement. But at the same time, it also aims to take a holistic view of climate displacement as a broadly unified phenomenon that raises distinctive questions of responsibility.

The pluralist theory aims both to clarify the structure of the problem of climate displacement and to provide us with normative guidance as we address it. The problem-based method that I have adopted in constructing the pluralist theory suggests that instead of proceeding by applying general principles of justice to climate displacement, we should begin with an investigation of the moral contours of the phenomenon itself. So, my first aim here has been to give a more concrete shape to the inchoate sense that we have that climate displacement represents a great moral challenge. I have identified five contexts in which climate change and displacement interact—community relocation, territorial sovereignty, labour migration, refugee movement, and internal displacement—with a view to identifying the different moral problems that arise in these contexts. These contexts are focal points for analysing climate displacement, which give us a map for understanding the different moral questions that it raises.

This map remains only a rough outline. I have no doubt that there are many cases of climate displacement that fit uneasily with these contexts, and that there are many moral problems associated with climate displacement that I have not even begun to address here. The closer the attention we pay to the specific dynamics of climate displacement in particular contexts, the more difficult it is to develop generally applicable normative guidance for addressing it. And the more general the normative guidance that we develop, the more difficult it is to be faithful to the specific dynamics of climate displacement in particular contexts. I have sought to strike a balance between the general and the specific. No doubt I have not captured the full breadth of the phenomenon of climate displacement. But I hope to have encouraged political theorists to move past unhelpful and simplistic idealizations and to take a more contextual view of the problem of climate displacement. Those who disagree with the arguments that I have made can now, I hope, make those disagreements on a shared terrain of debate.

The problem-based method enjoins us to begin theorizing climate displacement with the practical contexts in which it emerges. But although it begins with our existing institutions and practices, the pluralist theory does not end with them. Now that we have analysed the various contexts in which climate displacement arises, we are in a position to see that the pluralist theory has revisionary implications when it comes to our existing institutions and practices. Achieving a just future for climate displacement will involve—among other things—unprecedented forms of international cooperation in funding and implementing both *in situ* adaptation and relocation projects; significant changes in international law and practice to ensure the robust protection of the rights of internally displaced persons; a renegotiation of states' territorial sovereignty to enable small-island peoples to exercise self-determination; far-reaching changes to high-income states' labour migration policies; a wholesale transformation in the paradigms of refugee protection in the Global North; and extensive redistribution between states to fund these projects. These are ambitious goals. I have not provided a blueprint for the institutional changes that will be necessary to achieve them here. But achieving justice in climate displacement undoubtedly requires significant transformations in the international order.

The theory that I have developed here remains provisional as well as contextual. Although I have attempted to give a reasoned defence of the pluralist theory of climate displacement, its ultimate test will be its utility as we begin to confront the moral challenge of climate displacement in practice. And one important feature of climate displacement is that its future is uncertain. The nature and scale of climate displacement will depend on the emissions pathway that humanity follows in the near future and on the efforts that we make to adapt to a changing climate. Over the course of this book, I have envisaged a relatively moderate scenario of climate displacement. This decision is based on two judgements, one empirical and one normative. The empirical judgement is that, as we saw in Chapter 1, this is the scenario that is best supported by the evidence that we have available to us, at least for the near- to medium-term future. The normative judgement is that it is important to keep firm in our commitment to tackling climate change. The moderate scenario does not presuppose our collective failure in our efforts to tackle climate change, and we should not allow consideration of our duties with respect to climate displacement to be an excuse for defeatism and inaction on climate change.

But it is also important to reflect on the open future of climate displacement, including on the possibility of our failure to bring climate change under control. Although it is certainly not inevitable, there is a plausible future in which humanity's failure to mitigate climate change and to adapt to its effects creates more catastrophic displacement scenarios. The unpleasant truth is that we are not doing nearly enough to tackle climate change, and if we do not make serious attempts to ramp up our efforts, then we may face new and unprecedented displacement scenarios. This puts us in the somewhat strange position of anticipating our own moral failure.[1]

Here, I close our inquiry by reflecting on the possibility of a more catastrophic scenario of climate displacement. My aim is not to determine what we should *do* in such a future. Rather, my aim is to think about how the prospect of our failure to tackle climate change can orient our reflection on climate displacement in the here-and-now. This involves an—inevitably somewhat speculative—exercise of prospection. I imagine a catastrophic scenario of climate displacement that could occur because of our failure to tackle climate change. Such a future is a fearsome prospect, but I argue that our response to climate displacement should not be motivated by fear. Instead, I suggest that we have rational grounds for a politics of hope for the future of climate displacement.[2]

Fear and the Future of Climate Displacement

The moral imagination is a central part of our critical faculties. For John Dewey, imagination is an important part of the process of deliberative inquiry.[3] The 'dramatic rehearsal' of the consequences of our actions can inform our judgements today. As he put it, 'thought runs ahead and foresees outcomes, and thereby avoids having to await the instruction of actual failure and disaster'.[4] The process of dramatic rehearsal reveals to us our response to the future that we imagine, and this enables us to make judgements about what to do today:

> In imagination as in fact we know a road only by what we see as we travel on it . . . In thought as well as in overt action, the objects experienced in following out a course of action attract, repel, satisfy, annoy, promote and retard. Thus deliberation proceeds.[5]

Envisaging future scenarios can play an important role in orienting our moral reflection. By reflecting on the future of climate displacement, we can make better judgements about what we ought to do today. With this perspective in mind, we can reflect on the possibility of our failure to bring climate change under control. What might such a future of climate displacement look like?

In the Intergovernmental Panel on Climate Change (IPCC) reports, scientists use different 'Representative Concentration Pathways' (RCPs) to model future scenarios of climate change.[6] RCP 2.6 is a scenario in which humanity manages to limit temperature increases to below 2°C above the pre-industrial baseline. RCP 8.5 is a high-emission scenario, in which temperatures reach between 4 and 5°C above the pre-industrial baseline, and possibly higher, by the end of the century.[7] Given recent developments in clean energy technology and emissions reductions,

RCP 8.5 is now probably closer to a 'worst-case' scenario than a 'business-as-usual' scenario.[8] But it is certainly not outside the bounds of possibility. RCP 8.5 tracks our cumulative CO_2 emissions fairly closely, and significant uncertainty about climatic feedback loops and future growth rates mean that this scenario could be more likely than scientists have assumed so far.[9] So, although it might not be the most likely outcome—and it certainly need not be, if we act rapidly to reduce our emissions—there is a real possibility that something like this 4 to 5°C scenario is the future that awaits us.

It is hard to overstate just how catastrophic RCP 8.5 could be.[10] The scale of the impacts means that it is hard to even imagine what such a world would look like. It would certainly involve critical tipping elements in the Earth's climate system being crossed, such as the collapse of the West Antarctic Ice Sheet and the release of large quantities of methane from previously frozen permafrost, locking in massive amounts of sea-level rise and rapid temperature increases.[11] The biogeophysical feedback loops in such a 'hothouse earth' would lead to cascading crises such as the dieback of boreal forests, massive flooding in deltaic regions, and instability in the South Asian Monsoon.[12] Extreme heatwaves, severe hurricanes and typhoons, and rapidly spreading vector-borne diseases would become common.[13] This level of warming would lead to a planet that is unrecognizable from the one that we inhabit today, with severe risks to the ecological systems that sustain human life as we know it. Agricultural production would be severely affected in many areas of the world, with crop failures, food insecurity, and commodity shocks becoming common, especially in already vulnerable areas such as sub-Saharan Africa.[14] Water availability would decrease in major river basins such as the Ganges and the Nile that supply water to millions of people.[15] And sea-level rise of up to 2 metres would affect around 187 million people on coastlines around the world over the course of the twenty-first century.[16]

The human consequences of such a scenario are easily imagined. As Darrel Moellendorf imagines it, this world is one of 'wars and walls'.[17] Major systemic crises would unfold as human societies struggle to cope, with the worst consequences felt in the poorest and most vulnerable regions of the world.[18] Food shortages, extreme weather events, and water stress would create major social upheavals. These escalating tensions would drive political conflict in already divided societies and lead to crises of mass displacement.[19] In other parts of the world, people would be driven to seek refuge simply because they can no longer survive in places no longer in the 'human climate niche'.[20] The most vulnerable would be left behind, trapped by extreme poverty.[21] The global rich would be best placed to protect themselves against the worst outcomes of catastrophic climate change. And if the border politics of today is anything to go by, we can expect that rich states in the Global North would continue to fortify and militarize their borders to deter and repel those seeking safety.[22] Existing trends towards the hardening of borders could reach new heights, with states abandoning any pretence of abiding by the norms of refugee protection.[23] Instead, the global rich would seek to insulate themselves against the damage wrought by their high-emission lifestyles, building walled cities and pushing back desperate people seeking protection. They would use their wealth to protect themselves against the conditions of extreme heat, conflict, and hunger that the masses of the poor and vulnerable would be left to endure. This is a world of 'islands of privilege' in a sea of desperation.[24]

In a 2007 report for the United Nations, Archbishop Desmond Tutu used the term 'climate apartheid' to describe the possibility of a future such as this.[25] Clearly, the comparison to the apartheid regime in South Africa is not one to be made lightly. But the comparison is not entirely inapt. Climate apartheid is a scenario of oppression and segregation on a global scale, undergirded by a structure of power that enables a privileged minority to enforce a system of domination of the poor and vulnerable, with a racialized division between the 'climate-privileged' and the 'climate-precarious'.[26] And the racialized nature of the division between the climate-privileged and the climate-precarious would not be accidental. As Nancy Tuana puts it, climate apartheid 'emerges from the complex exchanges between racism and environmental exploitation'.[27] Environmental justice activists have long recognized the ways in which environmental exploitation is intertwined with racialized hierarchies of oppression, whether through the siting of facilities that generate toxic pollutants in segregated neighbourhoods in the USA, the displacement and dispossession of Indigenous communities around the world by extractive industries that plunder natural resources, or the export of hazardous waste from rich states to the poor.[28] Catastrophic climate change would be no different. It would involve the reckless destruction of the planet largely by the Global North, with its consequences being felt most severely in the Global South. It would be an expansion and entrenchment of an order of global racial injustice.[29]

Clearly, the scenario of climate apartheid is one that we should do everything we can to avoid—we do not need to reflect much on the future of climate displacement to make this judgement. But a future of catastrophic climate change is not merely bad—it is *terrifying*. The scenario of catastrophic climate change elicits a profound sense of fear. What role should *fear* for the future of climate displacement play in our moral reflection today? Should our response to climate displacement today be driven by our fears for how it might turn out in the future?

Fear can be a powerful motivator. As psychologists understand it, fear is an adaptive response that can make danger salient and provoke responses that help us to avoid it.[30] Fear also has a rich pedigree in political theory: theorists from Thomas Hobbes to Judith Shklar have drawn on fear—either imagined or remembered—as a basis for a politics in the present that seeks to avoid the worst in the future.[31] More recently, Alison McQueen has defended the place of fear in responding to climate change.[32] She defends what social psychologists call 'fear appeals'—that is, attempts to 'arouse fear in order to promote precautionary motivation and self-protective action'—in the context of climate change.[33] Fear can make abstract dangers such as climate change more salient. It can also direct our limited attentional resources towards climate change rather than other issues with which it might otherwise compete. McQueen thus argues that fear can have an important motivational role in climate politics. If she is right, then perhaps the prospect of catastrophic climate change can play an important role in our moral reasoning today. The scenario of catastrophic climate change is a fearsome one, and the fear that it elicits could provide a basis for a politics in the present that seeks to avoid the worst dangers of climate displacement in the future.

Critics of the politics of fear have argued that it can be irrational and counterproductive. The charge of irrationality suggests that fear clouds our judgement, preventing us from acting on the basis of a sober analysis of the evidence available to us.[34] But this critique has little force in the context of climate change. For one thing, even if it is relatively unlikely, the gravity of the scenario of catastrophic climate change means that there is a clear precautionary argument for taking serious efforts to avoid it.[35] To do so would not be irrational—quite the opposite. For another thing, this critique depends on too sharp a distinction between rationality and emotion. Fear can have an important function in supporting rationality. As McQueen points out, we face a number of cognitive biases that make us prone to underestimating the risks of climate change, and the salience function of fear can be a powerful way of countering those biases.[36]

The charge of counterproductivity suggests that rather than being empowering, a politics of fear can provoke fatalism and disengagement.[37] The evidence suggests that while 'fear appeals' increase the salience of the threat of climate change, they also tend to make people feel powerless to address it.[38] At its worst, fear can become pathological: the phenomenon of 'climate anxiety' documented among young people is characterized by feelings of despair and powerlessness.[39] But the connection between fear and fatalism is not a necessary one. Fear can be disempowering, but as McQueen points out, when fear appeals are paired with information about actions that we can take to mitigate climate change, they need not lead to fatalism.[40]

Fear can be a powerful motivator, and it need not be irrational or counterproductive. I do not think we should reject the place of fear in climate politics entirely. But I do think there is a reason to avoid basing our response to climate displacement on our fear for its future. A politics of fear risks making the future of climate apartheid a self-fulling prophecy, by motivating action by citizens of the Global North that aims not at averting catastrophic climate change, but instead at shielding themselves from its worst consequences.

Fear is a fundamentally defensive emotion. The dangers to which it responds are typically dangers that we face ourselves, or dangers that face those with whom we share affective bonds.[41] For this reason, Martha Nussbaum describes fear as 'asocial' and 'narcissistic'.[42] Unlike compassion, which faces outwards towards others, fear faces inwards at threats to our own well-being. Psychologists point out that fear appeals typically work by presenting a severe threat 'to which the recipient is personally susceptible'.[43] The defensive impulse generated by fear is not usually an impulse to protect others from danger; it is an impulse to protect ourselves and members of our own group.

Fear is also malleable. Both the content of our fears—what we perceive as dangerous—and the implications of our fears—what we think we should do about those dangers—can be manipulated. The content of our fears can be shaped by 'framing effects' that affect what we perceive as a threat to our own well-being.[44] And although fear suggests responses that enable us to avoid danger, it leaves open significant room for different courses of action. As Nussbaum puts it, 'fear makes us want to avoid disaster. But it certainly does not tell us how.'[45] Fearful people are easily swayed by those who present themselves as having a means of saving them from danger. As history has shown, the malleability of fear makes it easy for demagogues to incite fear, scapegoat out-groups as threats, and then leverage fear to normalize exceptional forms of governance.[46] It is these features of fear that makes it particularly dangerous in the context of climate displacement.

Apocalyptic visions of climate displacement risk falling prey to these dangers. Those who have studied the 'securitization' of climate displacement have pointed out that the spectre of a future crisis of climate displacement is already being used to legitimate restrictive border policies.[47] In a political climate characterized by widespread hostility to migrants and refugees, it is easy for public officials to leverage fears of mass displacement to provide justifications for increased border security. In popular media, the figure of the 'climate refugee' is framed in racialized terms as a threat with 'enormous potential for disorder and disruption'.[48] Newspaper headlines predict 'waves' and 'floods' of desperate people arriving at the shores of rich states in the Global North. Citizens who are motivated by this perceived threat will seek to insulate themselves against it. Ultimately, the primary consequence of a politics of fear may not be increased political appetite for action on climate change. Instead, it may be increased political appetite for the fortification of borders to protect oneself from the perceived disorder associated with climate displacement. As Gregory White puts it:

> 'Climate refugees' is an easily invoked specter that ties into a citizenry's deepest fears about climate change. One might ultimately become resigned to the inevitability of warmer temperatures, harsher precipitation patterns, floods, droughts, pests, blighted crops, and so on. Yet droves of people invading a country? Immigrants and refugees streaming toward 'our' border? That fear is hard to bear and easily mobilized.[49]

The danger of a politics of fear for climate displacement is that instead of encouraging citizens of the Global North to tackle climate change, it will instead encourage them to double down on restrictive border policies in order to make sure that they are in the class of the 'climate-privileged' rather than the 'climate-precarious'.

At least part of the force of this objection to the politics of fear derives from a background judgement that this restrictive response to catastrophic climate change is itself morally objectionable. But David Miller has argued that it may be morally permissible for states to close their borders to at least some people in a scenario of catastrophic climate change. Even if he is right, I do not think that this conclusion would vindicate the politics of fear—it would still be better to motivate responses that seek to avoid catastrophic climate change in the first place—but it might give us less reason to worry about a response to climate displacement based in fear. Miller describes such a judgement as 'morally excruciating', but suggests that it would be within the prerogative of states to exclude those seeking protection in a scenario of catastrophic climate change:

> We can imagine a future in which the effects of global warming or resource depletion makes large parts of the Earth's surface virtually uninhabitable, and then the searching question is whether the societies that have escaped relatively unscathed would have an obligation to admit refugees in numbers that would transform their own cultures and political institutions . . . the obligation to admit would in these circumstances be humanitarian in nature, not something that justice demands, which also implies that it would be a matter for the citizens of the receiving society to decide upon—they could not be forced to comply, either by refugees themselves or by third parties.[50]

If Miller is right, then we might have less reason to be concerned about rich states fortifying their borders today to protect themselves against unwanted migration caused by catastrophic climate change in the future.

What should we make of this suggestion? In any plausible scenario of catastrophic climate change, the states that have 'escaped relatively unscathed' are also likely to be the ones that have played a significant role in bringing about catastrophe. This makes their decision to exclude the victims of catastrophic climate change seem straightforwardly indefensible. And Miller does admit that if would-be receiving states are 'partly responsible' for climate change, they would have compensatory obligations to admit a 'large number of unwanted refugees'.[51] But even if they did not bear responsibility, it would be impermissible for would-be receiving states to close their borders to the victims of catastrophic climate change in order to protect their culture and political institutions. To justify their exclusion, states would need to claim that protecting their culture and political institutions should take precedence over the lives and livelihoods of its victims of catastrophic climate change. They would need to claim that those seeking protection have no right to resist their attempts to control their borders. It is hard to see how a compelling case for these claims could be made. In a world of catastrophic climate change, the least that the safe and comfortable could do would be to accept some changes to the makeup of their societies in order to save the lives and livelihoods of the poor and vulnerable. Those at risk would have a clear claim of necessity to resist and evade attempts by rich states to enforce immigration control. We cannot vindicate the politics of fear by suggesting that the outcome that it is likely to produce is permissible.

Hope and the Future of Climate Displacement

The future scenario of climate displacement that I have outlined here is bleak. But we should not, I have argued, orient our action today in terms of our fear for that future. If not fear, then what? My suggestion is that we have rational grounds for hope for the future of climate displacement. Hope may seem misplaced in light of the bleak future outlined here. But that future is not yet written, and it is in times of deep uncertainty that we need hope the most. Like fear, hope is a response to an uncertain future. And like fear, hope can be a powerful motivator. Hope can sustain our commitment to act in pursuit of a future that we value in the face of adversity.

Philosophers tend to view hope as a motivating practical attitude that involves a desire for an outcome and a belief that its occurrence is possible but not certain.[52] The desire element captures the idea that hopes have a positive valence: we hope for things that we take to be valuable. The belief element captures the idea that hopes are oriented towards an uncertain future: if we knew that an outcome was inevitable or impossible, there would be no use in hoping for it. Philosophers also typically take our hopes—or at least our substantial rather than trivial hopes—to contain some third element that explains their motivating force. Various third elements have been proposed, including a cognitive resolve to act 'as if' the desired outcome will obtain, a disposition to focus on the outcome under the aspect of its possibility, and an interpretation of the belief as licensing hopeful activities.[53] For our purposes, it is not necessary to adjudicate between these views, but it is important to recognize that hope involves some such motivating practical commitment.

Hope's motivational force helps to explain why it is instrumentally valuable.[54] Our hopes can sustain our commitment to act in pursuit of goals that we value even in the face of a relatively low probability of success. In circumstances in which the object of our hopes is at least partially under our own control, this means that hope can help us to act in ways that make achieving the outcome for which we hope more likely.[55] And the context of climate change is one in which this motivational function of hope may be especially important.[56] Hope can play an important role in sustaining our commitment in circumstances in which the prospects for achieving the goal of tackling climate change appear dim.

But our hopes can also be subjected to critical scrutiny. As Darrel Moellendorf puts it, hope exists 'within the space of reasons'.[57] We evaluate our hopes in terms of both their moral status and their practical rationality. In moral terms, we want our hopes to be oriented towards the good or the right, and we criticize those who hope for things that we think are wrongful. In terms of practical rationality, we want our hopes to be justified. We want to distinguish our hopes from wishful thinking or mindless optimism. There is disagreement about what epistemic standards must be met for hope to be rational in this way: some argue that the object of our hopes must be merely possible, whereas others argue that the object of our hopes must meet some minimal threshold of probability.[58] Here, I follow those like Moellendorf who take hope to be 'evidence-relative' to at least some degree.[59] The idea is not that the object of our hope must be *likely* for hope to be justified. After all, a hope is not a belief that an outcome will occur, and so it is not governed by the epistemic norms governing beliefs. Hope is clearly consistent viewing an outcome as improbable. Rather, the idea is that we must have enough evidence for us to be justified in taking hope to bear *practically* on our actions. Hoping has costs as well as benefits—not least the costs of the disappointment of unsatisfied hopes—and so the epistemic standards for rational hopes should be calibrated to the potential costs of hoping as well as the benefits of hoping for our own moral agency.[60] We need what Moellendorf calls 'hope-makers'—pieces of evidence that support our practical commitments—to justify our hopes.[61]

What hopes for the future of climate displacement might we have, and what hope-makers might justify them? Gaia Vince has recently articulated what she takes to be a hopeful vision of the future of climate displacement. She expects migration and mobility to play an important role in adaptation to climate change over the course of what she calls the 'nomad century'.[62] The picture that she paints of the future is of a world that is fundamentally restructured by the mass movement of billions of people, mostly from hot, arid, flooded, and drought-stricken regions of the world, further north. But on her view, mass migration is not something to be feared. Instead, it is fundamental to our survival and flourishing as a species. The future that Vince envisages involves the construction of new cities in polar regions of the planet 'greened' by climate change, the receding of nationalist sentiments, and a new form of global citizenship for all through a UN passport.[63]

There is much to be admired in Vince's vision of the future. She makes a compelling case that migration is often a solution to the problems brought about by climate change, not something that we should fear. And the vision that she articulates offers an important counterpoint to the fearful visions of catastrophic climate displacement that predominate in the popular imagination. But Vince's vision of the future of climate displacement should not, in my view, be the object of our hopes. Vince's vision of the future treats catastrophic climate change as inevitable. In her view, a rise of at least 4°C above pre-industrial temperatures is almost unavoidable.[64] The picture that she paints is one of deep adaptation to a fundamentally inhospitable world. But this prematurely accepts the inevitability of our failure to bring climate change under our control.

In my view, the object of our hopes should be more open-textured. Over the course of this book, I have made some arguments about how we ought to address different forms of climate displacement. But I do not think that the object of our hopes should be that we carry out to the letter the details of the proposals that I have suggested. Hoping too narrowly for these specific outcomes is liable to misdirect us from the opportunities for action that arise in an unpredictable and changing world. Political action requires judgement, not just blueprints for a future society. We should not allow overly specific hopes to blind us to alternatives that can lead to a more just future of climate displacement.

Instead, our hopes should be oriented towards overcoming the pathologies of our politics that hinder the emergence of *any* just response to climate displacement. Some specific problems have been examined over the course of this book, but the big picture of these pathologies is relatively familiar. In the domain of climate change, obstacles include the entrenched private interests that profit from fossil fuel economies, the persistent failure of international cooperation, and the distributive conflicts that arise in the face of the imperative to shut down industries such as coal and oil.[65] In the domain of migration, they include the increasingly hostile policies adopted to prevent and deter migration to the Global North, the surge of populist and nationalist sentiments that sustains those policies, and the hollowing out of social and labour protections and the scapegoating that pits workers against immigrants.[66] A realistic and rational hope for the future of climate displacement is one that looks for the signs of the possibility of overcoming these pathologies.

What hope-makers could sustain a commitment to overcoming these barriers to a just future of climate displacement? We can look for inspiration to structural changes in our societies that create more fertile grounds for overcoming these pathologies, policies that promise to help us to overcome the conflicts that hinder progress, and social movements that contest the forces that would hold back the achievement of migration and climate justice. Here, I largely draw on Moellendorf's analysis of hope-makers in the domain of climate change, but I also identify some parallel developments in the domain of migration. These developments should not make us heedlessly optimistic, but they do give us grounds for a politics of hope that can sustain our commitment to achieving justice in climate displacement.

Structural changes give us grounds for hope for the future of climate displacement. In the domain of climate change, technological progress is making clean energy a viable alternative to fossil fuels. The price of renewable energy is falling, and data from the International Energy Agency (IEA) shows that renewable energy is now cheaper than ever, and at least as cheap as fossil fuels in most markets.[67] At the same time, investment in clean energy technology is rising and has largely rebounded from the pandemic-related dip in 2020.[68] In the USA, the

Biden Administration's Inflation Reduction Act of 2022 recently authorized $369 billion in spending on climate change and extended tax credits on investments in solar power.[69] On their own, these developments will not be enough to enable the rapid decarbonization that we need to limit global temperature increases to 1.5–2°C and so to prevent the occurrence of more dramatic displacement scenarios. But they are an important starting point that makes it easier to overcome the problem of structural dependence on fossil fuel energy.

At the same time, changes in the demographic structure of developed states are creating a practical imperative to admit greater numbers of migrants. Developed states are undergoing an important demographic transition.[70] Increasing life expectancies and decreasing fertility rates are increasing the 'old age dependency ratio', which makes it more difficult to sustain pensions and healthcare. Since one way of increasing the working-age population is through migration, this creates an incentive for states to relax their presently restrictive border policies.[71] Of course, this practical imperative alone is not sufficient to overcome the tendency towards anti-immigrant sentiment in the Global North, and it is consistent with harsh limitations on the rights of migrant workers and restrictive immigration selection policies. But it does create a leverage point for political action that aims to overcome the tendency towards the hardening of borders in developed states.

At the level of policy, there are also proposals that promise to help to overcome the pathologies of climate and migration politics. In climate politics, proposals for a Green New Deal offer a promising way forward. As Moellendorf points out, proposals for a Green New Deal are varied, but those with the most promise pair large-scale public investments in decarbonization with commitments to a just transition and strong labour protections in the jobs created in the new energy economy.[72] Such a Green New Deal would make action on climate change an investment that benefits the worst-off, including those who currently depend for their livelihoods on the fossil fuel economy, rather than a costly sacrifice. It would certainly not eliminate resistance to climate action—those invested in the continued extraction of fossil fuels stand to lose in any hopeful scenario—but it does have the potential to help us to overcome some of the distributive conflicts associated with decarbonization.

In migration politics, international legal and policy developments create an opportunity to push for more progressive migration and refugee policies. The Global Compact for Refugees and the Global Compact on Migration are in many ways deeply flawed, but they have played an important role in solidifying norms on burden-sharing in refugee protection, highlighting the need to protect those who fall outside the scope of the legal definition of the refugee, and promoting the idea that mobility is something to be facilitated rather than prohibited.[73] There are also progressive proposals for building on these forms of cooperation in the future. The Model International Mobility Convention, for example, aims to promote compliance with refugee burden-sharing by tying it to benefits such as priority access to an international clearinghouse for labour visas.[74] States stand to benefit from a stable regime of global mobility, which would stop them having to deal with refugee crises in ad hoc ways. Policies such as these can help to make vivid the benefits that states stand to gain, and so could help to overcome existing tendencies towards backsliding in refugee protection.

The work being done by social movements organizing for climate and migration justice also provides grounds for hope for the future of climate displacement. Youth and Indigenous-led movements such as Fridays for Future and the campaign against the Dakota Access Pipeline at Standing Rock have played an instrumental role in putting climate change on the political agenda in Western democracies.[75] Strategic and sustained mass mobilization is critical to breaking the power of entrenched fossil fuel interests. As Moellendorf puts it, 'the power of money in politics is best met by the power of mass mobilization'.[76] Existing popular pressure has yet not proved sufficient to force a confrontation with entrenched fossil fuel interests, and we should not expect quick and easy victories.[77] But movements such as these are a critical part of building the power necessary to stop vested fossil fuel interests holding back the project of decarbonization.

Refugee and migrant-led activism and strategic forms of non-compliance with immigration law also point towards promising avenues for resisting regressive developments in migration politics. Protests by the *sans-papiers* in France and the 'coming out' movement by DREAMers in the USA aim to challenge hostility to refugees and migrants by making the plight of undocumented migrants visible.[78] At the same time, solidarity movements aim to confront the deterrence paradigm in refugee and migration policy. In the USA, the Sanctuary City movement seeks to frustrate efforts to deport and detain undocumented migrants by limiting the cooperation of public services with Immigration and Customs Enforcement (ICE).[79] In the Mediterranean, activist organizations such as Alarm Phone—which provides an emergency hotline for those in distress at sea—contest non-arrival measures and save lives.[80] These forms of non-compliance and resistance will clearly not dismantle the deterrence paradigm on their own, but they are an important way of confronting the unjust border and migration policies pursued by states in the Global North.

These structural changes, policy proposals, and social movements provide a basis for a hope that we can overcome the pathologies that hold back the achievement of a just response to climate displacement. They can serve as a point of orientation for a politics of hope for the future of climate displacement. They do not give us reason to think that such an achievement is likely, and they should not make us complacent or optimistic about the prospects for success. We should be clear-minded about the very real obstacles that stand in the way. But at the same time, we should not submit to the pessimism of fear, which treats those obstacles as inevitable and inescapable. A politics of hope involves what Dewey called *meliorism*: 'the belief that the specific conditions which exist at one moment, be they comparatively bad or comparatively good, in any event may be bettered.'[81] A politics of hope can sustain our commitment to achieving a better future of climate displacement in the face of a difficult and uncertain future. It is precisely because of the daunting challenge that we face that we have reason to hope.

Notes

Chapter 1: The Moral Challenge of Climate Displacement

1. Quoted in IOM, *International Dialogue on Migration Vol. 18—Climate Change, Environmental Degradation and Migration* (IOM, 2012), 52–3.
2. Keffing Sissoko et al., 'Agriculture, Livelihoods and Climate Change in the West African Sahel', *Regional Environmental Change* 11, no. S1 (2011): S119–25.
3. Jon Pedersen, 'Drought, Migration and Population Growth in the Sahel: The Case of the Malian Gòurma: 1900–1991', *Population Studies* 49, no. 1 (1995): 111–26.
4. Esau Sinnok, 'My World Interrupted', *US Department of Interior* (blog post), 12 August 2015, available at https://www.doi.gov/blog/my-world-interrupted.
5. Quoted in Alex Randall, Jo Salsbury, and Zach White, *Moving Stories: The Voices of People Who Move in the Context of Environmental Change* (Climate Outreach, 2014).
6. Asia Development Bank, *Addressing Climate Change and Migration in Asia and the Pacific* (Asia Development Bank, 2012), 5.
7. OCHA, 'Pakistan Media Factsheet' (OCHA, 2011), available at https://reliefweb.int/sites/reliefweb.int/files/resources/Full_Report_51.pdf.
8. Clare M. Goodess, 'How Is the Frequency, Location and Severity of Extreme Events Likely to Change up to 2060?' *Environmental Science & Policy* 27, no. S1 (2013): S4–14.
9. Quoted in Tamer Afifi et al., *Climate Change, Vulnerability and Human Mobility: Perspectives of Refugees from the East and Horn of Africa* (UNU-EHS, 2012), 47.
10. Chris Funk, 'We Thought Trouble Was Coming', *Nature* 476, no. 7358 (2011): 7.
11. CARE International, 'Dadaab Refugee Camps, Kenya', *CARE* (blog post), 23 September 2013, available at https://www.care.org/emergencies/dadaab-refugee-camp-kenya.
12. Mohamed Nasheed, in UNGA, 'General Debate of the 64th Session', 24 September 2009, available at un.org/en/ga/64/generaldebate/pdf/MV_en.pdf.
13. Jon Barnett and W. Neil Adger, 'Climate Dangers and Atoll Countries', *Climatic Change* 61 (2003): 321–37.
14. Isak Stoddard et al., 'Three Decades of Climate Mitigation: Why Haven't We Bent the Global Emissions Curve?' *Annual Review of Environment and Resources* 46 (2021): 653–89; Dale Jamieson, *Reason in a Dark Time: Why the Struggle Against Climate Change Failed—and What It Means for Our Future* (Oxford University Press, 2014), 11–60.
15. Rainer Bauböck, 'Europe's Commitments and Failures in the Refugee Crisis', *European Political Science* 17 (2018): 140–50.
16. For a compelling analysis, see Serena Parekh, *No Refuge: Ethics and the Global Refugee Crisis* (Oxford University Press, 2020).
17. For 'duty of rescue' views, see Michael Walzer, *Spheres of Justice* (Basic Books, 1983); Matthew Gibney, *The Ethics and Politics of Asylum: Liberal Democracy and the Response to Refugees* (Cambridge University Press, 2004); David Miller, *Strangers in Our Midst: The Political Philosophy of Immigration* (Harvard University Press, 2016). For 'state system' views, see Chris Bertram, *Do States Have the Right to Exclude?* (Polity, 2018); David Owen, *What Do We Owe to Refugees?* (Polity, 2020); Gillian Brock, *Justice for People on the Move: Migration in Challenging Times* (Cambridge University Press, 2020).
18. See, for example, Matthew Taylor, 'Climate Change "Will Create World's Biggest Refugee Crisis"', *The Guardian*, 2 November 2017; Damian Carrington, 'Climate Change Will

Stir "Unimaginable" Refugee Crisis, Says Military', *The Guardian*, 1 December 2016; Ben Spencer, 'UK Warned of "Climate Change Flood of Refugees": Droughts and Heatwaves Could Force Millions to Flee their Country', *The Daily Mail*, 1 April 2014; Jonathan Leake, 'Climate Change "Could Create 200m Refugees"', *The Sunday Times*, 1 April 2007.

19. Etienne Piguet, 'From "Primitive Migration" to "Climate Refugees": The Curious Fate of the Natural Environment in Migration Studies', *Annals of the Association of American Geographers* 103, no. 1 (2013): 148–62.
20. Ellsworth Huntington, *The Pulse of Asia: A Journey in Central Asia Illustrating the Geographic Basis of History* (Houghton, Mifflin and Company, 1907), 382.
21. Huntington, *The Pulse of Asia*, 382–4.
22 Piguet, 'From "Primitive Migration" to "Climate Refugees"', 151–52.
23. See, for example, the discussion of 'ecological' migration in William Peterson, 'A General Typology of Migration', *American Sociological Review* 23, no. 3 (1958): 256–66.
24. Piguet, 'From "Primitive Migration" to "Climate Refugees"', 152.
25. See Emmanuel Marx, 'The Social World of Refugees: A Conceptual Framework', *Journal of Refugee Studies* 3, no. 3 (1990): 189–203.
26. Andrew Sluyter, 'Neo-Environmental Determinism, Intellectual Damage Control, and Nature/Society Science', *Antipode* 35, no. 4 (2003): 816. See, for example, the conspicuous absence of the environment as a causal factor in P. Neal Ritchey, 'Explanations of Migration', *Annual Review of Sociology* 2, no. 1 (1976): 363–404.
27. Essam El-Hinnawi, *Environmental Refugees* (UNEP, 1985), 4.
28. For example, Jodi Jacobson, *Environmental Refugees: A Yardstick of Habitability* (Worldwatch Institute, 1988).
29. Astri Suhrke, 'Environmental Degradation and Population Flows', *Journal of International Affairs* 47, no. 2 (1994): 473–96.
30. Norman Myers, *Ultimate Security: The Environmental Basis of Political Stability* (W.W. Norton, 1993), 191; Norman Myers, 'Environmental Refugees: A Growing Phenomenon of the 21st Century', *Philosophical Transactions of the Royal Society B: Biological Sciences* 357, no. 1420 (2002): 609–13. See also Norman Myers and Jennifer Kent, *Environmental Exodus: An Emergent Crisis in the Global Arena* (Climate Institute, 1995).
31. Nicholas Stern, *The Economics of Climate Change: The Stern Review* (Cambridge University Press, 2007), 91–2; Jane Lewis, Rachel Baird, and Angela Burton, *Human Tide: The Real Migration Crisis* (Christian Aid, 2007).
32. François Gemenne, 'How They Became the Human Face of Climate Change: Research and Policy Interactions in the Birth of the "Environmental Migration" Concept', in Etienne Piguet, Antoine Pécoud, and Paul De Guchteneire (eds) *Migration and Climate Change* (Cambridge University Press, 2011), 225–59.
33. Gaim Kibreab, 'Environmental Causes and Impact of Refugee Movements: A Critique of the Current Debate', *Disasters* 21, no. 1 (1997): 20–38; Astri Suhrke, 'Environmental Degradation and Population Flows'; Richard Black, 'Environmental Refugees: Myth or Reality?' *Working Paper: New Issues in Refugee Research* (UNHCR, 2001); Stephen Castles, 'Environmental Change and Forced Migration: Making Sense of the Debate', *Working Paper: New Issues in Refugee Research* (UNHCR, 2002).
34. Stephen Castles, 'Concluding Remarks on the Climate Change–Migration Nexus', in Etienne Piguet, Antoine Pecoud, and Paul De Guchteneire (eds) *Migration and Climate Change* (Cambridge University Press, 2011), 416.
35. Richard Black, 'Environmental Refugees: Myth or Reality?', 3.
36. Castles, 'Concluding Remarks on the Climate Change–Migration Nexus', 419; Suhrke, 'Environmental Degradation and Population Flows', 477.
37. Castles, 'Concluding Remarks on the Climate Change–Migration Nexus', 416.
38. See Thomas F. Homer-Dixon, 'On the Threshold: Environmental Changes as Causes of Acute Conflict', *International Security* 16, no. 2 (1991): 76–116; 'Environmental Scarcities

and Violent Conflict: Evidence from Cases', *International Security* 19, no. 1 (1994): 5–40. For a critical assessment, see Betsy Hartmann, 'Population, Environment and Security: A New Trinity', *Environment and Urbanization* 10, no. 2 (1998): 113–28.
39. Robert D. Kaplan, 'The Coming Anarchy', *The Atlantic*, 1 February 1994, front page.
40. Andrew Baldwin, 'Racialisation and the Figure of the Climate Change Migrant', *Environment and Planning A: Economy and Space* 45, no. 6 (2013): 1474–90; Giovanni Bettini, 'Climate Barbarians at the Gate? A Critique of Apocalyptic Narratives on "Climate Refugees"', *Geoforum* 45 (2013): 63–72. See also Ingrid Boas, *Climate Migration and Security: Securitisation as a Strategy in Climate Change Politics* (Routledge, 2015); Benoît Mayer, *The Concept of Climate Migration: Advocacy and Its Prospects* (Edward Elgar Publishing, 2016).
41. Peter Schwartz and Doug Randall, 'An Abrupt Climate Change Scenario and Its Implications for United States National Security' (2003), 18, available at https://apps.dtic.mil/docs/citations/ADA469325.
42. Giovanni Bettini, Sarah Louise Nash, and Giovanna Gioli, 'One Step Forward, Two Steps Back? The Fading Contours of (in)Justice in Competing Discourses on Climate Migration', *The Geographical Journal* 183, no. 4 (2017): 348–58; Romain Felli and Noel Castree, 'Neoliberalising Adaptation to Environmental Change: Foresight or Foreclosure?' *Environment and Planning A: Economy and Space* 44, no. 1 (2012): 1–4. See also the discussion in this book at C5P46–C5P48.
43. Stephen Castles, 'Environmental Change and Forced Migration: Making Sense of the Debate', 5.
44. IPCC, 'Summary for Policymakers', in C.B. Field et al. (eds) *Climate Change 2014: Impacts, Adaptation, and Vulnerability. Part A: Global and Sectoral Aspects. Contribution of Working Group II to the Fifth Assessment Report of the Intergovernmental Panel on Climate Change* (Cambridge University Press, 2014), 20.
45. Etienne Piguet, 'Linking Climate Change, Environmental Degradation, and Migration: A Methodological Overview', *Wiley Interdisciplinary Reviews: Climate Change* 1, no. 4 (2010): 517–24.
46. For example, Sergio O. Saldaña-Zorrilla and Krister Sandberg, 'Impact of Climate-Related Disasters on Human Migration in Mexico: A Spatial Model', *Climatic Change* 96 (2009): 97–118; Sabine Henry, Paul Boyle, and Eric F. Lambina, 'Modelling Inter-Provincial Migration in Burkina Faso, West Africa: The Role of Socio-demographic and Environmental Factors', *Applied Geography* 23, no. 2–3 (2003): 115–36; Salvador Barrios, Luisito Bertinelli, and Eric Strobl, 'Climatic Change and Rural–Urban Migration: The Case of Sub-Saharan Africa', *Journal of Urban Economics* 60, no. 3 (2006): 357–71.
47. For a large-scale qualitative survey, see Jill Jäger et al., *Environmental Change and Forced Migration Scenarios Project Synthesis Report* (2009), available at http://www.each-for.eu/documents/EACH-FOR_Synthesis_Report_090515.pdf, and Koko Warner, 'Environmental Change and Migration: Methodological Considerations from Ground-Breaking Global Survey', *Population and Environment* 33, no. 1 (2011): 2–27. For historical approaches, see Robert McLeman et al., 'Drought Adaptation in Rural Eastern Oklahoma in the 1930s: Lessons for Climate Change Adaptation Research', *Mitigation and Adaptation Strategies for Global Change* 13 (2008): 379–400; Sheila J. Arenstam Gibbons and Robert J. Nicholls, 'Island Abandonment and Sea-Level Rise: An Historical Analog from the Chesapeake Bay, USA', *Global Environmental Change* 16, no. 1 (2006): 40–7.
48. For example, Dominic Kniveton, Christopher D. Smith, and Sharon Wood, 'Agent-Based Model Simulations of Future Migration Flows for Burkina Faso', *Global Environmental Change* 21, no. S1 (2011): S34–40; Christopher D. Smith, 'Modelling Migration Futures: Development and Testing of the Rainfalls Agent-Based Migration Model—Tanzania', *Climate and Development* 6, no. 1 (2014): 77–91.

49. Etienne Piguet, Antoine Pécoud, and Paul de Guchteniere, 'Migration and Climate Change: An Overview', *Refugee Survey Quarterly* 33, no. 3 (2011): 1–23; Robert McLeman and Lori M. Hunter, 'Migration in the Context of Vulnerability and Adaptation to Climate Change: Insights from Analogues', *Wiley Interdisciplinary Reviews: Climate Change* 1, no. 3 (2010): 450–61; Robert McLeman and Barry Smit, 'Migration as an Adaptation to Climate Change', *Climatic Change* 76, no. 1–2 (2006): 31–53; Richard Black et al., 'Climate Change: Migration as Adaptation', *Nature* 478, no. 7370 (2011): 447–9; Richard Black et al., 'Foresight: Migration and Global Environmental Change', *Foresight Reports* (The Government Office for Science, 2011).

50. Piguet, Pécoud, and de Guchteniere, 'Migration and Climate Change: An Overview', 12–13; Black et al., 'Foresight: Migration and Global Environmental Change'; Richard Black et al., 'The Effect of Environmental Change on Human Migration', *Global Environmental Change* 21, no. S1 (2011): S3–11.

51. Olúfẹ́mi O. Táíwò, *Reconsidering Reparations* (Oxford University Press, 2022), esp. 157–72, 215–22. On the social nature of vulnerability, see W. Neil Adger, 'Vulnerability', *Global Environmental Change* 16, no. 3 (2006): 268–81; Nick Brooks, W. Neil Adger, and P. Mick Kelly, 'The Determinants of Vulnerability and Adaptive Capacity at the National Level and their Implications for Adaptation', *Global Environmental Change* 15, no. 2 (2005): 151–63; W. Neil Adger and P. Mick Kelly, 'Social Vulnerability to Climate Change and the Architecture of Entitlements', *Mitigation and Adaptation Strategies for Global Climate Change* 4 (1999): 253–66; Susan L. Cutter, 'Vulnerability to Environmental Hazards', *Progress in Human Geography* 20, no. 4 (1996): 529–39. On the relationship between vulnerability to climate change and colonialism, see also J. Timmons Roberts and Bradley C. Parks, *A Climate of Injustice: Global Inequality, North–South Politics, and Climate Policy* (MIT Press, 2006); Anil Agarwal and Sunita Narain, *Global Warming in an Unequal World: A Case of Environmental Colonialism* (Centre for Science and Environment, 1991).

52. Piguet, Pécoud, and de Guchteniere, 'Migration and Climate Change: An Overview', 13–14; Richard Black et al., 'Migration, Immobility and Displacement Outcomes Following Extreme Events', *Environmental Science & Policy* 27, no. S1 (2013): S32–43; Ben Wisner et al., *At Risk: Natural Hazards, People's Vulnerability and Disasters* (Routledge, 2004).

53. Piguet, Pécoud, and de Guchteniere, 'Migration and Climate Change: An Overview', 14–15; Walter Kälin, 'Conceptualising Climate-Induced Displacement', in Jane McAdam (ed.) *Climate Change and Displacement: Multidisciplinary Perspectives* (Hart, 2010), 81–104.

54. Onora O'Neill, 'Abstraction, Idealization and Ideology in Ethics', *Royal Institute of Philosophy Supplements* 22 (1987): 57–8. See also O'Neill, *Towards Justice and Virtue: A Constructive Account of Practical Reasoning* (Cambridge University Press, 1996): 38–44.

55. Lewis Carroll, *Sylvie and Bruno Concluded* (Macmillan and Co., 1893), 169. See also Umberto Eco, 'On the Impossibility of Drawing a Map with a Scale of 1 to 1', in *How to Travel With a Salmon and Other Essays*, trans. William Weaver (Harvest, 1994): 95–106.

56. See also Jamie Draper, 'Anticipatory and Reactive Displacement', in Jamie Draper and David Owen (eds) *The Political Philosophy of Internal Displacement* (Oxford University Press, forthcoming).

57. Anthony H. Richmond, 'Reactive Migration: Sociological Perspectives on Refugee Movements', *Journal of Refugee Studies* 6, no. 1 (1993): 7–24. See also Anthony H. Richmond, *Global Apartheid: Refugees, Racism and the New World Order* (Oxford University Press, 1994).

58. Richmond, 'Reactive Migration', 15–17. Richmond builds his theory on the basis of Anthony Giddens' theory of structuration. See Anthony Giddens, *The Constitution of Society: Outline of the Theory of Structuration* (John Wiley & Sons, [1984] 2013).

59. See Valeria Ottonelli and Tiziana Torresi, 'When Is Migration Voluntary?' *International Migration Review* 47, no. 4 (2013): 783–813.
60. Miller, *Strangers in Our Midst*, 94.
61. Ottonelli and Torresi, 'When Is Migration Voluntary?' 785–8.
62. The distinctions that I draw here are informed by the typology set out by Walter Kälin, but do not straightforwardly follow the distinctions that he draws. See Kälin, 'Conceptualising Climate-Induced Displacement'.
63. Simona Capisani, 'Territorial Instability and the Right to a Liveable Locality', *Environmental Ethics* 42, no. 2 (2020): 189–207.
64. Capisani, 'Territorial Instability and the Right to a Liveable Locality', esp. 198–203. For Capisani, the right to a liveable locality is grounded in a particular view of the normative commitments implicit in the shared social practice of the territorial state system. I am sympathetic to that grounding, but I do think that there are other possible ways of grounding such a right available to those who are not, so I do not wed my approach to it here.
65. See John Dewey, 'Ethics', in Jo Ann Boydston (ed.) *The Later Works of John Dewey: 1925–1953*, Vol. 7 (South Illinois University Press, 1985), esp. 162–6, 178–80. For other methodological approaches to political theory that follow in Dewey's footsteps, see Elizabeth Anderson, 'How to Be a Pragmatist', in Ruth Chang and Kurt Sylvan (eds) *The Routledge Handbook of Practical Reason* (Routledge, 2021), 83–94; Elizabeth Anderson, *The Imperative of Integration* (Princeton University Press, 2010); Joshua Forstenzer, *Deweyan Experimentalism and the Problem of Method in Political Philosophy* (Routledge, 2019); Samuel Bagg, 'Between Critical and Normative Theory: Predictive Political Theory as a Deweyan Realism', *Political Research Quarterly* 69, no. 2 (2016): 233–44; David Wiens, 'Prescribing Institutions without Ideal Theory', *Journal of Political Philosophy* 20, no. 1 (2012): 45–70; Jack Knight and James Johnson, *The Priority of Democracy: The Political Consequences of Pragmatism* (Princeton University Press, 2011).
66. John Dewey, 'Reconstruction in Philosophy', in Jo Ann Boydston (ed.) *The Middle Works of John Dewey: 1899–1924*, Vol. 12 (South Illinois University Press, 1982), 177.
67. John Dewey, 'The Quest for Certainty', in Jo Ann Boydston (ed.) *The Later Works of John Dewey: 1925–1953*, Vol. 4 (South Illinois University Press, 1984), 5–6.
68. A large part of the literature on climate change in political theory deals with the question of how our duties to achieve that goal should be understood. For some important contributions, see Darrel Moellendorf, *Mobilizing Hope: Climate Change and Global Poverty* (Oxford University Press, 2022); Megan Blomfield, *Global Justice, Natural Resources, and Climate Change* (Oxford University Press, 2019); Henry Shue, *Climate Justice: Vulnerability and Protection* (Oxford University Press, 2014); Jamieson, *Reason in a Dark Time*; Darrel Moellendorf, *The Moral Challenge of Dangerous Climate Change: Values, Poverty, and Policy* (Cambridge University Press, 2012); Catriona McKinnon, *Climate Change and Future Justice: Precaution, Compensation and Triage* (Routledge, 2012); Stephen M. Gardiner, *A Perfect Moral Storm: The Ethical Tragedy of Climate Change* (Oxford University Press, 2011); Steve Vanderheiden, *Atmospheric Justice: A Political Theory of Climate Change* (Oxford University Press, 2008); Roberts and Parks, *A Climate of Injustice*.
69. Kyle Fruh, 'Anticipatory Moral Failure: The Case of Climate Change-Driven Displacement', *Journal of Social Philosophy* 54, no. 2 (2023): 248–61.
70. For practice-dependence, see Andrea Sangiovanni, 'Justice and the Priority of Politics to Morality', *Journal of Political Philosophy* 16, no. 2 (2008): 137–64; Andrea Sangiovanni, 'How Practices Matter', *Journal of Political Philosophy* 24, no. 1 (2016): 3–23; Charles Beitz, *The Idea of Human Rights* (Oxford University Press, 2009); Miriam Ronzoni, 'The Global Order: A Case of Background Injustice? A Practice-Dependent Account', *Philosophy & Public Affairs* 37, no. 3 (2009): 229–56; Aaron James, 'Constructing Justice for Existing Practice: Rawls and the Status Quo', *Philosophy and Public Affairs* 33, no. 3 (2005): 281–316; Ayelet

Banai, Miriam Ronzoni, and Christian Schemmel, 'Global Social Justice: the Possibility of Social Justice Beyond States in a World of Overlapping Practices', in Ayelet Banai, Miriam Ronzoni, and Christian Schemmel (eds) *Social Justice, Global Dynamics: Theoretical and Empirical Perspectives* (Routledge, 2011), 46–60. For contextualism, see Joseph Carens, 'A Contextual Approach to Normative Political Theory', *Ethical Theory and Moral Practice* 7, no. 2 (2004): 117–32; David Miller, *Justice for Earthlings: Essays in Political Philosophy* (Cambridge University Press, 2013); Sune Lægaard, 'Contextualism in Normative Political Theory', in *Oxford Research Encyclopaedia of Politics* (Oxford University Press, 2016); Tariq Modood and Simon Thompson, 'Revisiting Contextualism in Political Theory: Putting Principles into Context', *Res Publica* 24, no. 3 (2018): 339–57.
71. There is a disagreement among even committed ideal theorists about whether or not the vision of an ideally just political order that they articulate should be sensitive to non-moral facts. For 'fact-sensitive' ideal theories see, for example, John Rawls, *A Theory of Justice* (Belknap, [1971] 1999); Ronald Dworkin, *Sovereign Virtue: The Theory and Practice of Equality* (Harvard University Press, 2000). For 'fact-insensitive' ideal theories see, for example, Cohen, *Rescuing Justice and Equality*; David Estlund, 'Utopophobia', *Philosophy & Public Affairs* 42, no. 2 (2014): 113–34; Simon Caney, *Justice Beyond Borders: A Global Political Theory* (Oxford University Press, 2005).
72. Laura Valentini, 'Ideal vs. Non-Ideal Theory: A Conceptual Map', *Philosophy Compass* 7, no. 9 (2012): 660.
73. See Joseph Carnes, *The Ethics of Immigration* (Oxford University Press, 2013), esp. 8–13.
74. A. John Simmons, 'Ideal and Nonideal Theory', *Philosophy & Public Affairs* 38, no. 1 (2014): 5–36; Ingrid Robeyns, 'Ideal Theory in Theory and Practice', *Social Theory and Practice* 34, no. 3 (2008): 341–62.

Chapter 2: Against a Treaty for Climate Refugees

1. UNGA, *New York Declaration on Refugees and Migrants*, A/RES/71/1 § (2016), article I.1.
2. UNHCR, *The Global Compact on Refugees*, A/73/12 (Part II) § (2018), article I.D.8; UNGA, *The Global Compact for Safe, Orderly and Regular Migration*, A/RES/73/195 § (2018), articles 18(b), 18(h)–(l), 21(h), 39(b).
3. UNFCCC, 'Report of the Conference of the Parties on Its Sixteenth Session. Part Two: Actions Taken by the Conference of the Parties at the Sixteenth Session', FCCC/CP/2010/7/Add.1 § (2011), sec. 13(f).
4. See https://unfccc.int/wim-excom/sub-groups/TFD.
5. IPCC, *Climate Change 2014: Impacts, Adaptation and Vulnerability. Part A: Global and Sectoral Aspects. Contribution of Working Group II to the Fifth Assessment Report of the Intergovernmental Panel on Climate Change*. Core Writing Team, C.B. Field and V.R. Barros (eds) (Cambridge University Press, 2014), 73. On the scale of climate displacement, see François Gemmene, 'Why the Numbers Don't Add Up: A Review of Estimates and Predictions of People Displaced by Environmental Changes', *Global Environmental Change* 21, no. S1 (2011): S41–S49.
6. François Gemenne, 'How They Became the Human Face of Climate Change: Research and Policy Interactions in the Birth of the "Environmental Migration" Concept', in Etienne Piguet, Antoine Pécoud, and Paul De Guchteneire (eds) *Migration and Climate Change* (Cambridge University Press, 2011).
7. Ludwig Wittgenstein, *Philosophical Investigations*, trans. G.E.M. Anscombe (Blackwell, 2007 [1953]), 53 (§115). On this idea of a picture, see David Owen, 'Criticism and Captivity: On Genealogy and Critical Theory', *European Journal of Philosophy* 10, no. 2 (2002):

216–30. Here I am influenced by David Owen's distinction between two 'pictures' of the institution of refugeehood in his *What Do We Owe to Refugees?* (Polity Press, 2020).
8. See Owen, 'Criticism and Captivity', 217–19.
9. Frank Biermann and Ingrid Boas, 'Preparing for a Warmer World: Towards a Global Governance System to Protect Climate Refugees', *Global Environmental Politics* 10, no. 1 (2010): 60–88. See also Frank Biermann and Ingrid Boas, 'Protecting Climate Refugees: The Case for a Global Protocol', *Environment: Science and Policy for Sustainable Development* 50, no. 6 (2008): 8–17.
10. Biermann and Boas, 'Preparing for a Warmer World', 75–6.
11. Biermann and Boas, 'Preparing for a Warmer World', 75, 79–82.
12. Bonnie Docherty and Tyler Giannini, 'Confronting a Rising Tide: A Proposal for a Convention on Climate Change Refugees', *Harvard Environmental Law Review* 33, no. 2 (2009): 349–403.
13. Docherty and Giannini, 'Confronting a Rising Tide', 376–8.
14. Sujatha Byravan and Sudhir Chella Rajan, 'The Ethical Implications of Sea-Level Rise Due to Climate Change', *Ethics & International Affairs* 24, no. 3 (2010): 239–60. See also Sujatha Byravan and Sudhir Chella Rajan, 'Sea Level Rise and Climate Change Exiles: A Possible Solution', *Bulletin of the Atomic Scientists* 71, no. 2 (2015): 21–8.
15. Byravan and Rajan, 'The Ethical Implications of Sea-Level Rise Due to Climate Change', 253.
16. Jane McAdam, *Climate Change, Forced Migration and International Law* (Oxford University Press, 2012), 191.
17. Environmental Justice Foundation, 'Beyond Borders: Our Changing Climate—Its Role in Conflict and Displacement' (Environmental Justice Foundation, 2017), available at https://ejfoundation.org/resources/downloads/BeyondBorders.pdf.
18. Volker Türk and Rebecca Dowd, 'Protection Gaps', in Elena Fiddian-Qasmiyeh, Gil Loescher, Katy Long, and Nando Sigona (eds) *The Oxford Handbook of Refugee and Forced Migration Studies* (Oxford University Press, 2014), 278–89.
19. For an argument that it is consistent with the 'logic' (though not the wording) of the refugee convention to grant refugee status to (some) people displaced by climate impacts, see Matthew Lister, 'Climate Change Refugees', *Critical Review of International Social and Political Philosophy* 17, no. 5 (2014): 618–34. See also the discussion in Chapter 6 at C6P48–C6P57.
20. Khalid Koser, 'Climate Change and Internal Displacement: Challenges to the Normative Framework', in Étienne Piguet, Antoine Pécoud, and Paul De Guchteniere (eds) *Migration and Climate Change* (Cambridge University Press, 2011), 289–305.
21. Jane McAdam, *Complementary Protection in International Refugee Law* (Oxford University Press, 2007).
22. Biermann and Boas, 'Preparing for a Warmer World', 72–4; Docherty and Giannini, 'Confronting a Rising Tide', 357–61.
23. Biermann and Boas, 'Preparing for a Warmer World', 76.
24. Byravan and Rajan, 'The Ethical Implications of Sea-Level Rise Due to Climate Change', 242–53.
25. Docherty and Gianni, 'Confronting a Rising Tide', 361.
26. Biermann and Boas, 'Preparing for a Warmer World', 64.
27. Byravan and Rajan, 'The Ethical Implications of Sea-Level Rise Due to Climate Change', 252.
28. McAdam, *Climate Change, Forced Migration and International Law*, 39–51.
29. See Aurelie Lopez, 'The Protection of Environmentally Displaced Persons in International Law', *Environmental Law* 37, no. 2 (2007): 378–86. For an analysis of the UNHCR's expanding *de facto* mandate with respect to climate displacement, see Nina Hall, *Displacement,*

Development, and Climate Change: International Organizations Moving Beyond Their Mandates (Routledge, 2016).
30. McAdam, *Climate Change, Forced Migration and International Law*, 42–8. For UNHCR's position, see UNHCR, 'Legal Considerations Regarding Claims to International Protection Made in the Context of the Adverse Effects of Climate Change and Disasters' (UNHCR, 2020), available at https://www.refworld.org/docid/5f75f2734.html.
31. UNHCR, 'Summary of Deliberations on Climate Change and Displacement' (the 'Bellagio Deliberations') (UNHCR, 2011). Available at https://www.unhcr.org/uk/protection/environment/542e95f09/unhcr-bellagio-expert-meeting-summary-deliberations-climate-change-displacement.html.
32. McAdam, *Climate Change, Forced Migration and International Law*, 40.
33. Quoted in McAdam, *Climate Change, Forced Migration and International Law*, 41.
34. Karen E. McNamara, 'Cross-Border Migration with Dignity in Kiribati', *Forced Migration Review* 49 (2015): 62.
35. Biermann and Boas, 'Preparing for a Warmer World', 67.
36. Prem Kumar Rajaram, 'Humanitarianism and Representations of the Refugee', *Journal of Refugee Studies* 15, no. 3 (2002): 247–64.
37. On the political uses of humanitarian representations of refugees, see Didier Fassin, *Humanitarian Reason: A Moral History of the Present* (University of California Press, 2002).
38. For the former, see Byravan and Rajan, 'The Ethical Implications of Sea-Level Rise Due to Climate Change'. For the latter, see Diane C. Bates, 'Environmental Refugees? Classifying Human Migrations Caused by Environmental Change', *Population and Environment* 23, no. 5 (2002): 465–77.
39. Robert D. Bullard, 'Differential Vulnerabilities: Environmental and Economic Inequality and Government Response to Unnatural Disasters', *Social Research* 75, no. 3 (2008): 754–6; Ben Wisner et al., *At Risk: Peoples' Vulnerability and Disasters* (Routledge, 1994).
40. On the state of the science of attributing events such as these to climate change, see Friederike E.L. Otto et al., 'The Attribution Question', *Nature Climate Change* 6 (2016): 813–16.
41. Mike Hulme, 'Climate Refugees: Cause for a New Agreement? Commentary on "Climate Refugees: Protecting the Future Victims of Global Warming" by Biermann, F. and Boas, I.', *Environment* 50, no. 6 (2008): 50.
42. Etienne Piguet, Antoine Pécoud, and Paul de Guchteniere, 'Migration and Climate Change: An Overview', *Refugee Survey Quarterly* 30, no. 3 (2011): 14.
43. For a classic articulation of this view, see John Dewey, 'The Historical Background of Corporate Legal Personality', *The Yale Law Journal* 35, no. 6 (1926): 655–73.
44. For the idea that this is a 'basic' or 'generic' principle of equality, see Ian Carter, 'Respect and the Basis of Equality', *Ethics* 121, no. 3 (2011): 541; Thomas Christiano, 'A Foundation for Egalitarianism' in Nils Holtug and Kasper Lipper-Rasmussen (eds) *Egalitarianism: New Essays on the Nature and Value of Equality* (Clarendon Press, 2007), 41–82; Joseph Raz, *The Morality of Freedom* (Oxford University Press, 1986), 219.
45. John Rawls, *A Theory of Justice* (Belknap Press, [1971] 1999), 5. See also H.L.A. Hart, *The Concept of Law* (Clarendon, [1961] 2012), 159–60.
46. Michelle Madden Dempsey and Matthew Lister, 'Applied Political and Legal Philosophy', in Kaspar Lippert-Rasmussen, Kimberly Brownlee, and David Coady (eds) *A Companion to Applied Philosophy* (Wiley-Blackwell, 2017), 217.
47. McAdam, *Climate Change, Forced Migration and International Law*, 187–8.
48. Phillip Cole, 'Climate Change and Global Displacement: Towards an Ethical Response', in Birgit Schippers (ed.) *The Routledge Handbook on Rethinking Ethics in International Relations* (Routledge, 2020), 179–94.
49. Joseph Carens, *The Ethics of Immigration* (Oxford University Press, 2013), 201.

50. McAdam, *Climate Change, Forced Migration and International Law*, 188.
51. Gemenne makes a related point about the language of climate refugees, arguing that it does at least connate our responsibility for the plight of those displaced by climate impacts. See François Gemenne, 'One Good Reason to Speak of "Climate Refugees"', *Forced Migration Review* 49 (2015): 70–1.
52. IPCC, *Climate Change 2014: Impacts, Adaptation and Vulnerability*, 767.
53. Richard Black et al., 'The Effect of Environmental Change on Human Migration', *Global Environmental Change* 21, no. S1 (2011): S3–11.
54. McAdam, *Climate Change, Forced Migration and International Law*, 197–8.
55. McAdam, *Climate Change, Forced Migration and International Law*, 36–8. Rob Nixon has labelled this kind of largely invisible environmental harm 'slow violence'. See Rob Nixon, *Slow Violence and the Environmentalism of the Poor* (Harvard University Press, 2011).
56. Alexander Betts and Angela Pilath, 'The Politics of Causal Claims: The Case of Environmental Migration', *Journal of International Relations and Development* 20, no. 4 (2017): 782–804; Callum T. Nicholson, 'Climate Change and the Politics of Causal Reasoning: The Case of Climate Change and Migration', *The Geographical Journal* 180, no. 2 (2014): 151–60.
57. Biermann and Boas, 'Preparing for a Warmer World', 67.
58. Biermann and Boas, 'Preparing for a Warmer World', 75.
59. McAdam, *Climate Change, Forced Migration and International Law*, 188.
60. Byravan and Rajan, 'The Ethical Implications of Sea-Level Rise Due to Climate Change', 253.
61. See https://www.nanseninitiative.org/. The Nansen Initiative has now been succeeded by the Platform on Disaster Displacement, see https://disasterdisplacement.org/.
62. Norwegian Refugee Council, 'The Nansen Conference: Climate Change and Displacement in the 21st Century' (Norwegian Refugee Council, 2011), Principle § IX, 5, available at https://www.unhcr.org/4ea969729.pdf.
63. The Nansen Initiative, *Agenda for the Protection of Cross-Border Displaced Persons in the Context of Disasters and Climate Change: Volume I* (The Nansen Initiative, 2015), 7, available at https://disasterdisplacement.org/wp-content/uploads/2014/08/EN_Protection_Agenda_Volume_I_-low_res.pdf.

Chapter 3: Climate Change and Community Relocation

1. Elizabeth Marino, *Fierce Climate, Sacred Ground: An Ethnography of Climate Change in Shishmaref, Alaska* (University of Alaska Press, 2015); Elizabeth Marino, 'The Long History of Environmental Migration: Assessing Vulnerability Construction and Obstacles to Successful Relocation in Shishmaref, Alaska', *Global Environmental Change* 22, no. 2 (2012): 374–81; Robin Bronen and F. Stuart Chapin, 'Adaptive Governance and Institutional Strategies for Climate-Induced Community Relocations in Alaska', *Proceedings of the National Academy of Sciences* 110, no. 23 (2013): 9320–5; Julie Koppel Maldonado et al., 'The Impact of Climate Change on Tribal Communities in the US: Displacement, Relocation, and Human Rights', *Climatic Change* 120, no. 3 (2013): 601–14; Christine Shearer, 'The Political Ecology of Climate Adaptation Assistance: Alaska Natives, Displacement, and Relocation', *Journal of Political Ecology* 19 (2012): 174–83.
2. Gigi Berardi, 'Schools, Settlement and Sanitation in Native Alaskan Villages', *Ethnohistory* 46, no. 2 (1999): 329–59; Frank Darnell, 'Education among the Native Peoples of Alaska', *Polar Record* 19, no. 112 (1979): 431–46; Kyle Powys Whyte, Jared L. Talley, and Julia D. Gibson, 'Indigenous Mobility Traditions, Colonialism, and the Anthropocene', *Mobilities* 14, no. 3 (2019): 319–35.

3. Marino, 'The Long History of Environmental Migration', 377.
4. Bronen and Chapin, 'Adaptive Governance and Institutional Strategies for Climate-Induced Community Relocations in Alaska', 9321.
5. Felicity Carus, 'Alaskan Community Revives Legal Bid for Global Warming Damages', *The Guardian*, 30 November 2011.
6. Bronen and Chapin, 'Adaptive Governance and Institutional Strategies for Climate-Induced Community Relocations in Alaska', 9324.
7. Shearer, 'The Political Ecology of Climate Adaptation Assistance', 177.
8. Alex De Sherbinin et al., 'Preparing for Resettlement Associated with Climate Change', *Science* 334, no. 6055 (2011): 456–7; Elizabeth Ferris and Sanjula Weerasinghe, 'Promoting Human Security: Planned Relocation as a Protection Tool in a Time of Climate Change', *Journal of Migration and Human Security* 8, no. 2 (2020): 134–59.
9. For Vietnam, see Lilly Salloum Lindegaard, 'Lessons from Climate-Related Planned Relocations: The Case of Vietnam', *Climate and Development* 12, no. 7 (2020): 600–9. For China, see Sarah Rogers and Tao Xue, 'Resettlement and Climate Change Vulnerability: Evidence from Rural China', *Global Environmental Change* 35 (2015): 62–9. For Fiji, see Karen E. McNamara and Helene Jacot Des Combes, 'Planning for Community Relocations Due to Climate Change in Fiji', *International Journal of Disaster Risk Science* 6 (2015): 315–19; Amanda Bertana, 'The Role of Power in Community Participation: Relocation as Climate Change Adaptation in Fiji', *Environment and Planning C: Politics and Space* 38, no. 5 (2020): 902–19. For Papua New Guinea, see Julia B. Edwards, 'The Logistics of Climate-Induced Resettlement: Lessons from the Carteret Islands, Papua New Guinea', *Refugee Survey Quarterly* 32, no. 3 (2013): 52–78. For the USA, see Maldonado et al., 'The Impact of Climate Change on Tribal Communities in the US: Displacement, Relocation, and Human Rights'. For Mozambique, see Alex Arnall, 'Resettlement as Climate Change Adaptation: What Can Be Learned from State-Led Relocation in Rural Africa and Asia?' *Climate and Development* 11, no. 3 (2019): 253–63.
10. Kirstin Dow et al., 'Limits to Adaptation', *Nature Climate Change* 3: 305–7. For this reason, some have argued that we should view community relocation as a *failure* of adaptation—captured more accurately under the rubric of 'loss and damage'—rather than as an instance of adaptation. In my view, viewing these categories as mutually exclusive is unhelpful. Community relocation is clearly a form of adaptation in the broad sense of it being part of a 'process of adjustment to actual or expected climate and its effects' (Intergovernmental Panel on Climate Change (IPCC), *Climate Change 2014: Impacts, Adaptation and Vulnerability. Part A: Global and Sectoral Aspects. Contribution of Working Group II to the Fifth Assessment Report of the Intergovernmental Panel on Climate Change*, C.B. Field et al. (eds) (Cambridge University Press, 2014), 5). This does not mean that it cannot *also* involve forms of loss and damage to which communities cannot adapt, as I discuss below. For a discussion, see Karen E. McNamara et al., 'The Complex Decision-Making of Climate-Induced Relocation: Adaptation and Loss and Damage', *Climate Policy* 18, no. 1 (2018): 111–17. For a discussion of different conceptions of adaptation, see Mark Pelling, *Adaptation to Climate Change: From Resilience to Transformation* (Routledge, 2011).
11. Rob Nixon, *Slow Violence and the Environmentalism of the Poor* (Harvard University Press, 2014), esp. 150–74; Anthony Oliver Smith, 'Development-Forced Displacement and Resettlement: A Global Human Rights Crisis', in Anthony Oliver Smith (ed.) *Development and Dispossession: The Crisis of Forced Displacement and Resettlement* (School for Advanced Research, 2009), 3–23.
12. Anna Stilz, *Territorial Sovereignty: A Philosophical Exploration* (Oxford University Press, 2019), 167.
13. Stilz, *Territorial Sovereignty*, 167–8.

14. Marino, *Fierce Climate, Sacred Ground*, 81–92; Josh Wisniewski, *Come On Ugzruk, Let Me Win: Experience, Relationality, And Knowing In Kigiqtaamiut Hunting And Ethnography*, PhD Diss. (University of Fairbanks, Alaska, 2010), 136–56.
15. Kyle Powys Whyte, 'Justice Forward: Tribes, Adaptation and Responsibility', *Climatic Change* 120, no. 3 (2013): 517–30.
16. W. Neil Adger et al., 'This Must Be the Place: Underrepresentation of Identity and Meaning in Decision-Making about Climate Change', *Global Environmental Politics* 11, no. 2 (2011): 1–25; Setha M. Low and Irwin Altman, 'Place Attachment: A Conceptual Inquiry', in Irwin Altman and Setha M. Low (eds) *Place Attachment* (Springer, 1992), 1–12.
17. I say 'typically' here because there may be some cases where the only way to enable communities to adapt *in situ* will require radical changes to a community's way of life that may themselves undermine practice-based interests. There may, as such, be some cases where *in situ* adaptation is technically feasible, but where it would lead to setbacks to residents' practice-based interests that are at least equally as significant as those involved in relocation. In such cases, community members may need to decide whether they view relocation or *in situ* adaptation as the best option for protecting their own practice-based interests.
18. A.R. Siders, 'Social Justice Implications of US Managed Retreat Buyout Programmes', *Climatic Change* 152, no. 2 (2019): 215–66.
19. Jeremy Martinich et al., 'Risks of Sea Level Rise to Disadvantaged Communities in the US', *Mitigation and Adaptation Strategies for Global Change* 18, no. 2 (2013): 169–85.
20. Martinich et al., 'Risks of Sea Level Rise to Disadvantaged Communities in the US', 179.
21. Robert Mendelsohn, 'Efficient Adaptation to Climate Change', *Climatic Change* 45, no. 3 (2000): 585.
22. Mendelsohn, 'Efficient Adaptation to Climate Change', 596.
23. Robin Kundis Craig, 'Coastal Adaptation, Government-Subsidized Insurance, and Perverse Incentives to Stay', *Climatic Change* 152, no. 2 (2019): 215–26.
24. Anna Stilz, 'Internal Climate Migration and Territorial Justice', in Jamie Draper and David Owen (eds) *The Political Philosophy of Internal Displacement* (Oxford University Press, forthcoming).
25. Elizabeth Brake, 'Rebuilding after Disaster: Inequality and the Political Importance of Place', *Social Theory and Practice* 45, no. 2 (2019): 179–204. Relatedly, Alexa Zellentin has argued that the 'cultural loss' experienced by members of communities that face relocation due to climate change can threaten the bases of their self-respect, though her focus is on societal cultures—particularly in small-island states (examined in the next chapter)—rather than more localized forms of cultural loss. See Alexa Zellentin, 'Climate Migration: Cultural Aspects of Climate Change', *Analyse & Kritik* 32, no. 1 (2016): 63–86; Alexa Zellentin, 'Climate Justice, Small Island Developing States and Cultural Loss', *Climatic Change* 133, no. 3 (2015): 491–8.
26. Stilz, 'Internal Climate Migration and Territorial Justice'.
27. For the idea of an 'expensive taste', see Ronald Dworkin, *Sovereign Virtue: The Theory and Practice of Equality* (Belknap Press, 2000), 48–59.
28. Alan Patten, *Equal Recognition: The Moral Foundations of Minority Rights* (Princeton University Press, 2014).
29. Stilz, 'Internal Climate Migration and Territorial Justice'.
30. Jonathan Lear, *Radical Hope: Ethics in the Face of Cultural Devastation* (Harvard University Press, 2006).
31. Lear, *Radical Hope*, 145.
32. Bernard Williams, *Problems of the Self: Philosophical Papers 1956–1972* (Cambridge University Press, 1973), 166–86.
33. Stilz, *Territorial Sovereignty*, 45.

34. Stilz, *Territorial Sovereignty*, 45.
35. Mindy Thompson Fullilove, *Root Shock: How Tearing Up City Neighborhoods Hurts America, and What We Can Do About It* (NYU Press, 2016).
36. Fullilove, *Root Shock*, 14.
37. Marino, *Fierce Climate, Sacred Ground*, 15.
38. For the idea of brute luck, see Dworkin, *Sovereign Virtue*, 73.
39. Katharine J. Mach et al., 'Managed Retreat Through Voluntary Buyouts of Flood-Prone Properties', *Science Advances* 5, no. 10 (2019): eaax8995; Miyuki Hino, Christopher B. Field, and Katharine J. Mach, 'Managed Retreat as a Response to Natural Hazard Risk', *Nature Climate Change* 7, no. 5 (2017): 364–70.
40. Tatiana Filatova, 'Market-Based Instruments for Flood Risk Management: A Review of Theory, Practice and Perspectives for Climate Adaptation Policy', *Environmental Science & Policy* 37 (2014): 227–42.
41. Samuel Fankhauser, Joel B. Smith, and Richard S.J. Tol, 'Weathering Climate Change: Some Simple Rules to Guide Adaptation Decisions', *Ecological Economics* 30, no. 1 (1999): 69–70.
42. Nicholas Stern, *The Economics of Climate Change: The Stern Review* (Cambridge University Press, 2007), 406.
43. For concept of collective goods, see Russel Hardin, *Collective Action* (Routledge, 2015), 17–20.
44. For a good overview of the ways in which adaptation may depend on the provision of collective goods, see Daniel Osberghaus et al., 'The Role of the Government in Adaptation to Climate Change', *Environment and Planning C: Government and Policy* 28, no. 5 (2010): 834–50.
45. Bronen and Chapin, 'Adaptive Governance and Institutional Strategies for Climate-Induced Community Relocations in Alaska', 9323.
46. Shearer, 'The Political Ecology of Climate Adaptation Assistance', 177.
47. Christian Huggel et al., 'Early Warning Systems: The "Last Mile" of Adaptation', *Eos, Transactions, American Geophysical Union* 93, no. 22 (2012): 209–10. I say 'effectively' here, because there are conceivable ways in which early warning systems could be made to be excludable, such as through the use of proprietary technology for broadcasting and receiving warning messages.
48. James Buchanan, *The Demand and Supply of Public Goods* (Liberty Fund, 1999), 83.
49. John Rawls, *A Theory of Justice* (Belknap Press, [1971] 1999), 237–8.
50. Rawls, *A Theory of Justice*, 236.
51. Marino, *Fierce Climate, Sacred Ground*, 72.
52. Elinor Ostrom, *Governing the Commons: The Evolution of Institutions for Collective Action* (Cambridge University Press, 1990).
53. Ostrom, *Governing the Commons*, esp. 182–216.
54. W. Neil Adger, 'Social Capital, Collective Action, and Adaptation to Climate Change', *Economic Geography* 79, no. 4 (2003): 387–404.
55. David Schlosberg, 'Climate Justice and Capabilities: A Normative Framework for Adaptation Policy', *Ethics & International Affairs* 26, no. 4 (2012): 445–61; David Schlosberg, 'Justice, Ecological Integrity and Climate Change', in Allen Thompson and Jeremy Bendik-Keymer (eds) *Ethical Adaptation to Climate Change: Human Virtues of the Future* (MIT Press, 2012), 165–83; David Schlosberg and David Carruthers, 'Indigenous Struggles, Environmental Justice, and Community Capabilities', *Global Environmental Politics* 10, no. 4 (2010): 12–35.
56. Schlosberg, 'Climate Justice and Capabilities', 455–6.
57. Schlosberg, 'Climate Justice and Capabilities', 455. For Nussbaum's rejection of community-level capabilities, see Martha Nussbaum, *Women and Human Development: The Capabilities Approach* (Cambridge University Press, 2000), 74. For Page's capabilities

approach to climate justice, see Edward Page, 'Intergenerational Justice of What: Welfare, Resources or Capabilities?' *Environmental Politics* 16, no. 3 (2007): 453–69.
58. Schlosberg, 'Climate Justice and Capabilities', 455.
59. Schlosberg, 'Justice, Ecological Integrity, and Climate Change', 173; Breena Holland, 'Procedural Justice in Local Climate Adaptation: Political Capabilities and Transformational Change', *Environmental Politics* 26, no. 3 (2017): 391–412; Craig Johnson, 'Governing Climate Displacement: The Ethics and Politics of Human Resettlement', *Environmental Politics* 21, no. 2 (2012): 308–28.
60. Breena Holland, 'Procedural Justice in Local Climate Adaptation: Political Capabilities and Transformational Change', *Environmental Politics* 26, no. 3 (2017): 397.
61. Craig Johnson, 'Governing Climate Displacement: The Ethics and Politics of Human Resettlement', *Environmental Politics* 21, no. 2 (2012): 317.
62. Ingrid Robeyns, *Wellbeing, Freedom and Social Justice: The Capability Approach Re-Examined* (Open Book Publishers, 2017), 57. See also Nussbaum, *Women and Human Development*, 56; Rawls, *A Theory of Justice*, 233–4.
63. See Robeyns, *Wellbeing, Freedom and Social Justice*, 183–9.
64. Will Kymlicka, *Multicultural Citizenship: A Liberal Theory of Minority Rights* (Oxford University Press, 1995), 75–106. See also Joseph Carens, *Culture, Citizenship, and Community: A Contextual Exploration of Justice as Evenhandedness* (Oxford University Press, 2000); Patten, *Equal Recognition*, esp. 69–103.
65. See, for example, Anne Phillips, *The Politics of Presence* (Oxford University Press, 2000); Young, *Justice and the Politics of Difference*, 183–91.
66. See Whyte, 'Justice Forward'.
67. For accounts of the jurisdictional rights of Indigenous peoples, see James Tully, *Strange Multiplicity: Constitutionalism in an Age of Diversity* (Cambridge University Press, 1995); Allen Buchanan, *Justice, Legitimacy and Self-Determination* (Oxford University Press, 2004); Burke Hendrix, *Ownership, Authority and Self-Determination: Moral Principles and Indigenous Rights Claims* (Oxford University Press, 2010).
68. Alex Arnall, Chris Hilson, and Catriona McKinnon, 'Climate Displacement and Resettlement: The Importance of Claims-Making "From Below"', *Climate Policy* 19, no. 6 (2019): 669; Jean-Phillippe Platteau and Frédéric Gaspart, 'The Risks of Resource Misappropriation in Community-Driven Development', *World Development* 31, no. 10 (2003): 1687–703.
69. Kyle Powys Whyte, 'The Recognition Dimensions of Environmental Justice in Indian Country', *Environmental Justice* 4, no. 4 (2011): 204.
70. Iris Marion Young, *Inclusion and Democracy* (Oxford University Press, 2002), 87–8.
71. Iris Marion Young, *Justice and the Politics of Difference* (Princeton University Press, [1990] 2011), 234–6.
72. Young, *Inclusion and Democracy*, 87–92.
73. Rawls, *A Theory of Justice*, 109–10; David Hume, *A Treatise of Human Nature* (The Floating Press, [1740] 2009), 725–65.
74. Rainer Bauböck, 'A Pluralist Theory of Citizenship', in *Democratic Inclusion: Rainer Bauböck in Dialogue* (Manchester University Press, 2018), 3–102.
75. Bauböck, 7–18.
76. For this idea of a 'public', see John Dewey, *The Public and Its Problems: An Essay in Political Inquiry*, in Jo Ann Boydston (ed.) *The Later Works of John Dewey, 1925–1953, Volume 2* (University of South Illinois Press, 1984), 235–372.
77. Bauböck, 'A Pluralist Theory of Citizenship', 8.
78. Thomas Christiano, *The Constitution of Equality: Democratic Authority and Its Limits* (Oxford University Press, 2008).
79. See James Bohman and William Rehg (eds) *Deliberative Democracy: Essays on Reason and Politics* (MIT Press, 1997) for an overview.

80. Simone Chambers, 'Deliberative Democratic Theory', *Annual Reviews of Political Science* 6 (2003): 307–26; Young, *Inclusion and Democracy*.
81. Harald Winkler and Joanna Depledge, 'Fiji-in-Bonn: Will the Talanoa Spirit Prevail?' *Climate Policy* 18, no. 2 (2018): 141–5.
82. Elizabeth Anderson, 'The Epistemology of Democracy', *Episteme* 3, no. 1–2 (2006): 8–22.
83. Amy Gutmann and Dennis Thompson, *Why Deliberative Democracy?* (Princeton University Press, 2004). For the idea that being in the majority can involve a kind of power, see Arash Abizadeh, 'The Power of Numbers: On Agential Power-With-Others Without Power-Over-Others', *Philosophy & Public Affairs* 49, no. 3 (2021): 290–318.
84. Arash Abizadeh argues that when persistent minorities are systematically disadvantaged in majoritarian decision-making, this is a failure of political equality: Arash Abizadeh, 'Counter-Majoritarian Democracy: Persistent Minorities, Federalism, and the Power of Numbers', *American Political Science Review* 115, no. 3 (2021): 742–56. In the context of a 'one-shot' problem like community relocation, minorities whose interests are not represented in the outcomes of decision-making are not 'persistent', but neither do they have an opportunity to 'win' in other decisions, and so it is likewise important that they have a genuine opportunity to influence the outcome of relocation decisions.
85. Samuel Bagg, 'Can Deliberation Neutralize Power?' *European Journal of Political Theory* 17, no. 3 (2018): 257–79.
86. Albert O. Hirschman, *Exit, Voice, and Loyalty: Responses to Decline in Firms, Organizations, and States* (Harvard University Press, 1970).
87. Robert S. Taylor, *Exit Left: Markets and Mobility in Republican Thought* (Oxford University Press, 2017), 11–18.
88. Keith Dowding et al., 'Exit, Voice, and Loyalty: Analytic and Empirical Developments', *European Journal of Political Research* 37, no. 4 (2000): 472.
89. Hirschman, *Exit, Voice, and Loyalty*, 79–82.
90. Marino, *Fierce Climate, Sacred Ground*, 61–2.
91. Shishmaref Inter-Agency Planning Work Group, 'Shishmaref Strategic Management Plan, September 2016' (2016), available at: https://www.commerce.alaska.gov/web/Portals/4/pub/1_Shishmaref_SMP_September_2016.pdf.
92. Bronen and Chapin, 'Adaptive Governance and Institutional Strategies for Climate-Induced Community Relocations in Alaska', 3922.
93. See https://www.commerce.alaska.gov/web/dcra/PlanningLandManagement/ShishmarefInter-AgencyPlanningWorkGroup.aspx.
94. Marino, *Fierce Climate, Sacred Ground*, 66–7.
95. Robin Bronen, 'Climate-Induced Community Relocations: Creating an Adaptive Governance Framework Based in Human Rights Doctrine', *New York Review of Law and Social Change* 2 (2011): 357–407.
96. Bronen, 'Climate-Induced Community Relocations', 399.
97. Bronen, 'Climate-Induced Community Relocations', 401–2.
98. Bronen, 'Climate-Induced Community Relocations', 396.
99. Whyte, 'Justice Forward'.
100. Whyte, Talley, and Gibson, 'Indigenous Mobility Traditions, Colonialism, and the Anthropocene'; Kyle Powys Whyte, 'Is This Colonial Déjà Vu? Indigenous Peoples and Climate Injustice', in Joni Adamson and Michael David (eds) *Humanities for the Environment: Integrating Knowledge, Forging New Constellations of Practice* (Routledge, 2016), 88–104.
101. Roger Few, Katrina Brown, and Emma L. Tompkins, 'Public Participation and Climate Change Adaptation: Avoiding the Illusion of Inclusion', *Climate Policy* 7, no. 1 (2007): 46–59.
102. Peter Penz, Jay Drydyk, and Pablo S. Bose, *Displacement by Development: Ethics, Rights and Responsibilities* (Cambridge University Press, 2011), esp. 79–81.

103. See Samuel Bagg, *The Dispersion of Power: A Critical Realist Theory of Democracy* (Oxford University Press, forthcoming).
104. Alfred Moore, *Critical Elitism: Deliberation, Democracy, and the Problem of Expertise* (Cambridge University Press, 2017), 34.
105. Moore, *Critical Elitism*, 34–7.
106. Heather Douglas, *Science, Policy, and the Value-Free Ideal* (University of Pittsburgh Press, 2009), 87–114.
107. Marino, *Fierce Climate, Sacred Ground*, 77–8.
108. James C. Scott, *Seeing Like a State: Why Certain Schemes to Improve the Human Condition Have Failed* (Yale University Press, 1998), esp. 309–41. We need not posit any deep divide between 'scientific' and 'Indigenous' knowledge to make sense of this claim. See Arun Argawal, 'Dismantling the Divide Between Indigenous and Scientific Knowledge', *Development and Change* 26, no. 3 (1995): 413–39.
109. Marino, *Fierce Climate, Sacred Ground*, 32–8.
110. Kyle Powys Whyte and Robert P. Crease, 'Trust, Expertise, and the Philosophy of Science', *Synthese* 117, no. 3 (2010): 411–25.
111. Marino, *Fierce Climate, Sacred Ground*, 58–60.
112. Moore, *Critical Elitism*, 54–7.
113. For a similar idea in relation to anti-corruption, see Samuel Bagg, 'Sortition as Anti-Corruption: Popular Oversight Against Elite Capture', *American Journal of Political Science* (forthcoming).
114. Schlosberg, 'Climate Justice and Capabilities'.
115. Nadia Urbinati and Mark E. Warren, 'The Concept of Representation in Contemporary Democratic Theory', *Annual Review of Political Science* 11 (2008): 388. For one articulation of this standard view, see Robert A. Dahl, 'What Political Institutions Does Large-Scale Democracy Require?' *Political Science Quarterly* 120, no. 2 (2005): 187–97. For my purposes here, I am interested in the potential for representation to overcome the problem of scale. But it is worth noting that many contemporary democratic theorists do not view representation as *merely* a way of overcoming the problem of scale, but instead highlight the other functions that it can serve, including the ways in which it can itself encourage political participation. See Nadia Urbinati, *Representative Democracy: Principles and Genealogy* (University of Chicago Press, 2006).
116. See Hanna Pitkin, *The Concept of Representation* (University of California Press, 1967).
117. Pitkin, *The Concept of Representation*, 145–67.
118. John Parkinson, 'Legitimacy Problems in Deliberative Democracy', *Political Studies* 51, no. 1 (2003): 180–96.
119. For a pessimistic view of the accountability function of elections, see Christopher H. Achen and Larry Bartels, *Democracy for Realists: Why Elections Do Not Produce Responsive Government* (Princeton University Press, 2016).
120. Archon Fung and Erik Olin Wright, 'Thinking about Empowered Participatory Governance', in Archon Fung and Erik Olin Wright (eds) *Deepening Democracy: Institutional Innovations in Empowered Participatory Governance* (Verso, 2003).
121. See T.M. Thomas Isaac and Patrick Heller, 'Democracy and Development: Decentralized Planning in Kerala' and Gianpaolo Baiocchi, 'Participation, Activism, and Politics: The Porto Alegre Experiment', both in Archon Fung and Erik Olin Wright (eds) *Deepening Democracy: Institutional Innovations in Empowered Participatory Governance* (Verso, 2003).
122. Fung and Wright, 'Thinking about Empowered Participatory Governance', 20–3.
123. Baiocchi, 'Participation, Activism, and Politics: The Porto Alegre Experiment', 47–57. See also Gianpaolo Baiocchi, *Militants and Citizens: The Politics of Participatory Democracy in Porto Alegre* (Stanford University Press, 2005).

124. See Bagg, *The Dispersion of Power.*
125. Fung and Wright, 'Thinking about Empowered Participatory Governance', 37–8.
126. Marino, *Fierce Climate, Sacred Ground,* 72–4.

Chapter 4: Climate Change and Territorial Sovereignty

1. Intergovernmental Panel on Climate Change (IPCC), *Climate Change 2014: Synthesis Report. Contribution of Working Groups I, II and III to the Fifth Assessment Report of the Intergovernmental Panel on Climate Change.* Core Writing Team, R.K. Pachuari and L.A. Meyer (eds) (IPCC, 2014), 60.
2. Stefan Rahmstorf et al., 'Recent Climate Observations Compared to Projections', *Science* 316, no. 5825 (2007): 709.
3. IPCC, *Climate Change 2014: Synthesis Report,* 11.
4. Jonathan L. Bamber et al., 'Ice Sheet Contributions to Future Sea Level Rise from Structured Expert Judgement', *Proceedings of the National Academy of Sciences* 116, no. 23 (2019): 11195–200.
5. Jon Barnett and W. Neil Adger, 'Climate Dangers and Atoll Countries', *Climatic Change* 61 (2003): 321–37.
6. Susin Park, 'Climate Change and the Risk of Statelessness: The Situation of Low-Lying Island States', *Legal and Protection Policy Research Series* (UNHCR, 2011), 2.
7. Milla Emilia Vaha, 'Drowning Under: Small-Island States and the Right to Exist', *Journal of International Political Theory* 11, no. 2 (2015): 206–23.
8. *Montevideo Convention on the Rights and Duties of States* (1934), article §1(a), article §1(b).
9. Jane McAdam, '"Disappearing States", Statelessness and the Boundaries of International Law', in Jane McAdam (ed.) *Climate Change and Displacement: Multidisciplinary Perspectives* (Hart, 2010), 119–60.
10. David Miller, 'Territorial Rights: Concept and Justification', *Political Studies* 60, no. 2 (2012): 252–68. Territorial rights are also usually taken to include various other associated rights, such as the right to control the flow of people and goods across the borders of the territory and the right to control and extract benefits from natural resources located within that territory.
11. On the resilience of coral atolls to sea level rise, see Roger McLean and Paul Kench, 'Destruction or Persistence of Coral Atoll Islands in the Face of 20th and 21st Century Sea Level Rise?' *Wiley Interdisciplinary Reviews: Climate Change* 6, no. 5 (2015): 455–63. On the effects of limiting global temperature increases for small-island states, see IPCC, *Global Warming of 1.5°C. An IPCC Special Report on the Impacts of Global Warming of 1.5°C above Pre-industrial Levels and Related Global Greenhouse Gas Emission Pathways, in the Context of Strengthening the Global Response to the Threat of Climate Change, Sustainable Development, and Efforts to Eradicate Poverty* (Valérie Masson-Delmotte et al. (eds)) (Cambridge University Press, 2018), 232; D.J. Rasumussen et al., 'Extreme Sea Level Implications of 1.5 °C, 2.0 °C, and 2.5 °C Temperature Stabilization Targets in the 21st and 22nd Centuries', *Environmental Research Letters* 13 (2018): 034040; Rosanne Martyr-Koller et al., 'Loss and Damage Implications of Sea-Level Rise on Small Island Developing States', *Current Opinion on Sustainability* 50 (2021): 245–59.
12. Timothée Ourbak and Alexandre K. Magnan, 'The Paris Agreement and Climate Change Negotiations: Small Islands, Big Players', *Regional Environmental Change* 18, no. 8 (2018): 2201–7.
13. Joeri Rogelj et al., 'Paris Agreement Climate Proposals Need a Boost to Keep Warming Well below 2 °C', *Nature* 534, no. 7609 (2016): 631–9.

14. Jane McAdam, *Climate Change, Forced Migration and International Law* (Oxford University Press, 2012) 119–61; James Crawford, *The Creation of States in International Law* (Clarendon, 2006), 715.
15. Mathias Risse, 'The Right to Relocation: Disappearing Island Nations and Common Ownership of the Earth', *Ethics & International Affairs* 23, no. 3 (2009): 281–300.
16. Clare Heyward and Jorgen Ödalen, 'A Free Movement Passport for the Territorially Dispossessed', in Clare Heyward and Dominic Roser (eds) *Climate Justice in a Non-Ideal World* (Oxford University Press, 2015), 208–26; Robyn Eckersley, 'The Common But Differentiated Responsibilities of States to Assist and Receive "Climate Refugees"', *European Journal of Political Theory* 14, no. 4 (2015): 481–500.
17. *The Charter of the United Nations* (1945), article §1(2); *International Covenant on Civil and Political Rights* (1966), article §1(1); *Declaration on the Granting of Independence to Colonial Countries and Peoples* (1960), article §2.
18. Avishai Margalit and Joseph Raz, 'National Self-Determination', *Journal of Philosophy* 87, no. 9 (1990): 439.
19. One issue here is whether it is nations or 'peoples' (defined in various ways) that have a right to self-determination. For nationalist views, see Margalit and Raz, 'National Self-Determination'; David Miller, *On Nationality* (Oxford University Press, 1997), esp. 81–118. For peoplehood views, see Margaret Moore, *A Political Theory of Territory* (Oxford University Press, 2015); Anna Stilz, *Territorial Sovereignty: A Philosophical Exploration* (Oxford University Press, 2019).
20. Antonio Cassese, *Self-Determination of Peoples: A Legal Reappraisal* (Cambridge University Press, 1995), 5–12; Anna Stilz, 'The Value of Self-Determination', in David Sobel, Peter Vallentyne, and Steven Wall (eds) *Oxford Studies in Political Philosophy: Volume 2* (Oxford University Press, 2016), 98.
21. Iris Marion Young, 'Two Concepts of Self-Determination', in Stephen May, Tariq Modood, and Judith Squires (eds) *Ethnicity, Nationalism, and Minority Rights* (Cambridge University Press, 2004), 176–96.
22. For the idea of an ameliorative concept, see Sally Haslanger, *Resisting Reality: Social Construction and Social Critique* (Oxford University Press, 2011), 366–7.
23. Young, 'Two Concepts of Self-Determination', 181. See also Iris Marion Young, *Inclusion and Democracy* (Oxford University Press, 2002), 236–76.
24. Jean L. Cohen, 'Whose Sovereignty? Empire versus International Law', *Ethics & International Affairs* 18, no. 3 (2004): 15. The historical event of the Peace of Westphalia functions as an 'origin myth' that has lent credence to the idea of an international society based on the mutual recognition of equal sovereignty. See Andreas Osiander, 'Sovereignty, International Relations, and the Westphalian Myth', *International Organization* 55, no. 2 (2001): 251–87.
25. For a thoroughgoing analysis of the changing normative terrain of the international order, see Jean L. Cohen, *Globalization and Sovereignty: Rethinking Legality, Legitimacy and Constitutionalism* (Cambridge University Press, 2012).
26. David Held, 'Regulating Globalization? The Reinvention of Politics', *International Sociology* 15, no. 2 (2000): 394–408.
27. Rauna Kuokkanen, *Restructuring Relations: Indigenous Self-Determination, Governance and Gender* (Oxford University Press, 2019), 27.
28. Young, *Inclusion and Democracy*, 257.
29. Young, 'Two Concepts of Self-Determination', 184.
30. Allen Buchanan, 'The Right to Self-Determination: Analytical and Moral Foundations', *Arizona Journal of International and Comparative Law* 8, no. 2 (1991): 46.
31. Allen Buchanan, *Justice, Legitimacy and Self-Determination: Moral Foundations for International Law* (Oxford University Press, 2004), 206.

32. E.g., Margalit and Raz, 'National Self-Determination'.
33. Buchanan, *Justice, Legitimacy and Self-Determination*, 248–62; Will Kymlicka, *Multicultural Citizenship: A Liberal Theory of Minority Rights* (Oxford University Press, 1996), esp. 107–31.
34. Avner de Shalit, 'National Self-Determination: Political, Not Cultural', *Political Studies* 44, no. 5 (1996): 906–20.
35. Petra Gümplová, 'Sovereignty over Natural Resources: A Normative Reinterpretation', *Global Constitutionalism* 9, no. 1 (2020): 20–1.
36. Jacob T. Levy, *The Multiculturalism of Fear* (Oxford University Press, 2000), esp. 40–66.
37. Young, 'Two Concepts of Self-Determination', 185–9.
38. Young, 'Two Concepts of Self-Determination', 187.
39. Young draws on Philip Pettit's work on domination. See Young, 'Two Concepts of Self-Determination', 184; Philip Pettit, *Republicanism: A Theory of Freedom and Government* (Oxford University Press, 1997). Since then, there have been debates among republican theorists about what exactly makes the exercise of power arbitrary. Some important contributions include Cécile Laborde, 'Republicanism and Global Justice: A Sketch', *European Journal of Political Theory* 9, no. 1 (2010): 48–69; Frank Lovett, *A General Theory of Domination and Justice* (Oxford University Press, 2010); Nicolas Vrousalis, 'Exploitation, Vulnerability, and Social Domination', *Philosophy & Public Affairs* 41, no. 2 (2013): 131–57; Christopher McCammon, 'Domination: A Rethinking', *Ethics* 125, no. 4 (2015): 1028–52.
40. Young, 'Two Concepts of Self-Determination', 187–8. For the idea that non-interference may still have some value as a jurisdictional rule, see Jacob T. Levy, 'Self-Determination, Non-Domination, and Federalism', *Hypatia: A Journal of Feminist Philosophy* 23, no. 3 (2009): 60–78.
41. Young, 'Two Concepts of Self-Determination', 187.
42. Cécile Laborde and Miriam Ronzoni, 'What Is a Free State? Republican Internationalism and Globalisation', *Political Studies* 64, no. 2 (2016): 279–96.
43. Young, 'Two Concepts of Self-Determination', 188.
44. Young, 'Two Concepts of Self-Determination', 187.
45. Young, 'Two Concepts of Self-Determination', 180–1; Kuokkanen, *Restructuring Relations*, 22–59.
46. Buchanan, *Justice, Legitimacy and Self-Determination*, 220–2.
47. Adom Getachew, *Worldmaking after Empire: The Rise and Fall of Self-Determination* (Princeton University Press, 2019), 71–106.
48. Cara Nine, 'Ecological Refugees, States Borders and the Lockean Proviso', *Journal of Applied Philosophy* 27, no. 4 (2010): 359–75.
49. Nine, 'Ecological Refugees, States Borders and the Lockean Proviso', 360.
50. For the idea of downsizing see A. John Simmons, 'Historical Rights and Fair Shares', *Law and Philosophy* 14, no. 2 (1995): 163.
51. The Lockean proviso to which Nine appeals is modified in the sense that it applies to *holdings* rather than to *acquisition*, as in the case of property. See Nine, 'Ecological Refugees, States Borders and the Lockean Proviso', 367–9.
52. Nine, 'Ecological Refugees, States Borders and the Lockean Proviso', 362.
53. Frank Dietrich and Joachim Wündisch, 'Territory Lost—Climate Change and the Violation of Self-Determination Rights', *Moral Philosophy and Politics* 2, no. 1 (2015): 97–100.
54. For a view consistent with nationalist premises, see Kim Angell, 'New Territorial Rights for Small-Island States', *European Journal of Political Theory* 20, no. 1 (2021): 95–115. Lea Ypi also suggests that her Kantian 'permissive' theory of territorial rights could be used to justify this kind of territorial redistribution, though she does not develop this argument in detail: see Lea Ypi, 'A Permissive Theory of Territorial Rights', *European Journal of Philosophy* 22,

no. 2 (2014): 308. Another possibility is based on Avery Kolers' 'plenitude' theory, though strictly speaking this would not count as 'territorial redistribution' as I have articulated it here, since Kolers adopts an idiosyncratic conception of territory as the 'ratio of land to justice' that complicates the claim that territory is straightforwardly being redistributed; see Avery Kolers, 'Floating Provisos and Sinking Islands', *Journal of Applied Philosophy* 29, no. 4 (2012): 333–43.

55. Nine, 'Ecological Refugees, States Borders and the Lockean Proviso', 363.
56. Nine, 'Ecological Refugees, States Borders and the Lockean Proviso', 362.
57. Nine, 'Ecological Refugees, States Borders and the Lockean Proviso', 363, 366, emphasis added.
58. Nine, 'Ecological Refugees, States Borders and the Lockean Proviso', 372.
59. Dietrich and Wündisch, 'Territory Lost', 103, 88.
60. Nine, 'Ecological Refugees, States Borders and the Lockean Proviso', 373.
61. Cara Nine, *Sharing Territories: Overlapping Self-Determination and Resource Rights* (Oxford University Press, 2022).
62. A similar 'viability proviso' plays a role in discussions of secession. See Andrew Altman and Christopher H. Wellman, *A Liberal Theory of International Justice* (Oxford University Press, 2009), 46.
63. Dietrich and Wündisch specify two conditions, the 'cultural identity' condition and the 'appropriate size' condition, for viable territories. See Dietrich and Wündisch, 'Territory Lost', 95–6.
64. See Steven R. Ratner, 'Drawing a Better Line: *Uti Possidetis* and the Borders of New States', *The American Journal of International Law* 90, no. 4 (1996): 590–624.
65. For a discussion, see Allen Buchanan, 'Secession, State Breakdown, and Humanitarian Intervention', in Dean Chatterjee and Donald Scheid (eds) *Ethics and Foreign Intervention* (Cambridge University Press, 2003), 189–211.
66. Among theorists of territorial rights, differences in the ways in which people value territories and resources have led to disagreements about the best way of calculating whether different states enjoy more than their 'fair share' of territory. For some important contributions, see Hillel Steiner, 'Territorial Rights and Global Redistribution', in Gillian Brock and Harry Brighouse (eds) *The Political Philosophy of Cosmopolitanism* (Cambridge University Press, 2005), 28–38; Chris Armstrong, *Justice and Natural Resources: An Egalitarian Theory* (Oxford University Press, 2017), esp. 9–27; Avery Kolers, *Land, Conflict, and Justice* (Cambridge University Press, 2009), esp. 100–38; Stilz, *Territorial Sovereignty*, esp. 157–77.
67. Dietrich and Wündisch, 'Territory Lost', 100–2.
68. Anna Stilz, 'Occupancy Rights and the Wrong of Removal', *Philosophy & Public Affairs* 41, no. 4 (2013): 324–56; Margaret Moore, *A Political Theory of Territory* (Oxford University Press, 2015), esp. 36–40. See also the discussion in Chapter 7 at C7P29–C7P37.
69. Jonathan Quong, 'In Defense of Functionalism', in Jack Knight and Melissa Schwartzberg (eds) *Political Legitimacy: NOMOS LXI* (New York University Press, 2019), 47–64.
70. For an analysis of the conditions under which development-induced displacement might be permissible and the terms on which it should take place, see Peter Penz, Jay Drydyk, and Pablo S. Bose, *Displacement by Development: Ethics, Rights and Responsibilities* (Cambridge University Press, 2011).
71. Cara Nine, 'Water Crisis Adaptation: Defending a Strong Right Against Displacement from the Home', *Res Publica* 22, no. 1 (2016): 37–52.
72. Quong, 'In Defense of Functionalism', 58. For a defence of the claim that this problem affects all theories of secession, see Matthew Lister, 'Self-Determination, Dissent, and the Problem of Population Transfers', in Fernando R. Tesón (ed.) *The Theory of Self-Determination* (Cambridge University Press, 2015), 145–65.

73. Avner de Shalit similarly argues that compensation is unlikely to make up for the losses faced by relocated small-island peoples. See Avner de Shalit, 'Climate Change Refugees, Compensation, and Rectification', *The Monist* 94, no. 3 (2011): 310–28.
74. Penz, Drydyk, and Bose, *Displacement by Development*, 118.
75. Jörgen Ödalen, 'Underwater Self-Determination: Sea Level Rise and Deterritorialized Small-Island States', *Ethics, Policy & Environment* 17, no. 2 (2014): 225–37. For other discussions, see Rosemary Rayfuse, 'International Law and Disappearing States: Using Marine Entitlements to Overcome the Statehood Dilemma', *UNSW Law Research Paper*, no. 2010-52 (2010): 1–13; Maxine Burkett, 'The Nation *Ex-Situ*: On Climate Change, Deterritorialised Nationhood and the Post-Climate Era', *Climate Law* 2 (2011): 345–74.
76. Ödalen, 'Underwater Self-Determination', 227.
77. Ödalen, 'Underwater Self-Determination', 227.
78. Ödalen, 'Underwater Self-Determination', 227.
79. Chris Armstrong and John Corbett, 'Climate Change, Sea Level Rise, and Maritime Baselines: Responding to the Plight of Low-Lying Atoll States', *Global Environmental Politics* 21, no. 1 (2021): 89–107.
80. Ian Brownlie, *Principles of Public International Law* (Oxford University Press, 2019), 114. See also Noel Cox, 'The Continuing Question of the Sovereignty of the Sovereign Military Order of Jerusalem, of Rhodes and Malta', *Australasian International Law Journal* 13 (2006): 211–32.
81. See Rayfuse, 'International Law and Disappearing States'; Burkett, 'The Nation *Ex Situ*'.
82. Ödalen, 'Underwater Self-Determination', 232.
83. Ödalen, 'Underwater Self-Determination', 231; Buchanan, 'The Right to Self-Determination', 46.
84. Ödalen, 'Underwater Self-Determination', 230.
85. Ödalen, 'Underwater Self-Determination', 232.
86. A similar objection is made by Rainer Bauböck to the idea that 'cloud communities' could supplant membership in territorial states. See Rainer Bauböck, 'Citizenship in Cloud Cuckoo Land?', in Rainer Bauböck (ed.) *Debating Transformations of National Citizenship* (Springer, 2018), 261–66.
87. Helder De Schutter, 'Non-Territorial Jurisdictional Authority: A Radical Possibility in Need of a Critique', in Jean François-Grégoire and Michael Jewkes (eds) *Redistribution and Recognition in Multinational Federations* (Leuven University Press, 2015), 35–56.
88. See Stuart Elden, *The Birth of Territory* (Chicago University Press, 2013).
89. Karl Renner, 'State and Nation' (1899), reprinted in Ephraim Nimni (ed.) *National-Cultural Autonomy and its Contemporary Critics* (Routledge, 2005), 15–47.
90. On competing national groups that share territory, see De Schutter, 'Non-Territorial Jurisdictional Authority'. On language policy, see Alan Patten, *Equal Recognition: The Moral Foundations of Minority Rights* (Princeton University Press, 2014), 186–231. On hypermobile societies, see Rainer Bauböck, 'Democratic Representation in Mobile Societies', in Anna Triandafyllidou (ed.) *Multicultural Governance in a Mobile World* (Edinburgh University Press, 2017), 283–306.
91. Michael Blake makes a similar objection to 'cloud communities', though his focus is on the need for coercive power in securing the conditions for political justice within geographical space. See Michael Blake, 'Virtual Politics, Real Guns: On Cloud Community, Violence, and Human Rights', in Rainer Bauböck (ed.) *Debating Transformations of National Citizenship* (Springer, 2018), 289–93.
92. Rainer Bauböck, 'Multinational Federalism: Territorial or Cultural Autonomy?' *Willy Brandt Series of Working Papers in International Migration and Ethnic Relations* 2/01 (2001): 25–6.
93. De Shutter, 'Non-Territorial Jurisdictional Authority', 41.

94. Philippe Van Parijs, *Linguistic Justice for Europe and the World* (Oxford University Press, 2011), 148.
95. For one prominent articulation of this principle, see Ronald Dworkin, *Sovereign Virtue: The Theory and Practice of Equality* (Harvard University Press, 2002), 1–2.
96. For example, Simon Caney, *Justice Beyond Borders: A Global Political Theory* (Oxford University Press, 2005).
97. Christian Schemmel, 'Why Relational Egalitarians Should Care about Distributions', *Social Theory and Practice* 37, no. 3 (2011): 365–90. Given that proximity only tracks the density of social relations imperfectly in a globalized world, this may have broader implications for the reduction of inequalities in transnational contexts of social interaction.
98. For a wide range of examples, see Hurst Hannum, *Autonomy, Sovereignty and Self-Determination: The Accommodation of Conflicting Rights* (University of Pennsylvania Press, 1996).
99. See, respectively, Buchanan, *Justice, Legitimacy and Self-Determination*, 257–60; Jacob T. Levy, 'Federalism, Liberalism, and the Separation of Loyalties', *American Political Science Review* 101, no. 3 (2007): 459–77; Daniel Weinstock, 'Towards a Normative Theory of Federalism', *International Social Science Journal* 53, no. 167 (2002): 75–83.
100. Anna Stilz, *Territorial Sovereignty: A Philosophical Exploration* (Oxford University Press, 2019), 177–85.
101. Stilz, *Territorial Sovereignty*, 167.
102. Stilz, *Territorial Sovereignty*, 174.
103. Stilz, *Territorial Sovereignty*, 178.
104. Stilz, *Territorial Sovereignty*, 179 n60.
105. Stilz, *Territorial Sovereignty*, 179. I think that the best interpretation of Stilz's claim here is not that *actual* state–tribal government relations are a good model for intra-state territorial autonomy, given the manifest moral failings of the US government to interact on fair terms with tribal governments. Rather, I think the best interpretation of her claim is that a suitably reformed version of US–tribal government relations could serve as a good model. Below, I suggest some alternative models that I take to be more appropriate for the context of small-island states.
106. See John Campbell, 'Climate-Induced Community Relocation in the Pacific: The Meaning and Importance of Land', in Jane McAdam (ed.) *Climate Change and Displacement: Multidisciplinary Perspectives* (Hart, 2010), 57–79.
107. Stilz, *Territorial Sovereignty*, 181.
108. Campbell, 'Climate-induced Community Relocation in the Pacific', 63–4.
109. On the Nauru case, see Jane McAdam, 'The High Price of Resettlement: The Proposed Environmental Relocation of Nauru to Australia', *Australian Geographer* 48, no. 1 (2017): 7–16. For other historical precedents, see Jane McAdam, 'Historical Cross-Border Relocations in the Pacific: Lessons for Planned Relocations in the Context of Climate Change', *Journal of Pacific History* 49, no. 3 (2014): 301–27.
110. McAdam, *Climate Change, Forced Migration, and International Law*, 153–8.
111. New Zealand is permitted to act on behalf of Niue and the Cook Islands upon their request and within the bounds of their 'advice and consent'.
112. Eve Hepburn, 'Recrafting Sovereignty? Lessons from Small Island Autonomies', in Alain G. Gadon and Michael Keating (eds) *Political Autonomy and Divided Societies: Imagining Democratic Alternatives in Complex Settings* (Palgrave Macmillan, 2012), 123.
113. Hepburn, 'Recrafting Sovereignty?' 122–3; Daniel J. Elazar, 'Federalism and Consociational Regimes', *Plubius: A Journal of Federalism* 15, no. 2 (1985): 17–34.
114. Hepburn, 'Recrafting Sovereignty?' 123–4.

115. This distinction is due to James Anaya, *Indigenous Peoples in International Law* (Oxford University Press, 1996), 80–2. See also Buchanan, *Justice, Legitimacy, and Self-Determination*, 206; Margaret Moore, 'The Moral Value of Collective Self-Determination and the Ethics of Secession', *Journal of Social Philosophy* 50, no. 4 (2019): 620–41.
116. Hendrik Spruyt, *The Sovereign State and Its Competitors* (Princeton University Press, 1994).
117. Jacob T. Levy, 'Contra Politanism', *European Journal of Political Theory* 19, no. 2 (2020): 162–83.

Chapter 5: Climate Change and Labour Migration

1. Michael Mortimore, 'Adapting to Drought in the Sahel: Lessons for Climate Change', *Wiley Interdisciplinary Reviews: Climate Change* 1, no. 1 (2010): 137. On the rationality of agrodiversity, see James C. Scott, *Seeing Like a State: How Certain Schemes to Improve the Human Condition Have Failed* (Yale University Press, 1998), 273–86.
2. Catherine Porter, 'Shocks, Consumption and Income Diversification in Rural Ethiopia', *Journal of Development Studies* 48, no. 9 (2012): 1209–22.
3. Dejene Aredo, 'The *Iddir*: An Informal Insurance Arrangement in Ethiopia', *Savings and Development* 34, no. 1 (2010): 53–72.
4. For up-to-date figures, see https://gain.nd.edu/our-work/country-index/.
5. Temesgen Tadesse Deressa and Rashid M. Hassan, 'Economic Impact of Climate Change on Crop Production in Ethiopia: Evidence from Cross-Section Measures', *Journal of African Economies* 18, no. 4 (2009): 529–54.
6. Stefan Dercon, 'Growth and Shocks: Evidence from Rural Ethiopia', *Journal of Development Economics* 74, no. 2 (2004): 309–29.
7. Porter, 'Shocks, Consumption and Income Diversification', 1216.
8. Clark Gray and Valerie Mueller, 'Drought and Population Mobility in Rural Ethiopia', *World Development* 40, no. 1 (2012): 135.
9. Markos Ezra and Gebre-Egzaibher Kiros, 'Rural Out-Migration in the Drought-Prone Areas of Ethiopia: A Multilevel Analysis', *International Migration Review* 35, no. 3 (2001): 766.
10. Peter D. Little et al., '"Moving in Place": Drought and Poverty Dynamics in South Wollo, Ethiopia', *Journal of Development Studies* 42, no. 2 (2006): 217.
11. Intergovernmental Panel on Climate Change (IPCC), *Climate Change 2014: Impacts, Adaptation and Vulnerability. Part A: Global and Sectoral Aspects. Contribution of Working Group II to the Fifth Assessment Report of the Intergovernmental Panel on Climate Change*, C.B. Field et al. (eds) (Cambridge University Press, 2014), 796–7.
12. Asia Development Bank, 'Facing the Challenge of Environmental Migration in Asia and the Pacific', *ADB Briefs* (Asia Development Bank, 2011); Michael Webber and Jon Barnett, *Accommodating Migration to Promote Adaptation to Climate Change* (The World Bank, 2010); Richard Black et al., 'Foresight: Migration and Global Environmental Change', *Foresight Reports* (The Government Office for Science, 2011); Nicole de Moor, 'Labour Migration for Vulnerable Communities: A Strategy to Adapt to a Changing Environment', *COMCAD Working Papers* 101 (2011).
13. Etienne Piguet, Antoine Pécoud, and Paul de Guchteneire, 'Migration and Climate Change: An Overview', *Refugee Survey Quarterly* 30, no. 3 (2011): 1–23; Black et al., 'Foresight: Migration and Global Environmental Change', 50.

14. Among social scientists, one concern that is sometimes raised is that increased rural–urban migration relating to climate change will put pressure on cities that are already vulnerable to climatic hazards (Black et al., 'Foresight: Migration and Global Environmental Change', 155–61). But restricting intra-state migration would—as well as drastically restricting a basic liberty—address this challenge only at the cost of preventing some vulnerable persons from being able to protect themselves against climate impacts. The better option is to invest in climate-proofing infrastructure that enables these cities to safely grow and develop as they incorporate internal labour migrants. Vulnerable states can rightly claim that the costs of making these infrastructural investments should be shared between states, with higher-income states bearing the lion's share of the costs, on the basis that they are part of the international community's broader duty to promote adaptation to climate change.
15. Among political theorists, the idea that restrictions on intra-state mobility are impermissible is sufficiently uncontroversial that it is often taken as a shared premise in arguments about whether the values that underpin it also imply that restrictions on inter-state mobility are impermissible. See, for example, David Miller, 'Is There a Human Right to Immigrate?' in Sarah Fine and Lea Ypi (eds) *Migration in Political Theory: The Ethics of Movement and Membership* (Oxford University Press, 2013), 11–31; Carens, *The Ethics of Immigration* (Oxford University Press, 2013), 237–45. For an analysis of the Hukou system, see Dorothy Solinger, 'Human Rights Issues in China's Internal Migration: Insights from Comparisons with Germany and Japan', in Joanne R. Bauer and Daniel A. Bell (eds) *The East Asian Challenge for Human Rights* (Cambridge University Press, 1999), 285–312. For a defence of the Hukou system, see Daniel A. Bell, *Beyond Liberal Democracy: Political Thinking for an East Asian Context* (Princeton University Press, 2006), 235–9.
16. IPCC, *Climate Change 2014: Impacts, Adaptation, and Vulnerability*, 5.
17. For an overview of the concept of resilience, see Carl Folke, 'Resilience: The Emergence of a Perspective for Social–Ecological Systems Analyses', *Global Environmental Change* 16, no. 3 (2006): 253–67. The broad conception of resilience that I adopt here differs from the conception developed by Mark Pelling, who uses it more narrowly to refer to strategies of adaptation that seek to preserve the status quo, as opposed to transition (promoting incremental change) or transformation (promoting radical change). See Mark Pelling, *Adaptation to Climate Change: From Resilience to Transformation* (Routledge, 2010), 50–1.
18. IPCC, *Climate Change 2014: Impacts, Adaptation, and Vulnerability*, 6–8.
19. Amartya Sen, *Development as Freedom* (Oxford University Press, 1999), esp. 87–110; Jonathan Wolff and Avner De-Shalit, *Disadvantage* (Oxford University Press, 2007), esp. 63–73.
20. Jessica Ayers and David Dodman, 'Climate Change Adaptation and Development I: The State of the Debate', *Progress in Development Studies* 10, no. 2 (2010): 161–8; Thomas C. Schelling, 'Some Economics of Global Warming', *American Economic Review* 82, no. 1 (1992): 6.
21. I have benefited from Kieran Oberman's parsing of the empirical literature here. See Kieran Oberman, 'Poverty and Immigration Policy', *American Political Science Review* 109, no. 2 (2015): 239–51.
22. For the canonical statement of the economic logic of labour migration, see Oded Stark and David Bloom, 'The New Economics of Labor Migration', *The American Economic Review* 75, no. 2 (1985): 173–8. See also Douglas Massey et al., 'Theories of International Migration: A Review and Appraisal', *Population and Development Review* 19, no. 3 (1993): 431–66; Oded Stark, *The Migration of Labour* (Blackwell, 1991).
23. J. Edward Taylor, 'The New Economics of Labour Migration and the Role of Remittances in the Migration Process', *International Migration* 37, no. 1 (1999): 63–88.
24. Christian Dustmann and Josep Mestres, 'Remittances and Temporary Migration', *Journal of Development Economics* 92, no. 1 (2010): 62–70; Oded Galor and Oded Stark,

'Migrants' Savings, the Probability of Return Migration and Migrants' Performance', *International Economic Review* 31, no. 2 (1990): 463-7. 'Circular' migration here refers to iterated forms of temporary migration.

25. Hein de Haas, 'International Migration, Remittances and Development: Facts and Myths', *Third World Quarterly* 26, vol. 8 (2005): 1269-84; Oberman, 'Poverty and Immigration Policy', 242-3.

26. François Gemmene and Julia Blocher, 'How Can Migration Serve Adaptation to Climate Change? Challenges to Fleshing Out a Policy Ideal', *The Geographical Journal* 183, no. 4 (2017): 336-47; Douglas K. Bardsley and Graeme J. Hugo, 'Migration and Climate Change: Examining Thresholds of Change to Guide Effective Adaptation Decision-Making', *Population and Environment* 32, no. 2-3 (2010): 238-62; Cecilia Tacoli, 'Crisis or Adaptation? Migration and Climate Change in the Context of High Mobility', *Environment & Urbanization* 21, no. 2 (2009): 513-25.

27. See, respectively, W. Neil Adger et al., 'Migration, Remittances, Livelihood Trajectories and Social Resilience', *AMBIO: A Journal of the Human Environment* 31, no. 4 (2002): 258-66; Douglas S. Massey et al., 'Environmental Change and Out-Migration: Evidence from Nepal', *Population and Environment* 32, no. 2-3 (2010): 109-36; Lori M. Hunter, Sheena Murray, and Fernando Riosmena, 'Rainfall Patterns and U.S. Migration from Rural Mexico', *International Migration Review* 47, no. 4 (2013): 874-909; Dean Yang and HwaJung Choi, 'Are Remittances Insurance? Evidence from Rainfall Shocks in the Philippines', *The World Bank Economic Review* 21, no. 2 (2007): 219-48; Amina Maharjan et al., 'Migration and Household Adaptation in Climate-Sensitive Hotspots in South Asia', *Current Climate Change Reports* 6 (2020): 1-16; Koko Warner, 'Environmental Change and Migration: Methodological Considerations from a Ground-Breaking Global Survey', *Population and Environment* 33, no. 1 (2011): 3-27; Koko Warner and Tamer Afifi, 'Where the Rain Falls: Evidence from 8 Countries on How Vulnerable Households Use Migration to Manage the Risk of Rainfall Variability and Food Insecurity', *Climate and Development* 6, no. 1 (2014): 1-17.

28. Richard Black et al., 'Migration as Adaptation', *Nature* 478, no. 7370 (2011): 447-9; Robert McLeman and Barry Smit, 'Migration as an Adaptation to Climate Change', *Climatic Change* 76, no. 1-2 (2006): 31-53; Robert McLeman and Lori Hunter, 'Migration in the Context of Vulnerability and Adaptation to Climate Change: Insights from Analogues', *Wiley Interdisciplinary Reviews: Climate Change* 1, no. 3 (2010): 450-61.

29. Webber and Barnett, *Accommodating Migration to Promote Adaptation to Climate Change*, 32.

30. Asia Development Bank, 'Addressing the Challenge of Migration and Climate Change in the Pacific', 72-3.

31. Black et al., 'Foresight: Migration and Global Environmental Change', 175-6, 183-5.

32. Richard Black, Dominic Kniveton, and Kerstin Schmidt-Verkerk, 'Migration and Climate Change: Towards an Integrated Assessment of Sensitivity', *Environment and Planning A: Economy and Space* 43, no. 2 (2011): 431-50.

33. Alex de Sharbinin, 'Climate Change Hotspots Mapping: What Have We Learned?' *Climatic Change* 123, no. 1 (2014): 23-37.

34. World Bank, *Migration and Remittances Factbook 2016* (World Bank, 2016); Richard H. Adams Jr and John Page, 'Do International Migration and Remittances Reduce Poverty in Developing Counties?' *World Development* 33, no. 10 (2005): 1645-69.

35. Gemmene and Blocher, 'How Can Migration Serve Adaptation to Climate Change?' 342-3.

36. Siri Eriksen et al., 'Adaptation Interventions and their Effect on Vulnerability in Developing Countries: Help, Hindrance, or Irrelevance?' *World Development* 141 (2021): 105383.

37. Samuel Fankhauser, Joel B. Smith, and Richard S.J. Tol, 'Weathering Climate Change: Some Simple Rules to Guide Adaptation Decisions', *Ecological Economics* 30, no. 1 (1999): 69-70.

38. Rasumus Heltberg, Paul Bennett Siegel, and Steen Lay Jorgensen, 'Addressing Human Vulnerability to Climate Change: Towards a "No-Regrets" Approach', *Global Environmental Change* 19, no. 1 (2009): 89–99.
39. Asia Development Bank, 'Addressing the Challenge of Migration and Climate Change in the Pacific', 55; Black et al., 'Foresight: Migration and Global Environmental Change', 183–4.
40. Black et al., 'Foresight: Migration and Global Environmental Change', 183; de Moor, 'Labour Migration for Vulnerable Communities', 13–15.
41. George Borjas, *Heaven's Door: Immigration Policy and the American Economy* (Princeton University Press, 1996); see also Stephen Macedo, 'The Moral Dilemma of U.S. Immigration Policy', in Carol M. Swain (ed.) *Debating Immigration* (Cambridge University Press, 2007), 63–81.
42. On complementarity, see David Card, 'Immigration and Inequality', *American Economic Review* 99, no. 2 (2009): 1–21; Gianmarco Ottaviano and Giovanni Peri, 'Rethinking the Effect of Immigration on Wages', *Journal of the European Economic Association* 10, no. 1 (2012): 152–97. On the role of the declining power of labour in driving wage depression, see Ruth Milkman, *Immigrant Labor and the New Precariat* (Polity, 2020); Douglas S. Massey, *Categorically Unequal: The American Stratification System* (Russell Sage, 2007). I have benefited here from Anna Stilz's parsing of the empirical literature. See Anna Stilz, 'Economic Migration: On What Terms?' *Perspectives on Politics* 20, no. 3 (2022): 983–98.
43. Ottaviano and Peri, 'Rethinking the Effect of Immigration on Wages'; Arash Abizadeh, Manish Pandey, and Sohrab Abizadeh, 'Wage Competition and the Special Obligations Challenge to Open Borders', *Politics, Philosophy & Economics* 14, no. 3 (2015): 255–69.
44. Stilz, 'Economic Migration: On What Terms?' Stilz argues that liberalized labour migration policies should be made *conditional* on adopting redistributive policies, such that liberal labour migration policies are only permissible if they are accompanied by redistributive policies that protect domestic workers (Stilz, 'Economic Migration: On What Terms?' 993). I do not believe that making labour migration conditional on redistribution can be justified in the context of climate change. Given that states have a *duty* to promote labour migration, this restriction would be unjustified for the same reasons that I articulate in the final section of this chapter: it would unfairly shift the costs of adaptation onto those most vulnerable to climate change.
45. George Borjas, *Immigration Economics* (Harvard University Press, 2014); Stilz, 'Economic Migration: On What Terms?' 990.
46. Frédéric Docquier and Hillel Rapaport, 'Globalization, Brain Drain, and Development', *Journal of Economic Literature* 50, no. 3 (2012): 681–730; Lise Widding Isaksen, Sambasivan Uma Devi, and Arlie Russell Hochschild, 'Global Care Crisis: A Problem of Capital, Care Chain, or Commons?' *American Behavioural Scientist* 52, no. 3 (2008): 405–25.
47. De Haas, 'Internal Migration, Remittances and Development', 1272–73.
48. Oded Stark, Christian Helmenstein, and Alexia Prskawetz, 'A Brain Drain with a Brain Gain', *Economics Letters* 55, no. 2 (1997): 227–34.
49. Devesh Kapur and John McHale, *Give Us Your Best and Brightest: The Global Hunt for Talent and Its Impact on the Developing World* (Centre for Global Development, 2005); Anca Gheaus, 'Care Drain: Who Should Provide for the Children Left Behind?' *Critical Review of International Social and Political Philosophy* 16, no. 1 (2013): 15–20.
50. For an argument that receiving states have duties to compensate sending states, see Paul Bou-Habib, 'The Brain Drain as Exploitation', *Politics, Philosophy & Economics* 21, no. 3 (2022): 449–68.
51. See Kieran Oberman, 'Can Brain Drain Justify Immigration Restrictions?' *Ethics* 123, no. 3 (2013): 427–55.

52. Stephanie J. Nawyn, 'Gender and Migration: Integrating Feminist Theory into Migration Studies', *Sociology Compass* 4, no. 9 (2010): 749–65; Silvia Pedraza, 'Women and Migration: The Social Consequences of Gender', *Annual Review of Sociology* 17 (1991): 303–25.
53. Grey and Mueller, 'Drought and Population Mobility in Rural Ethiopia', 142–3.
54. Douglas S. Massey, 'The Social and Economic Origins of Immigration', *Annals of the American Association of Political and Social Science* 510 (1990): 60–72; B. Davis and P. Winters, 'Gender, Networks, and Mexico–US Migration', *Journal of Development Studies* 38, no. 2 (2001): 1–26.
55. Emilio A. Parrado and Chenoa A. Flippen, 'Migration and Gender among Mexican Women', *American Sociological Review* 70, no. 4 (2005): 608–9; Jacqueline Maria Hagan, 'Social Networks, Gender, and Immigrant Incorporation', *American Sociological Review* 63, no. 1 (1998): 55–67.
56. Serene J. Khader, *Decolonizing Universalism: A Transnational Feminist Ethic* (Oxford University Press, 2019), esp. 21–49.
57. For an argument that interventions such as these that aim to reduce gender inequality can be justified even within the strict justificatory framework of political liberalism, see Gina Schouten, *Liberalism, Neutrality, and the Gendered Division of Labour* (Oxford University Press, 2019).
58. Kieran Oberman, 'Immigration, Global Poverty, and the Right to Stay', *Political Studies* 59, no. 2 (2011): 239–51; Oberman, 'Poverty and Immigration Policy'.
59. Oberman, 'Immigration, Global Poverty, and the Right to Stay', 258–60. For an alternative conception and justification of the right to stay, see Valeria Ottonelli, 'The Right to Stay as a Control Right', in David Sobel, Peter Vallentyne, and Steven Wall (eds) *Oxford Studies in Political Philosophy: Volume 6* (Oxford University Press, 2020), 87–117.
60. See Anna Stilz, *Territorial Sovereignty: A Philosophical Exploration* (Oxford University Press, 2019), 33–59; Margaret Moore, *A Political Theory of Territory* (Oxford University Press, 2015), 36–46. See also the discussion in Chapter 7 at C7P28–C7P38.
61. Oberman, 'Immigration, Global Poverty, and the Right to Stay', 258; 'Poverty and Immigration Policy', 246–7.
62. Oberman, 'Immigration, Global Poverty, and the Right to Stay', 260–2.
63. Charles Beitz, *The Idea of Human Rights* (Oxford University Press, 2009), esp. 106–17.
64. Beitz, *The Idea of Human Rights*, 109.
65. Michael Blake, *Justice, Migration, and Mercy* (Oxford University Press, 2020), 70–1.
66. Laura Valentini, 'Justice, Charity and Disaster Relief: What Do We Owe to Haiti, New Zealand and Japan?' *American Journal of Political Science* 57, no. 2 (2013): 491–503; David Miller, *National Responsibility and Global Justice* (Oxford University Press, 2007), 247–9.
67. Robert E. Goodin, 'Duties of Charity, Duties of Justice', *Political Studies* 65, no. 2 (2017): 268–83; Laura Valentini, 'Social Samaritan Justice: When and Why Needy Fellow Citizens Have a Right to Assistance', *American Political Science Review* 109, no. 4 (2015): 5.
68. For evidence of the former claim, see Daron Acemoglu, Simon Johnson, and James A. Robinson, 'The Colonial Origins of Comparative Development: An Empirical Investigation', *The American Economic Review* 91, no. 5 (2001): 1369–1401. For the latter claim, see Thomas Pogge, *World Poverty and Human Rights* (Blackwell, 2002). Oberman himself points towards this latter strategy (see his 'Immigration, Global Poverty, and the Right to Stay', 262) and Valentini endorses a related claim, that the global economic order amounts to a system of coercion that triggers duties of justice (see her 'Coercion and (Global) Justice', *American Political Science Review* 105, no. 1 (2011): 205–20).
69. Jouni Paavola and W. Neil Adger, 'Fair Adaptation to Climate Change', *Ecological Economics* 56, no. 4 (2006): 594–609.
70. Oberman, 'Poverty and Immigration Policy', 248.

216 NOTES

71. Oberman, 'Immigration, Global Poverty, and the Right to Stay', 260; Oberman, 'Poverty and Immigration Policy', 247. Emphasis added.
72. Oberman, 'Immigration, Global Poverty, and the Right to Stay', 260. See also G.A. Cohen, 'The Structure of Proletarian Unfreedom', *Philosophy & Public Affairs* 12, no. 1 (1983): 3–33.
73. Strictly speaking, it is possible for a would-be migrant to choose to migrate voluntarily *even if* they lack acceptable alternatives, if the reason why they choose to migrate is not *because* they lack acceptable alternatives (see Serena Olsaretti, *Liberty, Desert, and the Market: A Philosophical Study* (Cambridge University Press, 2004), 138–9). But unless would-be migrants have acceptable alternative options, we cannot know whether or not they would have otherwise chosen to migrate. The criterion that there should be acceptable alternatives provides an important 'political' and publicly verifiable standard for judgements about when migration is forced (see Valeria Ottonelli and Tiziana Torresi, 'When Is Migration Voluntary?' *International Migration Review* 47, no. 4 (2013): 792–801).
74. Valeria Ottonelli and Tiziana Torresi, *The Right Not to Stay* (Oxford University Press, 2022).
75. For an overview, see Clare Heyward, 'Ethics and Adaptation to Climate Change', in Stephen M. Gardiner and Allen Thompson (eds) *The Oxford Handbook of Environmental Ethics* (Oxford University Press, 2017), 474–86.
76. Ottonelli and Torresi, 'When Is Migration Voluntary?' 798–801.
77. Ottonelli and Torresi, 'When Is Migration Voluntary?' 800; Olsaretti, *Liberty, Desert, and the Market*, 140.
78. Jonathan Wolff, 'Fairness, Respect, and the Egalitarian Ethos', *Philosophy & Public Affairs* 27, no. 2 (1998): 97–122.
79. Samuel Fankhauser, 'The Costs of Adaptation', *Wiley Interdisciplinary Reviews: Climate Change* 1, no. 1 (2010): 23–30. For the less optimistic estimate, see Urvashi Narain, Sergio Margulis, and Timothy Essam, 'Estimating the Costs of Adaptation to Climate Change', *Climate Policy* 11, no. 3 (2011): 1001–19.
80. Daniel Callies and Darrel Moellendorf, 'Assessing Climate Change Policies: Catastrophe Avoidance and the Right to Sustainable Development', *Politics, Philosophy and Economics* 20, no. 2 (2021): 132. For up-to-date figures, see https://www.greenclimate.fund/about/resource-mobilisation.
81. Demond King and David Rueda, 'The New Politics of "Bread and Roses" in Industrialized Democracies', *Perspectives on Politics* 6, no. 2 (2008): 279–97.
82. Romain Felli, 'Managing Climate Insecurity by Ensuring Continuous Capital Accumulation: "Climate Refugees" and "Climate Migrants"', *New Political Economy* 18, no. 3 (2013): 337–63. See also Romain Felli and Noel Castree, 'Neoliberalising Adaptation to Environmental Change: Foresight or Foreclosure?' *Environment and Planning A: Economy and Space* 44, no. 1 (2012): 1–4.
83. Felli, 'Managing Climate Insecurity by Ensuring Continuous Capital Accumulation', 352–3.
84. Patti Tamara Lenard and Christine Straehle, 'Temporary Migration, Global Redistribution and Democratic Justice', *Politics, Philosophy and Economics* 11, no. 2 (2011): 212–13; Martin Ruhs, *The Price of Rights: Regulating International Labour Migration* (Princeton University Press, 2013), 65–71.
85. Black et al., 'Foresight: Migration and Global Environmental Change', 184; de Moor, 'Labour Migration for Vulnerable Communities', 8–9; Tacoli, 'Crisis or Adaptation?' 520–1.
86. Joseph Carens, *The Ethics of Immigration* (Oxford University Press, 2013), 45–61.
87. Martin Ruhs and Philip Martin, 'Numbers vs. Rights: Trade-Offs and Guest-Worker Programs', *International Migration Review* 42, no. 1 (2008): 249–65; Ruhs, *The Price of Rights*.
88. Eric Posner and Glen Weyl, 'A Radical Solution to Global Income Inequality: Make the U.S. More Like Qatar', *The New Republic*, 7 November 2014; see also Glen Weyl, 'The

Openness–Equality Trade-off in Global Redistribution', *The Economic Journal* 128, no. 612 (2018): F1–F36; Eric Posner and Glen Weyl, *Radical Markets: Uprooting Capitalism and Democracy for a Just Society* (Princeton University Press, 2018).
89. Branko Milanovic, *Global Inequality: A New Approach for the Age of Globalization* (Belknap Press, 2016), 147–54.
90. Ruhs, *The Price of Rights*, 172–6; see also Gillian Brock, *Justice for People on the Move: Migration in Challenging Times* (Cambridge University Press, 2020), 156–64. For other versions of this 'trade-off' argument, see Daniel Bell and Nicola Piper, 'Justice for Migrant Workers? The Case of Foreign Domestic Workers in Hong Kong and Singapore', in Will Kymlicka and Baogang He (eds) *Multiculturalism in Asia* (Oxford University Press, 2006), 196–222; Dani Rodrik, *The Globalization Paradox: Why Global Markets, States, and Democracy Can't Coexist* (Oxford University Press, 2011), 266–72.
91. See Rachel Brickner and Christine Straehle, 'The Missing Link: Gender, Immigration Policy and the Live-in Caregiver Programme in Canada', *Policy and Society* 29, no. 4 (2010): 309–20; Brock, *Justice for People on the Move*, 143–5; Joseph Carens, 'Live-in Domestics, Seasonal Workers, and Others Hard to Locate on the Map of Democracy', *Journal of Political Philosophy* 16, no. 4 (2008): 419–45.
92. Patti Tamara Lenard and Christine Straehle, 'Temporary Labour Migration: Exploitation, Tool of Development, or Both?' *Policy and Society* 29, no. 4 (2010): 287–8; Bridget Anderson, 'Migration, Immigration Controls, and the Fashioning of Precarious Workers', *Work, Employment and Society* 24, no. 2 (2010): 300–17.
93. Brock, *Justice for People on the Move*, 161–2. For arguments that more expansive rights protections can be justified on the grounds of non-domination, see Megan Benton, 'The Problem of Denizenship: A Non-Domination Framework', *Critical Review of International Social and Political Philosophy* 17, no. 1 (2014): 49–69; Alex Sager, 'Political Rights, Republican Freedom, and Temporary Workers', *Critical Review of International Social and Political Philosophy* 17, no. 2 (2014): 189–211.
94. See, e.g., Milanovic, *Global Inequality*, 153; Rodrik, *The Globalization Paradox*, 269.
95. Chris Bertram, 'The Openness–Rights Trade-Off in Labour Migration, Claims to Citizenship, and Democratic Justice', *Ethical Theory and Moral Practice* 22, no. 2 (2019): 283–96.
96. Robert Mayer, 'Guestworkers and Exploitation', *The Review of Politics* 67, no. 2 (2005): 319.
97. Ottonelli and Torresi, *The Right Not to Stay*; Valeria Ottonelli and Tiziana Torresi, 'Inclusivist Liberal Egalitarianism and Temporary Migration: A Dilemma', *Journal of Political Philosophy* 20, no. 2 (2012): 202–24.
98. For responsibility-based views, see Paul Baer, 'Adaptation: Who Pays Whom?' in W. Neil Adger, Jouni Paavola, Saleemul Huq and M.J. Mace (eds) *Fairness in Adaptation to Climate Change* (MIT Press, 2006), 131–54; Marco Grasso, 'An Ethical Approach to Climate Adaptation Finance', *Global Environmental Change* 20, no. 1 (2010): 74–81. For a capacity-based view, see Darrel Moellendorf, *The Moral Challenge of Dangerous Climate Change: Values, Poverty, and Policy* (Cambridge University Press, 2014), 186–89. For a benefit-based view, see Christian Baatz, 'Responsibility for the Past? Some Thoughts on Compensating Those Vulnerable to Climate Change in Developing Countries', *Ethics, Policy & Environment* 16, no. 1 (2013): 94–110. For a hybrid view, see Sverker C. Jagers and Göran Duus-Otterstrom, 'Dual Climate Change Responsibility: On the Moral Divergences Between Mitigation and Adaptation', *Environmental Politics* 17, no. 4 (2008): 576–91. For an overview of these debates, see Lauren Hartz-Nicholls, 'Responsibility for Meeting the Costs of Adaptation', *Wiley Interdisciplinary Reviews: Climate Change* 2, no. 5 (2011): 687–700.
99. Henry Shue, 'Historical Responsibility, Harm Prohibition, and Preservation Requirement: Core Practical Convergence on Climate Change', *Moral Philosophy and Politics* 2, no. 1 (2015): 7–31.

100. Shue, 'Historical Responsibility, Harm Prohibition, and the Preservation Requirement', 8.
101. Shue, 'Historical Responsibility, Harm Prohibition, and the Preservation Requirement', 16.
102. Rob Dellink et al., 'Sharing the Burden of Financing Adaptation to Climate Change', *Global Environmental Change* 19, no. 4 (2009): 411–21.
103. Henry Shue, *Climate Justice: Vulnerability and Protection* (Oxford University Press, 2014), 46.

Chapter 6: Climate Change and the Refugee Regime

1. Cortez's story is reported in Abraham Lustgarten, 'The Great Climate Migration', *The New York Times*, 23 July 2020, available at https://www.nytimes.com/interactive/2020/07/23/magazine/climate-migration.html.
2. Celia Medrano, 'Securing Protection for De Facto Refugees: The Case of Central America's Northern Triangle', *Ethics & International Affairs* 31, no. 2 (2017): 129–42; Nicolás Rodríguez Serna, 'Fleeing Cartels and *Maras*: International Protection Considerations and Profiles from the Northern Triangle', *International Journal of Refugee Law* 28, no. 1 (2016): 25–54.
3. For an analysis of the Trump Administration's family separation policies at the US–Mexico border, see Allison B. Wolf, *Just Immigration in the Americas: A Feminist Account* (Rowman and Littlefield, 2020), 85–108.
4. Oliver Milman, Emily Holden, and David Agren, 'The Unseen Driver Behind the Migrant Caravan: Climate Change', *The Guardian*, 30 October 2018, available at https://www.theguardian.com/world/2018/oct/30/migrant-caravan-causes-climate-change-central-america.
5. Jane McAdam, *Climate Change, Forced Migration, and International Law* (Oxford University Press, 2012), 39–51.
6. Joseph Carens, *The Ethics of Immigration* (Oxford University Press, 2013), 11.
7. Sarah Fine, 'The Ethics of Immigration: Self-Determination and the Right to Exclude', *Philosophy Compass* 8, no. 3 (2013): 254.
8. *Convention Relating to the Status of Refugees* (1951), article 33.1.
9. A strict reading of the principle of non-refoulement is ambiguous. It could mean either that those *already* admitted as refugees cannot be returned once their status has been determined, as was the argument of the Dutch delegation to the draft meetings for the Refugee Convention. But in practice, states have recognized that 'non-refoulement applies to the moment at which asylum seekers present themselves for entry' (Guy Goodwin-Gill and Jane McAdam, *The Refugee in International Law* (Oxford University Press, 2007), 280). For the Dutch delegation's view during the drafting of the convention, see Conference of Plenipotentiaries on the Status of Refugees and Stateless Persons, 'Summary Record of the Thirty-Fifth Meeting', A/CONF.2/SR.35 (1951), available at https://www.unhcr.org/uk/protection/travaux/3ae68ceb4/conference-plenipotentiaries-status-refugees-stateless-persons-summary.html.
10. *Convention Relating to the Status of Refugees*, article 31.1.
11. See James C. Hathaway, *The Rights of Refugees under International Law* (Cambridge University Press, 2005).
12. Hathaway, *The Rights of Refugees under International Law*, 258–656.
13. Hathaway, *The Rights of Refugees under International Law*, 657–912.
14. UNHCR, 'Framework for Durable Solutions for Refugees and Persons of Concern' (UNHCR, 2003), available at https://www.unhcr.org/partners/partners/3f1408764/framework-durable-solutions-refugees-persons-concern.html.

15. Hathaway, *The Rights of Refugees under International Law*, 913–90. In order to be consistent with the principle of non-refoulement, repatriation must either involve the return of a person who has ceased to be a refugee, because of a change of circumstances in their home state, or the voluntary decision of a refugee to their home state even in circumstances where they face persecution or other forms of ill-treatment. Hathaway argues that we should distinguish between 'repatriation' and 'voluntary reestablishment', which correspond to these two situations. See Hathaway, *The Rights of Refugees under International Law*, 916.
16. *Convention Relating to the Status of Refugees*, article 1.A.1.
17. *Protocol Relating to the Status of Refugees* (1967), article 1.
18. Goodwin-Gill and McAdam, *The Refugee in International Law*, 37.
19. James C. Hathaway, 'The Evolution of Refugee Status in International Law: 1920–1950', *The International and Comparative Law Quarterly* 33, no. 2 (1984): 380.
20. Alexander Betts, 'Global Governance and Forced Migration', in Anna Triandafyllidou (ed.) *Routledge Handbook of Immigration and Refugee Studies* (Routledge, 2015), 29–36.
21. Goodwin-Gill and McAdam, *The Refugee in International Law*, 23–32.
22. Alexander Betts, *Survival Migration: Failed Governance and the Crisis of Displacement* (Cornell University Press, 2013), 135–59. As Betts points out, this more inclusive reading of who counts as a refugee has often been accompanied by highly restrictive policies of 'humanitarian containment'.
23. UNHCR, 'Note on International Protection', A/AC.96/830 (UNHCR, 1994), 6, available at https://www.unhcr.org/uk/excom/excomrep/3f0a935f2/note-international-protection-submitted-high-commissioner.html. For a normative theory of refugeehood that puts 'international protection' at its centre, see T. Alexander Aleinikoff and Leah Zamore, *The Arc of Protection: Reforming the International Refugee Regime* (Stanford University Press, 2019).
24. For the qualification directives, see Directive 2004/83/EC, Pub. L. No. 32004L0083, OJ L 304 (2004), available at http://data.europa.eu/eli/dir/2004/83/oj/eng and Directive 2011/95/EU, Pub. L. No. 32011L0095, OJ L 337 (2011), available at http://data.europa.eu/eli/dir/2011/95/oj/eng. For an analysis, see Goodwin-Gill and McAdam, *The Refugee in International Law*, 60–3. For the 'lack of state protection' interpretation of persecution, see James C. Hathaway and Michelle Foster, *The Law of Refugee Status* (Cambridge University Press, 2014), 185.
25. Organization for African Unity (OAU), *Convention Governing the Specific Aspects of Refugee Problems in Africa* (1969), article 2.
26. *Cartagena Declaration on Refugees* (1984), article III.3.
27. Strictly, Price uses the term 'refugee' more broadly, but divorces the concept of the refugee from the provision of asylum. He argues that only 'persecuted peoples' or 'convention refugees' have justified claims to asylum. But if we take the concept of the 'refugee' to be connected to the provision of asylum, as I do here, then his is a version of the persecution view. See Matthew Price, *Rethinking Asylum: History, Purpose, and Limits* (Cambridge University Press, 2009), 17.
28. Max Cherem, 'Refugee Rights: Against Expanding the Definition of a "Refugee" and Unilateral Protection Elsewhere', *Journal of Political Philosophy* 24, no. 2 (2016): 191–2 (emphasis original); Matthew Lister, 'Who Are Refugees?' *Law and Philosophy* 32, no. 5 (2013): 662.
29. Michael Walzer, *Spheres of Justice: A Defense of Pluralism and Equality* (Robertson, 1983), 48.
30. Lister, 'Who Are Refugees?' 661; Cherem, 'Refugee Rights', 191–2. The phrase 'necessitous strangers' is due to Walzer, *Spheres of Justice*, 41–2.
31. Price, *Rethinking Asylum*, 69–94. For the distinction between 'burdened' and 'outlaw' societies, see John Rawls, *The Law of Peoples; with the Idea of Public Reason Revisited* (Harvard University Press, 1999).

32. According to Price, there are three principal ways in which granting asylum can induce changes in state behaviour: 'coercion' (including 'soft' forms of coercion such as reputational pressures), 'persuasion', and 'acculturation'. See Price, *Rethinking Asylum*, 76–85.
33. Price, *Rethinking Asylum*, 94.
34. For this distinction, used in a slightly different way, see David Owen, What Do We Owe to Refugees? (Polity, 2020), 76.
35. Those affected in these contexts might face persecution on the broader 'lack of state protection' interpretation developed by courts and in the work of Hathaway and Foster (see Hathaway and Foster, *The Law of Refugee Status*). But adopting this interpretation of 'persecution' would mean that the persecution view is no longer distinctive—it would bring the view much closer to what I call the 'membership view' below.
36. See Price's historiographical account of the political roots of asylum in *Rethinking Asylum*, 24–59.
37. T. Alexander Aleinikoff, 'State-Centred Refugee Law: From Resettlement to Containment', *Michigan Journal of International Law* 14, no. 1 (1992): 120–38.
38. Kieran Oberman, 'Refugee and Economic Migrants: A Morally Spurious Distinction', *The Critique*, 6 January 2016, available at http://www.thecritique.com/articles/refugees-economic-migrants-a-morally-spurious-distinction-2/.
39. Oberman, 'Refugee and Economic Migrants: A Morally Spurious Distinction'; see also Chandran Kukathas, 'Are Refugees Special?' in Sarah Fine and Lea Ypi (eds) *Migration in Political Theory: The Ethics of Movement and Membership* (Oxford University Press, 2016), 249–68.
40. Oberman considers this argument and replies that those whose basic needs are not *in fact* met in other ways still have claim to asylum (Oberman, 'Refugee and Economic Migrants: A Morally Spurious Distinction'). This may be right, but we can still draw a distinction in principle between refugees—whose plight can be remedied best through asylum—and those who should be provided asylum as a second-best solution to their plight, given failings of states to supply international assistance.
41. For example, Matthew Gibney, *The Ethics and Politics of Asylum: Liberal Democracy and the Response to Refugees* (Cambridge University Press, 2004); David Miller, *Strangers in Our Midst: The Political Philosophy of Immigration* (Harvard University Press, 2016).
42. Miller, *Strangers in Our Midst*, 83.
43. Miller, *Strangers in Our Midst*, 83–5.
44. Eilidh Beaton, 'Against the Alienage Condition for Refugee Status', *Law and Philosophy* 39, no. 2 (2020): 147–76.
45. Astri Suhrke and Kathleen Newland, 'UNHCR: Uphill into the Future', *International Migration Review* 35, no. 1 (2001): 284–302.
46. 'Membership' need not only mean 'citizenship'. Members, as I understand them here, are those whose day-to-day lives are structured by their participation in a state. Long-term residents qualify as 'members' in this sense, though transient visitors such as tourists do not.
47. I say that protection is 'usually' best provided through asylum since there are other ways in which states can provide international protection, such as through protection in 'safe zones'. Often, however, there are significant problems with such forms of protection: they typically involve warehousing refugees in camps in ways that cannot usually be justified.
48. Owen, *What Do We Owe to Refugees?* 50. I do not adopt Owen's view wholesale here; in particular, I do not adopt his 'differentiated' approach to refugee protection. For a discussion of that aspect of Owen's view, see Rebecca Buxton and Jamie Draper, 'Refugees, Membership, and State System Legitimacy', *Ethics & Global Politics* 15, no. 4 (2022): 113–30.
49. Owen, *What Do We Owe to Refugees?* 45.

50. Owen, *What Do We Owe to Refugees?* 46.
51. Owen, *What Do We Owe to Refugees?* 47.
52. Emma Haddad, *The Refugee in International Society: Between Sovereigns* (Cambridge University Press, 2008), 69.
53. Carens, *The Ethics of Immigration*, 196; Owen, *What Do We Owe to Refugees?* 48–9. See also Gillian Brock, *Justice for People on the Move: Migration in Challenging Times* (Cambridge University Press, 2020), 113.
54. I do think that this is broadly consistent with Owen's view. Though Owen does not use the language of 'standing' to capture this aspect of the membership view, I take something like this to be implicit in his distinction between cases in which the international community 'supplements' and 'substitutes' for the state.
55. Owen, *What Do We Owe to Refugees?* 51.
56. Haddad, *The Refugee in International Society*, 44.
57. Matt McDonald, 'Discourses of Climate Security', *Political Geography* 33 (2013): 42–51.
58. Ban Ki Moon, 'A Climate Culprit in Darfur', *The Washington Post*, 16 June 2007, available at: https://www.washingtonpost.com/wp-dyn/content/article/2007/06/15/AR2007061501857.html.
59. Vally Koubi, 'Climate Change and Conflict', *Annual Reviews of Political Science* 22 (2019): 343–60.
60. The classic articulation of this argument is given in Thomas Homer-Dixon, *Environment, Scarcity, and Violence* (Princeton University Press, 2001).
61. Koubi, 'Climate Change and Conflict', 348–51. For a discussion of the case of Darfur, see Idean Salehyan, 'From Climate Change to Conflict? No Consensus Yet', *Journal of Peace Research* 45, no. 3 (2008): 315–26.
62. Jon Barnett and W. Neil Adger, 'Climate Change, Human Security, and Violent Conflict', *Political Geography* 26, no. 6 (2007): 639–55; Clionadh Raleigh, Andrew Linke, and John O'Loughlin, 'Extreme Temperatures and Violence', *Nature Climate Change* 4 (2014): 76–7.
63. See Barnett and Adger, 'Climate Change, Human Security, and Violent Conflict'.
64. Koubi, 'Climate Change and Conflict', 347–8. For the idea that political transitions are more likely in situations in which the costs of political turmoil are lower, see Daron Acemoglu and James A. Robinson, 'A Theory of Political Transitions', *American Economic Review* 91, no. 4 (2001): 913–63.
65. Michael Brzoska and Christiane Fröhlich, 'Climate Change, Migration and Violent Conflict: Vulnerabilities, Pathways and Adaptation Strategies', *Migration and Development* 5, no. 2 (2016): 190–210.
66. Koubi, 'Climate Change and Conflict', 348, 354–5.
67. See Colin P. Kelley et al., 'Climate Change in the Fertile Crescent and Implications of the Recent Syrian Drought', *Proceedings of the National Academy of Sciences* 112, no. 11 (2015): 3241–6 (especially for climate modelling); Peter H. Gleick, 'Water, Drought, Climate Change, and Conflict in Syria', *Weather, Climate, and Society* 6, no. 3 (2014): 331–40; Caitlin E. Werrell, Francesco Femia, and Troy Sternberg, 'Did We See It Coming? State Fragility, Climate Vulnerability, and the Uprisings in Syria and Egypt', *SIAS Review of International Affairs* 35, no. 1 (2015): 29–46.
68. See, for example, Tom Bawden, 'Refugee Crisis: Is Climate Change Affecting Mass Migration?' *The Independent*, 7 September 2015, available at https://www.independent.co.uk/news/world/refugee-crisis-is-climate-change-affecting-mass-migration-10490434.html; Henry Fountain, 'Researchers Link Syrian Conflict to a Drought Made Worse by Climate Change', *New York Times*, 2 March 2015, available at https://www.nytimes.com/2015/03/03/science/earth/study-links-syria-conflict-to-drought-caused-by-climate-change.

html; Richard Grey, 'Did Climate Change Trigger the War in Syria? Severe Drought May Have Contributed to Uprising, Study Reveals', *Mail Online*, 2 March 2015, available at https://www.dailymail.co.uk/sciencetech/article-2976063/Did-climate-change-trigger-war-Syria-Severe-drought-contributed-uprising-study-reveals.html.

69. Jan Selby et al., 'Climate Change and the Syrian Civil War Revisited', *Political Geography* 60 (2017): 232–44; Francesca De Châtel, 'The Role of Drought and Climate Change in the Syrian Uprising: Untangling the Triggers of the Revolution', *Middle Eastern Studies* 50, no. 4 (2014): 521–35; Christiane J. Frölich, 'Climate Migrants as Protestors? Dispelling Misconceptions about Global Environmental Change in Pre-Revolutionary Syria', *Contemporary Levant* 1, no. 1 (2016): 38–50.

70. Jeroen Warner and Ingrid Boas, 'Securitization of Climate Change: How Invoking Global Dangers for Instrumental Ends Can Backfire', *Environment and Planning C: Politics and Space* 37, no. 8 (2019): 1471–88; Giovanni Bettini, 'Climate Barbarians at the Gate? A Critique of Apocalyptic Narratives on "Climate Refugees"', *Geoforum* 45 (2013): 63–72; Chris Methmann and Delf Rothe, 'Preparing for the Day After Tomorrow: The Logic of Apocalypse in Global Climate Politics', *Security Dialogue* 43, no. 4 (2012): 323–44; Betsy Hartmann, 'Rethinking Climate Refugees and Climate Conflict: Rhetoric, Reality, and the Politics of Policy Discourse', *Journal of International Development* 22, no. 2 (2010): 233–46.

71. For example, research on climate change and conflict suffers from a 'streetlight effect' (i.e., researchers typically study only a handful of particularly salient and/or accessible cases) and tends to involve selection on the dependent variable (i.e., researchers select only cases in which conflict occurs, rather than selecting cases on the basis of hypothesized causes of conflict). See Courtland Adams, Tobias Ide, Jon Barnett, and Adrian Detges, 'Sampling Bias in Climate–Conflict Research', *Nature Climate Change* 8 (2018): 200–3. For methodological reflections on climate-conflict research more generally, see Halvard Buhaug, 'Climate-Conflict Research: Some Reflections on the Way Forward', *Wiley Interdisciplinary Reviews: Climate Change* 6, no. 3 (2015): 269–75; Tobias Ide, 'Research Methods for Exploring the Links Between Climate Change and Conflict', *Wiley Interdisciplinary Reviews: Climate Change* 8, no. 3 (2017): e456.

72. Intergovernmental Panel on Climate Change (IPCC), *Climate Change 2014: Impacts, Adaptation and Vulnerability. Part A: Global and Sectoral Aspects. Contribution of Working Group II to the Fifth Assessment Report of the Intergovernmental Panel on Climate Change*, C.B. Field et al. (eds) (Cambridge University Press, 2014), 796–7.

73. For an analysis of socio-economic claims to refugee status, see Michelle Foster, *International Refugee Law and Socio-Economic Rights: Refuge from Deprivation* (Cambridge University Press, 2007). Since Foster's focus is on international refugee law, she takes the concept of persecution to be central in her analysis, though she does adopt a broad interpretation of 'persecution'. On the view that I defend, whether or not socio-economic deprivation can be understood in terms of persecution (even in this broad sense) is less important than whether we are given reason to judge that the state has lost its standing to act as the guarantor of its members' human rights.

74. Betts, *Survival Migration*, 15–22.

75. Elizabeth Kennedy, 'Refugees from Central American Gangs', *Forced Migration Review* 43 (2013): 50–2.

76. Matthew Lister, 'The Place of Persecution and Non-State Action in Refugee Protection', in Alex Sager (ed.) *The Ethics and Politics of Immigration: Core Issues and Emerging Trends* (Rowman and Littlefield, 2017), 53–4.

77. Medrano, 'Securing Protection for De Facto Refugees'; Serna, 'Fleeing Cartels and *Maras*'.

78. Celia A. Harvey et al., 'Climate Change Impacts and Adaptation among Smallholder Farmers in Central America', *Agriculture & Food Security* 7 (2018): 57.

79. World Food Programme, *Food Security and Emigration: Why People Flee and the Impact on Family Members Left Behind in El Salvador, Guatemala and Honduras*

(2017), available at https://www.wfp.org/publications/2017-food-security-emigration-why-people-flee-salvador-guatemala-honduras.
80. María José Méndez, 'The Silent Violence of Climate Change in Honduras', *NACLA Report on the Americas* 52, no. 4 (2020): 436–41.
81. Clare M. Goodess, 'How is the Frequency, Severity, and Location of Extreme Weather Events Likely to Change Up to 2060', *Environmental Science & Policy* 27, no. S1 (2013): S4–S14.
82. Richard Black et al., 'Migration, Immobility and Displacement Outcomes Following Extreme Events', *Environmental Science & Policy* 27, no. S1 (2013): S32–S43; Ben Wisner et al., *At Risk: Natural Hazards, Peoples' Vulnerability and Disasters* (Routledge, 2004).
83. Fraser C. Lott, Nikolaos Christidis, and Peter A. Stott, 'Can the 2011 East African Drought Be Attributed to Climate Change?' *Geophysical Research Letters* 40, no. 6 (2013): 1177–81.
84. Amartya Sen, *Poverty and Famines: An Essay on Entitlement and Deprivation* (Oxford University Press, 1983).
85. Daniel Maxwell and Merry Fitzpatrick, 'The 2011 Somalia Famine: Contexts, Causes and Complications', *Global Food Security* 1, no. 1 (2012): 5–12.
86. Mehdi Achour and Nina Lacan, 'Drought in Somalia: A Migration Crisis', in François Gemenne, Pauline Brücker, and Dina Ionesco (eds) *The State of Environmental Migration 2011* (IOM and Sciences Po, 2012), 75–90.
87. Serena Parekh, *No Refuge: Ethics and the Global Refugee Crisis* (Oxford University Press, 2020), 161.
88. Parekh, *No Refuge*, 8.
89. Molly Conisbee and Andrew Simms, *Environmental Refugees: The Case for Recognition* (New Economics Foundation, 2003), 33.
90. Conisbee and Simms, 30. For legal defences of the idea of 'environmental persecution', see Jessica B. Cooper, 'Environmental Refugees: Meeting the Requirements of the Refugee Definition', *New York University Environmental Law Review* 6, no. 2 (1998): 480–529; Christopher M. Kozoll, 'Poisoning the Well: Persecution, the Environment, and Refugee Status', *Colorado Journal of International Environmental Law and Policy* 15, no. 2 (2004): 271–307.
91. McAdam, *Climate Change, Forced Migration and International Law*, 43–8.
92. Matthew Lister, 'Climate Change Refugees', *Critical Review of International Social and Political Philosophy* 17, no. 5 (2014): 621. As we have already seen, Lister is a proponent of the persecution view of refugee status. But he does not think that this subset of those displaced by climate change must meet the persecution condition to be eligible for refugee status. So, there is an apparent inconsistency between his view of refugee status and his claims about the role of the refugee regime for climate displacement. Lister squares this circle by arguing that we only have 'shallow' rather than 'deep' reasons to endorse the persecution condition—it typically, but not necessarily, picks out those with a valid normative claim to refugee status, because what is of basic moral significance is whether asylum is the appropriate remedy for the plight of the displaced person (see Lister, 'Climate Change Refugees', 630 n14; Lister, 'Who Are Refugees?' 661–71). In my view, if we take seriously Lister's claim that what is of basic moral significance is whether or not asylum is the appropriate remedy, then we do not even have 'shallow reasons' to endorse the persecution condition since, as we have seen, there are many other ways in which displaced people can find themselves in this predicament.
93. Lister, 'Climate Change Refugees', 619. For the idea of 'progressive conservatism', see Allen Buchanan, *Justice, Legitimacy and Self-Determination: Moral Foundations for International Law* (Oxford University Press, 2004), 63.
94. Helen Xanthaki, *Drafting Legislation: Art and Technology of Rules for Regulation* (Bloomsbury, 2014), esp. 1–20.

95. Aleinikoff and Zamore, *The Arc of Protection*, 93. Eligibility for international protection, on Aleinikoff and Zamore's view, is a broader category than eligibility for refugee status.
96. Aleinikoff and Zamore, 95.
97. Luara Ferracioli, 'The Appeal and Danger of a New Refugee Convention', *Social Theory and Practice* 40, no. 1 (2014): 123–44.
98. Guy Goodwin-Gill, 'Asylum: The Law and Politics of Change', *International Journal of Refugee Law* 7, no. 1 (1995): 1–18; Joan Fitzpatrick, 'Revitalizing the Refugee Convention', *Harvard Human Rights Journal* 9 (1996): 229–53; Betts, *Survival Migration*, 186.
99. Betts, *Survival Migration*, 178–81.
100. Ferracioli, 'The Appeal and Danger of a New Refugee Convention', 137. For the idea of 'dynamic duties', see Pablo Gilabert, 'Justice and Feasibility: A Dynamic Approach', in Michael Weber and Kevin Vallier (eds) *Political Utopias: Contemporary Debates* (Oxford University Press, 2017), 95–126.
101. Thomas Gammeltoft-Hansen and Nikolas F. Tan, 'The End of the Deterrence Paradigm? Future Directions for Global Refugee Policy', *Journal of Migration and Human Security* 5, no. 1 (2017): 28–56.
102. Tilman Rödenhauser, 'Another Brick in the Wall: Carrier Sanctions and the Privatization of Immigration Control', *International Journal of Refugee Law* 26, no. 2 (2014): 223–47.
103. Matthew Gibney, 'A Thousand Little Guantanamos: Western States and Measures to Prevent the Arrival of Refugees', in Kate E. Tunstall (ed.) *Displacement, Asylum, Migration: The Oxford Amnesty Lectures 2004* (Oxford University Press, 2006), 139–69.
104. There is now a significant legal and sociological literature documenting the ways in which states in the Global North seek to deter refugees. See, among others, David Scott Fitzgerald, *Refuge Beyond Reach: How Rich Democracies Repel Asylum Seekers* (Oxford University Press, 2019); Ayelet Shachar, *The Shifting Border: Legal Cartographies of Migration and Mobility* (Manchester University Press, 2020); Parekh, *No Refuge*, 121–50; Reece Jones, *Violent Borders: Refugees and the Right to Move* (Verso, 2016); Rebecca Hamlin, *Let Me Be a Refugee: Administrative Justice and the Politics of Asylum in the United States, Canada, and Australia* (Oxford University Press, 2014); Thomas Gammeltoft-Hansen, *Access to Asylum: International Refugee Law and the Globalisation of Migration Control* (Cambridge University Press, 2013); Matthew Longo, *The Politics of Borders: Sovereignty, Security, and the Citizen after 9/11* (Cambridge University Press, 2017); Emily Ryo, 'Detention as Deterrence', *Stanford Law Review* 71 (2019): 237–50.
105. Parekh, *No Refuge*, 130.
106. Parekh, *No Refuge*, 139–41. On the limited effectiveness of deterrence policies, see Gammeltoft-Hansen and Tan, 'The End of the Deterrence Paradigm?' 43–5; Douglas S. Massey, 'Borderline Madness: America's Counterproductive Immigration Policy', in Carol M. Swain (ed.) *Debating Immigration* (Cambridge University Press, 2007), 129–38.
107. Parekh, *No Refuge*, 145.
108. Parekh, *No Refuge*, 142–6. For discussions of the ethics of people smuggling, see Javier Hidalgo, 'The Ethics of People Smuggling', *Journal of Global Ethics* 12, no. 3 (2016): 311–26; Mollie Gerver, 'Decriminalising People Smuggling', *Moral Philosophy and Politics* 8, no. 1 (2019): 131–53; Eamon Aloyo and Eugenio Cusumano, 'Morally Evaluating Human Smuggling: The Case of Migration to Europe', *Critical Review of International Social and Political Philosophy* 24, no. 2 (2021): 133–56; Julian F. Müller, 'The Ethics of Commercial Human Smuggling', *European Journal of Political Theory* 20, no. 1 (2021): 138–56.
109. Jason De León, *The Land of Open Graves: Living and Dying on the Migrant Trail* (University of California Press, 2015), esp. 23–37.
110. James Verini, 'How U.S. Policy Turned the Sonoran Desert into a Graveyard for Migrants', *The New York Times*, 18 August 2020, available at: https://www.nytimes.com/2020/08/18/magazine/border-crossing.html; Jess Beck et al., 'Animal Scavenging and Scattering and

the Implications for Documenting the Deaths of Undocumented Border Crossers in the Sonoran Desert', *Journal of Forensic Sciences* 60, no. S1 (2015): S11–S20.
111. De Léon, *The Land of Open Graves*, 214.
112. Shane C. Cambell-Staton et al., 'Physiological Costs of Undocumented Human Migration Across the Southern United States Border', *Science* 374, no. 6574 (2021): 1499.
113. Fitzgerald, *Refuge Beyond Reach*, 6–9.
114. Shachar, *The Shifting Border*, 82–8; Michael Blake, *Justice, Migration, and Mercy* (Oxford University Press, 2020), 110–16. On Blake's view, the provision of carriers for refugees can include using coercive force in defence of refugees whose states are not willing to cooperate. The use of coercive force within refugees' home states raises a whole set of questions about the legitimacy of foreign intervention, and I am much more sceptical than Blake that this kind of intervention is typically prudent or justifiable.
115. For an analysis of Canada's Refugee Resettlement Program, see Shauna Labman, *Crossing Law's Border: Canada's Refugee Resettlement Program* (UBC Press, 2019).
116. Bill Frelick, 'In-Country Refugee Processing of Haitians: The Case Against', *Refuge: Canada's Journal on Refugees* 21, no. 4 (2003): 66–72.
117. For the idea of 'mixed migration', see Nicholas Van Hear, 'Mixed Migration: Policy Challenges', *The Migration Observatory Policy Primer* (2011), available at: https://migrationobservatory.ox.ac.uk/wp-content/uploads/2016/04/PolicyPrimer-Mixed_Migration.pdf.
118. Matthew Lister, 'Enforcing Immigration Law', *Philosophy Compass* 15, no. 3 (2020): e12653; José Jorge Mendoza, *The Moral and Political Philosophy of Immigration: Liberty, Security, and Equality* (Lexington, 2016), esp. 95–119.
119. For an argument that the impermissibility of enforcing most border controls should lead us to adopt much more open borders, see Alex Sager, 'Immigration Enforcement and Domination: An Indirect Argument for Much More Open Borders', *Political Research Quarterly* 70, no. 1 (2017): 42–54.
120. Gibney, *The Ethics and Politics of Asylum*, 195.
121. Statistics in this paragraph are from UNHCR, 'Global Trends: Forced Displacement in 2020' (UNHCR, 2021), available at https://www.unhcr.org/60b638e37/unhcr-global-trends-2020.
122. Stephen M. Gardiner, *A Perfect Moral Storm: The Ethical Tragedy of Climate Change* (Oxford University Press, 2011), 31.
123. For the Fragile States Index, see Fragile States Index, 'Fragile States Index Annual Report 2021' (Fund For Peace, 2021), available at: https://fragilestatesindex.org/2021/05/20/fragile-states-index-2021-annual-report/. For the ND-GAIN Index, see https://gain.nd.edu/our-work/country-index/rankings/. The two states not in the top ten are Syria (ranked 150th most vulnerable to climate change out of 182 states) and South Sudan (for which no adaptation data are available).
124. *Global Compact on Refugees* (2018), paragraph I.A.1.
125. James C. Hathaway, 'The Global Cop-Out on Refugees', *International Journal of Refugee Law* 30, no. 4 (2018): 594.
126. See, e.g., Miller, *Strangers in Our Midst*, 86–8, 162–3; David Owen, 'Refugees and Responsibilities of Justice', *Global Justice: Theory, Practice, Rhetoric* 11, no. 1 (2018): 23–44; Carens, *The Ethics of Immigration*, 206–17; Matthew Gibney, 'Refugees and Justice Between States', *European Journal of Political Theory* 14, no. 4 (2015): 488–63.
127. There may be some non-material costs associated with refugee protection that cannot be redistributed between states. Since those costs cannot be redistributed between states, they may be relevant to the question of where refugees should be hosted and may be appealed to as part of a state's claim about the number of refugees that it should be required to host.

128. Alexander Betts and Paul Collier, *Refuge: Transforming a Broken Refugee System* (Oxford University Press, 2017). See also James C. Hathaway and Alexander Neve, 'Making International Refugee Law Relevant Again: A Proposal for Collectivized and Solution-Oriented Protection', *Harvard Human Rights Journal* 10 (1998): 115–211.
129. For a fuller articulation of this critique, see Jamie Draper, 'Domination and Misframing in the Refugee Regime', *Critical Review of International Social and Political Philosophy* 25, no. 7 (2022): 939–62.
130. Will Jones and Alexander Teytelboym, 'The International Refugee Match: A System that Respects Refugees' Preferences and the Priorities of States', *Refugee Survey Quarterly* 36, no. 2 (2017): 84–109.
131. Gibney, 'Refugees and Justice Between States', 456–7. For a discussion of the factors affecting the 'integrative capacities' of states, see David Owen, 'Refugees, Fairness and Taking Up the Slack', *Moral Philosophy and Politics* 3, no. 2 (2016): 141–64.
132. Zosia Wasik and Henry Foy, 'Poland Favours Christian Refugees from Syria', *The Financial Times*, 21 August 2015, available at: https://www.ft.com/content/6edfdd30-472a-11e5-b3b2-1672f710807b. The preference-matching proposal is consistent with restrictions of this kind. See Jones and Teytelboym, 'The International Refugee Match', 94.
133. Alexander Betts, 'Public Goods Theory and the Provision of Refugee Protection: The Role of the Joint-Product Model in Burden-Sharing Theory', *Journal of Refugee Studies* 16 (2003): 274–96; Astri Suhrke, 'Burden-Sharing during Refugee Emergencies: The Logic of Collective versus National Action', *Journal of Refugee Studies* 11, no. 4 (1998): 396–415. The refugee regime may be best described as an *impure* public good, since it may create some benefits, such as reputational benefits that come from hosting refugees, that accrue to states individually.
134. The idea that states have special responsibilities towards refugees they have produced has widespread appeal in the broader literature on refugees (see James Souter, *Asylum as Reparation: Refuge and Responsibility for the Harms of Displacement* (Palgrave Macmillan, 2022); Carens, *The Ethics of Immigration*, 195; Miller, *Strangers in Our Midst*, 90). Often, however, this is understood as an obligation to host, rather than as an obligation to bear costs, as I am suggesting here.
135. I say 'wrongfully' here because there may be some cases in which states permissibly engage in actions that produce refugees—for example, where a state engages in a justified military intervention on behalf of the international community—such that the costs of refugee protection should be borne collectively. For related discussions, see Fredrik D. Hjorthen, 'Humanitarian Intervention and Burden-Sharing Justice', *Political Studies* 68, no. 4 (2020): 936–53; Cécile Fabre, *Cosmopolitan War* (Oxford University Press, 2012), 187–92.

Chapter 7: Climate Change and Internal Displacement

1. IDMC and IOM, 'The Evolving Picture of Displacement in the Wake of Typhoon Haiyan' (IOM, 2014), 2, available at https://www.iom.int/files/live/sites/iom/files/Country/docs/The-Evolving-Picture-of-Displacement-in-the-Wake-of-Typhoon-Haiyan.pdf.
2. '"It's Time to Stop this Madness"—Philippines Plea at UN Climate Talks', *Climate Home News*, 11 November 2013, available at https://www.climatechangenews.com/2013/11/11/its-time-to-stop-this-madness-philippines-plea-at-un-climate-talks/. See also Isabel Makoul, 'Recovery and Return After Typhoon Haiyan/Yolanda', in François Gemenne, Pauline Brücker, and Dina Ionesco (eds) *The State of Environmental Migration 2014: A Review of 2013* (IOM and Sciences Po, 2014), 13–30.

3. IDMC, *Global Report on Internal Displacement 2022* (IDMC, 2022), 16, available at https://www.internal-displacement.org/sites/default/files/publications/documents/IDMC_GRID_2022_LR.pdf.
4. On the development of the international protection framework surrounding internal displacement, see Thomas G. Weiss and David A. Korn, *Internal Displacement: Conceptualization and its Consequences* (Routledge, 2006). On the exclusion of internal displacement from the legal frameworks of the international order before the 1990s, see Phil Orchard, 'The Contested Origins of Internal Displacement', *International Journal of Refugee Law* 28, no. 2 (2016): 210–33.
5. The landmark statement of this international protection framework is Roberta Cohen and Francis M. Deng, *Masses in Flight: The Global Crisis of Internal Displacement* (Brookings, 1998).
6. Francis M. Deng, 'Guiding Principles on Internal Displacement', *The International Migration Review* 33, no. 2 (1999): 484–93; *Protocol on the Protection and Assistance to Internally Displaced Persons*, 30 November 2006, available at https://www.refworld.org/docid/52384fe44.html; *African Union Convention for the Protection and Assistance of Internally Displaced Persons in Africa ('Kampala Convention')*, 23 October 2009, available at https://www.refworld.org/docid/4ae572d82.html; IASC, *IASC Framework on Durable Solutions for Internally Displaced Persons* (Brookings-Bern Project on Internal Displacement, 2010).
7. For some recent exceptions, see the contributions in Jamie Draper and David Owen (eds) *The Political Philosophy of Internal Displacement* (Oxford University Press, forthcoming).
8. Deng, 'Guiding Principles on Internal Displacement', 484.
9. Walter Kälin, 'Internal Displacement', in Elena Fiddian-Qasmiyeh, Gil Loescher, Katy Long, and Nando Sigona (eds) *The Oxford Handbook of Refugee and Forced Migration Studies* (Oxford University Press, 2014), 163–4.
10. Phil Orchard, 'Protection of Internally Displaced Persons: Soft Law as a Norm-Generating Mechanism', *Review of International Studies* 36, no. 2 (2010): 281–303.
11. Anne Willem Bijleveld, 'Towards More Predictable Humanitarian Responses—Inter-Agency Cluster Approach to IDPs', *Refugee Survey Quarterly* 25, no. 4 (2006): 28–34.
12. Cohen and Deng, *Masses in Flight*, 16.
13. Eilidh Beaton, 'Against the Alienage Condition for Refugee Status', *Law and Philosophy* 39, no. 2 (2020): 147–76; David Owen, '*In Loco Civitatis*: On the Normative Basis of the Institution of Refugeehood and Responsibilities for Refugees', in Sarah Fine and Lea Ypi (eds) *Migration in Political Theory: The Ethics of Movement and Membership* (Oxford University Press, 2016), 279–80; Andrew Shacknove, 'Who Is a Refugee?' *Ethics* 95, no. 2 (1985): 274–84.
14. On the 'respect, promote, and fulfil' formulation for human rights protection, see David Karp, 'What Is the Responsibility to Protect Human Rights? Reconsidering the "Respect, Promote, Fulfil" Framework', *International Theory* 12, no. 1 (2020): 83–108. For the idea of a 'division of labour' between states in protecting human rights, see Charles Beitz, *The Idea of Human Rights* (Oxford University Press, 2009), 108–9.
15. David Owen, *What Do We Owe to Refugees?* (Polity Press, 2020), 51.
16. Tamar Schapiro, 'Kantian Rigorism and Mitigating Circumstances', *Ethics* 117, no. 1 (2006): 54.
17. Veridiana Sedeh, 'Floods and Displacement in Bolivia', in François Gemenne, Pauline Brücker, and Dina Ionesco (eds) *The State of Environmental Migration 2014: A Review of 2013* (IOM and Sciences Po, 2014), 179–80.
18. For the idea of complementary protection in the law, see Jane McAdam, *Complementary Protection in International Refugee Law* (Oxford University Press, 2007). For a philosophical analysis of complementary protection (which differs from the view I express

here), see Matthew Lister, 'Philosophical Foundations for Complementary Protection', in David Miller and Christine Straehle (eds) *The Political Philosophy of Refuge* (Cambridge University Press, 2019), 211–30.
19. James C. Hathaway, 'Forced Migration Studies: Could We Agree Just to "Date"?' *Journal of Refugee Studies* 20, no. 3 (2007): 356.
20. See the regional overview in Cohen and Deng, *Masses in Flight*, 39–72.
21. Joseph Raz, *The Morality of Freedom* (Clarendon Press, 1988), 373–7. This does not mean that an adequate range of options is *sufficient* for movement to be autonomous, nor that any movement which is not involuntary is autonomous, since other conditions (such as a capacity for autonomy and independence) may be necessary for genuinely autonomous action. See Raz, *The Morality of Freedom*, 369–73, 377–8.
22. Anthony Richmond, 'Reactive Migration: Sociological Perspectives on Refugee Movement', *Journal of Refugee Studies* 6, no. 1 (1993): 7–24.
23. Richmond, 'Reactive Migration', 16.
24. Richmond, 'Reactive Migration', 12, 15–17.
25. Anna Stilz, 'Occupancy Rights and the Wrong of Removal', *Philosophy & Public Affairs* 41, no. 4 (2013): 335. See also Margaret Moore, *A Political Theory of Territory* (Oxford University Press, 2015), 36–40 and, on the importance of micro-level spaces such as the home, Cara Nine, 'The Wrong of Displacement: The Home as Extended Mind', *Journal of Political Philosophy* 26, no. 2 (2018): 240–57; Katy Wells, 'The Right to Housing', *Political Studies* 67, no. 2 (2019): 406–21.
26. For a fuller analysis of the harms of anticipatory displacement, see Jamie Draper, 'Anticipatory and Reactive Displacement', in Draper and Owen (eds) *The Political Philosophy of Internal Displacement*.
27. Anna Stilz, *Territorial Sovereignty: A Philosophical Exploration* (Oxford University Press, 2019), 33–58; Stilz, 'Occupancy Rights and the Wrong of Removal'; Moore, *A Political Theory of Territory*, 36–40.
28. Stilz, 'Occupancy Rights and the Wrong of Removal', 327–8; Moore, *A Political Theory of Territory*, 36.
29. Clearly, the notion of a 'reasonable person' here is somewhat vague. There is room for disagreement about what level of risk is tolerable. Some people might also argue that those who exercise a responsible choice in knowingly moving to a high-risk area can be reasonably required to bear a higher burden of displacement risk. This formulation leaves open space for these disagreements.
30. IASC, *IASC Framework on Durable Solutions for Internally Displaced Persons*. For an analysis, see Megan Bradley, 'Durable Solutions and the Right of Return for IDPs: Evolving Interpretations', *International Journal of Refugee Law* 30, no. 2 (2018): 218–42.
31. See Bradley, 'Durable Solutions and the Right to Return for IDPs', 235–40. The idea that those who have been expelled from their lands and homes have a right to return enjoys broad support among theorists of territorial rights. See Moore, *A Political Theory of Territory*, 139–48; Stilz, *Territorial Sovereignty*, 74–8; David Lefkowitz, 'Autonomy, Residence, and Return', *Critical Review of International Social and Political Philosophy* 18, no. 5 (2015): 529–46.
32. Walter Kälin, *Guiding Principles on Internal Displacement: Annotations* (American Society for International Law and Brookings-Bern Project on Internal Displacement, 2008), 125.
33. Stilz, *Territorial Sovereignty*, 41–3.
34. Khalid Koser, 'Climate Change and Internal Displacement: Challenges to the Normative Framework', in Etienne Piguet, Antoine Pécoud, and Paul De Guchteneire (eds) *Migration and Climate Change* (Cambridge University Press, 2011), 289.
35. IDMC, *Global Report on Internal Displacement 2022*, 16.

36. Clare M. Goodess, 'How Is the Frequency, Location and Severity of Extreme Events Likely to Change up to 2060?' *Environmental Science & Policy* 27, no. S1 (2013): S4–14.
37. Anthony Oliver-Smith, '"What Is a Disaster?": Anthropological Perspectives on a Persistent Question', in Anthony Oliver-Smith and Susannah M. Hoffman (eds) *The Angry Earth: Disaster in Anthropological Perspective* (Psychology Press, 1999).
38. Mike Hulme et al., 'Unstable Climates: Exploring the Statistical and Social Constructions of "Normal" Climate', *Geoforum* 40, no. 2 (2009): 197–206.
39. For reviews, see Friederike E.L. Otto, 'Attribution of Weather and Climate Events', *Annual Review of Environment and Resources* 42 (2017): 627–46; Peter A. Stott et al., 'Attribution of Extreme Weather and Climate-Related Events', *Wiley Interdisciplinary Reviews: Climate Change* 7, no. 1 (2016): 23–41.
40. Benjamin Wisner et al., *At Risk: Natural Hazards, People's Vulnerability and Disasters* (Psychology Press, 2004); W. Neil Adger, 'Vulnerability', *Global Environmental Change* 16, no. 3 (2006): 268–81.
41. Richard Black et al., 'Migration, Immobility and Displacement Outcomes Following Extreme Events', *Environmental Science & Policy*, 27, no. S1 (2013): S32–43.
42. Gregory Squires and Chester Hartman (eds), *There Is No Such Thing as a Natural Disaster: Race, Class, and Hurricane Katrina* (Routledge, 2007); Olúfẹ́mi O. Táíwò, *Reconsidering Reparations* (Oxford University Press, 2022), 150–7; Iris Marion Young, 'Katrina: Too Much Blame, Not Enough Responsibility', *Dissent* 53, no. 1 (2006): 41–6.
43. Patrick Sharkey, 'Survival and Death in New Orleans: An Empirical Look at the Human Impact of Katrina', *Journal of Black Studies* 37, no. 4 (2007): 482–501.
44. Bob Bolin and Lisa C. Kurtz, 'Race, Class, Ethnicity, and Disaster Vulnerability' in Havidán Rodríguez, William Donner, and Joseph E. Trainor (eds) *Handbook of Disaster Research* (Springer, 2007), 194.
45. Robert D. Bullard, 'Differential Vulnerabilities: Environmental and Economic Inequality and Government Response to Unnatural Disasters', *Social Research* 75, no. 3 (2008): 754–6.
46. Elizabeth Fussell, Narayan Sastry, and Mark Van Landingham, 'Race, Socioeconomic Status, and Return Migration to New Orleans after Hurricane Katrina', *Population and Environment* 31, no. 1–3 (2010): 20–42.
47. Camilla Stivers, '"So Poor and So Black": Hurricane Katrina, Public Administration, and the Issue of Race', *Public Administration Review* 67, no. S1 (2007): 48–56.
48. See, for example, United Nations, 'Cuba: A Model in Hurricane Risk Management' [press release], 14 September 2004, available at https://www.un.org/press/en/2004/iha943.doc.htm.
49. Gonzalo Lizarralde et al., 'A Systems Approach to Resilience in the Built Environment: The Case of Cuba', *Disasters* 39, no. 1 (2015): S76–S95.
50. Holly Sims and Kevin Vogelmann, 'Popular Mobilization and Disaster Management in Cuba', *Public Administration and Development* 22, no. 5 (2002): 389–400.
51. Lizarralde et al., 'A Systems Approach to Resilience in the Built Environment: The Case of Cuba', S91.
52. Kirstin Dow et al., 'Limits to Adaptation', *Nature Climate Change* 3, no. 4 (2013): 305–7; W. Neil Adger et al., 'Are There Social Limits to Adaptation to Climate Change?' *Climatic Change* 93, no. 3 (2009): 335–54.
53. Jon Barnett and Saffron O'Neill, 'Maladaptation', *Global Environmental Change* 20, no. 2 (2010): 211–13; A.K. Magnan et al., 'Addressing the Risk of Maladaptation to Climate Change', *Wiley Interdisciplinary Reviews: Climate Change* 7, no. 5 (2016): 646–65.
54 James Fairhead, Melissa Leach, and Ian Scoones, 'Green Grabbing: A New Appropriation of Nature?' *The Journal of Peasant Studies* 39, no. 2 (2012): 238, 252–3. On land-grabbing more

broadly, see Anna Jurkevics, 'Land Grabbing and the Perplexities of Territorial Sovereignty', *Political Theory* 50, no. 1 (2022): 32–58.
55. T.F. Keenan and C.A. Williams, 'The Terrestrial Carbon Sink', *Annual Review of Environment and Resources* 43 (2018): 219–43.
56. Arun Argawal and Kent Redford, 'Conservation and Displacement: An Overview', *Conservation & Society* 7, no. 1 (2009): 1–10.
57. Anne M. Larson, 'Forest Tenure Reform in the Age of Climate Change: Lessons for REDD+', *Global Environmental Change* 21, no. 2 (2011): 540–9; Jacob Phelps, Edward L. Webb, and Arun Argawal, 'Does REDD+ Threaten to Recentralize Forest Governance?' *Science* 328, no. 5976 (2010): 312–13.
58. Quoted in Indigenous Environmental Network and Carbon Trade Watch (eds), *No REDD Papers, Vol. 1* (Eberhardt Press, 2011), 64.
59. Chris Armstrong, *Justice and Natural Resources* (Oxford University Press, 2017), 120–7; Chris Armstrong, 'Climate Justice and Territorial Rights', in Jeremy Moss (ed.) *Climate Change and Justice* (Cambridge University Press, 2015), 59–72. For Armstrong's defence of the background claim that developing countries should be compensated for foregoing the economic benefit of exploiting their rainforests, see Chris Armstrong, 'Fairness, Freeriding, and Rainforest Protection', *Political Theory* 44, no. 1 (2016): 106–30.
60. Arnim Scheidel et al., 'Environmental Conflicts and Defenders: A Global Overview', *Global Environmental Change* 63 (2020): 102104.
61. Megan Blomfield, 'Land as a Global Commons?' *Journal of Applied Philosophy* 40, no. 4 (2023): 577–92; see also Megan Blomfield, 'Global Common Resources and the Just Distribution of Emissions Shares', *Journal of Political Philosophy* 21, no. 3 (2013): 283–304.
62. Deng, 'Guiding Principles on Internal Displacement', 486.
63. Draper, 'Anticipatory and Reactive Displacement'; Cara Nine, 'Water Crisis Adaptation: Defending a Strong Right Against Displacement from the Home', *Res Publica* 22, no. 1 (2016): 37–52.
64. For an analysis in the context of development, see Peter Penz, Jay Drydyk, and Pablo S. Bose, *Displacement by Development: Ethics, Rights and Responsibilities* (Cambridge University Press, 2011).
65. Deng, 'Guiding Principles on Internal Displacement', 485.
66. Catherine Phuong, *The International Protection of Internally Displaced Persons* (Cambridge University Press, 2005), 76–116.
67. Laura Valentini, 'Justice, Charity, and Disaster Relief: What, If Anything, Is Owed to Haiti, Japan, and New Zealand?' *American Journal of Political Science* 57, no. 2 (2013): 491–503. See also Laura Valentini, 'Social Samaritan Justice: When and Why Needy Fellow Citizens Have a Right to Assistance', *American Political Science Review* 109, no. 4 (2015): 735–49.
68. Valentini, 'Justice, Charity, and Disaster Relief', 500.
69. For a discussion of the relationship between responsibility and remedial duties, see David Miller, *National Responsibility and Global Justice* (Oxford University Press, 2007), 81–109.
70. For the idea of positive sovereignty, see Miriam Ronzoni, 'Two Conceptions of State Sovereignty and Their Implications for Global Institutional Design', *Critical Review of International Social and Political Philosophy* 15, no. 5 (2012): 573–91.
71. For the idea of background justice, see Miriam Ronzoni, 'The Global Order: A Case of Background Injustice? A Practice-Dependent Account', *Philosophy & Public Affairs* 37, no. 3 (2009): 242–9.
72. For the idea of a standard threat, see Henry Shue, *Basic Rights: Subsistence, Affluence, and U.S. Foreign Policy* (Princeton University Press, 1996).
73. Roberta Cohen, 'Response to Hathaway', *Journal of Refugee Studies* 20, no. 3 (2007): 371.
74. Deng, 'Guiding Principles on Internal Displacement', 492.

75. Phil Orchard, 'Implementing a Global Internally Displaced Persons Protection Regime', in Alexander Betts and Phil Orchard (eds) *Implementation and World Politics: How International Norms Change Practice* (Oxford University Press, 2014), 106–14.
76. Roberta Cohen and Francis M. Deng, 'The Genesis and the Challenges', *Forced Migration Review*, Special Issue: Ten Years of the Guiding Principles on Internal Displacement (2008): 4.
77. Orchard, 'Implementing a Global Internally Displaced Persons Protection Regime', 117.
78. Elizabeth Ferris, Erin Mooney, and Chareen Stark, *From Responsibility to Response: Assessing National Approaches to Internal Displacement* (Brookings Institution, 2011), 23–9.
79. David Strömberg, 'Natural Disasters, Economic Development, and Humanitarian Aid', *Journal of Economic Perspectives* 21, no. 3 (2007): 199–222; A. Cooper Drury, Richard Stuart Olson, and Douglas A. Van Belle, 'The Politics of Humanitarian Aid: U.S. Foreign Disaster Assistance, 1964–1995', *Journal of Politics* 67, no. 2 (2005): 454–73; Alberto Alesina and David Dollar, 'Who Gives Foreign Aid to Whom and Why?', *Journal of Economic Growth* 5, no. 1 (2000): 33–63.
80. Richard S.J. Tol, 'The Economic Impacts of Climate Change', *Review of Environmental Economics and Policy* 12, no. 1 (2021): 4–25.
81. For the distinction between 'soft' and 'hard' law, see Kenneth W. Abbott and Duncan Snidal, 'Hard and Soft Law in International Governance', *International Organization* 54, no. 3 (2000): 421–56.
82. Abbott and Snidal, 'Hard and Soft Law in International Governance', 427–8.
83 Walter Kälin, 'Guiding Principles on Internal Displacement: The Way Ahead', *Proceedings of the ASIL Annual Meeting* 102 (2008): 199.
84. Kälin, 200.
85. Chaloka Beyani, 'The Politics of International Law: Transformation of the Guiding Principles on Internal Displacement from Soft Law into Hard Law', *Proceedings of the ASIL Annual Meeting* 102 (2008): 194–8.
86. My use of the idea of an 'internalist bias' here extends its usage from the context of refugee studies. See B.S. Chimni, 'The Geopolitics of Refugee Studies: A View from the South', *Journal of Refugee Studies* 11, no. 4 (1998): 350–74; Astride R. Zolberg, Astri Suhrke, and Sergio Aguayo, *Escape from Violence: Conflict and the Refugee Crisis in the Developing World* (Oxford University Press, 1989).

Chapter 8: Sharing the Costs of Climate Displacement

1. My focus in this chapter is on the financial costs of addressing climate displacement. There may also be some non-financial costs involved in discharging our duties to the displaced. Since those costs cannot always be easily redistributed, they are often best viewed as moral claims that figure in the balance of reasons in our judgements about the content and bearer of different first-order duties in the first place.
2. Henry Shue, 'Global Environment and International Inequality', *International Affairs* 75, no. 3 (1999): 533.
3. David Miller, *National Responsibility and Global Justice* (Oxford University Press, 2007), 82.
4. R. Jay Wallace, *Responsibility and the Moral Sentiments* (Harvard University Press, 1996). This view broadly follows practice-based theories of responsibility, which build on P.F. Strawson's claim that we should think about responsibility from the perspective of our participation in practices of responsibility attribution (P.F. Strawson, 'Freedom and Resentment', *Proceedings of the British Academy* 48 (1962): 1–25). This is in opposition to a 'metaphysical' view of responsibility that holds that whether or not someone is responsible

can be settled independently of any normative commitments. Such a view, in G.A. Cohen's words, 'subordinates political philosophy to metaphysical questions' (G.A. Cohen, 'On the Currency of Egalitarian Justice', *Ethics* 99, no. 3 (1989): 934; see also Carl Knight, 'The Metaphysical Case for Luck Egalitarianism', *Social Theory and Practice* 32, no. 2 (2006): 173–89). For a defence of the practice-based view over the metaphysical view, see Emily McTernan, 'How to Be a Responsibility-Sensitive Egalitarian: From Metaphysics to Social Practice', *Political Studies* 64, no. 3 (2016): 748–64.

5. Miller, *National Responsibility and Global Justice*, 83–4. Here Miller is building on Tony Honoré, 'Responsibility and Luck', in Tony Honoré (ed.) *Responsibility and Fault* (Hart, 1999), 14–40. A similar distinction is made between 'responsibility as attributability' and 'substantive responsibility' in T.M. Scanlon, *What We Owe to Each Other* (Harvard University Press, 1998), 248, and between 'blame-responsibility' and 'task-responsibility' in Anna Stilz, 'Collective Responsibility and the State', *Journal of Political Philosophy* 19, no. 2 (2011): 194. Stilz and Scanlon, however, see 'blame-responsibility' and 'responsibility as attributability' as being essentially related to moral appraisal, whereas Miller does not take outcome responsibility itself to be sufficient for moral appraisal. I appeal to Miller's distinction here because nothing in my argument hangs on ascribing moral blame to agents that are outcome-responsible—though such blame may well be justified.
6. Miller, *National Responsibility and Global Justice*, 83.
7. Miller, 87–8.
8. Miller, 96.
9. Miller, 98–99.
10. Miller, 100–4. Miller takes moral responsibility to be concerned with the aptness of issuing moral blame and praise.
11. Miller, 93.
12. Miller, 101.
13. Scanlon, *What We Owe to Each Other*, 253.
14. For the former reason, see Robert Jubb, 'Contribution to Collective Harms and Responsibility', *Ethical Perspectives* 19, no. 4 (2012): 740–1. For the latter, see Zofia Stemplowska, 'Responsibility and Respect: Reconciling Two Egalitarian Visions', in Carl Knight and Zofia Stemplowska (eds) *Responsibility and Distributive Justice* (Oxford University Press, 2011), 115–35.
15. Robert O. Keohane and David Victor, 'The Regime Complex for Climate Change', *Perspectives on Politics* 9, no. 1 (2011): 7–23; Joyeeta Gupta, 'A History of International Climate Change Policy', *Wiley Interdisciplinary Reviews: Climate Change* 1, no. 5 (2010): 636–53.
16. Darrel Moellendorf, *The Moral Challenge of Dangerous Climate Change: Values, Poverty, and Policy* (Cambridge University Press, 2014); Darrel Moellendorf, 'Treaty Norms and Climate Mitigation', *Ethics & International Affairs* 23, no. 3 (2009): 247–66.
17 Alexandra Lesnikowski et al., 'What Does the Paris Agreement Mean for Adaptation?' *Climate Policy* 17, no. 7 (2017): 825–31.
18 Sverker C. Jagers and Göran Duus-Otterström, 'Dual Climate Change Responsibility: On Moral Divergences between Mitigation and Adaptation', *Environmental Politics* 17, no. 4 (2008): 577–8. Darrel Moellendorf has recently argued that global solidarity in financing adaptation can be motivated by an appeal to a shared interest in peace and security that is threatened by climate change. On his view, the potential for climate change to lead to destabilizing forms of mass migration provides a reason for states to cooperate in financing adaptation (see Darrel Moellendorf, *Mobilizing Hope: Climate Change and Global Poverty* (Oxford University Press, 2022), 97–119). In my view, there are two problems with this argument. First is that it depends on an unhelpful and inaccurate picture of climate displacement as a threat to national security that is more likely to provide a rationalization for the fortification of borders than a basis for cooperation on adaptation—especially since,

as we have seen, adaptation in some cases may well require states to facilitate cross-border migration. Second is that even if it does motivate global action on adaptation, it does not seem appropriate to describe this action as being based in *solidarity*. On Moellendorf's view, reasons of solidarity are reasons to act for the sake of a collective benefit (Moellendorf, *Mobilizing Hope*, 90–5). But the reason to which Moellendorf appeals here has more to do with the self-interest of states in the Global North that seek to insulate themselves against the effects of climate displacement than it does with a genuinely collective interest in global peace and security.

19. Darrel Moellendorf, 'Taking UNFCCC Norms Seriously', in Clare Heyward and Dominic Roser (eds) *Climate Justice in a Non-Ideal World* (Oxford University Press, 2016), 104–22.
20. John Rawls, *Political Liberalism* (Columbia University Press, [1993] 2005), 265–9.
21. Blake Francis, 'In Defense of National Climate Change Responsibility: A Reply to the Fairness Objection', *Philosophy & Public Affairs* 49, no. 2 (2021): 115–55.
22. Bård Lahn, 'A History of the Global Carbon Budget', *Wiley Interdisciplinary Reviews: Climate Change* 11, no. 3 (2020): e636.
23. See Simon Caney, 'Just Emissions', *Philosophy & Public Affairs* 40, no. 4 (2012): 525–30; Lukas H. Meyer and Dominic Roser, 'Distributive Justice and Climate Change: The Allocation of Emissions Rights', *Analyse & Kritik* 28, no. 2 (2006): 223–49.
24. Moellendorf, *The Moral Challenge of Dangerous Climate Change*.
25. For discussions of the excusable ignorance objection, see Alexa Zellentin, 'Compensation for Historical Emissions and Excusable Ignorance', *Journal of Applied Philosophy* 32, no. 3 (2015): 258–74; Derek Bell, 'Global Climate Justice, Historic Emissions, and Excusable Ignorance', *The Monist* 94, no. 3 (2011): 391–411.
26. Miller, *National Responsibility and Global Justice*, 96.
27. Miller, *National Responsibility and Global Justice*, 96.
28. Intergovernmental Panel on Climate Change (IPCC), *Climate Change: The IPCC Impacts Assessment*, eds W.J. McG. Tegart, G.W. Sheldon, and D.C. Griffiths (IPCC, 1990), chap. 5.
29. For an overview of paradigmatic kinds of climate impacts to be avoided, see Mark G. New, Diana M. Liverman, Richard A. Betts, Kevin L. Anderson, and Chris C. West (eds), 'Four Degrees and Beyond: the Potential for a Global Temperature Increase of Four Degrees and its Implications', [special issue] *Philosophical Transactions of the Royal Society A: Mathematical, Physical and Engineering Sciences* 369, no. 1934 (2011), especially François Gemmene, 'Climate-Induced Population Displacements in a 4°C+ World'; Philip K. Thornton et al., 'Agriculture and Food Systems in Sub-Saharan Africa in a 4°C+ World'; and Rachel Warren, 'The Role of Interactions in a World Implementing Adaptation and Mitigation Solutions to Climate Change', all in that issue.
30. David Coady et al., 'How Large are Global Fossil Fuel Subsidies?' *World Development* 91 (2017): 11–27; David Victor, 'The Politics of Fossil-Fuel Subsidies', in *Untold Billions: Fossil Fuel Subsidies, Their Impacts and the Path to Reform* (International Institute for Sustainable Development, 2009), 9–32.
31. In making the claim that inaction can be sufficient for the attribution of outcome responsibility, I am not making the further claim that there is no moral difference between doing and allowing. Only the weaker claim that allowing can itself be morally significant in a way that justifies the imposition of liabilities is necessary for my argument. On the relevance of the state for discussions of the doing/allowing distinction, see Adam Omar Hossein, 'Doing, Allowing, and the State', *Law and Philosophy* 33, no. 2 (2014): 235–64.
32. Etienne Piguet, Antoine Pécoud, and Paul de Guchteniere, 'Migration and Climate Change: An Overview', *Refugee Survey Quarterly* 33, no. 3 (2011): 1–23; Richard Black et al., 'Foresight: Migration and Global Environmental Change', *Foresight Reports* (The Government Office for Science, 2011); Richard Black et al., 'The Effect of Environmental Change

on Human Migration', *Global Environmental Change* 21, no. S1 (2011): S3–11; and the discussion in this book at C1P26–C1P27 and C2P20–C2P21.

33. For the idea of structural injustice, see Iris Marion Young, *Responsibility for Justice* (Oxford University Press, 2011). For diagnoses of climate change in these terms, see Robin Eckersley, 'Responsibility for Climate Change as a Structural Injustice', in Teena Gabrielson, Cheryl Hall, John M. Meyer, and David Schlosberg (eds) *The Oxford Handbook of Environmental Political Theory* (Oxford University Press, 2016), 346–61; Michael Christopher Sardo, 'Responsibility for Climate Change: Political Not Moral', *European Journal of Political Theory* 22, no. 1 (2023): 26–50; Lukas Sparenborg, '"Power Concedes Nothing Without Demand": The Structural Injustice of Climate Change', *Critical Review of International Social and Political Philosophy* (forthcoming).
34. See Stephen R. Perry, 'The Moral Foundations of Tort Law', *Iowa Law Review* 77 (1992): 449–514 and, more broadly, John Oberdiek (ed.) *Philosophical Foundations of the Law of Torts* (Oxford University Press, 2014).
35. Dale Jamieson, 'Ethics, Public Policy and Global Warming', *Science, Technology & Human Values* 17, no. 2 (1992): 149.
36. Eric Posner and David Weisbach, *Climate Change Justice* (Princeton University Press, 2010), 84.
37. For a recent attempt to reconcile theories of structural injustice and backward-looking judgements of responsibility, see Maeve McKeown, 'Reparations and Structural Injustice', *Contemporary Political Theory* 20, no. 4 (2021): 771–94.
38. See Fanny Thornton, *Climate Change and People on the Move: International Law and Justice* (Oxford University Press, 2018), 96–127; Peter Penz, 'International Ethical Responsibilities to "Climate Change Refugees"', in Jane McAdam (ed.) *Climate Change and Displacement: Multidisciplinary Perspectives* (Hart, 2010), 151–74.
39. I am indebted here to Thornton, *Climate Change and People on the Move*, 98–101.
40. Richard A. Epstein, 'The Historical Origins and Economic Structure of Workers' Compensation Law', *Georgia Law Review* 16, no. 4 (1982): 775–819; Robert E. Goodin and David Schmidtz, *Social Welfare and Individual Responsibility* (Cambridge University Press, 1998), 156–8.
41. Goodin and Schmidtz, *Social Welfare and Individual Responsibility*, 156.
42. In discussions of climate displacement, climate change is sometimes described as a 'threat multiplier' (see, for example, Patrick Huntjens and Katharina Nachbar, 'Climate Change as a Threat Multiplier for Human Disaster and Conflict', *The Hague Institute for Global Justice Working Paper* 9 (The Hague Institute for Global Justice, 2015)). I avoid this terminology and instead speak of it as a 'risk multiplier', because the term 'threat multiplier' is often associated with a securitized perspective on climate displacement which sees the reasons we have to avert it as a matter of self-interest and national security, rather than moral obligation.
43. The doctrine of market share liability was developed in the case of *Sindell v Abbott Laboratories et al.* (1980), in which drug manufacturers were held liable for the harmful effects of diethylstilbestrol (DES)—a drug prescribed to prevent miscarriages which was found to be carcinogenic—in proportion to their share of the market for the drug. See Mary Jane Sheffet, 'Market Share Liability: A New Doctrine of Causation in Product Liability', *Journal of Marketing* 47, no. 1 (1983): 35–45.
44. For a defence of the idea of assigning liability in this way, see Lewis Ross, 'Justice in Epistemic Gaps: The "Proof Paradox" Revisited', *Philosophical Topics* 31, no. 1 (2021): 315–33.
45. Thornton, *Climate Change and People on the Move*, 96–127; Penz, 'International Ethical Responsibilities to "Climate Change Refugees"', 167–71.
46. Thornton, *Climate Change and Peoples on the Move*, 98.

47. François Gemenne, 'Why the Numbers Don't Add Up: A Review of Estimates and Predictions of People Displaced by Environmental Changes', *Global Environmental Change* 21, no. S1 (2011): S41–9.
48. Dominic Kniveton et al., *Climate Change and Migration: Improving Methodologies to Estimate Flows* (IOM, 2008).
49. Robert McLeman, 'Developments in Modelling of Climate Change-Related Migration', *Climatic Change* 117, no. 3 (2013): 607.
50. Rachel Z. Friedman, *Probable Justice: Risk, Insurance, and the Welfare State* (Princeton University Press, 2020); Aaron Doyle and Diana Erikson, *Uncertain Business: Risk, Insurance, and the Limits of Knowledge* (University of Toronto Press, 2004).
51. Shue, 'Global Environment and International Inequality', 534.
52. The canonical statements of this idea in economic theory are Kenneth Arrow, 'Uncertainty and the Welfare Economics of Medical Care', *American Economic Review* 53, no. 5 (1963): 941–73, and Mark V. Pauly, 'The Economics of Moral Hazard', *American Economic Review* 58, no. 3 (1968): 531–7.
53. Mina Fazel et al., 'Prevalence of Serious Mental Disorder in 7000 Refugees Settled in Western Countries: A Systematic Review', *The Lancet* 365 (2005): 1309–14; Samantha L. Thomas and Stuart D.M. Thomas, 'Displacement and Health', *British Medical Bulletin* 69, no. 1 (2004): 115–27. For a philosophical analysis that emphasizes this aspect of displacement, see Laura Santi Amantini, 'The Harms of Internal Displacement Beyond Human Rights Violations', in Jamie Draper and David Owen (ed.) *The Political Philosophy of Internal Displacement* (Oxford University Press, forthcoming).
54. United Nations Environment Programme, *Adaptation Gap 2022: Too Little, Too Slow: Climate Adaptation Failure Puts the World at Risk* (UNEP, 2022), available at https://www.unep.org/adaptation-gap-report-2022.
55. For an overview of the relationship between mining and displacement, see John R. Owen and Deanna Kemp, 'Mining-Induced Displacement and Resettlement: A Critical Appraisal', *Journal of Cleaner Production* 87 (2015): 478–88.
56. This problem mirrors a debate in both political philosophy and political economy about whether the rules of the global order or the quality of domestic institutions are the primary cause of poverty. For philosophical arguments that draw on the claim that the global order causes poverty, see Thomas Pogge, *World Poverty and Human Rights* (Polity, 2002); Leif Wenar, *Blood Oil: Tyrants, Violence and the Rules that Run the World* (Oxford University Press, 2016). For empirical support for this claim, see Adam Prezworski and James Raymond Vreeland, 'The Effect of IMF Programs on Economic Growth', *Journal of Development Economics* 62, no. 2 (2000): 385–421; Robert Hunter Wade, 'What Strategies are Viable for Developing Countries Today? The World Trade Program and the Shrinking of "Development Space"', *Review of International Political Economy* 10, no. 4 (2003): 621–44; Joanne Gowa and Soo Yeon Kim, 'An Exclusive Country Club: The Effects of GATT on Trade, 1950–94', *World Politics* 57, no. 4 (2005): 453–78. For philosophical arguments that draw on the claim that the quality of domestic institutions causes poverty, see Matthias Risse, 'How Does the Global Order Harm the Poor?' *Philosophy & Public Affairs* 33, no. 4 (2005): 349–76; Shmuel Nili, 'Liberal Global Justice and Social Science', *Review of International Studies* 42, no. 1 (2016): 136–55. For empirical support for this claim, see Daron Acemoglu, Simon Johnson, and James A. Robinson, 'The Colonial Origins of Comparative Development: An Empirical Investigation', *American Economic Review* 91, no. 5 (2001): 1369–1401; Dani Rodrik, Arvind Subramanian, and Francesco Trebbi, 'Institutions Rule: The Primacy of Institutions Over Geography and Integration in Economic Development', *Journal of Economic Growth* 9, no. 2 (2004): 131–65; William Easterly and Ross Levine,

'Tropics, Germs, and Crops: How Endowments Influence Economic Development', *Journal of Monetary Economics* 50, no. 1 (2003): 3–39. For a recent philosophical analysis of this debate, including a parsing of this empirical literature to which I am indebted here, see Chris Armstrong, 'Domestic Institutions, Growth, and Global Justice', *European Journal of Political Theory* 22, no. 1 (2023): 4–25.

57. UNFCCC, *United Nations Framework Convention on Climate Change* (1992), article 2.
58. Other measures have also been proposed, such as atmospheric concentrations of CO_2, with 350 parts per million being a popular target. For the scientific basis of the 350ppm target, see James Hansen et al., 'Target Atmospheric CO_2: Where Should Humanity Aim?' *The Open Atmospheric Science Journal* 2, no. 1 (2008): 217–31.
59. UNFCCC, *Copenhagen Accord* (2010), article 1; UNFCCC, *Paris Agreement* (2015), article 1(a). For overviews of the development of climate negotiations, see Gupta, 'A History of International Climate Change Policy'; Dale Jamieson, *Reason in a Dark Time: Why the Struggle Against Climate Change Failed—And What It Means for Our Future* (Oxford University Press, 2014), 11–60.
60. Moellendorf, *The Moral Challenge of Dangerous Climate Change*, 9–29.
61. Simon Caney, 'Climate Change', in Serena Olsaretti (ed.) *The Oxford Handbook of Distributive Justice* (Oxford University Press, 2018), 665–6.
62. IPCC, *Climate Change 2014: Synthesis Report*, ed. R.K. Pachauri and Leo Mayer (IPCC, 2015), 6–10.
63. On the prospects for clean energy technology, see Robert Pollin, *Greening the Global Economy* (MIT Press, 2015), 45–61.
64. See Michael Oppenheimer and Annie Petsonk, 'Article 2 of the UNFCCC: Historical Origins, Recent Interpretations', *Climatic Change* 73, no. 3 (2005): 195–226; Stephen M. Gardiner, 'Ethics and Global Climate Change', *Ethics* 113, no. 3 (2004): 555–600; William Nordhaus, *A Question of Balance: Weighing the Options on Global Warming Policies* (Yale University Press, 2014).
65. For example, Ted Nordhaus, 'The Two Degree Delusion', *Foreign Affairs*, 8 February 2018, available at https://www.foreignaffairs.com/world/two-degree-delusion. For a response, see Daniel Callies and Darrel Moellendorf, 'Assessing Climate Policies: Catastrophe Avoidance and the Right to Sustainable Development', *Politics, Philosophy & Economics* 20, no. 2 (2021): 127–50.
66. Moellendorf, *Mobilizing Hope*, 21–30.
67. UNFCCC, *United Nations Framework Convention on Climate Change*, article 3.4.
68. Moellendorf, *Mobilizing Hope*, 26.
69. Darrel Moellendorf, 'A Right to Sustainable Development', *The Monist* 94, no. 3 (2011): 437.
70. Moellendorf, *Mobilizing Hope*, 74–85; *The Moral Challenge of Dangerous Climate Change*, 128–31.
71. Moellendorf, *The Moral Challenge of Dangerous Climate Change*, 133–4.
72. Henry Shue, *Climate Justice: Vulnerability and Protection* (Oxford University Press, 2014), 50–1.
73. Paul Baer et al., 'Greenhouse Development Rights: A Proposal for a Fair Global Climate Treaty', *Ethics, Place & Environment* 12, no. 3 (2009): 270.
74. Yoshiro Matsui, 'Some Aspects of the Principle of "Common But Differentiated Responsibilities"', *International Environmental Agreements* 2, no. 2 (2002): 151–70.
75. UNFCCC, *Kyoto Protocol* (1997), article 3.1.
76. UNFCCC, *Paris Agreement*, article 4.3 and 4.4.
77. Emilio L. La Rovere, Laura Valente de Macedo, and Kevin A. Baumert, 'The Brazilian Proposal on Relative Responsibility for Global Warming', in Kevin A. Baumert et al.

(eds) *Building on the Kyoto Protocol: Options for Protecting the Climate* (World Resources Institute, 2002), 157–74.

78. For expressions and defences of this principle, see Simon Caney, 'Cosmopolitan Justice, Responsibility, and Global Climate Change', *Leiden Journal of International Law* 18, no. 4 (2005): 752; Gardiner, 'Ethics and Global Climate Change', 580; Eric Neumayer, 'In Defence of Historical Accountability for Greenhouse Gas Emissions', *Ecological Economics* 33, no. 2 (2000): 185–92; Shue, 'Global Environment and International Inequality'.

79. For defences of the BPP, see Edward Page, 'Give It Up for Climate Change: A Defence of the Beneficiary Pays Principle', *International Theory* 4, no. 2 (2012): 300–30; Axel Gosseries, 'Historical Emissions and Free-Riding', *Ethical Perspectives* 11, no. 1 (2004): 36–60. For criticisms of it, see Simon Caney, 'Environmental Degradation, Reparations, and the Moral Significance of History', *Journal of Social Philosophy* 37, no. 3 (2006): 464–82; Lukas H. Meyer and Dominic Roser, 'Climate Justice and Historical Emissions', *Critical Review of International Social and Political Philosophy* 13, no. 1 (2010): 229–53. For an argument that the BPP is not better placed to avoid the problems associated with the PPP, see Laura Garcia-Portela, 'Backward-Looking Principles of Climate Justice: The Unjustified Move from the Polluter Pays Principle to the Beneficiary Pays Principle', *Res Publica* (forthcoming).

80. Shue, 'Global Environment and International Inequality', 537; Moellendorf, *The Moral Challenge of Dangerous Climate Change*, 173–7.

81. Edward Page, 'Distributing the Burdens of Climate Change', *Environmental Politics* 17, no. 4 (2008): 561.

82. Caney, 'Cosmopolitan Justice, Responsibility, and Global Climate Change', 763. For the interpretation of the principle that the least developed states should not bear significant costs as an exemption, see Alex McLaughlin, 'The Limit of Climate Justice: Unfair Sacrifice and Aggregate Harm', *Critical Review of International Social and Political Philosophy* 26, no. 6 (2023): 942–63.

83. Simon Caney, 'Climate Change and the Duties of the Advantaged', *Critical Review of International Social and Political Philosophy* 13, no. 1 (2010): 203–28; Baer et al., 'Greenhouse Development Rights'. Moellendorf is an exception here: he defends the APP and provides a more revisionary interpretation of the concept of responsibility that draws on the forward-looking 'social' conception of responsibility developed by Iris Marion Young. See Moellendorf, *The Moral Challenge of Dangerous Climate Change*, 154–7, 173–7; Iris Marion Young, 'Responsibility and Global Justice: A Social Connection Model', *Social Philosophy and Policy* 23, no. 1 (2006): 102–30.

84. Cass R. Sunstein, 'Incompletely Theorized Agreements', *Harvard Law Review* 108, no. 7 (1995): 1733–72.

85. Henry Shue, 'Historical Responsibility, Harm Prohibition, and Preservation Requirement: Core Practical Convergence on Climate Change', *Moral Philosophy and Politics* 2, no. 1 (2015): 8.

86. Stephen M. Gardiner, *A Perfect Moral Storm: The Ethical Tragedy of Climate Change* (Oxford University Press, 2011), 119.

87. IPCC, *Climate Change 2014: Synthesis Report*, 54.

88. Moellendorf, *Mobilizing Hope*, 25.

89. Luke Tomlinson, *Procedural Justice in the United Nations Framework Convention on Climate Change* (Springer, 2015), esp. 29–83.

90. J. Timmons Roberts and Bradley C. Parks, *A Climate of Injustice: Global Inequality, North-South Politics, and Climate Policy* (MIT Press, 2007), esp. 14–19.

91. UNFCCC, *Procedural, Institutional and Legal Matters. Rules of Procedure of the Conference of the Parties and Its Subsidiary Bodies* (1995), rule 42, available at https://unfccc.int/index.php/documents/1184.

92. David Victor, *Global Warming Gridlock: Creating More Effective Strategies for Protecting the Planet* (Cambridge University Press, 2011); Robyn Eckersley, 'Moving Forward in Climate Negotiations: Multilateralism or Minilateralism?' *Global Environmental Politics* 12, no. 2 (2012): 24–42.
93. Allen Buchanan, 'Institutional Legitimacy', in David Sobel, Peter Vallentyne, and Steven Wall (eds) *Oxford Studies in Political Philosophy* (Oxford University Press, 2018), 53–78.
94. Moellendorf, 'Taking UNFCCC Norms Seriously'.
95. Climate Action Tracker, 'Warming Projects Global Update' (2022), ii, available at https://climateactiontracker.org/documents/1094/CAT_2022-11-10_GlobalUpdate_COP27.pdf.
96. For an analysis, see Robert Faulkner, 'The Paris Agreement and the New Logic of International Climate Politics', *International Affairs* 92, no. 5 (2016): 1107–25.
97. Paul Bou-Habib, 'Climate Justice and Historical Responsibility', *Journal of Politics* 81, no. 4 (2019): 1298–310.
98. Bou-Habib, 'Climate Justice and Historical Responsibility', 1301.
99. For an alternative response, which focuses on the relationship between states' 'promotional duties' to put in place legitimate climate governance institutions and their own emissions, see Göran Duus-Otterström, 'Liability for Emissions Without Laws or Political Institutions', *Law and Philosophy* 42, no. 5 (2023): 461–86.

Chapter 9: The Future of Climate Displacement

1. Kyle Fruh, 'Anticipatory Moral Failure: The Case of Climate Change-Driven Displacement', *Journal of Social Philosophy* (forthcoming).
2. In this general approach, I am indebted to Darrel Moellendorf, *Mobilizing Hope: Climate Change and Global Poverty* (Oxford University Press, 2022).
3. John Dewey, *Human Nature and Conduct*, in Jo Anne Boydston (ed.) *The Middle Works of John Dewey: 1899–1924, Vol. 14* (South Illinois University Press, 1982), 4–227.
4. Dewey, *Human Nature and Conduct*, 133.
5. Dewey, *Human Nature and Conduct*, 134.
6. Deltef P. van Vuuren et al., 'The Representative Concentration Pathways: An Overview', *Climatic Change* 109 (2011): 5–31.
7. Keywan Riahi et al., 'RCP 8.5—A Scenario of Comparatively High Greenhouse Gas Emissions', *Climatic Change* 109 (2011): 33–57.
8. Zeke Hausfather and Glen P. Peters, 'Emissions—the "Business as Usual" Story Is Misleading', *Nature* 577 (2020): 618–20.
9. Christopher R. Schwalm, Spencer Glendon, and Philip B. Duffy, 'RCP8.5 Tracks Cumulative CO_2 Emissions', *Proceedings of the National Academy of Sciences* 117, no. 33 (2020): 19656–7; Pierre Friedlingstein et al., 'Uncertainties in CMIP5 Climate Projections Due to Carbon Cycle Feedbacks', *Journal of Climate* 27, no. 2 (2014): 511–26; P. Christensen, K. Gillingham, and W. Nordhaus, 'Uncertainty in Forecasts of Long-Run Economic Growth', *Proceedings of the National Academy of Sciences* 115, no. 21 (2018): 5409–14.
10. See Mark Lynas, *Our Final Warning: Six Degrees of Climate Emergency* (Harper–Collins, 2020).
11. Timothy Lenton et al., 'Tipping Elements in the Earth's Climate System', *Proceedings of the National Academy of Sciences* 105, no. 6 (2008): 1786–93.
12. Will Steffen et al., 'Trajectories of the Earth System in the Anthropocene', *Proceedings of the National Academy of Sciences* 115, no. 33 (2018): 8252–9.
13. Luke Kemp et al., 'Climate Endgame: Exploring Catastrophic Climate Change Scenarios', *Proceedings of the National Academy of Sciences* 119, no. 34 (2022): e108146119.

14. Philip K. Thornton et al., 'Agriculture and Food Systems in Sub-Saharan Africa in a 4C+ World', *Philosophical Transactions of the Royal Society of London A: Mathematical, Physical and Engineering Sciences* 369, no. 1934 (2011): 117–36.
15. Fai Fung, Ana Lopez, and Mark New, 'Water Availability in +2°C and +4°C Worlds', *Philosophical Transactions of the Royal Society of London A: Mathematical, Physical and Engineering Sciences* 369, no. 1934 (2011): 99–116.
16. Robert J. Nicholls et al., 'Sea-Level Rise and Its Possible Impacts Given a "Beyond 4C World" in the Twenty-First Century', *Philosophical Transactions of the Royal Society of London A: Mathematical, Physical and Engineering Sciences* 369, no. 1934 (2011): 161–81.
17. Moellendorf, *Mobilizing Hope*, 179–81.
18. Kemp et al., 'Climate Endgame', 3.
19. Carl-Friedrich Schleusser, 'Armed-Conflict Risks Enhanced by Climate-Related Disasters in Ethnically Fractionalized Countries', *Proceedings of the National Academy of Sciences* 113, no. 33 (2016): 9216–21.
20. Chi Xu et al., 'The Future of the Human Climate Niche', *Proceedings of the National Academy of Sciences* 117, no. 21 (2020): 11350–5.
21. François Gemenne, 'Climate-Induced Population Displacements in a 4°C+ World', *Philosophical Transactions of the Royal Society of London A: Mathematical, Physical and Engineering Sciences* 369, no. 1934 (2011): 182–95.
22. Reece Jones and Corey Johnson, 'Border Militarisation and the Re-Articulation of Sovereignty', *Transactions of the Institute of British Geographers* 41, no. 2 (2016): 187–200.
23. Robert McLeman, 'International Migration and Climate Adaptation in an Era of Hardening Borders', *Nature Climate Change* 9 (2019): 911–8.
24. Moellenorf, *Mobilizing Hope*, 181.
25. Desmond Tutu, 'We Do Not Need Climate Change Apartheid in Adaptation', in Kevin Watkins, *Human Development Report 2007/2008* (Palgrave Macmillan, 2007), 166. See also Olúfẹ́mi O. Táíwò, 'Climate Apartheid Is the Coming Police Violence Crisis', *Dissent*, 12 August 2020, available at https://www.dissentmagazine.org/online_articles/climate-apartheid-is-the-coming-police-violence-crisis; Ashley Dawson, *Extreme Cities: The Peril and Promise of Urban Life in the Age of Climate Change* (Verso, 2017), esp. 189–232.
26. Jennifer L. Rice, Joshua Long, and Anthony Levenda, 'Against Climate Apartheid: Confronting the Persistent Legacies of Expendability for Climate Justice', *Environment and Planning E: Nature and Space* 5, no. 2 (2022): 625–45.
27. Nancy Tuana, 'Climate Apartheid: The Forgetting of Race in the Anthropocene', *Critical Philosophy of Race* 7, no. 1 (2019): 6.
28. Paul Mohai, David Pellow, and J. Timmons Roberts, 'Environmental Justice', *Annual Review of Environment and Resources* 34 (2009): 405–30.
29. Olúfẹ́mi O. Táíwò, *Reconsidering Reparations* (Oxford University Press, 2022), esp. 14–68.
30. Arne Öhman, 'Fear and Anxiety: Overlaps and Dissociations', in Michael Lewis et al. (eds) *Handbook of Emotions* (The Guilford Press, 2008), 709–28.
31. Thomas Hobbes, *Leviathan* (Oxford University Press, 1998 [1651]); Judith Shklar, 'The Liberalism of Fear', in Nancy L. Rosenblum (ed.) *Liberalism and the Moral Life* (Harvard University Press, 1989), 21–38.
32. Alison McQueen, 'The Wages of Fear: Toward Fearing Well About Climate Change', in Mark Budolfson, Tristram McPherson, and David Plunkett (eds) *Philosophy and Climate Change* (Oxford University Press, 2021), 152–77.
33. Robert A.C. Ruiter, Charles Abraham, and Gerjo Kok, 'Scary Warnings and Rational Precautions: A Review of the Psychology of Fear Appeals', *Psychology and Health* 16, no. 6 (2001): 614.
34. McQueen, 'The Wages of Fear', 157–8; Martha Nussbaum, *The Monarchy of Fear: A Philosopher Looks at Our Political Crisis* (Oxford University Press, 2018), 27.

35. Catriona McKinnon, 'Runaway Climate Change: A Justice-Based Case for Precaution', *Journal of Social Philosophy* 40, no. 2 (2009): 187–203.
36. McQueen, 'The Wages of Fear', 158. On the relationship between emotions and rationality more generally, see Ronald de Sousa, *The Rationality of Emotions* (MIT Press, 1987).
37. McQueen, 'The Wages of Fear', 159–61. This criticism is made by those who denounce 'doomism' about climate politics. See, for example, Michael E. Mann, *The New Climate War: The Fight to Take Back Our Planet* (Scribe, 2021).
38. Saffron O'Neill and Sophie Nicholson-Cole, '"Fear Won't Do It": Promoting Positive Engagement with Climate Change through Visual and Iconic Representations', *Science Communication* 30, no. 3 (2009): 355–79; Saffron O'Neill et al., 'On the Use of Imagery for Climate Change Engagement', *Global Environmental Change* 23, no. 2 (2013): 413–21.
39. Caroline Hickman et al., 'Climate Anxiety in Children and Young People and Their Beliefs About Government Responses to Climate Change: A Global Survey', *Lancet Planetary Health* 5 (2021): e863–73.
40. McQueen, 'The Wages of Fear', 160–1.
41. Christine Tappolet argues that it is possible to fear for perfect strangers (Christine Tappolet, 'Emotion, Motivation, and Action: The Case of Fear', in Peter Goldie (ed.) *The Oxford Handbook of Philosophy of Emotion* (Oxford University Press, 2010)). But fear is nonetheless *typically* oriented towards threats to our own well-being, or the well-being of those with whom we share some affective connection, which is sufficient for my purposes here.
42. Nussbaum, *The Monarchy of Fear*, 22.
43. Ruiter, Abraham, and Kok, 'Scary Warnings and Rational Precautions', 614. McQueen argues that fear appeals need not be personal: 'we can feel fear on behalf or for those with whom we have some kind of moral or affective connection' (McQueen, 'The Wages of Fear', 155 n7). For my purposes, it is enough that the scope of fear is limited to threats to members of an 'in-group' with whom we share these kinds of bonds.
44. For the idea of framing effects, see Amos Tversky and Daniel Kahneman, 'The Framing of Decisions and the Psychology of Choice', *Science* 211, no. 4481 (1981): 453–8.
45. Nussbaum, *The Monarchy of Fear*, 26.
46. Nussbaum, *The Monarchy of Fear*; see also Corey Robin, *Fear: The History of a Political Idea* (Oxford University Press, 2004).
47. Betsy Hartmann, 'Rethinking Climate Refugees and Climate Conflict: Rhetoric, Reality, and the Politics of Policy Discourse', *Journal of International Development* 22, no. 2 (2010): 233–46; Giovanni Bettini, 'Climate Barbarians at the Gate? A Critique of Apocalyptic Narratives on "Climate Refugees"', *Geoforum* 45 (2013): 63–72; Andrew Baldwin, Chris Methmann, and Delf Rothe, 'Securitizing "Climate Refugees": The Futurology of Climate-Induced Migration', *Critical Studies on Security* 2, no. 2 (2014): 121–30; Gregory White, *Climate Change and Migration: Security and Borders in a Warming World* (Oxford University Press, 2011).
48. Chris Methmann, 'Visualising Climate Refugees: Race, Vulnerability, and Resilience in Global Liberal Politics', *International Political Sociology* 8, no. 4 (2014): 431; see also Andrew Baldwin, 'Racialisation and the Figure of the Climate Change Migrant', *Environment and Planning A: Economy and Space* 45, no. 6 (2013): 1474–90.
49. Gregory White, 'The "Securitization" of Climate-Induced Migration', in Kavita R. Khory (ed.), *Global Migration: Challenges in the Twenty-First Century* (Springer, 2012), 19.
50. David Miller, *Strangers in Our Midst: The Political Philosophy of Immigration* (Harvard University Press, 2016), 163.
51. Miller, *Strangers in Our Midst*, 209 n16.

52. Catherine Rioux, 'Hope: Conceptual and Normative Issues', *Philosophy Compass* 16, no. 3 (2021): e1274. Dissenting views see hope as a 'simple' rather than a 'compound' psychological state. See, e.g., Claudia Blöser, 'Hope as an Irreducible Concept', *Ratio* 32, no. 3 (2019): 205–14.
53. See, respectively, Philip Pettit, 'Hope and Its Place in the Mind', *Annals of the American Academy of Political and Social Science* 592 (2004): 152–65; Andrew Chignell, 'The Focus Theory of Hope', *The Philosophical Quarterly* 73, no. 1 (2023): 44–63; Adrienne M. Martin, *How We Hope: A Moral Psychology* (Princeton University Press, 2013). The 'third element' of hope also needs to solve another problem with the 'desire plus belief' model, which is that this model cannot by itself distinguish hope from other attitudes such as despair. To see this, consider that two people can both believe that an outcome is possible but highly unlikely (say, escaping from prison) and have the same desire for that outcome (say, the desire that escaping prison would be good), while one hopes for this outcome and the other despairs. For this point, see Luc Bovens, 'The Value of Hope', *Philosophy and Phenomenological Research* 59, no. 3 (1999): 667–81.
54. Hope may also have intrinsic value. On this, see Bovens, 'The Value of Hope'.
55. On the motivational role of hope in general, see Pettit, 'Hope and Its Place in the Mind'; Cheshire Calhoun, *Doing Valuable Time: The Present, the Future and Meaningful Living* (Oxford University Press, 2018), 68–89. On its motivational role in politics, see Jakob Huber, 'Defying Democratic Despair', *European Journal of Political Theory* 20, no. 4 (2021): 719–38; Darrel Moellendorf, 'Hope as a Political Virtue', *Philosophical Papers* 35, no. 3 (2006): 413–33.
56. For philosophical arguments to this effect, see Moellendorf, *Mobilizing Hope*; Catriona McKinnon, 'Climate Change: Against Despair', *Ethics & the Environment* 19, no. 1 (2014): 31–48. There is also some psychological evidence that supports the idea that hope can sustain commitment to climate action. See Simon M. Bury, Michael Wenzel, and Lydia Woodyatt, 'Against the Odds: Hope as an Antecedent of Support for Climate Change Action', *British Journal of Social Psychology* 59, no. 2 (2020): 289–310; Paul C. Stern, 'Hope and Fear in Climate Messages', *Nature Climate Change* 2 (2012): 572–3.
57. Darrel Moellendorf, 'Hope for Material Progress in the Anthropocene', in Claudia Blöser and Titus Stahl (eds) *The Moral Psychology of Hope* (Rowman and Littlefield, 2020), 251.
58. For the former view, see Chignell, 'The Focus Theory of Hope'; for the latter view, see Miriam Schleifer McCormick, 'Rational Hope', *Philosophical Explorations* 20, no. S1 (2017): 127–41.
59. Moellendorf, 'Hope for Material Progress in the Anthropocene', 251.
60. McCormick, 'Rational Hope'. McCormick argues that as the stakes of our hopes increase, the standards of evidence to which we should hold them decrease, because it is particularly important to sustain hope in conditions in which doing so can bear on the prospects for achieving a valuable outcome. Moellendorf understands the epistemic demands of rational hope in terms of the 'opportunity costs' of hoping (see Moellendorf, 'Hope for Material Progress in the Anthropocene', 253–4).
61. Moellendorf, *Mobilizing Hope*, 30–4; 'Hope for Material Progress in the Anthropocene', 252.
62. Gaia Vince, *Nomad Century: How to Survive the Climate Upheaval* (Allen Lane, 2022).
63. Vince, *Nomad Century*, 84–9, 107–20.
64. Vince, *Nomad Century*, 1–9.
65. Moellendorf, *Mobilizing Hope*, 125–8.
66. Christian Joppke, *Neoliberal Nationalism: Immigration and the Rise of the Populist Right* (Cambridge University Press, 2021).
67. International Energy Agency, 'Projected Costs of Generating Renewable Energy: 2020 Edition' (IEA Publications, 2020), 13, available at https://www.iea.org/reports/projected-

costs-of-generating-electricity-2020. See also Moellendorf, *Mobilizing Hope*, 124–5; Robert Pollin, *Greening the Global Economy* (MIT Press, 2015).
68. International Energy Agency, *World Energy Investment 2021* (IEA Publications, 2021), 15–7, available at https://www.iea.org/reports/world-energy-investment-2021.
69. Emily von Loesecke and Charlie Chermak, 'The Inflation Reduction Act: Impacts on Utilities and Power Producers', *Climate and Energy* 39, no. 7 (2023): 1–10.
70. Ronald Lee, 'The Demographic Transition: Three Centuries of Fundamental Change', *Journal of Economic Perspectives* 17, no. 4 (2003): 167–90.
71. For defence of 'replacement migration' as a response to the demographic transition, see Paul Bou-Habib, 'The Case for Replacement Migration', *Journal of Political Philosophy* 27, no. 1 (2019): 67–86.
72. Moellendorf, *Mobilizing Hope*, 130–3. For such a vision, see Kate Aronoff et al., *A Planet to Win: Why We Need a Green New Deal* (Verso, 2019).
73. T. Alexander Aleinikoff, 'The Unfinished Work of the Global Compact on Refugees', *International Journal of Refugee Law* 30, no. 4 (2018): 611–17; Walter Kälin, 'The Global Compact on Migration: A Ray of Hope for Disaster-Displaced Persons', *International Journal of Refugee Law* 30, no. 4 (2018): 664–7; François Crépaux, 'Towards a Mobile and Diverse World: "Facilitating Mobility" as a Central Objective of the Global Compact on Migration', *International Journal of Refugee Law* 30, no. 4 (2018): 650–6.
74. The Model International Mobility Commission, 'The Model International Mobility Convention', *Columbia Journal of Transnational Law* 56, no. 2 (2018): 342–465. On the benefits that accrue to compliant states on this model, see Michael W. Doyle, 'The Model International Mobility Convention', *Columbia Journal of Transnational Law* 56, no. 2 (2018): 229–32.
75. Dana R. Fisher and Sohana Nasrin, 'Climate Activism and Its Effects', *Wiley Interdisciplinary Reviews: Climate Change* 12, no. 1 (2021): e683.
76. Moellendorf, *Mobilizing Hope*, 129. Moellendorf draws on Martin Luther King's conception of mass mobilization in making this argument, but empirical research also supports the idea that successful large-scale political transformations depend on mass mobilization. See Erica Chenoweth and Maria Stephan, *Why Civil Resistance Works: The Strategic Logic of Nonviolent Conflict* (Columbia University Press, 2011).
77. For this reason, Andreas Malm has recently argued that the climate movement should abandon its commitment to non-violence and embrace more confrontational tactics such as sabotage. See Andreas Malm, *How to Blow Up a Pipeline: Learning to Fight in a World on Fire* (Verso, 2021).
78. On the *sans-papiers* movement, see Anne McNevin, 'Political Belonging in a Neoliberal Age: The Struggle of the Sans-Papiers', *Citizenship Studies* 10, no. 2 (2006): 135–51. On the DREAMers's movement, see Matthew Lister, '"Dreamers" and Others: Immigration Protests, Enforcement and Civil Disobedience', *APA Newsletter on Hispanic/Latino Issues in Philosophy* 17, no. 2 (2018): 15–7.
79. For an argument that such policies are best interpreted as an act of resistance, see Shelley Wilcox, 'How Can Sanctuary Policies Be Justified?' *Public Affairs Quarterly* 33, no. 2 (2019): 89–113.
80. Maurice Stierl, 'A Sea of Struggle—Activist Border Interventions in the Mediterranean Sea', *Citizenship Studies* 20, no. 5 (2016): 561–78.
81. John Dewey, *Reconstruction in Philosophy*, in Jo Anne Boydston (ed.) *The Middle Works of John Dewey, 1899–1924: Volume 12* (South Illinois University Press, 1982), 181–2.

Index

For the benefit of digital users, indexed terms that span two pages (e.g., 52–53) may, on occasion, appear on only one of those pages.
'n.' after a paragraph number indicates the endnote number.

A
Abizadeh, Arash, 205 n.84
activism, 1, 144–145, 180, 188
   climate action and hope, 251 n.56
   mass mobilization, 188
   non-violence *vs* confrontational tactics, 188, 252 n.77
Adger, Neil, 45
Afghanistan, 127
agent-based modelling, 8, 165
Åland Islands, 83
Alaskan communities (Native)
   climate change impact on, 1–2, 35
   hunting, 35, 37, 40–41, 44
   sea-level rise, 1, 35
   Shishmaref, 1–2, 35, 37
   shoreline erosion, 1–2, 35, 44, 55
   see also community relocation: Shishmaref
Aleinikoff, T. Alexander, 111, 122
anticipatory displacement, 9–11, 36, 138
   anticipatory forms of involuntary movement, 138–139
   forms of, 11
   harm of, 139
   see also climate displacement contexts
AOSIS (Alliance of Small Island States), 64
Armstrong, Chris, 145
Asia Development Bank, 89–90
asylum
   asylum claiming, 112, 123–125
   asylum provision and refugee regime, 110, 225 n.27
   asylum seeking, dangerous routes to 123–126
   asylum seeking and people smugglers, 123–126
   function of asylum: expressing condemnation of 'outlaw' states, 110–111, 225 n.32
   giving priority to those in need, 111–112
   providing safe and legal routes to, 123, 125, 130
   refugee movement and asylum provision, 110–113, 225 n.27, 226 n.47
   right to seek asylum, 125–126
   see also refugee movement
Australia, 24, 80, 82–84, 123–124

B
Bangladesh, 127
Ban Ki Moon, 114–115
Barnett, Jon, 89–90
Bauböck, Rainer, 50–51, 77–78, 213 n.86
Beaton, Eilidh, 112
Betts, Alexander, 123, 128, 224 n.22
Biermann, Frank, 20, 22, 23–26, 29–30
Bismarck, Otto von, 163
Black, Richard, 6–7, 89–90, 142–143
Blake, Michael, 213 n.91, 231 n.114
Boas, Ingrid, 20, 22, 23–26, 29–30
Bolivia, 136
Bose, Pablo S., 74
Bou-Habib, Paul, 174–175
Brake, Elizabeth, 39
Bronen, Robin, 55–56
Buchanan, Allen, 67, 69, 75–76
Byravan, Sujatha, 20–23, 30

C
Canada, 102
   Refugee Resettlement Program, 125
Caney, Simon, 168
Capisani, Simona, 12, 195 n.64
Caplan, Robert, 7
Carens, Joseph, 27, 107
Carroll, Lewis, 9
Central African Republic, 127
Central America, 106, 118
Chad, 1, 127
Cherem, Max 110
clean energy, 169–170, 186–187
climate apartheid, 180

climate change
  accelerating nature of, 14–15
  as *anthropogenic*, 4, 14–15, 119, 142
  development and, 168–169, 172
  impact of, 1, 37, 86–87, 106
  internal displacement and, 131–132, 142, 151, 153
  as risk multiplier, 163–164
  'social complexity' of, 174
  as structural injustice, 161
climate change adaptation
  adaptation costs/finance, 99–100, 103, 157–158, 166, 240 n.18
  benefits of, 157–158
  community relocation as adaptation to climate change, 36, 61–62
  definition, 88
  disaster displacement and, 143
  duty to promote climate change adaptation, 96, 103
  fairness in sharing the costs of adaptation, 103–104
  internal displacement and, 140, 144
  labour migration as adaptation to climate change, 17, 86, 88, 99, 100–101, 104–105
  labour migration policy as tool of climate change adaptation, 17, 87, 89–90, 93–94, 96–98, 104–105
  limits to, 144
  maladaptation, 144
  poverty and, 88
  see also in situ adaptation; resilience
climate change mitigation, 145, 157–158
  climate change mitigation duties, 14–15
  poverty and, 169, 172
  states' climate mitigation duties, 18, 129
climate displacement, 1–2
  as *anthropogenic*, 154, 175
  climate change/displacement interaction, 4–5, 19
  failure to address crises of displacement, 4
  international governance and, 19
  modelling climate displacement, 165
  'moderate' scenario of, 14–15
  as moral challenge, 3–4, 9, 11, 13, 19, 176
  moral terrain of, 4–5, 8–9, 15, 16, 176
  political significance of, 3–4, 19
  quantifying climate displacement, 6, 164–165
  as threat to national security, 240 n.18
  see also displaced, the; pluralist theory of climate displacement
climate displacement contexts, 9, 16, 176
  anticipatory/reactive displacement, 9–11
  community relocation, 11
  internal displacement, 11–12
  labour migration, 11–12
  refugee movement, 11–12
  territorial instability and, 12
  territorial sovereignty, 11
  see also anticipatory displacement; community relocation; internal displacement; labour migration; reactive displacement; refugee movement; territorial sovereignty
climate displacement costs, 18, 154, 175
  adaptation costs/finance, 99–100, 103, 157–158, 166, 240 n.18
  APP ('Ability to Pay Principle'), 103, 129, 170–171
  BPP ('Beneficiary Pays Principle'), 103, 170, 171
  climate refugee treaty and sharing costs, 22
  complexity of climate displacement, 18, 154–155, 161, 175
  'core practical convergence', 103–104
  disagreement about states' climate duties, 18, 154–155, 161, 167, 175
  displacement risk, holding responsible for, 33–34, 162–165, 167, 172, 175
  distributed according to hybrid approach, 103
  equal burdens principle, 129, 152
  fairness in sharing the costs of adaptation, 103–104
  high-income states, required to bear the lion's share of costs, 22, 103–104, 171, 172–173, 215 n.14
  IDP protection costs, 146–147, 150–151, 153
  IDP protection costs, sharing between states, 146–147, 152
  insurance model of responsibility, 162–167, 175
  labour migration, 215 n.14
  LDCs (Least Developed Countries), 103–104, 127, 172–173
  non-financial costs, 239 n.1
  non-material costs, 232 n.127
  outcome responsibility, 160–161
  PPP ('Polluter Pays Principle'), 170–171
  remedial responsibility, 157–158
  responsibility principle, 18, 33–34, 103–104, 129, 152–155, 157, 175, 199 n.51
  sharing costs between states, 18, 28, 103, 128, 130, 154, 157–158
  state inaction, 160–161
  states as primary bearers of responsibility, 158–162, 165–167, 172–175
  unfairness in distribution of costs, 87, 101, 104–105, 126–129, 151, 165–166, 171
  see also refugee protection costs; responsibility

INDEX 245

climate displacement dynamics, 5, 19, 176
  agent-based modelling, 8, 165
  climate change/displacement
    interaction, 4–5, 19
  complexity of climate displacement, 7–9,
    16, 19–20, 25, 26, 28–29, 31, 34, 118,
    120–122, 176
  complexity of climate displacement and
    climate displacement costs, 18, 154–155,
    161, 175
  consensus view, 26, 28
  heterogeneity of climate displacement, 8–9,
    16, 19–20, 25, 26, 29–31, 34, 176
  maximalist view, 25–26
  multiple causality of climate
    displacement, 7–8, 25, 28, 90
  political views, 25–26
  social injustice and climate displacement, 8
  structural constraints and climate
    displacement, 28, 138, 142–143, 166
  traditional approaches, 26
  unpredictable nature of climate change
    impacts, 29–30
climate displacement future, 18, 177–178
  activism, 180, 188
  border policies and migration, 179–180,
    182–184, 186, 187–188
  'business-as-usual' scenario, 178–179
  climate apartheid, 180
  fear and, 178, 188–189
  hope and, 18, 184
  RCP 2.6, 178–179
  RCP 8.5, 178–179
  RCPs ('Representative Concentration
    Pathways'), 178–179
  uncertain future, 7–8, 18, 177
  'worst-case' scenario, 14–15, 18, 177–180, 183
  see also fear; hope
climate policy (global)
  CBDR-RC ('common but differenti-
    ated responsibilities and respective
    capabilities'), 170–171
  climate change mitigation, 157–158, 172
  'dangerous climate change', 169, 171–172
  disagreement in global climate policy,
    157, 167
  fairness in, 172–175
  global carbon budget, 159, 168–169
  'incompletely theorized agreement'
    about, 171
  'pillars' of, 157–158
  'right to sustainable development', 169–172
  states and, 158, 160
  temperature targets, 168–169, 173–174

  see also climate change adaptation; emissions
    reductions; temperature targets
climate refugees
  climatic/non-climatic displacement
    distinction, 27–29
  climate refugee treaty and 'climate refugee'
    concept, 19–20, 23, 27–32, 34
  as legal status, 20, 23, 24–26, 33
  media and, 5
  misunderstandings on, 5
  not recognized as refugees, 23–24
  politics of fear and, 182
  race and, 7, 182
  stigma/moral failing associated with,
    24–25, 182
  term as 'inaccurate and misleading', 23–24
  term as insulting or degrading for those
    displaced by climate impacts, 24
  under-/over-inclusion, 29
  see also environmental refugees; refugee
climate refugee treaty, 20, 34, 107
  Biermann and Boas' proposal, 20, 22, 23–26,
    29–30
  Byravan and Rajan's proposal, 20–23, 30
  climate displacement, concept of, 27
  'climate refugee', concept of, 19–20, 23,
    27–32, 34
  complexity of climate displacement
    and, 9, 16, 19–20, 25, 26, 28–29,
    31, 34
  critique of, 9, 16, 19–22, 25–26, 165–166
  Docherty and Gianni' proposal, 20–21, 23
  failure to treat like cases alike, 16, 19–20,
    22–23, 26–29, 31, 33–34
  failure to treat relevantly different cases
    differently, 16, 19–20, 22–23, 26–27,
    29–31, 33, 34
  heterogeneity of climate displacement and, 9,
    16, 19–20, 25, 26, 29–31, 34
  idealized picture of climate displacement, 9,
    16, 19–20, 22–23, 26
  moral arbitrariness of, 16, 19–20, 22–23, 26,
    31–34
  pluralist theory of climate displacement
    and, 19–20, 31, 34
  popularity/attractiveness of, 19–22, 34
  practical irrelevance of, 9, 19–20, 31
  'protection gap' related to climate
    displacement, 21–22, 33, 34
  responsibility issues, 22, 28, 33, 155, 165–166
Cohen, G.A., 239 n.4
Cohen, Roberta, 133–134, 148, 149
Cold War, 111
Cole, Phillip, 27

Collier, Paul, 128
Colombia, 127
community relocation, 16–17, 61–62
  as adaptation to climate change, 36, 61–62
  as anticipatory displacement, 11, 36, 138–139
  basic territorial interests and, 37–39, 44, 61–62
  circumstances of relocation, 50–51
  collective goods, 43–46
  communitarian model of relocation, 16–17, 36–37, 46
  communitarian model of relocation: shortcomings, 16–17, 36–37, 47–49, 62
  conservation projects and, 145–146
  cultural loss/cultural devastation, 40–41, 202 n.25
  definition, 11
  deliberative justification, 51–54, 62
  democratic model of relocation, 16–17, 36–37, 49, 56, 62
  democratic model of relocation: advantages, 16–17, 54
  disruption of social networks and practices, 41–42, 45, 61–62
  effective right of exit, 53–54, 62
  empowered participatory governance, 60–62
  expertise problem, 16–17, 36–37, 56–58, 61, 62
  as failure of adaptation, 201 n.10
  Fiji, 51–52
  funding, 35–36, 39
  injustices, 38, 42, 56
  in situ adaptation, 11, 36, 38–40, 43–44, 55–56, 58–59, 61–62, 202 n.17
  institutional framework, 55–58, 62
  justice in adaptation, 46–48
  Kiribati, 24
  as last-resort option, 58–59
  loss and damage, 201 n.10
  market model of relocation, 16–17, 36–37, 42
  market model of relocation: shortcomings, 16–17, 36–37, 42, 43–45, 62
  political equality principle, 51, 54, 62
  practice-based interests and, 37, 43, 44–45, 47, 49, 62
  procedural dimensions of, 36
  procedural justice, 36, 41–42
  relocation decisions, 16–17, 36, 43, 47–54, 56, 57, 59–60, 205 n.84
  scale problem, 16–17, 36–37, 58–62, 207 n.115
  USA, 38–39, 42–43
community relocation: Shishmaref (Alaska), 41, 45, 47–49, 55
  challenges, 54–55, 61
  expertise and local knowledge, 57
  Iñupiaq village, 16–17
  Kivalina village, 35–36
  Newtok village, 35–36
  Newtok Planning Group, 35–36
  NRCS (Natural Resources Conservation Service), 55
  scale of relocation, 58–59
  Shishmaref Erosion and Relocation Coalition, 35–36, 45, 55
  Tin Creek site, 55–56
  USACE (United States Army Corps of Engineers), 55
  West Tin Creek Hills site, 55
conflict
  climate change, direct/indirect role in driving conflict, 115
  climate change and conflict: 'streetlight effect', 228 n.71
  Darfur, 114–115
  economic drivers of, 115
  'environmental conflict', 7
  internal displacement and civil conflict, 137
  political conflict, 3
  refugee movement and political conflict, 114–117, 129–130
  sociopolitical drivers of, 115
  Somalia, 2–3
Consibee, Molly, 121
Cook Islands, 83
coral bleaching, 3, 11, 63
Cortez Barrera, Delmira de Jesús, 106, 118
Cuba, 143

D

Dakota Access Pipeline (Standing Rock), campaign against, 188
'dangerous climate change', 169–172
Darfur, 114–115
De Guchteniere, Paul, 25–26
De Léon, Jason, 124–125
Deng, Francis, 133–134, 149
Denmark, 83
De Shalit, Avner, 67–68, 212 n.73
determinism, 115
  environmental determinism, 5–7, 116–117
  natural determinism, 5–6
development
  climate change and, 168–169, 172
  emissions and poverty-alleviating development, 168–170
  'Greenhouse Development Rights' framework, 169–170

development (*Continued*)
  HDI (Human Development Index), 169–170
  'right to sustainable development', 169–172
Dewey, John, 13–14, 178, 188–189
Dietrich, Frank, 70–71, 73, 211 n.63
disaster displacement
  climate change adaptation, 143
  climate change/disaster displacement relationship, 131–132, 142, 144
  complexity of, 142–144
  disaster risk reduction, 140, 143
  extreme weather events and, 131–132, 142
  IDP and, 118–119
  as internal displacement, 118–119
  internal displacement and, 131–132, 142, 144
  refugee movement and, 118–119, 129–130
  state and, 137
disasters, 142
  Cuba, disaster management system, 143
  extreme weather events and, 142
  resilience and, 131–132, 142–143
  as social phenomena, 142–143
  vulnerability and, 142–143, 151
displaced, the
  climatic/non-climatic displacement distinction, 27–29
  'right to a liveable locality', 12
  see also climate displacement; duties to the displaced
Docherty, Bonnie, 20–21, 23
DRC (Democratic Republic of the Congo), 127
drought, 116, 118
  East Africa, 119
  Ethiopia (rural), 86
  impact of, 1
  labour migration and, 86, 92–93
  risk-management strategies, 86
  Sahel, the, 1
  Somalia, 2, 119
Drydyk, Jay, 74
duties to the displaced, 4–5, 19, 154, 157, 164
  'anticipatory moral failure', 14–15
  climate change mitigation duties, 14–15
  IDP, duties owed to, 139–141, 151, 152
  institutions relied on for discharging duties to, 4, 19
  moral duties owed to, 4, 12
  reaching net zero emissions, 14–15
  states' climate mitigation duties, 18

E
earthquakes, 147
El Salvador, 106, 118

emissions reduction, 64, 85, 158, 169, 170, 173–174, 178–179, 186–188
  decoupling emissions from economic growth, 168–169
  NDC ('Nationally Determined Contribution'), 170, 173
  reaching net zero emissions, 14–15
  see also climate policy
environment
  'environmental conflict', 7
  environmental determinism, 5–7, 116–117
  environmental drivers of displacement, 121
  'environmental persecution', 121
  environmental refugees, 6–7, 23–24
  see also climate refugees
Environmental Justice Foundation, 20–21
erosion: shoreline erosion, 1–3, 35, 44, 55, 63
equality/inequality
  equal burdens principle, 129, 152
  political equality principle, 51, 54, 62
  proximate inequalities, 78–79
Ethiopia, 86, 127
  drought, 86
  labour migration, 17, 86, 92–93
extreme weather events, 3, 9–10, 25, 118–119
  as aberrations from otherwise stable climatic conditions, 142
  internal displacement and, 12, 142, 153
  Pakistan, 2
  'probabilistic event attribution', 142
  see also flooding; storms; typhoons; wildfires

F
Faroe Islands, 83
fear
  'climate anxiety', 181
  climate displacement future and, 178, 188–189
  'fear appeals', 180–182
  politics of fear, 181–184
  see also climate displacement future
Felli, Romain, 100–101
Ferracioli, Luara, 123
Fiji, 51–52
Fine, Sarah, 107
Finland, 83
Fitzgerald, David Scott, 125
flooding, 2, 12, 37, 131–132, 142, 153
food (in)security
  climate change and, 87, 117, 118
  Ethiopia, food insecurity, 86
  Somalia, food crisis and famine, 3, 119
fossil-fuel energy/economies, 3–4, 160–161, 171, 186–188

Foster, Michelle, 228 n.73
Fragile States Index, 127
Fridays for Future, 188
Fruh, Kyle, 14–15
Fullilove, Mindy, 41
Fung, Archon, 60–61

G
Gammeltoft-Hansen, Thomas, 123
Gemenne, François, 20, 199 n.51
Getachew, Adom, 69
Gianni, Tyler, 20–21, 23
Gibney, Matthew, 127
global citizenship, 185
Global Compact on Migration, 187–188
Global Compact for Refugees, 187–188
globalization, 66–67
Global North, 96, 171, 180, 240 n.18
　costs of refugee protection, 128–129
　deterrence paradigm in international refugee policy, 123–124, 126, 127
Global South, 7, 128, 129, 180
global warming, 6, 168, 183
Goodin, Robert, 163
governance
　climate displacement and international governance, 19
　empowered participatory governance, 60–62
　'failed governance', 117
　internal displacement governance regime, 132–133, 144, 149–152
　intra-state territorial autonomy and self-governance, 82–84
　legitimate climate-governance institutions, 174
　self-determination and self-governance, 66–69, 76, 77–79, 81, 84
Green Climate Fund, 99–100
Greenland, 83
Green New Deal, 187
Guatemala, 118
Gulf states, 102

H
Haddad, Emma, 113–114
Hasina, Sheikh, 20–21
Hathaway, James, 108, 128, 137, 224 n.15
Hawai'i, 83–84, 125, 147
Hirschman, Albert O., 53
Hobbes, Thomas, 180–181
Holland, Breena, 46–47, 49–50
Honduras, 118
Honoré, Tony, 240 n.5
hope, 184
　climate action and, 251 n.56
　hopeful vision of future of climate displacement, 18, 185–189
　'hope-makers', 184–186
　as motivational force, 184
　'opportunity costs' of, 251 n.60
　rational hope, 184–185
　see also climate displacement future
Horn of Africa, 2–3, 119
Hulme, Mike, 25–26
human rights, 10–11, 27
　IDP and, 133–137
　international order and, 113–114, 148
　refugee movement and, 109, 113–114, 117, 119, 129–130
　'right to stay' as human right, 94–95
　self-determination and, 69–70
　state and, 113–114, 129–130, 134–137, 147, 152
Hume, David 50
Huntington, Ellsworth, 5–6

I
Ibrahim, Hindou Oumarou, 1
ideal theory/ideal theorists, 15–16, 196 n.71
　idealized picture of climate displacement, 9, 16, 19–20, 22–23, 26
IDMC (Internal Displacement Monitoring Centre), 131–132
IDP (internally displaced person), 12
　'complementary protection' status, 136–137
　concept of, 132–133
　disaster displacement and, 118–119
　duties owed to, 139–141, 151, 152
　human rights and, 133–137
　involuntariness, 133–134, 136, 137
　involuntariness, narrow view of, 138–139, 141
　involuntariness and autonomous action, 137–138
　non-alienage, 133–134
　normative status of, 17–18, 132, 133–134, 138, 141, 152
　occupancy rights, 139–140, 144–146, 153
　as refugee, 118–119, 134, 137, 142
　refugee/IDP distinction, 113–114, 134–136, 147, 152
　rights of, 133, 136–137, 140–141, 149, 152
　right to background of relative stability restored quickly and effectively, 140–141, 152
　right to choose freely between return, local integration, or resettlement, 141, 152

IDP (internally displaced person), (*Continued*)
  right to reduction of risks of displacement to tolerable levels, 140, 152
  status of, 17–18, 132, 133, 137, 139–140, 150
  see also IDP, international legal frameworks; IDP protection; internal displacement
IDP, international legal frameworks
  1998 *Guiding Principles on Internal Displacement*, 132–134, 138–139, 145, 146, 148, 149–151
  2006 *Great Lakes Protocol*, 132–133, 150
  2009 *Kampala Convention*, 132–133
  2010 IASC *Framework on Durable Solutions for Internally Displaced Persons* (Inter-Agency Standing Committee), 132
  soft/hard law nature of, 149–151, 153
IDP protection, 137–139, 144, 152
  as charity, 148–149
  climate change and international protection of IDPs, 132, 146, 152
  costs of, 146–147, 150–151, 153
  costs sharing between states, 146–147, 152
  as domestic issue, 146–148, 151, 152
  humanitarian character of, 17–18, 132, 149–150
  internalist bias in, 17–18, 151
  responsibility issues, 147–148, 153
  state capacity and, 147–149
IMF (International Monetary Fund), 147
in situ adaptation, 117
  community relocation and, 11, 36, 38–40, 43–44, 55–56, 58–59, 61–62, 202 n.17
  internal displacement, 140
  labour migration and *in situ* adaptation opportunities, 17, 87, 98–101, 104–105
  sea-level rise, 58–59, 85
  state financing of, 166
internal displacement, 12, 17–18, 131–132, 152–153
  Bolivia, 136
  causes of, 133, 138–139, 151
  civil conflict and, 137
  climate change and, 131–132, 142, 151, 153
  climate change adaptation and, 140, 144
  conservation projects/'green-grabbing' and, 144–146, 153
  cross-border/internal displacement distinction, 118–119
  disasters/disaster displacement, 131–132, 142, 144
  external causes of, 151
  extreme weather events and, 12, 142, 153
  Hurricane Katrina (New Orleans), 143
  in situ adaptation, 140

internal displacement governance regime, 132–133, 144
internal displacement governance regime: dysfunctions in, 132, 149–152
lack of international cooperation in tackling displacement, 132
moral concerns, 134–135
political theory on, 132
proposed reforms, 132, 150–151, 153
as reactive displacement, 11, 138, 139–140, 145–146, 152
return, local integration, and resettlement as 'durable solutions' to, 141
Typhoon Haiyan (the Philippines), 131–132, 142
see also disaster displacement; IDP
international order
  climate change and, 3–4, 64, 157
  climate change and international protection of IDPs, 132, 146, 152
  climate displacement and international governance, 19
  failure of international cooperation, 132, 186
  human rights and, 113–114, 148
  need of transformation, 177
  political inertia and short-termism, 3–4
  refugee movement (regime) and international community, 113–114, 117, 119–120, 122, 129–130
  Westphalian international order, 66, 209 n.24
  see also climate policy
intra-state territorial autonomy, 17, 64–65, 72, 79, 85
  challenges, 84–85
  constituent units of federations, 83–84
  'federacy'/'asymmetric federalism', 83
  identifying suitable territories, 82–83
  models of, 83–84
  self-determination and, 64–65, 72, 79–82, 84, 85
  self-governance and, 82–84
  self-governance in 'free association' with another state, 83
  see also territorial sovereignty
IOM (International Organisation for Migration), 146
IPCC (Intergovernmental Panel on Climate Change), 7–8, 28, 63, 160, 165, 172, 178

J
Japan, 147
Johnson, Craig, 46–47, 49–50
Jones, Will, 128–129

justice
  climate change as structural injustice, 161
  community relocation and injustices, 38, 42, 56
  community relocation and procedural justice, 36, 41–42
  corrective justice, 164
  duties of justice, 96, 99, 100, 147–148
  duties of justice/duties of charity distinction, 95–96, 147
  duties to the poor as duties of justice, 95–96
  global economic order and duties of justice, 220 n.68
  justice in adaptation, 46–48, 97–98
  procedural injustices, 173
  rectificatory justice, 79–80
  refugee movement and injustices, 120
  social injustice and climate displacement, 8
  vulnerability to climate displacement and injustice, 161

K
Kälin, Walter, 150, 194 n.62
Khader, Serene J., 93
King, Martin Luther, 252 n.76
Kiribati, 3, 24
  'migration with dignity' policy, 24
  relocation to New Zealand and Australia, 24, 80
  sea-level rise, 17, 63
Kolers, Avery, 211 n.54
Kuokkanen, Rauna, 66–67
Kymlicka, Will, 47–48, 67
Kyoto Protocol, 170

L
labour migration, 12, 17, 86–88, 104–105
  abuse/violation of migrants' rights, 101–103
  as adaptation to climate change, 17, 86, 88, 99, 100–101, 104–105
  advantages, 90–91
  as anticipatory displacement, 11, 138–139
  'brain drain'/'care drain', 92
  Canada, 102
  as cost-effective adaptation alternative, 99–100, 104–105
  discrimination and, 9–10
  downsides/criticism of, 91–94, 100–101
  droughts and, 86, 92–93
  duty to promote labour migration, 99, 103, 104–105
  effects on domestic workers, 91–92
  Ethiopia, 17, 86, 92–93
  expanding opportunities for, 17, 87–90, 95
  fair terms for labour migration as climate adaptation, 100
  forms of, 12
  from low- to high-income states, 88–91
  gendered dynamics of, 92–93
  Gulf states, 102
  in situ adaptation opportunities, 17, 87, 98–101, 104–105
  international labour migration, 87–88
  intra-state labour migration, 87–88, 215–216 nn.14–15
  labour migration policy as conditional, 91–92, 98, 99, 104–105, 218 n.44
  labour migration policy as tool of climate change adaptation, 17, 87, 89–90, 93–94, 96–98, 104–105
  local costs of, 91–92
  moral concerns, 94–95, 98, 99, 102
  over-inclusivity, 90–91
  poverty and, 88–91, 93–97, 99, 101–103
  receiving states, facilitating mobility for labour migrants, 17, 87–90, 92
  receiving states, restrictive terms for labour migrants, 101–105
  resilience and, 89–90, 93–94, 99, 104–105
  right to stay, 93
  rural–urban migration, 215 n.14
  sharing costs between states, 103–104, 215 n.14
  temporary and 'circular' labour migration, 88–90, 101–103
  USA, 92–93, 101–102
  voluntary/forced migration and acceptable alternatives to labour migration, 97–98, 101, 102–103, 137–138, 220 n.73
  as 'win-win' or 'triple-win' strategy, 91, 100–101
  see also remittances; right to stay
La Niña event, 3
LDCs (Least Developed Countries), 103–104, 127, 172–173
Lear, Jonathan, 40
Lister, Matthew, 110, 121–122, 229 n.92
Locke, John, 70–71

M
Maldives, the, 3, 17, 63
Malm, Andreas, 252 n.77
Margalit, Avishai, 65
Marino, Elizabeth, 41
Marshall Islands, 3
Mayer, Robert, 102–103
McAdam, Jane, 27, 29, 30
McCormick, Miriam Schleifer, 251 n.60

McLeman, Robert, 165
McQueen, Alison, 180–181, 249 n.43
media and climate refugees, 5
Méndez, María José, 118
methodology, 13
  normative theorizing, 5, 24
  methods of inquiry and morals, 13–14
  'moderate' scenario of climate displacement, 14–15, 177
  problem-based approach, 13–16, 176, 177
migration
  economic explanations of, 5–7
  environment, 'disappearance' of, as causal factor in explanations of migration, 5–6
  environment as causal factor in explanations of, 6
  forced/voluntary migration, 10–11
  modernity and social migration, 5–6
  political causes of forced migration, 5–6
  sociological theory of, 9–10, 138
  undocumented migration, 106, 125, 126, 188
  USA and migration as threat, 7, 188
migrants
  distinction between voluntary/'economic' migrants and forced migrants/refugees, 10–11
  economic migrants, 10–11
  migrant caravans, 106
Milanovic, Branko, 101–102
Miller, David, 10–11, 112, 155–156, 160, 183–184
Model International Mobility Convention, 187–188
Moellendorf, Darrel, 169–170, 172, 179–180, 184–188, 240 n.18, 246 n.83, 251 n.60
Moore, Alfred, 58
Moore, Margaret, 139–140
morals/morality
  climate displacement, moral terrain of, 4–5, 8–9, 15, 16, 176
  climate displacement as moral challenge, 3–4, 9, 11, 13, 19, 176
  'conventional view' of the morality of immigration, 107
  hope and, 184–185
  labour migration, moral concerns, 94–95, 98, 99, 102
  methods of inquiry and, 13–14
  moral duties owed to the displaced, 4, 12
  moral theories, 13–14
  political morality of climate displacement, 4–5
  resilience and moral reasoning, 155

self-determination, moral concerns, 68–70, 81–82, 85
territorial sovereignty proposals, moral concerns, 73–74, 79, 81–82
Myers, Norman, 6–25

N
Nansen Initiative, 32–33
Nasheed, Mohamed, 3
ND-GAIN Index (Notre Dame Global Adaptation Initiative), 86, 127
New Zealand, 24, 83
Nine, Cara, 70–76, 78
Niue Islands, 83
Norway: *Climate Change and Displacement in the 21st Century*, 32–33
Nussbaum, Martha, 46–47, 181–182

O
OAU (Organisation of African Unity): 1969 *Convention Governing the Specific Aspects of Refugee Problems in Africa*, 109, 111, 123
Oberman, Kieran, 94–98, 111–112, 226 n.40
Ödalen, Jörgen, 75–77
OHCHR (Office of the High Commissioner on Human Rights), 146
Olsaretti, Serena, 98
Orchard, Phil, 149
Ostrom, Elinor, 45–46
Ottonelli, Valeria, 97–98
Owen, David, 113, 197 n.7, 226 n.54

P
Pacific, the
  coral bleaching, 3
  sea-level rise, 3, 24
  talanoa deliberative practice, 51–52
Page, Edward, 46
Pakistan, 2, 127
Parekh, Serena, 120, 123–124
Paris Agreement, 170, 173–174
Patten, Alan, 39–40
Pécoud, Antoine, 25–26
Pelling, Mark, 216 n.17
Penz, Peter, 74, 164
Philippines, the, 131–132, 142
Piguet, Etienne, 25–26
pluralist theory of climate displacement, 16, 19–20, 176
  climate change/displacement interaction, 4–5
  climate displacement normativity, 176
  climate refugees treaty, alternative to, 19–20, 31, 34

contexts/background conditions of climate displacement, 14–15
disaggregation of climate displacement, 32–33, 176
integration of climate displacement with other forms of displacement, 32–33, 176
'internal' theory, 15
moral terrain of climate displacement, 4–5, 176
problem-based approach to normative theorizing, 13–16, 176, 177
provisional nature of, 14, 177
responsibility rationale, 33–34, 155, 176
revisionary implications, 177
Posner, Eric, 101–102
poverty, 244 n.56
  climate change and, 87–88, 117–118
  climate change adaptation and, 88
  climate mitigation and, 169, 172
  duties to the poor as duties of justice, 95–96
  emissions and poverty-alleviating development, 168–170
  labour migration and, 88–91, 93–97, 99, 101–103
  poverty reduction/alleviation, 88–91, 94, 95–96
  poverty traps, 87, 117
Price, Matthew, 110–111, 225 n.27, n.32

Q
Quong, Jonathan, 73

R
race, 8
  climate refugees and, 7, 182
  vulnerability and, 143
Rajan, Sudhir Chella, 20–23, 30
Ravenstein, Ernst, 5
Rawls, John, 26–27, 50
Raz, Joseph, 65, 137–138
reactive displacement, 9–11, 140
  forms of, 11
  harm of, 139
  internal displacement as, 11, 138, 139–140, 145–146, 152
  see also climate displacement contexts
refugee
  'alienage condition', 108, 112, 114
  border policies and, 4, 14–15, 90, 91, 116, 123–124, 126, 179–180, 182–184, 187, 188
  'convention refugee', 108, n.27
  cross-border migration and, 112
  definition of, 12, 17, 23–24, 106–109, 120, 130
  durable solutions for, 108
  IDP as refugees, 118–119, 134, 137, 142
  'internal refugees', 112, 118–119, 134, 135, 152
  local integration in the state of asylum, 108
  'necessary flight', 122
  non-refoulement principle, 107, 112, 123–124, 223 n.9
  'persecution condition', 108, 114, 121, 229 n.92
  refugee/IDP distinction, 113–114, 134–136, 147, 152
  refugee protection, 108, 111, 112, 120, 123, 127
  refugee status, 12, 21, 23–24, 107, 108–109, 111, 112–114, 118–123, 126
  repatriation to home country, 108, 125, 224 n.15
  resettlement in a third country, 108, 125
  rights of, 107–108, 126
  social deprivation and refugee status, 117
  'voluntary reestablishment', 224 n.15
refugee camps, 4, 120
  Dadaab Refugee Camp (Kenya), 3, 119
  Nakivale refugee settlement (Uganda), 2
refugee laws and instruments
  1951 Refugee Convention, 20–22, 107, 108–110, 120–121, 130, 133, 223 n.9
  1951 Refugee Convention, reform of, 121–123, 130
  1967 *Protocol Relating to the Status of Refugees*, 108–110, 133
  1969 OAU's *Convention Governing the Specific Aspects of Refugee Problems in Africa* (Organisation of African Unity), 109, 111, 123
  1984 *Cartagena Declaration on Refugees*, 109, 111
  2004 European Union Qualification Directives, 108
  2011 European Union Qualification Directives, 108
  2018 Global Compact on Refugees, 128
Refugee and Migration Compacts, 19
refugee movement (regime), 12, 17, 106–107, 129–130
  asylum provision, 110–113, 225 n.27, 226 n.47
  basic needs view, 17, 106–107, 111–112
  Central America/Northern Triangle, 106, 118
  climate refugees, 107
  climate refugees not recognized as refugees, 23–24
  climate refugee treaty, 107

refugee movement (regime), (*Continued*)
  deterrence paradigm, 17, 106–107, 120, 123, 127, 130
  El Salvador, 106, 118
  human rights and, 109, 113–114, 117, 119, 129–130
  injustices, 120
  international community and, 114, 117, 119–120, 129–130
  international community as *in loco civitatis*, 113–114, 122
  membership view, 17, 106–108, 113–114, 117, 118–120, 122–123, 225 n.35, 226 n.46
  over-inclusivity, 112
  persecution view, 17, 106–111, 121, 228 n.73, 229 n.92
  political membership and, 110, 113
  proposed reforms, 121–123, 125, 130
  as reactive displacement, 11
  refugee, definition of, 12, 17, 23–24, 106–109, 120, 130
  refugee regime, 107
  refugee regime as instrument of foreign policy, 110–111
  refugee regime as 'legitimacy repair mechanism', 113
  refugee status, 12, 23–24, 107, 108–109, 111, 112–114, 118–120, 126
  restrictive policies of 'humanitarian containment', 224 n.22
  'safe havens/zones', 112, 136, 226 n.47
  USA, 106, 118, 123–125
  violence, fleeing from, 106, 108, 109–110, 118
  see also asylum; refugee; refugee movement/climate change relationship; refugee protection costs
refugee movement/climate change relationship, 12, 106–107, 114, 120–121, 127, 129–130
  climate change as the 'unseen driver' behind the caravans, 106
  complexity of, 106, 114, 116–120
  Darfur, 114–115
  disasters, 118–119, 129–130
  Horn of Africa, 119
  political conflict, 114–117, 129–130
  refugee regime, dysfunctions exacerbated in climate change context, 106–107, 120, 130
  refugee status, recognition of climatic drivers of displacement as grounds for, 121–123
  social deprivation and gang violence, 106, 117–118, 129–130
  Somalia, 119
  Syria, 116–117
refugee protection costs
  'ability to pay' principle, 129
  countries producing the highest numbers of refugees, 127
  equal burdens principle, 129
  maldistribution between states, 17, 106–107, 120, 126, 130
  non-material costs, 232 n.127
  separation of costs and locus of refugee protection, 128–129
  sharing costs between states, 128, 130
  states' responsibilities towards refugees they have created, 129, 183–184
  unfairly shift onto the most vulnerable, 126–129
remittances, 1, 86, 88–90
  poverty reduction and, 90–91
  skilled emigration and, 92
  see also labour migration
Renner, Karl, 76–77
resilience, 88, 216 n.17
  disasters/disaster displacement and, 131–132, 142–143
  labour migration and, 89–90, 93–94, 99, 104–105
  moral reasoning and, 155
  see also climate change adaptation
responsibility
  'blame-responsibility'/'task-responsibility', 240 n.5
  climate displacement costs and responsibility principle, 18, 33–34, 103–104, 129, 152–155, 157, 175, 199 n.51
  climate refugees treaty and, 22, 28, 33
  'connection theory' of responsibility, 156
  differentiated responsibilities, 170
  IDP protection, 147–148, 153
  insurance model of responsibility, 162–167, 175
  'market-share liability' idea, 163–164, 243 n.43
  'metaphysical' view of responsibility, 239 n.4
  outcome responsibility, 155–157, 160
  pluralist theory of climate displacement, 33–34, 155, 176
  practice-based theories of responsibility, 239 n.4
  remedial responsibility, 155–158
  'responsibility as attributability'/'substantive responsibility', 240 n.5
  tort model of responsibility, 162–163, 165–166, 175

Richmond, Anthony, 9–10, 138
right to stay
  duties imposed on would-be admitting states, 94–97
  freedom of movement, cultural membership, and territorial attachment, 94–95
  labour migration and, 93
  violation of, 94–97
  see also labour migration
Ruhs, Martin, 101–102
Rwanda, 127

S
Sahel, the, 1
Saño, Yeb, 131
Scanlon, T.M., 156–157, 240 n.5
Schapiro, Tamar, 135
Schlosberg, David, 46–50, 58
Scott, James C., 57
sea ice reductions, 2
sea-level rise, 3
  coastal defence measures, 45, 58–59
  in situ adaptation, 58–59, 85
  IPCC projections, 63
  Kiribati, 17, 63
  Maldives, the, 17, 63
  Pacific, the, 3, 24
  Shishmaref (Alaska), 1, 35
  'state extinction' and, 63–64, 85
  territorial sovereignty and, 11, 17, 63, 70–71, 85
  Tuvalu, 17, 63
  Vanuatu, 63
  variation around the world, 63
'securitization'
  of climate change and displacement, 116, 182, 243 n.42
  climate displacement as threat to national security, 240 n.18
self-determination, 17, 63, 64–65
  'constitutive'/'ongoing' self-determination, 84
  as cultural autonomy, 67–70
  decolonization and, 67–69, 72–73
  demands of self-determination, 65, 67–68
  deterritorialized statehood and, 74–79, 85
  Indigenous self-determination, 66–67, 69
  as interdependence, 66, 68–70, 72, 77, 81
  internal/external aspects of, 65, 80–81
  intra-state territorial autonomy and, 64–65, 72, 79–82, 84, 85
  moral concerns, 68–70, 81–82, 85
  as non-interference, 66–72
  political demand, 67–68
  self-governance and, 66–69, 76, 77–79, 81, 84
  small-island peoples, 17, 63, 64, 70–82, 84, 85, 177
  sovereign statehood and, 84–85
  territorial redistribution and, 70–72, 74, 85
  Westphalian international order, 66, 209 n.24
  see also territorial sovereignty
Sen, Amartya, 46–47
Shklar, Judith, 180–181
Shue, Henry, 103–104, 154, 165–166, 169–171
Simms, Andrew, 121
Sinnok, Esau, 1
small-island peoples
  self-determination, 17, 63, 64, 70–82, 84, 85, 177
  'state extinction', 64, 85
  see also self-determination; territorial sovereignty
Solomon Islands, 3
Somalia, 127
  Al-Shabaab, 119
  drought, 2, 119
  food crisis and famine, 3, 119
  refugee movement, 119
  war, 2–3
South Sudan, 127
state
  climate mitigation duties, 18, 129
  disagreement about states' climate duties, 18, 154–155, 161, 167, 175
  disaster displacement and, 137
  financing of *in situ* adaptation, 166
  human rights and, 113–114, 129–130, 134–137, 147, 152
  IDP protection and state capacity, 147–149
  in situ adaptation, financing of, 166
  NDC ('Nationally Determined Contribution'), 170, 173
  as primary bear of responsibility for climate displacement/costs, 158–162, 165–167, 172–175
  sea-level rise and 'state extinction', 63–64, 85
  state inaction, 160–161
  see also self-determination; territorial sovereignty
Stern, Nicholas, 42–43
Stilz, Anna, 37, 39, 40–41, 47, 80–81, 139–140, 218 n.44, 240 n.5
storms, 2
Strawson, P.F., 239 n.4
Sudan, 127
Sunstein, Cass, 171
Syria, 4, 116–117, 127

T

Táíwò, Olúfẹ́mi O., 8
Tan, Nikolas F., 123
Tanzania, 127
Tasmania, 83–84
temperature targets, 168–169, 173–174
  1.5°C, 64, 159, 168–169, 186–187
  2°C, 64, 159, 168–169, 178–179, 186–187
  2.4°C, 173–174
  4–5°C, 178–179, 185
territorial issues
  basic territorial interests, 37–39, 44, 61–62, 80
  occupancy rights, 73, 139–140, 144–146, 153
  practice-based interests and, 37, 43, 44–45, 47, 49, 62, 80
  significance of place, 38
  territorial instability, 12
  territorial rights, 70–71, 73–74, 80, 81–82, 94–95, 208 n.10, 211 n.54, n.66
  use rights, 145
  see also community relocation; IDP; territorial sovereignty
territorial sovereignty, 17, 85, 154
  1933 *Montevideo Convention on the Rights and Duties of States*, 63
  as anticipatory displacement, 11
  community relocation/territorial sovereignty distinction, 11
  coral bleaching and, 11
  Kiribati, 17, 80
  Maldives, the, 17
  relocation, 73–74, 80, 83
  relocation rights (individual), 64
  sea-level rise and, 11, 17, 63, 70–71, 85
  secession, 69, 73–74
  self-determination, right to 17, 63, 64–65
  'state extinction', 63–64, 85
  territorial rights, 70–71, 73–74, 80, 81–82, 208 n.10, 211 n.54, n.66
  Tuvalu, 17
  Vanuatu, 63
  see also self-determination; territorial sovereignty: proposals
territorial sovereignty: proposals
  deterritorialized statehood, 17, 64–65, 74, 81, 84, 85
  deterritorialized statehood: challenges, 77–79
  intra-state territorial autonomy, 17, 64–65, 72, 79, 85
  moral concerns, 73–74, 79, 81–82
  statehood and, 84–85
  territorial redistribution, 17, 64–65, 70, 84

territorial redistribution: challenges, 72–74, 81–82
  see also intra-state territorial autonomy; territorial sovereignty
Teytelboym, Alexander, 128–129
Thornton, Fanny, 164
Tong, Anote, 24
Torresi, Tiziana, 97–98
Tuana, Nancy, 180
Turkey, 127
Tutu, Desmond, Archbishop, 180
Tuvalu, 3, 17, 63
typhoons, 142
  Typhoon Haiyan/Typhoon Yolanda (the Philippines), 131–132, 142

U

Uganda, 127
UK (United Kingdom), 123–124
unemployment, 1, 104, 115–116
UNEP (United Nations Environment Programme), 6
UNFCCC (United Nations Framework Convention on Climate Change), 157, 167–168, 173–174
  1992 Rio Declaration, 160, 174–175
  Article 3.4: 'right to sustainable development', 169–172
  COP13 (13th Conference of the Parties, Bali), 144–145
  COP15 (15th Conference of the Parties, Copenhagen), 3, 168
  COP16 (16th Conference of the Parties, Cancún), 19
  COP19 (19th Conference of the Parties, Warsaw), 131
  COP21 (21st Conference of the Parties, Paris), 168
  COP23 (23rd Conference of the Parties, Bonn), 51–52
  REDD+ (Reducing Emissions from Deforestation and Degradation), 144–146
UNGA (United Nations General Assembly), Resolution 71/1: *The New York Declaration for Refugees and Migrants*, 19
UNHCR (United Nations High Commissioner for Refugees), 23–24, 32–33, 108, 123, 146
  Comprehensive Refugee Policy, 112
  expanded mandate, 109–110
UNICEF (United Nations Children's Fund), 146
USA (United States of America), 186–187
  community relocation, 38–39, 42–43
  Hurricane Katrina (New Orleans), 143

labour migration, 92–93, 101–102
migration as threat, 7, 188
refugee regime, 106, 118, 123–125
Sanctuary City movement, 188
Sonoran Desert, 124–125
tribal sovereignty, 79–80
US–tribal government relations, 214 n.105

V
Valentini, Laura, 147
Van Parijs, Philippe, 78–79
Vanuatu, 3, 63
Venezuela, 127
Vietnam, 36, 45
Vince, Gaia, 185
violence
  people smugglers and sexual violence, 124
  'silent violence' of climate change, 118
  see also conflict
vulnerability
  climate displacement and, 161
  disasters and, 142–143, 151
  LDCs (Least Developed Countries) and climate change, 172
  race and, 143
  'skewed vulnerabilities' of climate change, 172

W
Walzer, Michael, 110
war *see* conflict
warning systems, 44, 88, 143, 203 n.47
Warsaw International Mechanism on Loss and Damage, 19
Webber, Michael, 89–90
Weyl, Glen, 101–102
WFP (World Food Programme), 118, 146
White, Gregory, 182
WHO (World Health Organisation), 146
Whyte, Kyle Powys, 37, 48–49
wildfires, 12, 37, 131–132, 142, 153
Wittgenstein, Ludwig, 20
World Bank, 89–91, 147
Wright, Erik Olin, 60–61
Wündisch, Joachim, 70–71, 73, 211 n.63

Y
Yemen, 127
Young, Iris Marion, 49, 66, 68–69
Ypi, Lea, 211 n.54

Z
Zamore, Leah, 122
Zellentin, Alexa, 202 n.25